C + H

W9-BBM-155

66-10515 (7-16-66)

The only existing oil portrait of Vidkun Quisling, painted at the request of Adolf Hitler to hang in Berchtesgaden *(reproduced by courtesy of Harald Franklin Knudsen)*

QUISLING

Prophet without Honour

By the same author

COUNT FOLKE BERNADOTTE
his life and work

MR FIVE PER CENT
the biography of Calouste Gulbenkian

THE RICHEST AMERICAN
J. Paul Getty

A GOLDEN DREAM
the miracle of Kuwait

Ralph Hewins

QUISLING
Prophet without Honour

THE JOHN DAY COMPANY

NEW YORK

WINGATE COLLEGE LIBRARY
WINGATE, N. C.

FIRST AMERICAN EDITION 1966

© Ralph Hewins, 1965. All rights reserved. This book, or parts thereof, must not be reproduced in any form without permission. Published by The John Day Company, Inc., 62 West 45th Street, New York, N.Y. 10036, and on the same day in Canada by Longmans Canada Limited, Toronto.

Library of Congress Catalogue
Card Number: 66-10515

PRINTED IN THE UNITED STATES OF AMERICA

Contents

32201

Illustrations

FOR REX
in twenty-five years' Nordic friendship

I

A Word is Coined

ON April 9, 1940, the six months of 'phoney' war—after the Russo-German partition of Poland—ended abruptly. The Germans occupied Denmark and the key points of Norway overnight, and came within striking distance of England. A new international word was coined—'quisling'.

At 7.32 p.m. on that cold and fateful day a husky, blond man with bulging eyes, dressed in a shiny dark suit and sweating, burst into the Oslo broadcasting station and seized a microphone to tell an astonished world that he was the new Prime Minister of stricken Norway. He was Major Vidkun Abraham Lauritz Jonssøn Quisling.

Like 'Judas', his name has stuck as a generic word for traitor. It forthwith superseded 'fifth columnist', the corresponding term that had emerged during the Spanish Civil War. By April 15 *The Times* was using the word in inverted commas and on the 19th carried a leading article entitled 'Quisling is as Quisling does'. Quite independently I invented the word on April 21st, when I was cut off from the rest of the world on the North Trondheim Front, and it appeared in the *Daily Mail* on the 23rd.

Somehow 'quisling' had a sinister ring. The letter Q only came into English and Scandinavian usage during the Renaissance and it still

9

seems a trifle odd. Many dubious English words begin with Q: quack, quake, qualified, qualm, quarrel, quandary, quasi, queasy, queer, question, quibble, quirk, quit, quite, quiver, quiz. Into that suspect company 'quisling' fitted neatly. It was a natural.

In the same breath a myth was born, impenetrable as the Norse sagas of Snorre Sturlason seven hundred years ago, and Quisling the man has become depersonalised. Norwegian school-children identified him as an actor in a recent quiz.

During the last quarter of a century a network of Norwegian, British, German and Russian vested interests has blackened Quisling's name with almost every imaginable crime from murder and theft to high treason, until his character and career have become completely distorted in history and in the popular imagination at home and abroad.

A vast literature has appeared in Norwegian and other languages about Quisling and his times since he was hastily executed before a gloating crowd in the old Akershus Fortress in Oslo during the small hours of October 24, 1945; but most of it is one-sided and the same old 'image' of Quisling repeatedly finds its way into print without proper qualification in the light of abundant new evidence.

He has been branded as the prototype of traitor—a degraded upstart who plotted the invasion of Norway with Hitler, betrayed Norwegian military secrets and arranged to serve as a puppet pro-German ruler, with the help of an imitation Nazi Party, as soon as the *Wehrmacht* moved into Norway. He is also blamed at home and abroad for the defeat of the Norwegian Armed Forces in April-June, 1940, for the failure of the Anglo-French-Polish Intervention, and for the subsequent horrors of the German Occupation—all because he is supposed to have had a mad lust for power which turned him into a willing stooge of the Germans and a malefactor in his own country.

In order to document that thesis and to give it official sanction, a prodigious legal process was staged in the Freemasons' Hall in Oslo from August 22 to September 10, 1945. He was found guilty of murder on several counts and of contributing to the death of a number of Jews; abetting the German Occupation and attempting to bring Norway into a Pan-German Federation; attempting to change the Constitution and securing for himself and his party a position alien to the Constitution. He was condemned to death. In addition 1,040,000 *kroner* were confiscated from him and he had to pay 1,500 *kroner* costs.*

The object of this book is to unravel the garbled facts which contributed to the current Quisling 'image' and produced the penalties which were inflicted upon him and his supporters. Was Quisling a quisling? Or was he a prophet without honour in his own country?

*The equivalent of $145,600 and $210

2

The Norwegian 'Image'

HAS Quisling, in fact, been used as a scapegoat for sins of omission and commission perpetrated in Norway since she parted from Sweden in 1905, and culminating in the German Occupation with its wretched aftermath?

In order to tackle that question, which is the theme of this book, one must examine his milieu.

First, some dangerous generalisations. Fielding's *Travel Guide to Europe 1963* says of the Norwegian people that they are: 'Handsome, gregarious, industrious; fond of parties, gaiety and good living; rich in wit and humour, with a love of practical jokes; honest, hard-working and meticulously sanitary; possessing a tough moral fibre, honed through centuries of battling the elements and an essentially barren landscape; rugged and courageous, inventive soldiers and sailors; two-fisted eaters and five-finger drinkers; fast friends and joyous uncomplicated companions; warm-hearted, hospitable and clean-living; too proud to be petty.'

Quisling called them 'a shirtsleeves people', which has the same implications and is true up to a point. It is also how Norwegians like to think of themselves: how a great many Britons usually think of this people with whom they have had close ties for 1,500 years: how two million Americans of Norse descent look back at their distant cousins. But all generalisations are misleading.

It would be equally true to agree with the many Norwegians who identify themselves gladly with Peer Gynt, meaning that they are daydreamers, idealists and rather above the usual wickedness of the outside world. But this charming idiosyncrasy may equally be dubbed as happy-go-lucky, feckless, wayward, casual, unreliable, irresponsible or indolent.

Second, some exceptions. Reaction against Peer Gyntism stimulated the towering figures of Norway's Golden Age, which produced independence and petered out as the grip of egalitarian Socialism tightened in the 1930s until it has become a stranglehold in the 1960s.

The immortal dramatist, Henrik Ibsen, who knew Norwegian failings better than anybody and personified them in *Peer Gynt*;

Edvard Grieg, who was inspired by Norwegian folk songs and set *Peer Gynt* to music;

Knut Hamsun, who is often rated a greater writer than Ibsen and who won the Nobel Prize for Literature;

Sigrid Undset, who, like Hamsun, was steeped in Norwegian tradition and won the Nobel Prize;

Edvard Munch, the great imaginative painter whose marvellous frescoes decorate the Oslo University Hall;

Kirsten Flagstad, the famous Wagnerian singer;

Bjørnstjerne Bjørnson, the national poet who composed the moving National Anthem, *Ja, vi Elsker* (Yes, we love);

Gustav Vigeland, the monumental sculptor, whose prodigious output in Frogner Park, Oslo, is one of the wonders of the world, like it or not;

Dr. Fridtjof Nansen, sportsman, scientist, explorer, author, king-maker and humanitarian, who might be regarded as the greatest European of the century;

Roald Amundsen, who first reached the magnetic Pole and beat Captain Robert Falcon Scott to the South Pole, then flew the North Pole, besides navigating the North West and North East Passages;

Sondre Nordheim, who came from Quisling's native Telemark and invented downhill skiing;

Oscar Mathisen, the greatest of all speed-skaters.

And who is left from the Golden Age? Only Tryggve Gran, who discovered Captain Scott's body near the South Pole in 1913

13

WINGATE COLLEGE LIBRARY
WINGATE, N. C.

and next year placed himself on a par with Louis Blériot and Charles Lindbergh by flying the North Sea; Bernt Balchen, the first man to fly both Poles (who has adopted American citizenship); Jonas Lied, who opened the Kara Sea Route between Siberia and England in 1913 and later wrote the best-selling autobiography *Return to Happiness* and who has followed the example of many disillusioned Norwegian industrialists and withdrawn from public life; and Sonja Henie, the greatest of all figure-skaters, who invented a popular new art form in the shape of the ice ballet. She has only recently resumed Norwegian citizenship after being unfairly criticised for spending the war in America.

All those splendid people overlapped Vidkun Quisling. Their example and the national pride which they expressed inspired him, for good or ill, to leave his mark, too.

Today the world knows only two new Norwegian names— Trygve Lie, the former General Secretary of the United Nations, and Thor Heyerdahl of Kon-Tiki fame, who is not universally popular because he prefers to live abroad. The efflorescence is over. The country has sunk into mediocrity and stagnation, and the faceless Socialists have grown wings.

The blackened spectre of Vidkun Quisling provides a useful contrast to the pink angels.

Third, geography. Norway is the fifth largest country in Europe and (after Iceland) has the lowest density of population—under thirty persons per square mile. From North to South is 1,100 miles as the crow flies—as far as London to Sicily. If Svalbard (Spitsbergen) is included, the distance is as far as Alaska to Mexico.

The mainland coast is 2,000 miles long, or 12,500 miles including inlets and 150,000 islands of which only 2,000 are inhabited. Fjords cut 100 miles or more inland and at one point Norway is only four miles wide. Mainland Norway is 124,710 square miles (including Svalbard, 150,000 square miles).

Three-quarters of the surface is unsuitable for cultivation or habitation. One-third lies north of the Arctic Circle, where the Midnight Sun reigns from May 12 to August 1, and there is a corresponding period of darkness in midwinter.

The Gulf Stream moderates the climate of the West Coast and all ports are ice-free, even in the Far North, except in landlocked creeks.

Extremes occur in the inland valleys and the uninhabited mountainous districts. The highest point is Guldhøpiggen (8,090 ft.).

Today Norway still only supports a population of 3,600,000. When Quisling was a boy it was only about 2,000,000. Half live in Eastern Norway, including Oslo, which is far the largest city, with 477,000 inhabitants. Bergen, with 116,500 inhabitants, comes next, and Trondheim with 56,000. The rest of the population falls far short of the average thirty per square mile.

Twenty per cent of the population farms the 2·5 per cent of the country which is arable. Fishing occupies 61,000 Norwegians and is one of the country's three main industries. Forests cover a quarter of the country and half of them belong to farmers.

Apart from fish and forests, Norway has few natural resources: no petroleum and only a little coal from Svalbard. However, abundant snow melting in the highlands provides limitless hydro-electric power, which runs the famous Norsk Hydro nitrogen and heavy-water plants and a thriving aluminium industry, as well as the white elephant ironworks at Mo-i-Rana. There is also uneconomic iron-ore mining at Kirkenes. Tourism is said to be Norway's sixth industry, but this has yet to be developed on a scale worthy of the superb scenery.

What keeps the country from bankruptcy is 14,000,000 tons of modern shipping. For years Norway has had not only a large foreign trade deficit but also a deficit in overall payments which has had to be met by foreign loans to a considerable extent. No less than 21 per cent of the working population is employed in public administration, the slender Armed Forces and other services.

In Quisling's day, conditions were even more primitive.

Norway, in short, is a poor country—poor by nature and poor in opportunities. Sweden would not have it back as a gift. The people were thrown back on their individual resources until the Socialists suborned the masses and soaked the rich, who long ago despaired of politics and often sympathised with Quisling's dynamic ideas in the thirties.

The amenities of modern urban life are sub-standard since there is only one considerable city and even Oslo is provincial compared with Copenhagen, Stockholm or several other Swedish towns. A malaise has settled over the capital because life there is unnatural for the peasants who have swelled the population. This maladjustment is illustrated by maniac driving and phenomenal drunkenness. Para-doxically there are strong local patriotisms, in Oslo, the coastal towns of the South, Bergen, Trondheim and remote Tromsö, where geo-graphy and history combine with a sense of 'belonging' to foster pride. But it is the country, as opposed to the town, which counts. Slacks and shirtsleeves are the mode everywhere and Oslo must be the shabbiest capital in Europe, with the worst restaurant service, and the worst town-planning.

It is a go-as-you-please existence. Hence the bewilderment which confronted the German Invasion; the dismay which faced the Occupa-tion; the wounded pride which turned into hatred and has outlasted similar hatreds in Western Europe; the necessity to find a scapegoat for the national conscience and the nation's shortcomings.

The very idea that anybody could seek a working arrangement with an Occupant of the sacred Norwegian soil is blasphemy to ordinary Norwegians. Being a little people, they always want to achieve the impossible, which they do with amazing frequency, although the workaday chores often defeat them.

They must have the biggest City Hall, the biggest ski-jump, the monstrous Vigeland sculptures, the biggest modern tanker fleet. They must catch whales. They must beat the world at winter sports. It is no accident that a Norwegian was the first to set foot in Antarctica and to reach the South Pole; that a Norwegian first navigated the North West and North East Passages and was first to fly across both Poles; that a Norwegian (Leiv Eiriksson) discovered America; that a Norwegian first flew the North Sea. Quisling has to be the biggest and foremost traitor since Judas Iscariot. This has all become part of Norwegian folklore.

This 'sturdy individualism' is esteemed at home and abroad as a national characteristic and virtue. But it has almost become a vice. The result is a strange, happy-go-lucky, hand-to-mouth, undisciplined existence which is undoubtedly attractive, but at the same time ineffectual in modern times in peace or war.

The fisherman goes out in his little boat just when he feels like it, sells his catch and refuses to be organised into an efficient trawling industry. The farmer just cuts down some trees when he needs money and extracts fringe benefits from big business and the State to see him through the off-season. Any Norwegian who feels restless can take to the sea for a spell and come back for a spending spree with substantial savings. Absenteeism in offices and factories is colossal, considering the remarkable number of official and unofficial holidays. In the Armed Services the men mostly look upon their duties as merely a pensionable job and have the vaguest ideas about ever fighting—an attitude which has been encouraged by Norwegian Labour Governments for thirty years. Life in Norway is in fact spasmodic, unstable and idiosyncratic. Even meals are movable feasts. The net result has been the chaos which has produced present discontents.

What mainly preoccupies the Norwegian mind is to 'get away from it all': to go on a ski tour in the beckoning mountains or a hike in the wilderness; to sail or swim in the surrounding waters or to skate on frozen lakes; to disappear into the remote family log cabin for a long weekend; or to go abroad. Norway is the land of escapism, where facts are not to be faced but avoided—the dream world of Peer Gynt. Hence the overwhelming apathy which preceded the German Invasion; the flight of thousands of Norwegians into the wilds, to Sweden or to England. Hence, too, the unpopularity of Vidkun Quisling who committed the unforgivable Norwegian sin of facing up to reality.

Living close to the soil has combined with centuries of foreign domination and the cherished memories of an heroic Viking Age a thousand years ago to create an overweening national pride. Norway is one of the loveliest countries in the world, winter and summer, and its beauties are on everybody's doorstep. An Olympic ski-run is only fifteen minutes by tram outside Oslo and the fjord teems with a thousand sailing boats for six months in the year—two glorious sights. Norwegians truly love their native land, as their National Anthem proclaims. There is not much else to enjoy.

This pathological longing for greatness in any shape or form is a reaction against the parochialism which the Norwegian terrain induces, just as the Golden Age at the turn of the century was a reaction against Peer Gyntism. Few Norwegians know the native land of which they are so fond and proud. Few have even been half-way up, north of Trondheim. Few take the slightest interest in the surrounding world, and politics at the national level are conducted by parish pump standards. Norwegians are very keen on minding other people's business, hence their interest in the United Nations and in humanitarianism;

this saves face abroad and induces a pleasant smug feeling at home, but they are singularly inefficient at setting their own house in order. It is chronic for sectional interests to precede the national interest.

The idea that Norwegians should sink their petty differences and unite to save their country, as urged for ten years by Quisling, was therefore foreign to Norwegian instincts and practice and thus brought all the ills predicted by him, including the subdivision of the North into weak, vulnerable and bickering components. Individualism makes Norwegians loath to admit that they are ever wrong and so Quisling committed another unforgivable sin. 'I told you so', he said.

Perhaps the true 'image' of Norway is best obtained by flying over this vast, straggling country. One is struck by innumerable scattered and isolated cottages and hamlets, poised on islands, alps and clearings, and one wonders how the people can endure such solitude. It requires knowledge and imagination to understand that this is every Norwegian's ideal—a cabin as far away from neighbours as possible, where one can do as one likes. They hate interference, discipline or anybody who rises above his fellows, unless it is in such harmless fields as the Arts, Exploration, Sport or Humanitarianism. The 'noble savage' myth of the nineteenth century still survives here and, like most savages, the Norwegian has a hard, cruel streak which came out during the war and afterwards, thus permanently marring an otherwise pleasant stereotype. Hence the bitterness of the Quisling controversy, and the subsequent lack of magnanimity.

The Norwegian inferiority complex goes into reverse and demands something big, spectacular and immediate. These people have little stamina but they can harbour a grudge or a delusion of grandeur indefinitely. Hence the Quisling and the Home Front myths.

Put in another way, the very real Norwegian sense of inferiority *vis à vis* Sweden and Denmark and the outside world at large stimulates an urge to be different at any price. For instance the artificial creation of a second official language based on dialect, as if the vocabulary of Ibsen were not good enough. Hitherto it was fairly easily understood by Danes and Swedes or anybody who took the trouble to learn the elements of 'Scandinavian'. Now it becomes more incomprehensible annually to foreigners, and further splinters not only Norway but the North. The result is chaos in education, embitterment between parent and children, the sabotage of the publishing industry, which is seriously threatened by an influx of English books, and another spoke in the wheel of 'Nordic solidarity'.

In such fundamental matters Norwegians go out of their way to seem petty, cantankerous and unreasonable, thus making their existence more difficult and turning them into very 'edgy' friends. The broad perspective is far from a Norwegian's ken. His outlook is inbred, introspective and legalistic. He is extremely difficult to deal with, as Danes, Swedes and Germans have found through the centuries. He is also suspicious of his own countrymen, however eminent—as Quisling found when he returned with an international outlook to his native land.

Quisling fits naturally into any realistic 'image' of his lopsided and eccentric country. He was born and raised in Telemark, which is a synthesis of all Norway. It is rugged and parochial to this day, and there was always something parochial about him. He was introspective, opinionated, stubborn, unclubbable and a law unto himself, like most of his countrymen. Like them, too, he was steeped in Norwegian folklore and a nature-lover, with a passion for his native soil. He was typical of the narrow Norwegian outlook which makes the nation so awkward to handle, as people or as individuals: a self-centred individualist, 'sturdy' but distorted.

He was also a Peer Gynt. Like so many Norwegian mariners, explorers and emigrants, Quisling also shared the national urge to 'get away from it all', either abroad or in the imagination. The average Norwegian does not get much further than his cabin in the wilds, where he can commune with Nature in the raw and build castles in the air. Quisling was an extreme case of Peer Gyntism, so extreme that he was actually carried away by his dreams and tried to make them come true. This was his undoing. Most Norwegians are more ineffectual. They mistake the dream for the substance.

This national paradox of individualism and Peer Gyntism produced the heroes of the Golden Age into which Quisling was born. They revolted against the limitations of their country and its parochialism. The result was a great wave of creative endeavour in Politics, the Arts and Exploration which covered Norway in glory. Collectively they released and expressed the national pride, which had been stultified and frustrated for centuries, and they carried Norway to independence and the heights of international fame. The epitome of this sudden efflorescence was Fridtjof Nansen, Quisling's hero. Like Nansen, Quisling was a fervent patriot, burning to add to his young country's greatness.

Such passion distorted Quisling, as it distorted most of his great contemporaries. They were eccentrics. Nansen scattered his first wife's ashes under a rosebush and never told their children where. Edvard Munch and Gustav Vigeland were recluses. Oslo took its time from Ibsen as he walked from his corner table in the window of the Grand Hotel Café to set his watch by the University clock. Hamsun took only his tie off when he went to bed after receiving the Nobel Prize for Literature in Stockholm; he left the money with a waiter. Sigrid Undset managed to write a history of Norwegian literature without mentioning Hamsun. Three of Amundsen's fellow conquerors of the South Pole committed suicide, as did Hjalmar Johansen, who dragged Nansen to safety on their trek from near the North Pole to Franz Josef Land. Such examples could be multiplied. Even the greatest Norwegians were unbalanced, and Quisling was no exception.

He was a typical Norwegian who fitted naturally into the national image: a product of his environment. No other country could have produced him.

He attempted the impossible, but, unlike many another Norwegian, he failed to achieve it. His efforts received too little response. He was a fuehrer without a folk. Hence the fierce controversy which still rages around his name in Norway.

Final judgement on his extraordinary career has yet to be passed in historical perspective and in the light of fresh evidence which constantly accumulates.

The net result is not a simple study in black and white. The problem is not to choose between right and wrong. That is fairly easy. The real problem is to choose between right and right and to strike a fair balance. That is the interest and the difficulty of the Quisling case. An offbeat character among an offbeat people, he is the catalyst of modern Norwegian history, the centre of an internecine and emotional argument which warps and weakens a whole nation.

3

Prodigy

QUISLING'S background was impeccable, like a Scottish manse; not at all the sort of broken home or irredentist area where rebellion and high treason thrive. It was more liable to produce a reformer, an evangelist or a prophet, which is just how he regarded himself and how many Norwegians accepted him at different times.

He was born of good yeoman stock at Fyresdal, a scattered village in the beautiful mountains of Telemark in south-west Norway, where the Quisling family had been respected as priests, farmers and officers for six hundred years. He was definitely not a mere 'peasant', as his detractors maintain.

'I grew up among Viking graves, between Bible history and old Saga tales', he said on trial. 'I belong to an ancient family and I was always injected with the ideas of family pride and family saga as well as with the sense of responsibility towards our people. Bjørnson and Ibsen were of the same family as I: so it was not dishwater in my veins. The name Quisling is not of foreign origin; it is an ancient Nordic name and indicates one who is a side branch of the royal family. The letter Q indicates an ancient (magic) protective rune.* I have grown up

* Gabriel Turville-Petre, Reader in Ancient Icelandic Literature at Oxford University, comments: 'The runic alphabet varied greatly from time to time and district to district, but I cannot think of anything that resembles a Q in it. I hardly think that Q would have been much used in Scandinavia until the

under these conditions and imbibed a most intense love for my country.'

He was born on July 18, 1887. His father, Jon Lauritz Quisling, was pastor in the village's Lutheran state church and dean of the pastors in that district—a little old bookworm who looked like a troll and spent most of his time writing treatises on God, the Devil and Angels or speculations about mediaeval history and socialism.

Pastor Quisling traced the family surname back to a paternal grandfather's maternal grandmother, Susanne Magdalene Quislin (without a g), who was the daughter of a priest. The Ibsen connection harked back to another priest named Lauritz Ibsen Quisling.

The mother was born Anna Caroline Bang, whose father was a cousin of Bjørnstjerne Bjørnson and also a cousin of Rikard Nordraak (the leading Norwegian composer of the time, who set *Ja, Vi Elsker* to music). She also belonged to the well-known Northern family of Hvide, which included Archbishop Absolon, founder of Copenhagen.

She had a straight back, and in her black dress with a thick gold chain round her neck she looked composed, cultivated and rather distant. To the villagers she was inclined to be condescending and she brought up her children to keep their distance. Ibsen's Hjördis was her type.

By all accounts the parsonage was a happy home and the mother's neat appearance, firmly closed mouth and coldly clever eyes belied her true nature, which was friendly, humorous and lovable. At any rate Vidkun worshipped her to his dying day and she was probably the strongest influence in his life.

She had no chance of fulfilling her ambitions through her husband, to whom she was sometimes intolerant, and so she planted them in her children, of whom there were four. Vidkun was the eldest. Jørgen, who became a chemist and doctor, came two years later. Esther, who died at the age of nineteen, was four years younger than Vidkun, and

---

Renaissance. There *was* a type of runes called *kvistrúnar*, meaning literally "branch-runes"—*kvistr* meaning twig, branch and perhaps tributary of a river. I would think the name Quisling is derived from *kvis(t)lingr*, meaning small branch or small tributary. A variant form of *kvistr* is *kvísl*, which could give the dimutive *kvíslingr* (the r would of course drop out). This could mean branch of a river.'

finally came Arne, who became an engineer and emigrated to America. All four were very clever.

Quisling explained in court: 'I grew up in an erudite home. My father was a pastor, but he was more of a scientist; he was an historian and a linguist. I was encouraged in the study of history. I read everything I could lay my hands on about the old sagas, the history of Norway and world history. All my savings went in books. I was perhaps a lonely lad, and I was lonely because I never found what I was willing to give in exchange for friendship, namely everything. . . . Aside from my wife, I have never found one who was willing to do what I wanted to do, namely to lay down my life for my friends. For such reasons I have been a lonely man, and for no other reason.'

Jørgen was better looking, livelier and not as shy as his elder brother, whom he admired, perhaps for his strength of character. 'I am ashamed of myself: he is even cleverer than I', he used to say. Like Vidkun, Jørgen was interested in mathematics, and they shared also a bent for philosophical speculation. But Jørgen played no part in the Quisling movement and after the war he repudiated it.

Esther's death was due to a brain haemorrhage brought on by cramming at school, where she got an A in every subject except one. Her mother could never forget her and called her 'the great sorrow of my life'. She was a sweet, saintly child and her loss was one of the reasons for Vidkun's earnestness. He longed to comfort his mother by atoning for Esther's death with his own intellectual prowess and success.

Anna Quisling expected her children to get A in everything—not only to make up for the shortcomings of her quaint husband, who could not even preach a good sermon, despite his ecclesiastical background, but in order to live up to her distinguished pedigree and to rise above the neighbours. Hence one of the family failings, an intellectual arrogance.

Constant study and the family air of superiority cut Vidkun off from other boys and girls and turned him into a solitary at an early age. Throughout his life he remained shy, with no gift for small talk and little of the camaraderie which develops from rubbing shoulders with one's fellows. This often made life difficult for him in a democratic age and handicapped his judgement of people and politics. He became wrapped up in his deep and far-ranging thoughts, swayed rather by learning and logic than instinct and intuition. Such one-sidedness cut both ways. It gave him a deep insight into the affairs of men, but it also blinded him to the profound political difference between what is possible and impossible.

When he was only seven, he was sent to school at Drammen, the capital of Vestfold County and a forestry centre, where his father had been transferred. This is the fifth city in Norway and on Oslo Fjord, only twenty-five miles from the capital—a sharp change from the fastnesses of Telemark. Vidkun was miserable.

He also told the court: 'I became overwhelmed with homesickness. The mere smell of cattle manure, and just to hear the rooster crow, were enough to make me so homesick that I could not sit still.' In fact he felt a part of his native soil.

When he arrived he could not read or write and had only the Catechism from his mother. He used his county dialect and was ridiculed by the more sophisticated children of the neighbourhood. 'I was at the bottom of my class, but within a few months I had become number one', he continued; 'and I remained number one always afterwards. But I was no scholastic light in the ordinary sense, cramming and cramming. For the subjects in school were the least of my troubles. They did not mean much to me. What I was yearning for lay outside the school subjects, and that I gobbled up with an unquenching desire for knowledge.' All of which was true, and not a boast.

He was moved up after his first term and remained top of every class until he went to Skien Latin School at the age of thirteen—back once more in his beloved Telemark—where his father was transferred again and taught some history. Here, too, he was always top of his class—the pride and joy of the school and his family. The curriculum presented no difficulty at all to him and only occupied a fraction of his time. Ibsen went to the same school and not even he showed comparable brilliance. His classmates placed Vidkun on a pedestal.

Rector Vilhelm Ullmann of Oslo Secondary School, who was one of Quisling's classmates at Skien, told the court before which his lifelong friend was pilloried: 'He was a very bright lad in school, and he had a most unusual receptive capacity. He had read and studied a great deal, had many interests very unusual for a boy at that age. I went along to his home, just outside the city (at Gjerpen Parsonage), almost every day, and it was a beautiful home where harmony reigned, and I loved the whole family . . . He and I had a great interest in common, namely mathematics. With that we were greatly occupied. He was greatly interested in history. . . . At that time he talked about becoming an officer or pastor; but he ought to have become a natural scientist on account of his genius for mathematics.'

Quisling himself told the court: 'As a very young lad I discovered higher mathematics all by myself—outside school. I studied Abel's collected works all by myself, and my teacher was sad when he learned that I chose to become an Army officer.' Indeed a standard Norwegian school mathematics book,* contained a footnote referring to Quisling, saying that 'A pupil at Skien Latin School discovered an alternative way of proving this equation'.

His interest shifted from subject to subject when he was a boy. He was fascinated by history and the Heroic Age of Scandinavia from about 500 to the death of St. Olav (King of Norway, 1016-1030) and Canute the Great (King of Denmark, Norway and England), who died in 1035. He was proud of the fact that his birthday fell on the same date as the naval Battle of Hafrsfjord (c. 885), when Norway was united for the first time, under Harald Fairhair, thus incidentally leading to the Norse conquest of the Shetlands, Orkneys, the Hebrides and Caithness and the colonisation of Iceland.

His peculiar Christian name harked back to the Heroic Age, in common with many other Viking names in usage in Norway and nowhere else in Scandinavia—all of them testifying to the general Norwegian nostalgia for the greatness of a bygone epoch.

One of his most treasured presents as a boy was a copy of St. Olav's flag with a gold cross on a red background, and as a man he cherished a club with his name on one side and that of Harald Fairhair on the other.

It is common nowadays to scoff at his admiration for Nordic virtues, which developed from his studies and eventually jelled into an ideology parallel with Hitler's disastrous conception of a Master Aryan Race. But perhaps there was something in it. Britain, for instance, is still permeated with legacies of the Norsemen. The English and Scottish monarchies trace back to the Normans, through William the Conqueror, who was only separated by four generations and 155 years from the first Viking Duke of Normandy. The Vikings also left behind

* Eliasen's *Laerebok i algebra for gymnasiet.*

the foundations of British parliamentary and seafaring traditions. Nor was Quisling's Nordic ideology new-fangled. Many well-educated people in Norway were likewise inspired by harking back to the traditional culture of their country and to the history of the Germanic nations. Patriotism along those lines was carefully instilled in schools and colleges. It had a deep philosophical and emotional appeal as expressed, for example, in the novels of Knut Hamsun, who systematically contrasted the virtues of the old Nordic culture with the slum civilisation and money-grabbing of the industrialised, multi-party, Socialist world at large. Quisling, the man of the soil, was perfectly sincere in contrasting the good, old godly culture with the distintegrating, 'alien' Marxist ideology. Such views as his were held to be respectable until the Nazis came along and botched the idea.

Nor are such attitudes dead in the Atlantic Community. In fact, racial dogmatism vies with the population explosion as one of the two great problems of the future. Each of us is entitled to his own views, and Quisling was entitled to his. He failed to get them across, but plenty of honourable people in the Western World still share them—rightly or wrongly.

Quisling also studied philosophy and theology—including Judaism, for which he learned Hebrew. All this, too, went towards forming his own ideology—long before Hitler was ever heard of—and eventually found form in what he called *Universalism*—950 pages that represented his life's work and found expression in his politics. The central theme was a reconciliation of Christian principles with modern science and its application to government.

It is a monumental thesis, which at present is deposited in his widow's bank and is suppressed.

Yet Quisling was no prig. He enjoyed the outdoors as thoroughly as any other Norwegian youth. Fyresdal was one of the last valleys to be civilised in the South, and wild animals sometimes roamed the streets in his childhood. He hiked miles, often disappearing for days at a time without causing alarm, because he was as strong as the peasants who fought savagely at festivals. He walked 'like an elk' and often jog-trotted for six hours. His favourite sport was bear-hunting and he claimed to have shot fifty.

He committed his father's tome of Norwegian placenames and parishes to his inexhaustible memory and never afterwards used a roadmap. He knew his native land like the palm of his hand, and often won notional bets with his friends about distances when they were driving.

To the end of his life he maintained the family cabin—five hours' stiff walk in the hills from the parsonage in Fyresdal—and he often disappeared there for a week or more, without attracting attention, before and during the war.

This suited his solitary nature and enabled him to work out his complicated thoughts to their logical conclusion. It provided useful camouflage for the secret political missions on which he also disappeared from time to time. Furthermore, it built up a phenomenal physique and an almost imperturbable mentality which stood him in good stead during his fiercely contested electioneering, the long strain of the German Occupation, and finally his State trial.

It also enabled him to retain his health during his forbidding routine of concentrated book-learning and the horrors of the great Russian famine after the Revolution and Civil War, which turned Nansen's hair white. He slept only six hours a night and could do with one hour!

Except that he was above the average height of Norwegian men, which was 5 ft. 7¾ in. in 1900 and is now two inches more, in appearance Quisling could hardly have looked more Norwegian. He was fair-haired, like many of the population who have not mingled with the dark little nomadic Lapps (Samer) of the North. Like 64 per cent of the population he had blue eyes. He was also sloppily dressed: usually in a dark suit, grey mackintosh and grey felt hat in town, or in plus-fours, thick stockings and a patterned home-knitted sweater or *genser* (the origin of Guernsey) in the country.

His 'special peculiarities' were bulging eyes, which were made the subject of much scandal by his enemies. It was said that they protruded because he had a tumour on the brain and was therefore mentally unbalanced, but a panel of doctors subjected him to the most searching and painful examinations during his trial and found no trace of any deformity.

It was also alleged that he had caught malaria during the resettlement of Armenian refugees after the First World War and that this too had affected his brain, but, again, the doctors found no vestige of evidence to support this slander.

Most damaging to his reputation were the allegations of his brother,

Dr. Jørgen Quisling, after the war. Jørgen said that Vidkun was impotent—to put it bluntly, that 'his testicles had never fallen'—and that in consequence all his energies went to his brain, thus making possible his terrific concentration and capacity for absorbing information. 'If it had not been for his strength of character', added Jørgen by way of mitigation, 'he would have become a homosexual.'

Coming from a brother, from whom Vidkun was inseparable for many years—and a doctor at that—such a diagnosis requires serious examination. For, if it were true, it would delight all Quisling's enemies and would support the popular theory that he was insane, unbalanced or at least a crank.

I am, however, as satisfied as one can be, without having inspected his body, that there is no truth in Jørgen Quisling's statement. Jørgen himself went to seed, if not mad, after the Occupation. In mid-war he wrote a long thesis attempting to prove that Jesus Christ and the Apostles were homosexuals, thus embarrassing his brother and obliging him to ban its publication. After Quisling was arrested, Jørgen refused to visit him, to give evidence on his behalf or even to see him before the execution, whereas many people, who were far less closely connected, were not too ashamed or scared to do so. Later Jørgen was one of Quisling's very few supporters to repudiate him or to disassociate themselves from him in order to jump on the band wagon of 'good Norwegians'. (As in no other Occupied country, the Norwegian 'Nazis' still sincerely protest their loyalty to Quisling's memory and have no sense of guilt over what they regard as their patriotic stand against the Germans.) Finally, Jørgen took to spiritualism and saw visions of Vidkun. He also took to drink and narcotics, from which he died. He is therefore a shaky source.

If there had been any sign of impotence the Court doctors would certainly have pounced on it and the Bench would have made the very most of it—much to the jubilation of the Press and the new authorities. (Incidentally, Quisling's corpse was exposed at Police Headquarters to gloating visitors for most of the day of the execution.)

I have approached Mrs. Quisling on this delicate but important subject. She informed me emphatically: 'Jørgen had an inferiority complex concerning his brother and tried to belittle him—to impress people by shocking them. My husband was a good and kind man—normal in every way—and we lived a normal life together as man and wife.' She was horrified that such a rumour about her husband should have reached the ears of a foreigner and implored me to deny it with all the force at my command. I have no compunction in doing so.

Not one of Vidkun Quisling's classmates could be produced, persuaded or provoked by the post-war authorities to smear or betray him. On the contrary, they banded together with remarkable honesty and courage to defend him in court, much to the anger of the Bench. Through their spokesman, Rector Ullmann, they concurred:

'I can give you only the finest picture of him as a person—his genuine friendship, and his fine association with friends. . . . It was not only I who thought so but the entire class without exception—and I have discussed him with some of our classmates after I was summoned as a witness in this case—and I am sure that I speak on behalf of all of them in saying that we found him a fast and genuine friend, very kind and considerate. He was a most exceptionally well informed person . . . we looked up to him and admired him. . . . We never noticed anything small and treacherous about him. . . . At least to some of us he was quite helpful in our studies, since he was so far ahead of us that it was easy for him to be so; and he was never afraid to let us know ahead of time the results of his own work and studies.'

So much for unworthy post-war allegations that Quisling's scholastic triumphs were won by cheating!

The Rector continued: 'He had a certain trait of character—possibly of psychological interest—in that he was fundamentally very bashful, and I have now come to the conclusion that he suffered from a strong inferiority complex. He possessed a large amount of information . . . and he was always present at the meetings of our student society, but he almost never participated in the discussions . . . I believe it was a trait of his that he never dared to get up and express his opinions; and this is the opinion of the other classmates.'

Certainly he was shy. All his surviving friends and associates testify that. But whether that was due to an inferiority complex, which later, it might be argued, turned into reverse to become a superiority complex, is doubtful. Instead, may not his silences have been due to intellectual and social good manners, stemming from the competitive erudition of his home and an inbred Norwegian diffidence about setting oneself above one's fellows? Again, may not intellectual honesty, based on copious study, also have deterred him from throwing

29

his weight about until later in life, when he had tested his opinions by experience, formed conclusions and deemed that the time had come for decisive action? He was a complicated and many-sided man and such speculations are apposite, though inconclusive.

Much capital has been made by Quisling's enemies out of Rector Ullmann's next statement:

'His great hero seemed to be Napoleon. . . . That became evident time and again . . . he dreamt about the wonderful man he would one day become. For this impression I found proof in the fact that he . . . once showed great interest in becoming an outstanding personality in our history. That was a very decided trait of his.'

It was argued from this that Quisling always harboured a 'lust for power', but it is not unknown for a youth to identify himself with some great historical figure and to dream of glorifying his country. What could be more usual, innocent or even laudable? How else do great men of action start? There is little or no evidence of overweening ambition or dictatorial instincts in Ullmann's recollection.

Certainly Quisling's classmates never interpreted his ambition against him. Mrs. Cecilie S. Dahl, an intelligent old lady, who was one of them and contributed to Ullmann's evidence, told me:

'At the twenty-fifth anniversary of passing our student examination at Skien, Quisling spoke seriously to our class about the danger of Russia, whence he had just returned (in 1930), and we told him that he ought to issue a warning. That was the start of his political career and movement (*Nasjonal Samling*, i.e.National Unification).'

In short, Quisling was far from being disliked, ridiculed or distrusted at school, after his first term. Not a word was heard against his character, attainments or ambitions until he clashed head-on with the near-Red Labour Party in 1932. He was not only regarded as a paragon and respected as such. He was liked.

Even his contentious biographer in the *Norsk Biografisk Lexicon* concedes that he was a 'serious, lonely boy, brusque and wary, but could brighten up and smile in a remarkably childlike and winning manner'.

4

Sword of Honour

PATRIOTIC fervour fused with a sense of Norwegian history
and an affinity with his native soil to sweep Quisling into the
Army when he matriculated with all honours from Skien in 1905.

In that year Norway regained her independence from Denmark or
Sweden after five centuries, thus becoming responsible for her own
security, and Quisling was moved to abandon his more obvious bent
for an academic career or the Church in order to play a part in building
his country's defence system.

The drama of Norway's bid for independence is, of course, part of
history—how Sweden haughtily refused to allow her to have her own
Consuls abroad to tend the growing Norwegian Mercantile Marine;
how this touched off the spark of Norwegian nationalism and nearly
led to war with the obdurate Swedes; how Edward VII warned King
Gustaf V that he would send the Royal Navy into the Baltic unless his
son-in-law, Prince Carl of Denmark, was allowed to ascend the
Norwegian throne; and how the grave national hero, Dr. Fridtjof
Nansen, abandoned his republican tendencies to combine with the
debonair Prime Minister, Christian Michelsen of Bergen, to put Prince
Carl across and to organise a plebiscite which enthroned him as King
Haakon VII by a large majority.

Exactly how the vast length of Norway, at the cross-roads of the
North, was to be defended by three million people with few resources

has never been explained. Kaiser Wilhelm was already sabre-rattling and visiting the Norwegian west coast annually, but this vital question was never faced until Norway half-heartedly joined the North Atlantic Treaty Organisation after the grim realities of the Second World War.

Unarmed 'neutrality' was the soporific which lulled Norway into a fatal state of false security between 1905 and 1940—as Quisling discovered and preached.

But were the King and successive Governments *really* so unrealistic and irresponsible as it seems?

Was there no *quid pro quo* for Edward VII's decisive intervention on behalf of King Haakon and Queen Maud and the dynastic link which he formed in an age of naval rivalry with a country less than 300 miles from the British Isles? Many Norwegians, Right and Left, have their suspicions.

Nansen was immediately sent to London as Minister, not merely to cut a figure as the leading citizen of his newly liberated country, but to conduct serious diplomacy. It is generally agreed that his mission was to seek an alliance between Britain and Norway and thus to fill the glaring gap in his country's status as an independent Power. That he failed is generally attributed to Britain's reluctance to assume responsibility for such a long and exposed coastline and to fear of mortally offending the Kaiser. At any rate Nansen returned home a bitterly disappointed man.

But was he entirely empty-handed? Again, many Norwegians think *not*. Edward VII, that stickler for formality, had laid aside all protocol for Nansen, whom he had known and admired since the latter's triumphant visit to London after beating the record to the North Pole and reappearing from the dead in 1895-96. The Royal Family held 'open house' for Nansen, whose manly charm soon captivated Princess Victoria and led to a long flirtation, besides adverse gossip in Norway. This unique mission culminated in Edward VII paying a State visit to Oslo in May, 1908, and Nansen receiving the Grand Cross of the Royal Victorian Order, which is in the gift of the Sovereign.

Did, in fact, the State visit mark the conclusion of at least a secret 'understanding' between Edward and Haakon, if not a secret treaty? Many Norwegians believe that the minimum Edward extracted from his son-in-law was a verbal agreement that Norwegian home waters and key bases ashore in the South would be put at the disposal of

Britain, if necessary, in case of a Continental war. It is even rumoured that a document to that effect is buried in the Norwegian State Archives.

Whether there is any truth in those suspicions, they are important because their very existence illustrates the distrust with which Right and Left have always treated each other in Norway. No study of the German Occupation, including its prelude and aftermath, is complete without taking the supposed English tie into account.

Note, too, that Nansen was always pro-British. Witness his unstinted help to Captain Robert Falcon Scott, RN, in 1910 in preference to his fellow Norwegian, Captain Roald Amundsen, when they were preparing their Polar expeditions. Soon Nansen was to become more than Quisling's distant hero and inspiration—his chief in stricken Russia and his political mentor at home. This should be taken into account, also, in judging Quisling's lifelong claim that he was Nansen's disciple and was always pro-British into the bargain.

Those were stirring times for Norway and Quisling responded with greater vigour than ever when he entered Krigskola, the equivalent of the Royal Military College, Sandhurst, or West Point, in 1905.

The courses presented no more difficulty to him than the Skien curriculum. They were child's play and he mastered them so quickly that he had time 'to devour the whole General Staff library', in the words of the *Norsk Biografisk Lexicon*. 'As usual he was always first.' In 1908 he passed out of Krigskola, the Military Academy, with 'the best average grade ever obtained by anyone in the more than one hundred years' existence of that school'. He also received the special honour of an audience with the King, the only graduate to do so. This *innstilling* was equivalent to winning the Sword of Honour at Sandhurst with the added and unprecedented distinction of receiving it from the hands of the Sovereign.

Major Tryggve Gran, DFC, MC, was two years younger than Quisling. He was the ski expert on Scott's Antarctic Expedition, planted Queen Maud's personal standard on Queen Maud Land and found Scott's body in 1913. Next year he was the first man to fly the North Sea and the length of Norway. Later he had a spectacular career with the Royal Flying Corps in France, being credited with downing twenty-seven Huns in single combat, and was the thirteenth officer

gazetted in the RAF. As a youth he graduated from the Norwegian Naval College with distinction in navigation. Most of the top brass in the present Norwegian Air Force were his 'boys'. He therefore speaks with the authority of a brave and efficient officer.

'Quisling was idolised by Norwegian officers as the best brain that ever came out of the Defence School,' Gran told me. 'We also looked up to him as the most experienced internationalist in Norway after Nansen. As an officer, I shared this opinion.'

Captain Odd Melsom told me: 'At Krigskol Quisling reconnoitred forty miles across country alone one winter night in the mountains and so astonished his fellow officers that his exploit was cited as an example of keenness decades later. His extreme reserve amounted to a "primitive force". He was hardy and could stand all extremes of climate. His physique was splendid and he had iron will-power.'

I believe that Gran and Melsom are honest men, but they both supported Quisling and are therefore suspect in Norway. So let General Otto Ruge, Commander-in-Chief during the Norwegian Campaign in 1940, assess Quisling as a soldier with whom he served on the General Staff:

'Even though Quisling was rather a puzzling fellow . . . he was a very intelligent person, a most excellent worker, and in his personal life he was an ascetic.'

Those were brave words to utter before the Court trying Quisling. 'Was he disregardful of other persons, cruel and brutal?' Ruge was asked. 'No,' came the reply, 'I have never seen anything of that—no symptoms of that kind.' His personal need for money was very limited. 'Was he dominated by ambition?' 'Yes,' said Ruge, 'if that word is used with a noble meaning, that is a man who is convinced about his own greatness and ability and who sought the chance to use his capacities.'

Major-General Halvor Hanson, a later C-in-C, was also man enough to speak up for Quisling in Court, being his contemporary in Military High School, and on the General Staff and in the Officer Corps' Military Association. Quisling 'did what he could' as Defence Minister, and as such he 'aroused no misgivings'. He was 'very sober in money matters and very honourable'. He was also 'an exceptionally clever man' with 'a high moral character'. Hanson saw 'no resemblance to the Quisling depicted in Court by the Prosecution'.

In his evidence regarding Quisling's personal habits, Rector Ullmann stated: 'It has been said in the newspapers that he is addicted to alcohol. I have associated with him from time to time clear to 1939, and I wish to assert categorically that he was always sober and that he hardly ever tasted alcoholic drinks of any kind, and he never smoked. His life and conduct were very discreet. He used money very sparingly; he had very plainly a very limited understanding of money and its worth. . . . When he became Defence Minister (in 1931), he did not even enquire about his salary. Thus I believe he was never hungry for money . . . he lived well within his means.'

As late as 1937, Quisling was lecturing to the Military Association and the King saw fit to attend!

In any case, he left the Military Academy—as he left Skien—a prodigy and a paragon.

5

The Russian Bug

AFTER his superb performance at the Military Academy, Quisling returned to Skien for a year to teach. 'As a small boy I had wanted to preach on Sundays and to be a school-teacher on weekdays', he wrote of himself in 1930. 'But as the result of intense reading of world and Norwegian history, and perhaps under the influence of the patriotic atmosphere of the time, I chose a military career.'

Those twin desires never left him. He preached and lectured to Norway for the last fifteen years of his life and actually planned to retire to the family parsonage towards the end.

But in 1911 the General Staff grabbed their most brilliant cadet.

For the third time he settled down to an orgy of study, this time specialising in science and mathematics in his spare time. By 1915 Lieutenant Quisling, aged twenty-eight, was in a different class intellectually from his brother officers. As the Senior Physician, Dr. Jon Leikvam, told the Court, after interviewing Quisling in prison: 'He is a very intelligent man and he likes to adopt such lofty themes as theology, philosophy and mathematical problems. He has been dis-cussing the Quantum Theory, the construction of atoms and matters which normally only occupy the minds of Nobel Prizewinners. His academic discussion of these problems is marked by a keen sense of logic and often by profound insight and the utmost knowledge.'

He also became the leading expert on ballistics in Norway* and in 1916-17 served with the General Inspector of Field Artillery.

Then came the turning point in his career and the strongest influence in his life—Russia.

In 1918 he became Adjutant to the General Staff, with the rank of Captain, and chose Russia as his field of study. He learned the language, geography, economy and industrial conditions of the Tsarist Empire with his usual thoroughness—everything which might affect Russian war potential—and wrote an assessment for the General Staff.

Naturally, he was appointed Military Attaché to Petrograd, and he served in that capacity from April 5, 1918, to October 8, 1920. He thus arrived in the Russian capital four months after the Revolution in November 1917, and was thus present at the birth of the most important single development in the twentieth century—the first serious challenge to Christian civilisation since the Arab incursions into Spain and France in the Middle Ages and the Turkish onslaught on Vienna in 1683. Since he already knew the language and the background, he was peculiarly well fitted to assess the implications on the spot and to advise his country in the brand-new crisis which burst on the whole North within a few months. Very properly he took his duties with the utmost solemnity.

The whole future of Arctic Scandinavia was at stake at the time, quite apart from the fact that newly-born Finland, until recently a Tsarist Grand Duchy, was in the throes of far-reaching internal strife. Geographically, the Scandinavian Peninsula is the tail end of the body of Euro-Asia, as represented by the Soviet Union, which occupies a sixth of the land surface of the world. Until this century, the tundra stretching from Arctic Norway, across Sweden and Finland, to the White Sea was no-man's-land, across which nomadic Lapps roamed with their reindeer herds almost at will; where fishermen muscled in together, undeterred by territorial waters, among the vast shoals of the rich feeding-grounds on the verge of the ice; where explorers of the surrounding nations competed to beat the elements and to bring the Arctic under control.

This object was at the back of the mind of Jonas Lied, when he opened the Kara Sea Route between Siberia, Norway and England in

* Only one other Artillery officer has ever been awarded the Royal Norwegian Gold Medal for Ballistics.

1913, and of Nansen, when he went with Lied on a personally conducted tour of Siberia in order to compile the available information into his book, *Through Siberia*. Quisling's mind when he secured his key post in Petrograd was working along the same geopolitical lines.

He knew that, historically, Norway and Russia had been linked since the Dark Ages. Olav Tryggvason, grandson of Harald Fairhair, was nephew of a Norseman named Sigurd, joint ruler of Russia with Valdimar (Wladimir, 972-1014). Olav's father was killed in battle, after which his mother, Astrid, sought asylum with Sigurd. On the way mother and child were captured by Baltic pirates and held in bondage until Sigurd ransomed them and brought them to Holmgard (Novgorod). As a boy Olav fought in Valdimar's army until he left to become a Viking in the Baltic, and then he harried North Germany and Denmark for three years. After three more years in Russia, he sailed west again in 991 to harry Germany, the Low Countries, England, Scotland, Ireland, the Isle of Man, Wales and France. In 994 he participated in an attack on London, which failed, and he was sponsored into the Christian religion at Andover by Ethelred the Unready. Next year he returned to Norway, aged about twenty-seven, and received homage as Harald Fairhair's heir. He destroyed the famous pagan temple at Trondheim and tore the jewels from the idols in a successful campaign to convert Norway to Christianity, at least in name. But after five years' tempestuous reign (995-1000), he perished aboard the Long Serpent, the finest fighting ship afloat, in a battle with the Danes, Swedes and rebels. His laws were enacted by an assembly of freemen (Ting) and they were enforced by his bodyguard (Hird).

Another Norwegian hero with Russian links was King Olav Haraldson (St. Olav). His father died early and he was brought up as a pagan. In 1007, aged twelve, he went to sea and lived as a Viking in the Baltic, where he began to 'redden the headlands with blood'. In 1009-10 he attacked London and next year Canterbury, but he was baptised at Rouen in Normandy when he was eighteen and joined Ethelred to chase King Canute of Denmark out of England. In 1014 or 1015 he returned to Norway, where he seized the West Coast provinces held by one of Olav Tryggvason's three successors, and within a year reunited the whole country. Although he was far from an ascetic and was known as 'The Fat', with a weakness for women, he brought English bishops with him. His idea was to build the Norwegian

Church on English lines, but deteriorating relations with Canute in England forced him close to the Archbishops of Bremen and Hamburg.

Olav appealed to national sentiment by rebelling against Norway's Danish and Swedish overlords, but in 1028 he was defeated by Canute, who annexed the whole country, and he fled through Sweden to Russia, where he was entertained by King Jaroslav and Queen Ingigerd, to whom he had been betrothed. In 1030, leaving his bastard son Magnus at the Russian Court, he sailed for Norway, collecting Swedish help on the way. But he was killed at Stiklastadir, forty miles northeast of Trondheim, in the biggest battle in Norwegian history. His 'martyrdom' occurred during an eclipse, and thenceforth he was regarded as an emanation of Christ. Within hours wounds were healed with his blood and when his body was recovered from the sandbanks of the River Nid five years later, to be buried in the Church of St. Clement, which he founded in Trondheim, his flesh was not corrupt. Miracles were reported through his intercession from London to Constantinople throughout the Middle Ages, and many churches were dedicated to him. In 1035 Magnus returned from Russia to claim the throne and was known as 'The Good' until his death in 1047.

Such epics may seem very remote to British readers, whose history books begin (unrealistically) with 1066, but the sagas were very real to Quisling, who constantly referred to the two great Olavs. Norway's two modern kings, Haakon and Olav, deliberately harked back to the Viking age in acquiring those names. The influence of the Norse heroes cannot therefore be dismissed as a far-fetched absurdity. History combines with geography to keep Norwegians Russia-conscious and Quisling undoubtedly felt that he was treading familiar ground during the ten years he was to spend there on and off, in different capacities. He also developed a missionary, almost Messianic, zeal in enlightening Norway in her relationship with the Soviet Union.

Politically, too, Norway was involved up to the hilt with Soviet Russia when Quisling went to Petrograd in 1918. During the First World War the fledgling Labour Party had become fiercely Radical and had strong Communist sympathies. It believed in revolution as a means of achieving power, and this became its official policy in 1918. Shortly afterwards the Labour Party joined the Third International and accepted its principles, the so-called 'Moscow Thesis', according to which the dictatorship of the proletariat and peasants was to be established, if necessary by force, as the form of government. The more moderate wing broke away to form a separate party, the Norwegian Social Democratic Labour Party, but they did not break with Moscow until 1923—and only then on the technical issue as to whether it would be convenient to advocate atheism in a Lutheran country. The Labour Party still kept their revolutionary programme. These Left-wing factions fought each other bitterly until the Labour Party and the Social Democrats merged in 1927 for tactical reasons and the minority formed the Norwegian Communist Party. In that year Labour became the largest group in the Storting (Parliament), with 59 out of 150 seats. In January, 1928, a Labour member, Christoper Hornsrud, became Prime Minister.

Meanwhile hatred of Labour's Marxism had been sown throughout the country and even the Party's patriotism was questioned. Labour's focus was the Soviet Union and before long the Norwegian Government became the most extreme in Western Europe. In Russia, Quisling therefore found himself at the fountain-head of the Labour Party's inspiration and in the thick of an ideological struggle, which coloured his subsequent life and still pervades the whole Norwegian body politic.

The history of the German Occupation is a continuation of the internecine feud, which was born after the First World War and was not settled until the Labour Government returned from exile, with the help of Britain and under the aura of the King, after the Second World War.

Quisling's fate is inexplicable unless this bitter background is taken into account. He was bitten by the Russian bug, like the Labour Party, but their reactions were poles apart.

6

Object Lesson

IN October 1920, Captain Quisling was transferred round the corner of the Gulf of Finland, from Petrograd to Helsinki, to be not only Military Attaché but Secretary in the newly opened Norwegian Legation. Diplomatic relations with the young Soviet Union had just been broken and his special duties were still Russian affairs: another key post.

No Iron Curtain yet sealed the long Finnish frontier running from the outskirts of Petrograd, through the great lakes of Ladoga and Onega, and then through the forests of Karelia to the Murmansk Peninsula. He could therefore watch world-shattering Russian developments at point-blank range from the new diplomatic vantage-point. With several years' hindsight and his existing contacts, he had a pull over his colleagues. He was able to continue his study of Communism in practice, on his threshold, and to develop his dawning ideology, which, he later claimed, dated from those days, as one might expect.

Finland was intrinsically interesting, too. What happened there was an object lesson on what could also happen in any neighbouring country, such as Norway, and Quisling was one of the very few Norwegians who observed it on the spot.

The way the Finns rallied, spiritually and militarily, was a first-hand example of how a small Northern country could stave off a mighty neighbour and preserve its independence.

The way they later bickered politically and provoked the rise of a violent nationalistic Right-wing movement, which saved the country from the extreme Left but eventually brought the country to the point of suicide in the Second World War, also contributed to Quisling's ideas a decade later.

The surrounding events of his time in Petrograd and Helsinki furthermore sowed some of the seeds of the Second World War. The unwillingness of Britain and France to grant Russia satisfactory guarantees for the integrity of Finland and the Baltic States precipitated the Molotov-Ribbentrop Pact, which led immediately to the Russian occupation of the Baltic States and to the invasion of Finland in November 1939.

The forgotten Russo-Finnish 'Winter War' revived the dormant struggle for power in the North and so led to a race between Germany and the Allies for Norway and beyond.

That in turn led to the German Occupation of Denmark and Norway and to Quisling's intervention.

Proper attention must therefore be paid to the Finnish situation, which Quisling understood far better than the vast majority of his countrymen. This is a neglected aspect of the Quisling story.

The price which he paid for imparting his inside knowledge at home was ostracism. Norway did not want to listen or to learn.

As J. Hampden Jackson says in his *Finland*,* 'The wars between the new nations of Sweden and Russia were a source of unmitigated misery to Finland. She was the anvil on which the fate of north-eastern Europe was forged.' Finland was an anomaly—until recently part of the Russian Empire, acknowledging the authority of the Tsar, not as Emperor but as a constitutionally-limited Grand Duke, and expecting Russian protection but making no contribution to the Russian conscript army; containing good Baltic ports, yet subjecting Russian goods to tariffs; extending to within a few miles of the Russian capital, yet free from the Russian writ.

Alexander II rejoiced in Finland's liberties. Alexander III believed in the value of a contented buffer state on Russia's north-west flank—a compromise which the Soviet Union seems to appreciate at long last. Nicholas II, however, was more inept. He believed that the religious and moral values which he cherished could best be secured by Russian

* Allen & Unwin.

autocratic government in the interests of the Slav peoples. Finland had to be brought into line with the rest of Russia. So General Bobrikov was sent to Helsinki in 1898 as Governor-General. He had made his name in the ruthless Russification of the Baltic States and immediately set about disbanding the Finnish army and incorporating it in the Russian Forces. The Russo-Finnish honeymoon was over. The country simply went into mourning, as Hampden Jackson calls the dour and dogged Finnish passive resistance, which is an emanation of this people's famous characteristic *sissu* (guts).

The Press was muzzled, the wires tapped and the mail censored. Yet 522,931 signatures were collected from a total population of 2,700,000 to protest to Nicholas. He refused to see the 500 parish representatives who brought the list to St. Petersburg. Nor would he see the international deputation bearing the signatures of Florence Nightingale, Herbert Spencer, Anatole France, Zola and Ibsen. A reign of oppression followed.

Bobrikov tried to enforce his Army Bill by calling up 25,000 conscripts, of whom 15,000 refused to serve. Seventeen writers and fifteen judges, who upheld the men, were banished. The Finnish police, provincial governors and mayors were replaced by Russians. Three hundred Civil Servants were dismissed. Russian was made compulsory as the first foreign language in schools. Barracks in Helsinki and other towns were filled with Russian troops.

Bobrikov was shot dead in 1904: Eugen Schauman, the young Civil Servant who committed the murder single-handed and then took his own life, left a letter for the Tsar, saying: 'Since there is no prospect of a truthful representation of the real state of affairs reaching Your Majesty within a measurable period, and of General Bobrikov being recalled in consequence, the only remaining thing is to act in self-defence and to render him innocuous. . . . I sacrifice my own life by my own hand in order to convince Your Majesty yet more fully what grave evils prevail in the Grand Duchy of Finland.'

Aspirations for independence had started among the Finnish-Swedish nobility in the eighteenth century, but it was neither they who reversed Tsarist policy, nor the formal politicians, nor the assassin. It was the national passive resistance, ably led by the newly formed Labour Party.

At the turn of the century the Finnish population was divided roughly into 111,000 landed families, 160,000 tenant families, 207,000 landless agricultural labourers and 80,000 mill- or factory-workers, who represented 12 per cent of the whole. By 1903 membership of the Labour Party still only amounted to 13,500. But Russia's defeat by Japan in 1905 encouraged Labour to think that this was their hour and they proclaimed a General Strike in sympathy with similar disturbances in Russia proper. The whole nation responded. The police went on strike and university students identified themselves by white armbands when they joined up to maintain order. Not to be outdone, the young Labour men wore red armbands. So the 'White Guards' and 'Red Guards' were born. On the sixth day Russia gave way. Bobrikov's innovations were withdrawn and the Four Estates transformed the Diet into a one-chamber Parliament or House of Representatives elected by universal suffrage for all men and women over twenty-four. Eighty-two of the 200 members elected in 1907 were Social Democrats.

This produced a second period of Russification even more intense and far-reaching than that following Bobrikov's Manifesto and it continued until the Russian Revolution in 1917. Protests poured in from all over Europe, including one from 120 MPs at Westminster. Finnish political consciousness heightened and Finnish self-confidence grew with an astonishing boom in the forest industries.

Finland's hope of liberation centred on a German victory over Russia in 1914, and 1,800 volunteers from the resistance movement were sent to Germany to form a corps known as the 27th Jäger Battalion, which was intended to help to throw the Russians out.

England's main interest in Finland before the Great War was in the growing forest industries, notably in cellulose for newsprint.

So, on the eve of the Russian Revolution, we find this small democratic Northern Country girding itself spiritually, politically and militarily to defend its liberty against the next round of Russian aggression, and seeking help from Germany.

This line-up was to continue after the Revolution, when Quisling entered the scene, and it is easy to imagine the impact the situation made on his eager mind.

What could have been more natural than for Norway to turn to Germany—failing England—when Russian imperialism revived under the Soviets in 1939-40 and all the Northern Countries were again threatened by Russian expansion through Finland, with armed intervention by the Western Powers thrown in as an additional danger?

There was already a parallel between Finland's predicament in the First World War and Norway's dilemma in the Second World War —a likeness which was to be intensified by subsequent events. Finland was going to be the anvil of the Great Powers once more.

Let Marshal Gustaf Mannerheim, the creator of modern Finland, take up his country's success story. It will be seen how closely his thoughts and actions corresponded with Quisling's later behaviour when Norway was heading for disaster. In his *Memoirs*★ Mannerheim wrote: 'The Socialist, Kerenski, contributed actively to the downfall of Russia because of his indifference towards extremists and his opposition to all attempts to strengthen the executive power. . . . Everything was done to facilitate Lenin's *coup d'état*, which was, indeed, not difficult. . . . The freedom so suddenly won had been too much for the Russian people. They sank back into a slavery which was to develop into a world menace. I had not been in Helsinki for a week in December 1917, before I realised how menacing the situation was.'

Quisling, too, feared that the very pink Norwegian Labour Party would pave the way for the Communists to seize control of his own country unless they were nipped in the bud.

Mannerheim continued: 'Our Defence Corps was in respect of arms heavily handicapped compared with the Reds. . . . In December the Red leaders organised the individual corps according to districts, as a basis for mobilisation. . . . In case of need there were Russian depots to draw upon. But our greatest danger were the Russian troops in the country (some 40,000 men).

'(On January 16, 1918) the head of the Government and I were in complete agreement that the task confided to me did not merely concern the restoration of order, but the liberation of the country. . . . I agreed to accept the task, but on one definite understanding—that the Senate did not ask for the armed intervention of Sweden, nor that of Germany.'

In fact Mannerheim relied on the fighting qualities of the Finns, hardened through centuries of battle with Russia, and on the German-trained officer corps of Finnish 'Jägers' to beat the Reds and save the country. He did not spurn German or Swedish forces when they were

★ Cassell.

45

offered, but his emphasis was on self-reliance, and the War of Independence was virtually won by the time the Germans arrived. Quisling, too, appealed for years to the martial spirit of Norway, but it was dormant, if not dead, and the Germans took the country overnight. Like Mannerheim, Quisling also sought an understanding with the Germans in order to save his country from Bolshevism. Unlike Mannerheim, he did not succeed in keeping the German intervention within bounds and that failure was largely due to the difference between the Finnish and the Norwegian character. The Finns are made of sterner stuff.

By March 5 the Jägers had knocked eighteen Finnish battalions into shape and Mannerheim was able to launch an offensive, although he had only 14,000 men against 30,000 Red Guards and the 40,000 Russian troops. General Count Rudiger von der Goltz did not arrive with the German Division until April 3-5. By then Tampere, the industrial capital, had fallen, and Mannerheim was at Mikkeli (his headquarters in two later wars against Russia), preparing to roll the enemy across Karelia to Petrograd.

The Germans took Helsinki on April 11 and Hämeenlinna on the 26th, after which they joined with the Finnish Army to attack Viipuri, the ancient Karelian capital, on the 20th. Five days later the Red Government fled ignominiously to Petrograd, leaving the Red Guards to fight a hopeless rearguard action, and the Whites celebrated victory on May 1.

Just what a small country could achieve by leadership, determination and bravery against a great foreign power was proved at the cost of 24,000 Finnish dead, indicating what Norway might have done had she followed Quisling's lead before 1940.

On May 18 Senator Per Svinhufvud, a rugged stalwart of the Resistance, and the brilliant banker, Dr. Juho Paasikivi, were appointed respectively Head of State and Prime Minister. In the hour of victory, Mannerheim proclaimed: 'Without unity a strong army cannot be created, and only a strong nation can face the future with security'— words which Quisling echoed a thousand times at home with no effect.

But Finland was not out of the wood yet. The Senate proposed to hand over responsibility for defence to the Germans and to allow them bases, whereupon Mannerheim went into exile in disgust. On October

9 Prince Frederick Charles of Hesse, the Kaiser's brother-in-law, was chosen by the Parliament to be King of Finland. This initiative came to naught as the Germans lost the war next month, but it indicates the deep fear and hatred of Russia and Communism in the North at the time and the comparatively tolerant view of German imperialism. This attitude, so different from that of the Western Powers, was prevalent as late as 1940.

Mannerheim reached London from Aberdeen as a private individual, having heard that the Kaiser had fled to Holland, and had a long talk with Lord Robert Cecil at the Foreign Office, which was vacillating between restoring the pre-war Russian frontiers and partition. 'I did not encounter much understanding', wrote Mannerheim, 'of my fears for the troubles which a Bolshevik Russia would cause Europe.... The Finnish question was one of those political matters which England did not desire to tackle'.

In Paris he heard that he had been appointed Regent of Finland and 'could act with all the authority invested in the Head of State'. He assumed office on December 12 and on the 22nd issued a manifesto again stressing the importance of national unity and a strong defence.

By the 30th Finnish troops had arrived in Estonia to help fling the Bolsheviks out as Mannerheim 'considered it important, both from the political and the operational point of view, to have Finnish forces on either side of the Gulf of Finland'.

On a round of state visits to the other Northern capitals Mannerheim was informed by the Norwegian Minister in Copenhagen of 'threats that were being expressed in radical Left-wing quarters in connection with my impending visit to Oslo'. At first these were restricted to street demonstrations, 'then they involved the electric light and water supply to the castle', and Mannerheim declined King Haakon's invitation on the grounds of 'a marked deterioration in my health'.

That incident perfectly illustrates the pro-Communist trend in Norway and indifference to the factors which saved Finnish independence. The perverse and lazy frame of mind in Norway was incapable of heeding Quisling's later warnings and his campaign for armed neutrality, which were based on his Finnish experience as well as on common sense.

In April 1919, a new Finnish Government took office under a Liberal Prime Minister with a 60-40 majority over the Social Democrats and

Finland received the Great Powers' recognition by the end of June, despite the machinations of the White Russian *émigré* authorities at the Paris Peace Conference. In July Mannerheim retired into private life.

Meanwhile the White Russian government, under Foreign Minister Sazonov in Paris, had been urging Finland to join in a campaign against Petrograd since the spring of 1918. The proposed onslaught was to be part of a three-pronged offensive against the Bolsheviks from the Urals, the Caucasus and the Kola Peninsula.

By March 1919, Admiral Kolchak had penetrated from Siberia as far west as Perm and Ufa. He proclaimed himself to be Supreme Ruler of the White Russians and was later recognised as such by the Entente. By May, General Denikin in the Caucasus was beginning to move north. Supreme command of the Northern Army Corps was in the hands of General Judenich, who had the political support of 'the Government of North-West Russia' established under British military protection on the Murmansk-Archangel Front. A smaller group under General Rodzianko, who had served with Mannerheim in the élite Chevalier Guards of Imperial Russia, was quartered in Estonia, whither Judenich departed from Helsinki in July, hoping somehow to launch the Petrograd offensive.

The Allied War Council sponsored the proposed attack and the desired participation of Finnish troops. But Kolchak sabotaged the plan by sticking to his Government's decision in Paris that it would never relinquish 'the rights which are the basis of the political and economic connections between Russia and Finland'.* A successful White Intervention might therefore have replaced Finland under Russian bondage, and the Finns accordingly hung fire. The Petrograd offensive never materialised and the whole misguided campaign fizzled out next year, but not before irreparable harm had been done.

Russia finally recognised the independence of Finland at Dorpat (Tartu) in October 1920, when Stalin, the Commissar for Minorities, and Leo Trotsky, the warlord, signed for the USSR; Paasikivi for Finland. This document has been Finland's title deed to a free existence ever since. The Russians, however, regarded it as an agreement made under duress. They never forgave the Finns for their participation in the White Intervention in Estonia, nor for their wavering over the

* This was again argued by the USSR in 1939.

Allied designs on Petrograd. No Soviet Government has ever forgotten the British and French co-operation with the White Russians in attempting to crush the Revolution at birth and to restore the Tsar, nor the invasion of the Kola Peninsula by British troops.

Those old sores were behind the Molotov-Ribbentrop Pact, which precipitated the Second World War and the Russo-Finnish 'Winter War'. The Russians were pining to reverse the 1920 settlement as eagerly as Hitler sought to undo Versailles. Quisling understood this and survived long enough to be able to say, 'I told you so'. For he saw the Red Army march into North Norway, annexing North Finland on the way, and bossing an Allied Control Commission in Helsinki. Another two-and-a-half years and he would have seen Russia trying to drag Finland behind the Iron Curtain* at the same time as Czechoslovakia.

It might have been Quisling talking when Mannerheim declared to the Finnish people, as he went into retirement in 1919: 'Only by being steadfast in our stand against Bolshevism could we count upon that interest on the part of the Great Powers that constituted one of the corner-stones of the national edifice.'

Yet in 1922 Finland returned twenty-seven Communists to Parliament. 'The passivity shown by the authorities amounted actually to a vindication of the Red Revolt', Mannerheim wrote. 'Finland's Social-Democrats were, in fact, nihilists in the matter of Defence. . . . Their draft programme of Defence stated: "Social-Democracy rejects such illusions as that the working class must always and in all circumstances be bound to defend their own country by military means. . . . A reduction in military strength is being increasingly urged by the whole of the working class and the workers' international." '

That was every bit as true of Norway, where Left-wing pacifism was rampant and where independence, won fifteen years earlier than in Finland and much more easily, was also being dissipated. As in Finland, the decadence of the Left eventually produced strong reaction from the Right.

* The 'Pact Crisis' of February-April, 1948, when Russia proposed a non-aggression pact. The fellow-travelling Prime Minister, Pekkala, and Minister of Internal Affairs, Leino, were outmanœuvred, but it was touch and go. Members of the Cabinet changed their address nightly lest they should be kidnapped by Communists.

In 1926, Vaino Tanner, the pillar of the Social Democrats, who had broken with Otto Wille Kuusinen* and the Reds during the Civil War, became Prime Minister of Finland. Mixed motives allowed him to give the Communists full rein: magnanimity; Marxist sympathies; political calculations to the effect that any stick should be used to cow the Opposition and thus to attract waverers.

That was playing with fire. In 1929 the League of Communist Youth staged a rally, 400 strong, at Lapua, which had been the scene of the first White rally in the Civil War. In answer to this blatant affront, the local farmers gave the red-shirted youths a hiding and packed them off on the train by which they had arrived. The pious and conservative yeomen's direct action struck a chord throughout the nation and a mass rally was organised at Lapua, calling for the suppression of Communism. The Communists had gone too far. President and Premier expressed their sympathy with what became known as the 'Lapua Movement'.

Nevertheless, the Social Democrats joined with twenty-three Communists in Parliament to stop the proposed muzzling of the Communist press. In disgust, the Right backed the formal creation of Suomen Lukko (Finland's Lock), an Association based on Lapua, to combat Communism by direct action. Communist presses were smashed, two Communist Members of Parliament were kidnapped, and a number of Communist Party members were driven across the Soviet border.

The Prime Minister resigned, after suppressing the Communist newspapers, and a National Government came in. Twelve hundred members of the 'Lapua Movement' marched on Helsinki, calling for the expulsion of Communists from every public field, and were welcomed by the President and Mannerheim. After a General Election, Communism was outlawed, but only by the narrowest possible Parliamentary majority.

That was the exact time when Quisling finally returned from Russia.

* Later one of the leading theoreticians and figureheads of the Russian Communist Party, and Secretary of Comintern and a member of the Praesidium until his death in 1964. He was father of Hertta Kuusinen, later Secretary of the Finnish Communist Party, whose husband, Yrjö Leino, fumbled the proposed 1948 Pact. In 1939 he was head of the ephemeral, puppet Terijoki Government in Finland.

He had watched Finnish developments at close quarters for ten formative years. He, like the Lapua farmers, was of yeoman stock. Like Mannerheim and supporters of the Lapua Movement, he was horrified by the excesses of the Reds in his native land. He, too, contemplated a national resurgence, along Lapua lines, and he found that many Norwegians were thinking along the same lines. Indeed, they had actually started a similar society, named *Federlandslaget* (Fatherland Front), and he soon found a prominent place in it.

Such was the real origin of his movement, *Nasjonal Samling* (National Unification). Contrary to the version which has been sedulously and successfully put about at home and abroad, *Nasjonal Samling* was *not* founded on either Italian Fascism or German National Socialism.

As Mannerheim says: 'The ultimate reason why the popular (Lapua) movement took place has to be sought in the Government's impotence in the face of political tendencies and underground intrigues which jeopardised the life and well-being of the country.' The same comment largely applies to *NS*.

'Thanks to the Lapua Movement', Mannerheim continues, 'it was possible to create a parliamentary basis for a Government that would have a quite different vitality and will to action than during the period of decay in the 1920s, that is to say a realistic Government which saved the country from Russia in 1939-40.' That is precisely what Quisling sought in Norway.

His tragedy is that *Nasjonal Samling* was not appreciated by the Norwegians, whereas the Lapua Movement regenerated Finland and saved the country. In Norway, Labour was allowed to gain a stranglehold on office and to lead the country to disaster. The Socialists let Norway down, as they did in Russia and nearly did in Finland.

Unless the Norwegian tragedy is contemplated in a Northern, as opposed to a Western, European context, and unless Quisling's experience in the Russo-Finnish theatre is given due emphasis, his fate is inexplicable. He and *NS* were indigenous to the North and owed their inspiration to a respectable and triumphant movement of the same sort across the border: to 'Finland's Lock'.

The Lapua Movement and *NS* both became extreme under duress, but in neither case was this due to exterior patronage or to foreign penetration, but to the failings of the equally indigenous Left. The struggle became polarised.

On a world scale this increasingly bitter struggle for power between Right and Left came to its inevitable conclusion in the Russo-German War of 1941-45, in which Finland found herself on the Right (with Germany) and Norway on the Left (with Russia). The ideological struggle for power, which is what all politics is about, has continued in the form of twenty years' Cold War, and is pinpointed in divided Berlin.

In that sense the 'phoney war' of September 1939, to its outcome in June 1940, when Hitler finally undid Versailles, was really a continuation of the First World War. The *real* beginning of a Second World War, different in origin from its predecessor, began with the German Invasion of Russia in June, 1941. If there is a Third World War, deriving from its predecessor and the Cold War, it will be a continuation of the Second World War.

The first spark in the great unsolved Russo-German, Slav-Teutonic, conflict between Left and Right, East and West, materialism and Christianity, was struck with the Soviet invasion of Finland in November 1939. That is certainly how Quisling saw it, and Mannerheim too.

As Mannerheim wrote: 'The situation after the two World Wars offers striking parallels to a careful observer. The Western Powers on both occasions concentrated on the problem of Germany and ignored the danger that threatened from the East. Their Russian policy has been decisively influenced by internal political doctrines, which have been allowed to determine the course of foreign policy.'*

That goes for Norway, too. It is the crux of the Quisling controversy.

* Lest it should be argued that Mannerheim was pro-German, let me mention Hitler's meeting with him on a train at Mikkeli in 1942. Mannerheim received him with icy dignity and at lunch plied him with schnaps in true Finnish style. By the time the strawberries and cream came round, Hitler's nerve broke and his hand began to shake. 'Ah, I see the Chancellor likes schnaps with his strawberries', remarked the Marshal with shattering sarcasm. Hitler left empty-handed. Similarly, Mannerheim rebuffed the efforts of the Kaiser, Hindenburg and Ludendorff when they attempted to collar the Finnish Army for their own ends during the War of Liberation. Mannerheim also, of course, went into exile when it was proposed that the Kaiser's brother-in-law should become King of Finland.

7

Humanitarian

IN mid-1921 Quisling returned home, having earned the highest regard of his chief, Minister Andreas T. Urbye,* in Finland, who spoke up for him at his trial thus: 'He was a most conscientious man, a man of his word, a man with wide interests and very well informed.'

He expected to rejoin the General Staff, where his intelligence and fantastic knowledge, combined with a photographic memory from which he could pick facts at will, had already made him into a legend; but Nansen demanded his services in the cause of humanity and Norwegian prestige. So two great minds met.

Like Quisling, Nansen was of part-Danish extraction; an ancestor had explored the White Sea and Petchora Peninsula for the Tsar, become Burgomaster of Copenhagen and written a book on cosmology. Both loved their native Norwegian soil and lived very close to nature. Both were outstandingly tough men physically, in a rugged country. Nansen was a celebrated oceanographer and scientist, while Quisling was a higher mathematician. Yet they were not overspecialised: their interests were wide, deep and varied. Neither man suffered fools gladly. Both were experts, in their different ways, on Russia. Nansen had lectured in Russia, after being rescued on Tsarist territory in Franz Josef Land. He had also travelled 12,000 miles to and

* Legal adviser to the Norwegian Goverment during the break with Sweden in 1905 and later doyen of the Diplomatic Corps in Moscow.

fro across the breadth of Russia as a tourist, and written about Siberia. They were two serious men who had much in common, and it is not surprising that Nansen asked the General Staff to second Quisling to the gigantic work of mercy which awaited them amid the ruins of the Tsarist Empire.

Since Nansen's disappointing diplomatic mission to London in 1905-8, he had lived in comparative obscurity. During the war he had been 'troubled by the thought of Norway's sitting on the fence . . . and that Norway was not playing the game', as one of his biographers (S. Stuart Starritt) puts it. In one way he had been glad of an opportunity to return to his scientific studies, but his prima donna nature and his patriotism beckoned him to more great deeds on the world stage.

In the spring of 1919, he met future-President Herbert Hoover, then US Food Administrator in charge of world relief, and wrote to Woodrow Wilson, Clemenceau, Lloyd George and Orlando of Italy, proposing international action to alleviate the post-war catastrophe in Eastern Europe. They agreed to help 'when hostilities ceased', that is when the White Intervention in Russia and Pilsudski's operations against the Bolsheviks in Poland ended. The White Russian *émigré* authorities in Paris also prevaricated lest relief should help the Reds. So it was not until 1921 that the newly born League of Nations appointed Nansen to be its High Commissioner for Repatriation of Prisoners of War and Director of European Famine Relief. Nansen had also managed to get a telegram through Berlin to Lenin, but he too would not accept relief until 1921 and then only through the agency of Nansen operating as an individual. Meanwhile the human tragedy had mounted from bad to worse until the death, disease and suffering far outstripped the indescribable horrors of the hostilities in the First World War.

So it was not until 1921 that Nansen got to work, with the help of the senior Prince Carl, brother of the Swedish King, who organised huge exchanges of prisoners of war between Russia on the one hand and Germany and Austro-Hungary on the other. The renowned Swedish humanitarian, Elsa Brändström, also brought comfort to teeming prisoners of war in Siberia. This was a tremendous exercise in international co-operation, which paved the way for even mightier 'foreign aid' programmes after the Second World War. As the titular head of the whole show, Nansen deserved and coveted the credit he got. He was received like a one-man, supra-national power at Geneva. Postage stamps with his likeness came into international usage. The stateless travelled on 'Nansen Passports'. Millions were raised in his name. Norway gloried in the kudos which accrued and salved the national conscience over war-profiteering. The national hero had made his mark again!

But it was not a one-man show. Hoover, Prince Carl, Elsa Brändström and many others also deserve credit, notably Vidkun Quisling, whose knowledge of Russia was far greater than Nansen's.

Nansen had been under a cloud in Imperial Russia because he disobeyed strict protocol during his lecture tour. He had offended the Grand Duke Alexander Mihailovich and was unpopular in the circles that mattered. Nor was he later in close touch with Soviet leaders— at any rate not on a personal level—as his biographers maintain. He could not speak a word of Russian.

On the other hand, Quisling, who was Secretary of the Relief Organisation and Nansen's chosen right-hand man, spoke perfect Russian and several dialects, besides having made a more profound study of Russian history and worked for several years under contemporary Bolshevik conditions. Quisling actually became an intimate associate of Leon Trotsky, whose name was invariably linked with Lenin as the second man in Russia. Nansen was entirely dependent on interpreters and translators, except in so far as German helped, in his dealings with the Soviet authorities, and it was Quisling who usually acted as the intermediary. It was also Quisling who was responsible for carrying out the practical relief work, under enormous difficulties, in the rolling steppes of the Ukraine and the fastnesses of the Crimea, the most sorely stricken areas. Quisling was Nansen's eyes, ears, mouthpiece and chief executive.

The *Norsk Biografisk Lexicon* joins in the chorus which tries to belittle Quisling's task and contribution. It says he 'exaggerated the difficulties'. This is not borne out by Nansen himself, who, in *Through the Caucasus to the Volga*, gives this typical glimpse of conditions:

'From home to home the same appalling sight of death. . . . Dried grass, leaves, crushed bones and horses' hooves instead of bread. No warmth, so that the pitiful bodies froze to the floor before life expired. In a children's home last night two infants died and they were still lying in their beds with the living ones at their side. . . . Dead bodies were dug up to be eaten. Distracted parents killed their children to satisfy their own hunger. Upwards of thirty million people were starving. In addition epidemics were raging. Worst was spotted fever, of which more than three million died despite relief. . . . Over these very same plains thousands of gaunt human beings fled, not knowing where they were going—just to get away—without food and through the hardening winter, their last horses and camels dying on the frozen roads. Ice halted all river traffic. The railways were disorganised and the few trains, packed to overflowing with refugees, remained stuck in sidings where people died in the carriages. Horror was all around.'

Indeed civilisation had broken down. The difficulties could not be exaggerated. Nansen said that, in 1922, 45 million people were starving: about 8 million in Ukraine, 4 million in the Crimea, Black Sea and Kuban area, and 25 million in the Volga District. In the drought there was nothing to live on except rotten fish and the residue of better times. Illness thrived on physical weakness.

Quisling had his headquarters in Kharkov—in the heart of the Ukrainian granary of Russia, which was empty—and so his was the key post. How he handled the problem there was the key to the whole situation. It was no exaggeration to say, as Quisling's supporters claimed, that the life or death of millions 'depended on him lifting his little finger'. Quisling himself dramatised his responsibility by likening his power at this time to that of Caesar Augustus. His lines of communication stretched from Kharkov to Berlin and Western Europe and then up to Moscow, out to the Volga and the Don, and down to Odessa. He controlled 60 per cent of the creaking Russian railways, which were nominally requisitioned by the Soviets for the military purposes of Trotsky and the Red Army. Hence subsequent denials by Moscow that they ever gave foreigners administrative authority over the railways. That is a quibble.

Quisling simply wangled control by means of his fluent Russian, his stubbornness and infinite patience. He actually seized horses from Marshal Budionny's famous cavalry to feed people.

Said Nansen: 'It was a ravaged and ruined land which Quisling reached on February 12, 1922, with the job of organising and setting in motion all possible help, which would span great areas with millions of sick and starving people, in a country where communications were destroyed and all means of help were lacking.' Nansen reported that it took three months for a train from Kazan on the Volga to reach the Polish frontier. Of the 1,948 refugees on board, only 649 lived. In Saratov thirty or forty children died daily in hospital. This was disaster on a semi-continental scale. From this holocaust and its counterpart of rotting remains of the trench-warfare in Flanders spread the virulent 'influenza' which blotted out 40 million people in the Western World, just as the Black Death spread from the East at the end of the thirteenth century. This was an international emergency almost as serious as the Great War itself.

Nansen estimated that $13\frac{1}{2}$ million people were fed in 1922 and that one-fifth of the million lives saved in the Ukraine were directly saved as the result of Quisling's efforts. But Quisling was not merely dealing with an emergency. There was the future to consider. He realised that famine begins slowly and builds up to a maximum in the next harvest but one. He believed that the Volga famine would never have happened on a big scale with a little League of Nations help from the start. So he also strove to obtain seed and farm machinery to forestall 1923.

A testimonial to Quisling was exhibited in the Revolution Museum in Moscow, alongside Churchill's order to tighten the blockade of Russia, saying on behalf of the Central Committee of the Communist Party: 'The people of the hungry regions of the Ukraine will never forget that the first appeal for help and the actual commencement of the work among us in the Ukraine was begun by Dr. Fridtjof Nansen's representative, his friend and fellow-countryman Captain Quisling.'

Now history has been re-written in Russia and Norway. Moscow has refused facilities for making sequences of Nansen's famous work in Russia, which would be an indispensable part of a documentary film of his life, because his handmen were Quisling and Colonel Konrad Sundlo. The latter was Quisling's only intellectual rival on the Norwegian General Staff, his predecessor as Nansen's assistant in Russia and a supporter of *Nasjonal Samling*. Nor is Norway keen on pressing the point.

Everything possible has been done in Norway to belittle or expunge Quisling's record of indispensable help to Nansen in Russia. The *Norsk Biografisk Lexicon* says: 'Quisling was in personal contact with Nansen as Secretary for seven or eight weeks. . . . Nansen only praised Quisling's work, not his politics, and apparently did not know him very well.' The whole point, of course, is not the precise number of days or nights the two men spent together but the fact that Nansen trusted and relied on Quisling out of his sight, used him as an interpreter and contact man on his two fact-finding tours of the Volga, Armenia and elsewhere, and insisted on Quisling standing by him when the narrow-minded Norwegian General Staff refused to prolong Quisling's leave of absence. As a matter of fact the two men's political ideas were almost identical and they worked in harness when they eventually got back home. As for not being friends, no man was an intimate friend of Nansen. He was too aloof, and Quisling was too modest and withdrawn to force himself on the great man. Nevertheless, Quisling was received in the Nansen household and Nansen's last sketch was sent to Quisling as a New Year card in 1930. This is still in Mrs. Quisling's possession.

Nansen's widow, Sigrun, stated in *Tidens Tegn* on October 11, 1933: 'Whether one agrees with Quisling's politics or not, I believe many people deplore the personal and insulting manner of the election campaign against him. It is certainly of interest to hear how Fridtjof Nansen rated his help—he often spoke of his joy at having such a man's assistance—an excellent administrator, self-sacrificing and upright. His face brightened at the mention of Quisling's name.'

Nansen's son, Odd, who was an early admirer and supporter of Quisling, later parted from him and was removed by the Germans to a concentration camp, where he wrote a book on his gruesome experience. So I was not surprised when he told me in his office at the new Oslo airport, of which he is the Government architect: 'Sigrun Nansen's election testimonial was put into her mouth by another woman* when she was old, and it was very unfortunate.' That follows the party line, but it does not square with Dr. Nansen's own printed recognition of Quisling, nor with the written evidence of many witnesses.

Actually Quisling's relief work was by no means confined to helping Nansen. Most of the time, from 1922 to 1930, he was on his own. The League of Nations took him from Nansen in 1924-25 to be its representative for Russian refugees in the Danubian States and the Balkans. In the summer of 1925 he was Secretary of the League's Armenian Committee and in that capacity guided Nansen through that sad and beautiful country. He remained in Armenia as Secretary during the

* Fru Nina Roll Anker.

1925-26 winter and kept an eye on the rest of the Caucasus, thus witnessing the consolidation of Georgia, Armenia and Azerbaijan in the Soviet Union, after their fleeting independence and membership of the League of Nations—a process which he had seen averted in the corresponding border states in the Baltic while he was in Petrograd and Helsinki.

From May 1927, to December 1929, he was Secretary of the Norwegian Legation in Moscow, a post specially created for him to watch over British interests in Russia after a rupture of diplomatic relations. For his services to Britain he was created a Commander of the Order of the British Empire. In this twin diplomatic role he completed his dossier of Norwegian Socialists' intrigues with the Third International —ammunition which he was to fire off at home when he went into politics shortly afterwards.

The *Norsk Biografisk Lexicon* alleges that: 'From Armenia Quisling went straight to work with his old friend Frederick Prytz, whose timber concession was in financial difficulties. Quisling was to be head of a new office in Moscow and represented Prytz with the authorities. The office opened in 1926 and was used for exchanging roubles aside from the Russian State Bank: an activity which continued when Quisling, six months later, moved into the British Embassy. Quisling virtually took roubles from Persian businessmen who had earned Russian currency, and gave a receipt which Prytz changed into pounds through his agents in London. Quisling had a salary.' Then one reads: 'The Russians accepted Quisling's explanation that these transactions were necessary for the Company's finance and that no illegal profit was made.' So the writer clears himself, yet leaves the smear.

A famous industrialist, whom I may not identify because any connection with Quisling might damage his clean reputation, told me the truth: 'Prytz was one of a number of Norwegians who had huge timber concessions in Russia. Before the Revolution he was small fry. But the Bolsheviks confirmed his concession. I knew him well for years. He often joined me to make up a bridge four with our mutual friend, Vidkun Quisling, who could have held his own at Crockford's . . . I remember the night before Prytz had to leave Russia under a cloud. He was so nervous that he dropped his cards and made many unusual mistakes. His nerve had gone because the Bolsheviks had found the equivalent of $560,000 in black market notes, belonging to him, in the Norwegian diplomatic bag and they had intimated that they might liquidate him.

'Prytz had access to the bag because he had Acting-Consular rank, and he paid his unsuspecting lumberjacks in the remote forests of Lake Onega with these debased roubles for years before he was exposed. He also paid his shareholders a mere 5 per cent. That is how he made the fortune with which he bought Storfoss, near Trondheim, one of the finest estates in Norway.

'There he died before the end of the war, having become Quisling's Minister of Finance and received the highest Norwegian decoration, the Grand Cross of St. Olav, as a reward, thus satisfying his vanity and realising a lifelong ambition. He had this order on his breast when he expired, believing that he was a patriot.

'Quisling was not implicated in Prytz's shady business. His sideline was buying up bargains in Old Masters which had been ransacked from the nobility. He eventually took them home, quite legitimately, through Norwegian diplomatic channels. He was not a financier. He liked to sit up half the night, talking about everything under the sun— except money. He was the most interesting man I have ever met in my long and varied life. I never tired of listening to him. He was an idealist and a genius—anything but venal.'

It is probably best to rely on the 'universal genius' Nansen for a true picture of Quisling as a man and a relief worker in Russia. In his Foreword to *Armenia and the Near East*, he says: 'Captain V. Quisling, a Norwegian, was Secretary of the Commission, and the present writer was its head. I avail myself of this opportunity to express my heartfelt thanks to my kind and indefatigable colleagues for their efficient and self-sacrificing work throughout the journey, and for their invaluable collaboration.'

He was even more fulsome in his *Through the Caucasus to the Volga*, saying in the Foreword: 'These introductory words cannot be brought to an end without my hearty thanks to Captain Vidkun Quisling for his untiring kindness as a travelling companion and for the valuable help he has given the author through his knowledge of Russian and his many-sided attainments.'

Even opponents have to concede something towards Quisling's reputation as a relief worker. Mr. Philip Noel-Baker, at one time personal assistant to Nansen, who has since won the Nobel Peace Prize and is therefore indebted to the Norwegian authorities, besides being a Labour MP, informs me, for example: 'Nansen said that Quisling was an efficient agent, and Nansen certainly gave me the impression that he (Quisling) was doing his work in a spirit of well-meaning philanthropy.'

Let us end this phase with the words of a friend, Albert Eines: 'I first met him in the late autumn of 1925, twenty kilometres outside Leningrad, at the china factory. Artists, technicians and workers still kept at their beautiful work, despite bloody revolution. They were also turning out Nansen and Quisling plates and statuettes. There were Nansen and Quisling cigarettes, too . . . the Tsarist corn depot was empty . . . millions of thirsty, starving rats went down to the Neva twice a day to drink.' (Such horrors not only turned Nansen's hair white. Three of his assistants died of pestilence within a year, and Quisling caught malaria.)

Nansen and Quisling statuettes were treasured by the thousand, as symbols of salvation, right up to the Second World War, and were found all over the Eastern Front by Norwegian 'Front Fighters' as they advanced and retreated with the *Wehrmacht* in the 'fight against Bolshevism'.

In short, it seems difficult to dispute that Quisling was anything but a great and noble humanitarian worker in Russia; where he risked his life for years on end; when his acknowledged brilliance and versatility could have got him a comfortable and profitable job in many other fields; and when Nansen and his collaborators of different nationalities placed the utmost confidence in him in word and deed. Upon investigation, the campaign to minimise Quisling's contribution in Russia collapses.

8

For Better or for Worse

MUCH work and little play did not make Vidkun Quisling a dull young man, and he always had a strange fascination for women. They were a solace to him all his life and many are still alive to speak of their regard: some fearlessly, some anonymously, some critically (on political grounds), but all affectionately. I have yet to find one woman in Norway, who knew him, without something good to say for him. That in itself is an extraordinary fact, considering his off-beat character and the nationwide hate which has been whipped up against him—among a people who actually boast of 'the famous Norwegian hate'.

His surviving henchmen all say that his female admirers were 'a positive nuisance' or 'a menace' at his office during his heyday, and that special precautions had to be taken to keep them at bay because they were numerous and importunate. One is tempted to say that he must have had some hypnotic power over women, like Hitler, whom he slightly resembled physically. Like Hitler, too, his eyes blazed and bulged when he was roused. Also they both claimed to be 'the saviour of the nation' and to be ushering in 'a new era', which has a certain drama and excitement. But there any resemblance ends.

Hitler came from an unhappy, low-class home, and his interest in women was always banal, whereas Quisling came from a happy, intellectual upper-class milieu, and the women around him were

outlook. Private enterprise is still planning to re-stake Norway's ancient Viking claim to East Greenland, and this was an aspect of Quisling's programme. Indeed it was a theme which evidently cropped up in his first, vital meeting with Hitler on December 14, 1939, and which had previously been a subject of bitter political controversy with his Liberal, Socialist and Communist opponents in Norway. The loss of Norwegian prestige in the Arctic (in Spitsbergen) and in the Antarctic (in Queen Maud Land) is, moreover, a living issue in Norwegian public life. In August 1963, the Labour Government was ousted for the first time (apart from the war period) in twenty-eight years over the matter—of all questions—of mismanagement of a Norwegian coal-mine in Spitsbergen!

New books frequently appear on the Norsemen's colonisation of Greenland and the discovery of America in the Middle Ages. The Socialists' failure to follow up the heritage of Norwegian exploration in Antarctica—starting with Henrik Bull in 1895 and culminating with Amundsen's conquest of the South Pole in 1911—is a recurring theme in the Norwegian Conservative press.

Anybody outside northern Europe who imagines that such dreams are mad, meaningless or dead, does not know the frustration and nostalgia which is never far beneath the surface, in different forms, among the thinking people of the Nordic countries. The Socialists try their best to transmute this racial pride into civic pride, but they have not yet ironed out 'the Viking spirit'. Quisling's identification of himself with his 'nordic' Russian bride and a Viking background on the steppes of the Volga and the Don was not far-fetched according to a prevalent mode of thought.

Russia has always been an obsession in Scandinavia, which is merely a peninsula of Euro-Asia, linked by the Gulf Stream in the Arctic, the Finnish lakes and forests to the east, and the waterways and islands of the Baltic Sea to the south. Quisling's marriage bridged this geography and its associated history. It was an extension of his pre-occupation with Russia—a personalisation of his life-work, an expression of his psychology, a physiological necessity, a geopolitical marriage. What other man would have solemnly described his wife to his old schoolmates as '*russerina av dinarisk-nordisk avstamning*' ('a Russian of East Alpine-Nordic extraction')?

The *Norsk Biografisk Lexicon* claims that Quisling first married a girl named Alexandra in the Ukraine in 1922. She is described as having been born in Sebastopol in 1904, which would have made her nineteen, and the wedding is supposed to have been a mere formality so that Quisling could get her to safety outside Russia—an over-the-counter affair in the Communist style of the time, and just as easily revoked. If this incident ever occurred, it must have been due to Quisling's compassion—although why he should have chosen this particular girl out of innumerable Russian damsels in distress is not explained. Nor is any documentary or other evidence produced—from the archives of the Norwegian Legation or Consulate in Moscow, for instance—to substantiate any such marriage. Quisling's widow denies that an 'Odessa marriage' ever took place and as far as I know none of his surviving friends from Russia at that time remembers Alexandra.

The available evidence suggests that Quisling sowed no wild oats after the fashion of young officers. His self-sufficient family with its studious atmosphere cut him off from girls of his own age. He did not dance and he was never gay. As a cadet and a lieutenant, his ambition to serve his newly freed country absorbed his mind. Then came the profound shock to his system in the form of the Red holocaust in Russia. No wonder he fell hard when he did fall for Maria Vasiljevna Pasak.

An anonymous industrialist from Moscow told me: 'At first I thought Quisling was just going to marry Maria so that she could be "dropped over the border" to escape from the Bolsheviks. But she was often in the Norwegian Legation and apparently some mysterious attraction developed between them. She was above medium height, distinguished-looking, always dressed in excellent taste. They made a handsome couple. Maria was also quiet, intelligent and nice to talk to. They often came to my flat for auction bridge and she played a very good hand.

'Her family had a valuable collection of pictures and, I understood, it was in connection with saving them from the Bolsheviks that her parents originally established contact with Quisling. Maria had been brought up among beautiful things and was knowledgeable about the Arts. He shared this interest and they found some fine bargains in the glutted art market of the time. By the time they left Russia, they had assembled an impressive gallery of Old Masters, which served them in good stead later in Norway. Rubens, Van Eyck, Murillo and Reynolds were represented.

'He hated diplomatic parties and so they didn't lead a very active life socially. She was not, it seemed, ambitious in that way. But she took the greatest interest in his work and obviously wanted her husband to be a success.'

There was in fact a meeting of minds. This is clear from the evidence which she gave in writing at Quisling's trial: 'I met my husband during the famine in the Ukraine. I had seen his devoted and enormously difficult work, which he performed to help the Soviet Russians during the famine. He daily risked his life in the battle not only against famine but also against sickness, including cholera, typhus and the smallpox epidemic in the country. Adults and children died in thousands daily. He himself was infected with cholera. Devoted and fearless, as he always has been, he went personally to the worst afflicted districts.

'He saved millions of people, including many Jews. Although he held different political views from the Soviet Russians, that did not interfere with his loving work for humanity. When he had finished his task he received a letter of thanks from the Soviet authorities, which thanked him heartily for his devoted and valuable work during the famine, and in conclusion said he would always be a welcome guest in the Soviet Union. I understand that letter disappeared after the capitulation.

'His humanitarian work in Armenia where he sought to help another people in need, again showed his willingness to shoulder difficult and heavy tasks to assist his fellow human beings. A man who took upon himself such great and responsible duties at that time, and on April 9 (1940), is now accused of drinking, theft and fraud! It may be said simply that he is a temperate and sober man, who neither drinks nor smokes. In the last fifteen years, particularly during the last five hard years, he has worked day and night without sparing himself. In those years he had only two or three days' holiday.

'I have been married to my husband for twenty-two years and all the time I have seen how the thought of serving his country and his people animated him. Vidkun Quisling who was willing to offer his life for starving Russians and Armenians, the same man who is accused of treason against his own country and people, has loved them in a higher degree than anything else.

'Just as his work in Russia was a sacrifice, I know, too, that April 9 was also a great sacrifice which he made to save his country in difficult times. Twice he suggested that he should retire from his post as Minister-President, which I saw was a mental strain on him—to struggle on the one hand against his own countrymen and on the other against Terboven and his people in the Reichcommissariat. He was positively indignant on that account. He said to me that the Norwegian people's existence was at stake and that the worst that could happen would be for Norway to become a German military dictatorship: "The Norwegian people don't themselves realise how awful that would be or what consequences it would have." '

Mrs. Quisling would have followed her husband to the grave, if he had not stopped her. His love also knew no limit. He told the Court: 'Since we have begun to psychoanalyse people, I will mention an incident from the days when I was a schoolboy—how I had a good friend who betrayed me. I nearly killed him for that. . . . I have met friends in my life—simple, steadfast, good friends who have given witness here—but with the exception of my wife I have never met anybody who was willing to do what I would do, namely lay down my life for my friends. Therefore I have been a lonely man—for no other reason.'

He added: 'I may say, when one talks of my being a covetous man, that during the seven years from 1933 to 1940, I was not paid a single øre (farthing) for all my work for *Nasjonal Samling*, for all the articles I wrote and all the speeches I made. On the contrary, I sold my own and my wife's property to finance *Nasjonal Samling*.'

Such loyalty between man and wife can only be admired, but whether this was helpful to his career in Norway is doubtful on balance. She learned Norwegian, with an accent, but her foreign origin cut her off from the feelings of Norwegians at large and contributed to her husband's isolation from reality. Her friends mostly had a Russian background.

She was inclined to be temperamental and the marriage cannot always have been restful, but she placed her husband on a pedestal, and was always dutiful, attending to all the innocent functions associated with his post as Minister-President—entertaining the *Nasjonal Samling* youth and appearing with him at the theatre—and she was a discreet hostess to visiting German dignitaries, although she was non-political and spoke the language even worse than her husband. But her dizzy regard for him drove him—like his mother—to attempt the wellnigh impossible, always to be first, never to give up and to seek the heights of ambition in what he deemed to be the good cause. Thus she contributed to the destruction of his sense of proportion.

She must have had her moments of dreadful doubt. Herbert S. Bodom, who lived in the Quislings' block of spacious flats in the 'diplomatic quarter', told me: 'In 1943 she asked me to say whether I thought the Germans would win the war. I told her that they would undoubtedly lose since so few of their leaders knew the outside world or had any idea what England and America could do. I knew because I had worked nineteen years in the States and five in Birmingham, and my answer made her pause to think. Then she said: "Do you really believe that?" and I replied "Yes". Since Quisling believed in a German victory or at least a negotiated peace, Mrs. Quisling was obviously hoping to calm her own, instinctive anxieties on this score when she questioned me.'

But Maria stuck to her husband for better or for worse to the bitter end and he never betrayed her trust. What more can one say of any marriage than that? Unlike Norway, to which she only belonged by proxy, she believed in him and his motives—and still does. She served as his anchor in sickness and sorrow, unto death—always there in triumph and disaster, and undistracted by children. Perhaps if they had had a baby she would have been less intense and he would have been more human and successful. Instead, he adopted his native land and sought to be a father to it. But Norway betrayed him by rejecting his paternalism. In his disappointment he turned on his countrymen and chastised them for their own good, just as he turned on the unfaithful friend of his boyhood. The one person who might have brought Quisling down to earth was Maria. But she pandered to him. He was her saint.

9

Home Work

AT Christmas 1929, Vidkun Quisling, aged forty-two, settled in Norway for good, with a reputation second only to that of his chief, Dr. Fridtjof Nansen, and an unsurpassed insight into the Soviet Union, which he had invigilated from the start. Such was his reputation as an organiser in Russia that Leon Trotsky had invited him to be his Chief of Staff in the reorganisation of the Red Army, and Imperial China had offered him a similar position, for which he learned Chinese, only to lose this opportunity through the Chiang Kai-shek Revolution.

It has become an axiom in Norway that Quisling was a Communist in the 1920s. Carl Joachim Hambro, President of the *Storting*, and as such the second man in Norway after the King, says in *I Saw it Happen in Norway* that 'Quisling came back (from Russia) a full-fledged Bolshevik'. His views have gained international currency through his prestige as the last President of the League of Nations and because the Norwegian Labour Party collaborated with the High Court in trying to brand Quisling for all time as an ex-Communist, but he admits in the Norwegian edition of his book that 'Its purpose was to influence opinion in America, not to give scientific statements of facts and trends', so too much reliance should not be placed on this statement.

Nansen's daughter, Liv Høyer, says in her *Nansen og Verden* that when Quisling ran the Kharkov office for relief he was then 'nearly a

Communist', and the *Norsk Biografisk Lexicon* alleges: 'Quisling offered his services [to Norwegian Labour Leaders] for the formation of a "Red Guard".' The Labour Party has always stuck vehemently to this interpretation and it was even said that he attempted to rejoin the Norwegian General Staff in order to spy for Russia. But if Quisling was a Communist in 1924-25, so were Nansen, Lied, and the many capitalists who shared in the general optimism about Russia.

In truth Quisling shared with Nansen and the rest of the world the perennial doubt, now nearly fifty years old, as to whether the Russian Revolution was basically good or evil, whether Russia is potentially friend or foe. This ambivalence is inherent in Russia's geographical position as a Euro-Asiatic colossus, facing two ways. Significantly, the Imperial Russian eagle faced outwards whereas the Austro-Hungarian eagle faced inwards. This inescapable dilemma has never been solved by the Russians, Tsarist or Bolshevik, nor by those Powers which have to conduct diplomacy with Russia in peace and war. The lumbering weight of Russia is thrown periodically East or West, according to where danger or opportunity arises, and the rest of the world reacts accordingly.

The West is currently experiencing a period of relaxation with Russia, due to the emergence of the Chinese danger, 'the yellow peril' in modern guise, and 'the cold war' is going into limbo. For the previous twenty years, since Potsdam, we were at daggers drawn. In 1939 we courted Russia, but hesitated to go the whole hog, as the West always does in dealing with Russia, thereby forcing the arch enemies, Stalin and Hitler, into each other's arms. From 1941 to 1945 we were allied with Russia.

This fluctuating attitude can be traced back through the centuries, certainly to the time of Peter the Great. Germany, which is only separated from Russia by the plains and rivers of Poland, has during this century sent Lenin to Russia in a special train, via Sweden and Finland, to subvert the country, and then concluded the devastating Treaty of Brest-Litovsk. In their post-war misery both countries intrigued together to re-create their military strength surreptitiously—a liaison which was interrupted by Stalin's purges of the 1930s and Hitler's *lebensraum* and 'Aryan' ideology. Then came the Molotov-Ribbentrop Pact in 1939, which precipitated World War II, in the middle of which Russia changed sides and was welcomed unequivocally by the Allies.

France has looked to Russia periodically since the Napoleonic era, and in the previous century it was largely the campaigns of Charles XII of Sweden against Russia which enabled the wars of Louis XIV and the Duke of Marlborough to be fought in isolation. Within recent memory France has veered from the 'Popular Front' of Léon Blum to the ultra-conservatism of de Gaulle, who is now rumoured to be contemplating a *rapprochement* with Red China as a counterpoise to Russia and the United States.

No country has gone to greater extremes than the United States in its attitude to the Soviet Union. In 1917 the Red Revolution was heralded with joy in America as a victory for democracy over 'Tsarist tyranny' and as a grand opportunity for big business. The USA defied Britain and France and gave with unparalleled generosity to Russian Relief. Hoover, as Relief Controller, infiltrated his henchmen into Russia to secure aluminium concessions; Averell Harriman obtained the manganese concession in the Caucasus; Harry Sinclair, the 'Napoleon of oil', went to Russia for petroleum concessions, as did the young J. Paul Getty. Yet later the pendulum swung so far back that in the McCarthy era even a liberal was in danger of being regarded as a Communist.

This allusion to the see-saw vacillation between Russia and other nations is necessary in order to correct the prejudices of the reader who imagines that relations with the Soviet Union are governed by ideology. They never have been. Labels such as 'Fascism' or 'Communism', 'Christian civilisation' or 'free enterprise' are the façade—like the League of Nations and the United Nations—behind which power politics are conducted; or, as Lenin put it in reference to religion, they are 'the opium of the masses'. Politics are fundamentally about power—in other words survival or expediency. The rest is window-dressing or an illusion.

Similarly the attitudes of the two Norwegian experts on Soviet Russia, Nansen and Quisling, were dictated by expediency. Their conclusions varied from time to time with developments inside Russia —as did the policy of the Norwegian Labour Party and indeed the rest of the world.

As Professor V. H. Galbraith says in *An Introduction to the Study of History*:* 'If we could perfectly understand the past, our prejudices—

* Oxford University Press.

74

race, religion, nationalism, politics—which are our limitations, would be swallowed up and disappear in perfect human sympathy, pity and wonder.'

That was the spirit in which Nansen and Quisling sought to understand the young Soviet Union. We must therefore follow the vicissitudes of the USSR and their impact if we are to comprehend the stand which Quisling eventually took in Norwegian and world politics.

Nansen and Quisling both held deep regard for Russia at first and had high hopes that the Revolution would take a different course.

In 1923 Nansen devoted his Nobel Peace Prize to model farms at Saratov and Ekaterinoslav, which were run on a commercial basis. In his speech he said: 'Let me say a few words about helping Russia. The League of Nations was not in favour of this, to my great regret; for I cannot but think that if the League had supported the suggestion with its weighty authority, before it was too late, the situation would have been saved in Russia, and the state of things in Russia and Europe would have been quite different, and much more satisfactory than it is now.'

In the same year, in his book *Russia and Peace*, he wrote: 'There can hardly be room for doubt that the Russian people has a great future before it, and a great mission to fulfil in the future life of Europe and the world. . . . Not yet has the soul of the Russian people been able to cast off the yoke of Western Europe, and to achieve its free development; not yet has it found a way to express its own truth. But its time will come.'

In practical terms he based his faith in the young USSR largely on Lenin's New Economic Policy. 'I was able to observe', he wrote, 'the serious and methodical way in which they were trying, by strenuous efforts, to carry out their economic reconstruction based on the principles of the NEP. Even the caution with which they proceed is really a reason for believing that their work will succeed. . . . They have a full understanding of the complexity of the economic phenomena and the dangers which lie in constant interference by the State in the life of industry, trade and agriculture.'

Quisling at this time shared, and possibly inspired, Nansen's optimism. In his book *Russia and Ourselves*, written in 1930 after Stalinism had come into being and changed his mind, Quisling, looking back,

75

wrote: 'When the Civil War came to an end, however, and the crops simultaneously failed in great parts of Russia, the Bolshevik peasant policy resulted in a fearful crisis and the well-known great famine. . . . To save the Revolution Lenin was forced, in 1921, to introduce the so-called NEP—in other words to revert to capitalistic methods. . . . No more than this was needed to start a rapid recovery.'

If neither Nansen nor Quisling was an economist, if perhaps they were naïve, they were nevertheless in good company. That hard-headed and successful industrialist Jonas Lied was equally enthusiastic. As founder of the famous Siberian Company in 1910, he knew Russia, Tsarist and Soviet, as well as anybody, and in *Return to Happiness* he declared: 'By 1922 there was only slight interference with Russian businessmen. . . . State trusts were springing up overnight. . . . At the time we only felt that the Red Leader was consolidating the position of the Nepmen, and that we held the future of Russian commerce in our hands. The optimism was next to incredible. . . . Like the rest of us I accepted the optimistic view. . . . The general optimism was so great that I had not much difficulty in floating a new company to exploit the new business. . . . England was on tiptoe to take up new Russian business.'

Thus we find the three leading Norwegian experts on Russia in 1923 agreeing that the Soviet Union, under NEP, had the possibility of a swift revival—a view which was also entertained by such major industrialists as Herbert Hoover, Averell Harriman, Harry Sinclair and President Wirth of Germany, and such concerns as Swedish General Electric and Metropolitan-Vickers. This constituted the most enlightened and objective opinion of the time.

Then one of those personal factors that change the course of history suddenly intervened and revised Quisling's opinion. In April 1923, Lenin had his second stroke and never spoke again. On January 21, 1924, he died. 'Had he lived and enjoyed better health, it is possible that NEP might have flourished for a much longer period,' says Jonas Lied. 'For there is no reason to think that in 1922, when Lenin said NEP must endure for a long while, that he was misleading his associates.' In April 1924, Stalin, aided by the diabolical Felix E. Dzerjinsky, ex-head of the Cheka Secret Police, then President of the Supreme Economic Council, started to reverse NEP and some 30,000 arrests were made. It was not until 1928-29, however, that NEP was finally liquidated, and many foreign tycoons were still engaged in business in Russia as late as 1927.

The perspicacity of Quisling, however, recognised the new trend which was to result in the Stalinist dictatorship, 'socialism in one country', 'collectivisation of agriculture', the 'liquidation of the *kulaks* (small farmers)', the 'state-organised famine', 'industrialisation' and the 'great purges'—all the notorious apparatus that has still to be dismantled thoroughly.

In 1923 Stalinism belonged to the future and the Norwegian Labour Party, in common with its brothers in the rest of the world, still shared the idealistic euphoria of 1917. It did not break with the Third International until 1923 and then only on the tactical issue of whether it could usefully propagate atheism in a Lutheran country. Most of the Labour leaders continued to look to Moscow for a lead. It was for this reason that Quisling approached them when he was on leave from Russia in 1924-25, to warn them of the dangerous new Stalinist trend in Russia and to suggest that they should form a Home Guard to counteract Stalinist or Trotskyist subversion. Later, when Quisling decided that the Norwegian Labour Party was incorrigible, his exposure of them from patriotic reasons infuriated them and started the distortion of his motives which embittered domestic politics beyond repair, thus leading eventually to his rise and fall.

Whatever may be thought about Quisling's attitude towards Communism in the 1920s, there can be no doubt that his first-hand knowledge and perception of Stalinism changed his mind in good time, and encouraged him to take appropriate political action—years before his Socialist opponents were convinced that the Russian Revolution was betrayed. For this foresight the Norwegian Labour Party will never forgive him. They therefore do their utmost to tar him with their own Red brush.

Quisling wrote in *Russia and Ourselves*: 'The peasants thought they had won. . . . But they soon learned their mistake. In point of fact the Bolshevik land policy had two aims: (1) to prevent the rise of a free and prosperous peasant class, whose naturally capitalistic and conservative leanings would imperil the organisation of the Socialist State, (2) to foster close relations between the proletariat in town and country, and to organise agriculture on a Communist basis in order that the towns might be regularly supplied with provisions and the industries with

77

raw materials. . . . NEP, in the words of Lenin, was merely one step back in order to take two steps forward. . . . The Bolsheviks have completely belied Nansen's hopes.'

Such was Nansen's early faith in the young USSR that Quisling actually visualised him as a potential 'President of a New Russia', reviving old Nordic traditions. Nansen was however one of the first to see the dangers of Communism.

Quisling's disillusionment with Russia was complete, bitter and lasting—one of the main driving forces of his subsequent career.

He and Nansen, who left Russia at the parting of Europe's way, were not alone in seeing the danger of Bolshevism to Norway in 1930. They regarded the Norwegian Labour movement as disruptive and felt the necessity for a national renaissance. They therefore embraced the patriotic movements which were already afoot at home. They embarked on twin political careers, based on their joint experience in the USSR.

Unfortunately Nansen was removed from the scene by sudden and unexpected death almost before they had gone into action.

Quisling was saddled with Nansen's mantle before he was ready. Then the horrors of Stalinism, combined with the meteoric rise of Adolf Hitler, altered the picture and produced a new sense of urgency.

In order to understand how Quisling's own *Nasjonal Samling* movement took shape, it is necessary to dip briefly into Norwegian history.

A nationalist Nordic movement in Norway was as old as Eilert Sundt (1817-75), the pioneer social anthropologist who anticipated Sidney and Beatrice Webb, the statisticians of the British Labour Party. After eight years' theological depression, he found his feet as Director of the Student Union in 1843 and his inspiration was the national poet, Henrik Wergeland.

Since Eilert Sundt was a sociological planner and loved the common people, the Norwegian Labour Party has adopted him as one of their own, erected statutes to him and called streets after him, perpetuated his name in school books and recurrent exhibitions. But he was *not* a socialist. His conclusions, reached by fact-finding, like the Webbs', led him in fact in the opposite direction.

In his biography of Sundt, Martin S. Allwood writes: 'Sundt's reasons for rejecting socialism are clear. Being a Christian, he could not condone materialism ("the flesh"). Further, socialism, in so far as it preached class consciousness and class war, thereby inculcating a partisan spirit, sinned against Christian charity, which could not set the goals of one group higher than that of another. On the political level, Sundt foresaw that socialism would disrupt the nation. . . . On the sociological level, Sundt had already placed himself in line with the people, and declared his faith in the grass roots of the nation; the socialists had no understanding of the people. . . . They were therefore, in a deeper sense, enemies of the people.' That is pure Quislingism.

Allwood goes on to explain how Sundt spiritually rejected socialism: 'To lose sight of the "human factor", or rather, the human being, in the interminable rows of figures and tables, was tantamount to understanding nothing at all of the social process. In his theory of social causation, Sundt would include as of primary importance a psycho-dynamic factor, the human heart with its profoundest longing and divinest potentialities.'

Quisling, not the Norwegian Labour Party, was the heir to that philosophy. So, too, was Nansen, who sought his inspiration, as lovingly as Quisling, in 'the grass roots'.

Quisling's ideology was not based on German National Socialism but was rooted in a hundred-years-old Norwegian tradition.

From Nordic nationalism stemmed the Norwegian Golden Age which flowered into Independence in 1905 and did not wither until the deaths of Edvard Munch, Vigeland and Undset in the 1940s and of Hamsun in 1952. Meanwhile a competitive driving-force was developing in Norway, alien, supra-national and impersonal—the antithesis of go-getting Viking individualism—namely socialism. The head-on clash came in the 1930s, when the incompatability developed first into abuse and insurrection, later into war, and finally into the triumph of socialism. That merciless struggle is the story of Quisling's last fifteen years.

The first Norwegian trade unions grew up in the 1870s and in 1899 were joined in a National Federation. Conditions were so bad that no less than 750,000 Norwegians emigrated to America during 1866-1915, and in 1884 a Liberal Government appointed a commission to consider labour problems. The first practical results did not come until the Factory Inspection and Accidents Insurance Acts of 1892-94. From 1906 to 1919 the foundations of a welfare state were laid by Liberal and Conservative Governments, but then the war boom ended in 1920 and a slump started. Economic and social unrest filled the years 1921-28. Marketing difficulties decreased exports and shipping rates, and caused bankruptcies, unemployment and labour conflicts. Nearly all producers had debts. The farmers particularly felt the fall in prices that followed the rise in the value of the *krone* which made the burden of debt heavier and increased their difficulties. After a fleeting recovery, the Great Depression hit Norway in 1931 and conditions became worse than in the 1920s—with the safety-valve in America jammed.

This was the crisis when Quisling entered the political scene. In these cosy mid-twentieth-century days of 'affluence' and socialist respectability, it is difficult to recapture the hatred and bitterness of the inter-war period. It blazed in Norway until the blood-letting of 1945, since when it only simmers. This is an essential ingredient of the Quisling controversy.

The zest of the Golden Age began to fade almost as soon as Independence was born. The Norwegians had achieved the impossible. All the best in them had combined to produce this quick and spectacular result—to realise their Peer Gynt dreams on an international scale. What more could they want? The answer is sad, simple and characteristic. All they wanted, with few exceptions, was to revert to their own petty, parochial ways—the mode of life dictated by their divisive geography and the magnitude of the problems presented by a harsh and only semi-viable habitat.

Faction revived immediately. Christian Michelsen, the forceful Bergen fish merchant, who had created a National Government to stand up to Sweden and break away, resigned two years after the objective was attained—officially for his health, actually in disgust. (He lived until 1925.) Norway never had another National Government until faction produced total defeat in 1940. Those thirty-five years, 1905-40, encompass Quisling's life between the ages of eighteen and fifty-three, when his ideas crystallised.

Prior to 1905, there was a widespread desire for Nansen as President of a Republican Norway. He himself was not averse to this solution since he was no respecter of persons. His own manner was imperious and he would have had no qualms over assuming the powers of a head of state—as he was to show at the League of Nations, where he was treated as an independent power in his own right, and in Russia, where his Relief organisation was autonomous. But he was a scientist and free-thinker, who lived as a Christian gentleman yet openly scoffed at Christian dogma and barely mentioned religion in his copious writing. Therefore he could not have taken the oath to the Lutheran State Church. Another obstacle was his basic belief in co-operation between people and nations as the sovereign solution of the manifold problems of his time.

So in the end he threw in his lot with the monarchists, believing that the election of King Haakon VII would be the most unifying course in Norway, and his whirlwind tour of the country clinched the plebiscite. Consequently the new king was beholden to Nansen. This afterwards made any participation by Nansen in parliamentarianism, under a constitutional monarchy, wherein the Sovereign in Council theoretically had greater powers than a British Monarch, so difficult that it never materialised. Conversely, the Left, which was outmanœuvred in 1905 and remained spiritually Republican, could never trust Nansen either. An uneasy balance was thus struck and was not unsettled until 1940.

It would, however, be a mistake to deduce from the eventual crystallisation of Norwegian opinion behind the monarchy that the institutions hurriedly evolved in 1905, around the 1814 Constitution, were unchangeable. A certain ferment and fluidity persisted from the moment of King Haakon's election until the Second World War. In the extremity of the German Occupation the King and Government did a deal in order to survive, and this has subsequently consolidated Norwegian institutions and public opinion. But it was not always so. First Nansen, then Quisling, his heir apparent, were involved in the prolonged malaise which set in after 1905. This explains much about Quisling's course of action during his fifteen years' political career in Norway. Indeed his life is inexplicable without the historical background from his eighteenth year onwards.

Michelsen opposed industrialisation because his fish business had often taken him to England, where he had seen the slums. Neither social legislation nor socialism, he said, could make sound and decent people out of proletarians such as now threatened Norway's culture and government. This problem crystallised into the 'Concessions Controversy', namely whether the huge water-power of Norway should be harnessed to industrialisation and, if so, how, by whom and to what extent? It preoccupied Gunnar Knudsen, the versatile ship-owner, industrialist and landowner from Telemark, first as Finance Minister in Michelsen's Coalition, from which he resigned because he was Republican, later as Liberal Prime Minister in 1908-10, also in the earlier part of his second Ministry in 1913-20. He became a pioneer of electrification, which is still revolutionising Norway. This in its turn led to the rapid growth of a proletariat and the spread of socialism, just as Michelsen had predicted.

The Great War boom camouflaged this parting of the ways in Norwegian political life, but when it collapsed in 1920 the process of polarisation had accelerated, and rivalry at once broke out with renewed vigour—until the first Labour Government attained office on January 27, 1928, when its flagrant extremism led to its swift fall after less than a fortnight. That was the heated situation when Quisling first intervened in home politics in 1924-26.

The Labour Government's extremism in early 1928 confirmed the impression that it had not abandoned, as it professed, its revolution-ary programme.* Bourgeois fears of long standing were confirmed up to the hilt. Counter-measures, which had been adumbrated for twenty years by Michelsen, Nansen and many other distinguished citizens, were seen to have been apposite. Efforts redoubled to stem the proletarian tide.

Nansen firmly believed in the individualism which he practised with genius in many fields. Egalitarianism was anathema to him. So was dogma of any sort. Socialism went against his grain and in his last years he became almost American in his zest for free enterprise. Witness his address on 'Adventure' when he was elected Rector of St. Andrew's University in 1923: 'Why do I give you these examples from the life of exploration and adventure? Because all of us are explorers in life, whatever trail we follow. Because it is the explorers with the true spirit of adventure we now need if humanity shall really overcome the present difficulties, and find the right course across the dangerous sea ahead of us. . . . You will all find your adventure, for life itself is an adventure. But try not to waste your time in doing

* Premier Christopher Hornsrud said that the purpose of the Labour Government was 'to prepare the transformation of our society into a socialist community', to tax the wealthy heavily, 'to abandon military activities' and to prepare for 'the final disestablishment of the entire military system'.

things which you know can be done equally well by others. Everyone
should hit upon his own trail. Do not lose your opportunities, and do
not allow yourselves to be carried away by the superficial rush and
scramble which is modern life. . . . Do not let your flight be clogged by
all those trifles which are now considered necessities of life. Mind you,
by making your baggage-train longer you clip your wings.'

Nansen, the scientist and very human being, believed in the diversity
of Man as the element which produces progress, not in 'fair shares' or
'affluence' with all their paraphernalia. The 'State' was no God to
Nansen, but a factor which should be manipulated pragmatically for
higher and more humane ends than its own.

Such was the thinking of Nansen, Michelsen and their numerous
admirers as the 'statism' of the socialists gathered impetus in the 1920s.
Quisling shared this elastic and idealist view. As the folly of Socialism
led irrevocably to the demoralisation of the nation and to the disaster
of 1940, he was driven to the logical conclusion that he, as the heir of
the Opposition, must assume control. The idea that he emerged from
some idiot fringe of Norwegian or foreign politics is utterly false.

The whole line of thought of Nansen and his supporters (including
Michelsen until near his end) from 1905 to 1930 was anti-socialist,
anti-party politics, anti-parliamentarian and in favour of 'national
unification', the name by which Quisling was to call his own broad
movement. NS was in fact the natural, logical and practical sequel
to the failure of Nansen and company to stem the oncoming defeatist
socialist tide. The failure of the old Opposition to rally behind Quisling,
and its degeneration into faction, prolonged the socialist stranglehold
on Norway and thus presented the country to Hitler on a plate. The
guilt therefore belongs to Right as well as Left. That explains why the
former has never regained office for more than a few weeks since 1935.
It is discredited and fractured, powerless and despairing.

10

Battle Stations

BY the mid-1920s Norway was drifting to the perdition which caught up with her in 1940, and many people foresaw calamity; but nothing effective was done about it. Nansen, the natural leader of the nation, failed it. In his mid-sixties he was already fading and disillusioned. He was also too grand, vain and irresolute to come down from his pedestal and enter the hurly-burly of the political chaos which prevailed. The idea, mooted by business, finance and intellectuals, of a 'concentrated government', embracing all parties and resolved to set the Norwegian house in order, came to nothing. So did the idea of a Folk Party, led by Nansen and appealing to all people of goodwill, irrespective of party. A 'Ministry of All Talents', led by Nansen, also appealed equally little to the parochial Norwegian mind. The best that can be said of these serious, prolonged and widespread attempts is that they indicated the way to salvation, kept discussion alive and fermented ideas which Quisling was later to employ.

The only practical results of this wavering were the Fatherland League, which had its ramifications all over the country and attracted patriots from all walks of life in the bourgeois ranks, and another parallel organisation, named *Samfundsvernet* (Community Guard). This was a private, semi-military body of men, scattered at potential trouble-spots and specifically intended to help the authorities to stave off the Red Revolution which the socialists contemplated. Its chief was Colonel

Ragnvald Hvoslef. In Quisling's Telemark, the organiser of this 'emergency police force' was Harald Franklin Knudsen, who collected about a hundred volunteers and played a prominent part in the notorious rising of Norsk Hydro workers at Menstad when Quisling was Defence Minister in 1931.

The Fatherland League and the Community Guard were formed independently of Quisling. Both were patriotic, anti-Bolshevik and idealistic. Both contributed to Quisling's movement.

The creation of the Community Guard caused much bitterness among the socialists, but they had only themselves to blame. They had hailed the Russian Revolution with enthusiasm and established Workers' Councils (*Soviets*) on the Bolshevik model. By 1919 the socialists had joined the Third International in Moscow, and in the following year they sent six representatives to plot international strategy. In Parliament the socialists voted against joining the League of Nations because they did not wish to be handicapped by Western connections. Strikes of a revolutionary nature were organised in 1921 and during widespread strikes and lockouts in 1923-24 the Communists received substantial financial aid from Moscow. Trygve Lie, legal counsel of the Labour Party, and many other prominent Labour members of the *Storting* in the 1940s received money or salaries from Moscow in the 1920s, as the *Storting* archives show, and as Quisling revealed in his famous farewell to Parliament as Defence Minister on April 7, 1932. When the Community Guard was formed, the socialists already had activist clubs in operation and they retaliated against the bourgeoisie by planning 'Red Guards'. A real danger to the country existed, and fear of Labour drove much capital from the country.

Yet the bourgeoisie could not combine. The development of Labour and Communist parties had resulted in a balance of forces in Parliament, so that no single party had a clear majority. After Labour's brief but terrifying début in 1928, the non-socialist parties succeeded each other in office until 1935, when Labour returned—never since to relinquish its grip, even in exile. The party system was, indeed, reduced to a dangerous absurdity, after the fashion of the Third Republic in France, with comparable results.

Such were the frustrating circumstances in which Nansen and his friends dithered and when Quisling entered the political stage.

In one important respect he differed from Nansen. For all his talk of co-operation, Nansen was predisposed towards the Right by the 1920s, and he failed to secure the confidence of the Left, which never forgave him for his 'treachery' to Republicanism and his 'defection' to the monarchists in 1905. Quisling was handicapped by no such past, as his approaches to Labour leaders in 1924-26 showed. Nor was he sold on the virtues of the Right, which was far from blameless in contributing to the revolutionary situation.

Wilhelm Keilhau, Professor of Economics and History at Oslo University, wrote in 1938 that the well-to-do bourgeois elements 'did not clothe themselves in sackcloth and ashes. Quite the contrary. . . . Why should their use of consumer goods be reduced? During the war years even the rich experienced poverty in the life of luxury. Now the threat of revolution hung over the country. Was it not more sensible to feast while there was yet time? Thus the nerves of the right of centre elements were constantly on edge in the face of conscious danger.'

Quisling, the ascetic, who was never interested in money, had no sympathy with profiteers, although he was born, bred and accepted in the ruling class. He had rubbed shoulders with common humanity in its death throes for too many years at shirtsleeves level to be a snob, whereas Nansen, the international figurehead, who hobnobbed with royalty and statesmen, was identified with the rich. In France, or any country with a tradition of grandeur and glory, Nansen might have succeeded, like de Gaulle, in attracting nationwide support; in England, too, where Churchill's wartime oratory did the trick—but not in parvenu Norway. Quisling realised Nansen's limitation and pitched his appeal on a classless basis, derived more from the Nordic nationalism of Eilert Sundt than from the grandiose statesmanship of a Nansen, a Churchill or a de Gaulle.

Given more time and better luck, this might have worked, but, under the circumstances, it proved a fatal miscalculation.

So, by 1930, little Norway was poised on the brick of catastrophe —with the Left openly in sympathy with Soviet Communism, surreptitiously receiving aid from the Third International, employing the Soviet 'cell' system and raising Red Guards at a time when the Stalinist purges were beginning and the forcible collectivisation of agriculture was in progress; with the selfish Right, antagonising the workers and peasants by extravagance and ostentation, contemplating supra-parliamentary action and also raising a private army, soon after the Wall Street crash in October 1929, the start of the Great Depression and the failure of international finance. Such was the desperate situation at home and abroad when Quisling entered the arena.

No sooner had he consulted Nansen and established contact with the Fatherland League and the Community Guard, than two further disasters for Quisling and Norway happened unexpectedly. On May 13, 1930, Fridtjof Nansen died. On January 30, 1933, Adolf Hitler became Chancellor of Germany.

A German phoenix had arisen from the ashes of the First World War and the dusty Weimar Republic, bent on revenge for the 'stab in the back' and the 'injustice' of Versailles, supported by the officer caste, the Junkers and big business, and brawling with the Communists.

How Nansen would have reacted to this had he lived can only be surmised. His inclination, based on knowledge of elementary 'fascism' which he rejected, would probably have been to cling harder than ever to the League of Nations. But who knows if his belief in the 'Nordic cult', coupled with the breakdown of statesmanship in the thirties and the Stalinist excesses, might not have tempted him to seek an understanding with anti-Bolshevik Germany? That great sailor and First Lord of the Admiralty, Lord Fisher, had warned Nansen in 1906-8 that Britain would require Norwegian bases in a war with Germany. This was narrowly avoided by British mine-laying in Norwegian waters in 1916-18, but the risk must have been apparent to Nansen in 1930, as it was to Quisling. On the other hand Germany's interest was in a neutral Norway, as the Kaiser and Hitler both argued. The Kaiser had used Norwegian waters to extricate his fleet to Kiel in July 1914, and Hitler had the additional reason, in the form of iron-ore from Narvik for his armaments, for taking advantage of Norwegian neutrality.

Alternatively, Nansen might have plumped for a British alliance. He had tried for this in 1906-8. He liked the British Royal Family. He had worked with the British and respected their integrity. Such an alliance would have been logical, since National Socialism as well as Bolshevism was alien to the majority of Norwegians, whereas there were affinities between the British and Norwegian ways of life at all levels. A British alliance, however, would have been ill-received at the time by the pro-Russian Norwegian Left, the Lutheran State

Church and admirers of German industry and learning. Hitler would naturally have objected to any such proposal as vehemently as the Kaiser, and the North, as a whole, would have been dragged into the international maelstrom immediately, with divisive results.

What other option was open to Nansen? Norway's interest seemed to sprout in all directions. The problem was so complicated that most Norwegians gave up trying to fathom it—with the exception of Quisling.

The ideal solution would have been a joint Russo-German-British guarantee of Northern neutrality—an idea with which Nansen had also toyed in 1906-8. But this was hardly feasible in 1930, when extremism was rampant in Europe.

The idea of 'Nordic solidarity' would still have appealed in the 1930s to the feeling of Scandinavian brotherhood, and if a neutral block of Finland, Sweden, Norway and Denmark could have been organised, it might still have saved the North from the fragmentation which it suffered during and after the Second World War, as Quisling foresaw. But Nansen would have been as disappointed as Sundt or Quisling. The meeting of the 'Four K's'—King Gustaf, King Haakon, King Christian and President Kyosti Kallio of Finland—in the autumn of 1939, when the war had started and Finland was threatened by Russia, ended in discord. Finland was left to her fate, to be mutilated, as Denmark had been in 1864.

Perhaps 'Nordic solidarity' could have been achieved in time to save the North if Nansen had lived a few years longer and thrown all his authority into the scales on the advent of Hitler; certainly if Nansen had been the man in 1930 that he was in 1905.

Another weak alternative would have been armed neutrality for Norway in isolation. This would have been better than nothing and might have saved the day on April 9, 1940. It was the policy to which Quisling was reduced as a last resort and which he advocated up to the eve of the German invasion. Nansen the internationalist, the man of peace, the 'co-operator', was also practical and he, too, might have sunk his scruples as the emergency increased, and anticipated Quisling.

Norway is one of the easiest countries in the world to defend with a minimal force. Finland had shown the North what could be achieved by resolution and action in 1918 and the Lapua Movement had also shown how socialist subversion could be contained. Finland continued

88

to practise armed neutrality, which saved her in the Second World War. Sweden was another neighbouring example of how a small Northern country might protect itself, thus making itself a worthy and useful partner in any potential defence pact, instead of a feeble encumbrance. Norway thought she knew better—at grievous cost to herself and her neighbours.

The remaining alternative was unarmed neutrality in isolation— the hopeless policy of the Norwegian Left and Right. This would not have made sense to Nansen, although whether he would have acquiesced in it and paid lip service to the League of Nations is another question. Perhaps he would have continued to dither over foreign policy as he did over home affairs. But one does not like to think so ill of this great man of action. There were alternatives and the business of statesmanship is to choose the best feasible one. The Finns chose and the Swedes did likewise. In each case it was a gamble that just came off. Like them, Quisling chose armed neutrality.

But unarmed neutrality was preferred by Norway and Denmark. The latter at least had some excuse, since it was wide open, with a third of the population in one city (Copenhagen) and with no wilderness for mustering a resistance. The Norwegians, with all their geographical advantage, turned deaf ears for ten years to Quisling's warning. They preferred to dream and bicker, rather than think and rally, lulling themselves into a state of false security. The instinct for self-preservation seems to have deserted them. They would not save themselves. Nor would they allow one of their own kith and kin to save them. Perhaps they would even have ignored Nansen.

No small country—not even the ephemeral Caucasian Republics of 1918-20—made less attempt to preserve newly won independence than Norway, except perhaps the Baltic States, which were as indefensible as Denmark. Quisling alone faced the alternatives amid the dangers of the thirties, squarely and vociferously—attempting to develop the ideas of Nansen. Yet Quisling, of all people, is blamed for the disaster of 1940 and its consequences!

Nansen's funeral was on the National Day, May 17, 1930. To mark the occasion, Ronald Fanger wrote a leading article headed 'Norway's Symbol' in *Tidens Tegn*, which had launched the 'Nansen for Premier' campaign in 1926-7. It said that he had 'attempted to create national unification on a broad front*... based on large, simple principles ... above party lines which divorced people from their natural allegiance. ... But they would not have him, as they would not have Michelsen in his time because he simply did not symbolise Norwegian politics.'

This expressed the line of thought behind the Fatherland League, which had emerged from *Tidens Tegn*'s initiative in 1926 and been adopted by Nansen as his instrument for forging a national front under his own aegis—the movement of which the Community Guard was the strong arm. Now the 'unification' cause was leaderless. Who was to fill the gap?

Obviously Quisling—Nansen's respected colleague and friend—now the leading internationalist in Norway—the best surviving brain in the country—a man without a stain on his character and uncontaminated by party politics—well-connected, known personally to the king since his youth and a confidant of Queen Maud, who frequently sought his views on his vacations from Russia.

Accordingly *Tidens Tegn* launched him as Nansen's successor the following week. On May 24 his 'Political thoughts on the death of Fridtjof Nansen' occupied the whole front page of the paper, saying: 'The political task which Nansen foresaw for himself in Norway was, as is known, to free the fatherland from class-warfare and party politics and to accomplish national unification and construction on a basis of sound political and economic principles. With Nansen's death our people have been left without a natural leader to look up to. The situation is all the more distressing in that it has not actually displayed any truly unifying course of political action. The overall tendency has been tantamount to a further splitting of the nation—setting bourgeois against worker and worker against bourgeois. Aside from that, alarm and uncertainty for the future increase, also embitterment concerning our powerless and miserable political situation, our meaningless labour conflicts, the Bolshevist and disorderly spirit which is spreading in our towns and villages. ... Such circumstances require a new political order, clear, definite and positive. ... Our people must find their way back to their original mode of thought and from that develop their strength ... a spiritual and responsible attitude to existence ... a sound

* '*å skape en bred nasjonal samling*'—the name Quisling was to give his movement.

blending of individualism and communal spirit . . . the best leader . . . freedom for private enterprise . . . security of life and property, employment and its fruits . . . goodwill and co-operation instead of class-war . . . sound economic conditions for the individual and the community . . . freedom of conscience and consolidation of the economic life . . . in short a new, almost religious, political doctrine.'

The next four months, when Norwegians take to the hills and fjords, were the dead political season, and Quisling occupied himself writing his book, *Russia and Ourselves*. This was a sort of sequel to Nansen's *Russia and Peace*, and brought the situation up to date. It contained Quisling's ideology, elaborating his article of May 24, and began to appear serially in *Tidens Tegn* on September 15.

Thus the continuity between Nansen's tentative essay into home affairs and Quisling's début is established—long before the full import of National Socialism was widely appreciated outside Germany. It is a coincidence that Hitler's movement and Quisling's *Nasjonal Samling* had the same initials. The theme of national unification had been discussed in Norway for years previously.

If Quisling's ideology owed anything to 'fascist' thought, it was to Mussolini, whose improvements in Italy, such as 'making the trains punctual' and 'clearing the beggars off the streets', had received world-wide acclaim. Any coincidental resemblance between *Nasjonal Samling* and Fascism actually created distrust of Quisling in Nazi Germany, although he did not contact Mussolini until the Fascist Conference at Montreux in 1935. This mutual suspicion lasted up to 1940.

It is alleged that Quisling visualised himself as a dictator from the start, modelling himself on Lenin and Hitler, but leadership and the '*führer prinzip*' are not necessarily the same. Again it is an unfortunate coincidence from Quisling's viewpoint that the Norwegian word for leader is *fører*. This did him no good. Had he been more experienced politically, he would not have called his party NS and himself *Fører*, since the German concept of those names is alien to Norway.

Elaborate research has been conducted to prove that Quisling was already in contact with Nazis when his *Tidens Tegn* Russian articles appeared (September 15-December 7), but all that has been established is that he met Max Pferdekämper, one of Hitler's old cronies from the Munich beer-cellar days, in Oslo on December 7 and probably attended the opening of the new Norwegian-German Association quarters with him on the same day. That Quisling sought a meeting with Hitler and tried to secure Nazi funds is mere speculation, far-fetched at that, for as yet Quisling had no real party, organisation or newspaper to support. He did not know Germany and had merely travelled through it on his way between Norway and Russia. Nor did he speak the language. It was not until mid-1939 that he first contacted any Nazi of importance. Even then it was not on his own initiative. Up to that time he did no more than take an intelligent interest in National Socialism, which was surely wise rather than culpable. If more statesmen had done likewise there might have been no war!

Quisling's publication of his thesis in newspaper and book form has also been compared with release of the Marxist Manifesto and *Mein Kampf*—the insinuation being that he borrowed from the Soviet and Nazi cell system and the other conspiratorial techniques of the Russian and German Revolutions. Again the comparison is superficial.

Quisling's movement was designed to appeal to neither extreme but to the broad centre of Norwegian opinion. It was not conspiratorial; it operated openly. Nor yet were his supporters violent, uniformed or armed. The nearest resemblance to Bolshevism or Fascism came in the appeal that Nansen and Quisling both made to the nation over the heads of the established political parties. This amounted to nothing more subversive than advocating a national or bi-partisan government. Personally, neither Nansen nor Quisling aspired to be a leader in the sense of a dictator, but rather the saviour of the country, like a Lloyd George or Churchill, a Clemenceau or de Gaulle, a Woodrow Wilson or a Roosevelt in times of national crisis.

The attitudes and trappings of dictatorship were forced on Quisling first by the desperate apathy of his countrymen and then by grim fact of the German Occupation. Since reason would not stir Norway, he later resorted to more sensational methods of persuasion. Only when they failed did he feel obliged to emulate the Germans in order to preserve, as he thought, the dignity of Occupied Norway and to appease the conquerors, thus staking a claim to a favoured place in the Greater Reich, which looked as if it might indeed last 'a thousand years'.

At its worst the Quisling movement was never more than a super-ficial imitation of National Socialism. At the beginning, Quisling was at the most only marginally influenced by Nazism or Bolshevism. He was an indigenous product of deep-rooted Northern origin.

From May to September 1930—at the very start of the Stalin and Hitler dictatorships—Quisling defined his ideology and programme with uncanny penetration and prescience. His preamble in *Russia and Ourselves* reads thus:

'An unspeakably dangerous enemy is threatening our civilisation, and primarily the British Empire. This enemy is Bolshevism, the master of Russia and the champion of World Revolution. . . . It may well prove a decisive factor in the fate of the world. For Russia is a very great country, with unique potentialities of becoming a world power: an enormous area, almost three times that of the USA, with inexhaustible reserves of manpower, immense natural wealth, and a central geographical position between East and West. . . . Above all others, the Russian question is an issue between Bolshevism and the Teutonic nations, especially Great Britain, the natural upholder of all that is threatened by Communism. I propose . . . to set forth the principles and objects of the counter-policy we must adopt, in the interests of the world, to ensure the vigorous survival of the Northern nations. . . .

'Russian Bolshevism is a product of two highly different influences —international Communism, and . . . tendencies of a characteristically Russian kind; the reaction against the old régime and the inheritance of the past.' This must be familiar language to Americans today and an uncomfortable reminder to the British of the collapse of their Empire after the Russian triumph in the Second World War.

Quisling continues: 'Communism goes further than socialism, inasmuch as it aims at the complete collective organisation of life and, ultimately, the abolition of the State itself. Socialism, therefore, is a transition stage on the road to Communism. . . . The real difference between Communism and Socialism lies, of course, in the method by which they propose to establish a socialist organisation of society. Communism—as expounded by Marx and Lenin—is pledged to violence. . . . Communists regard Social Democrats as virtual allies of the bourgeoisie, if not the main impediment to social revolution. The Social Democrats, with their superficial specifics for social ills, are considered by Communists to act as a safety-valve which prevents capitalist society from exploding.'

We now come to the emotional and controversial matter of race in relation to revolution, and it is important to read this with the 'Nordic cult' of Sundt, Nansen and many other prominent Scandinavians in mind—rather than the distortions of Hitler, Rosenberg, Streicher, Haushofer and other Nazi racists. It is also salutary to remember such slogans as 'the white man's burden' in Britain, 'the chosen race' in Jewry and 'the American way of life'. Racial superiority was not the monopoly of Nazis.

'To some extent Bolshevist policy even deliberately tried to bring about the physical destruction of the classes where the most intelligent human material was to be found . . . anybody can see how different the racial type is now, for example in Moscow, from what it was before the Revolution. The predominance of Asiatic and Oriental blood is particularly noticeable. . . . The extermination of highly developed hereditary material involves an irretrievable loss and, as a policy, amounts to national suicide. . . .

'Nevertheless, one often sees really fine types in the Russian villages —men who remind one of the best type of peasant in the Norwegian highlands and who sometimes have quite a Viking air about them. What I have seen of the Russian peasants has given me a great liking for them and belief in them. Their influence and the contribution they may make as a vital source of racial renewal, will decide the future of the Russian people. It is all the more sad therefore to see how the Bolsheviks are doing their level best to stamp out the best peasant stock. . . .

'Bolshevism has its base among the Finno-Slav population of Great Russia, as it derives its origin from them. If Bolshevism lost its strongholds there, it could not hold out for long in the other Soviet republics.'

From this romantic and overstrained Nordic interpretation of history arose the most unfortunate ingredient of Quisling's ideology, namely an artificial argument with the Jews. He goes on: 'Jews took a leading part in bringing about the first Russian Revolution in 1917. . . . The main reason for this was, of course, that the Jews in Russia, numbering 6 million, were subject to various restrictions. . . . This forced many of the Jewish intelligentsia to join the revolutionary parties. Moreover, it inflamed the Jews in all parts of the world against the Tsarist régime. One effect of this was that relations between the USA and Russia before the Revolution were largely determined by the Jewish question in the latter country. . . .

'On the other hand the Jews, as a whole, have suffered more in consequence of the Revolution than any other race in Russia. This stands to reason, as the bulk of the Jewish inhabitants are craftsmen and small traders, whose occupations have been ruined by the Revolution. . . . In the Ukraine alone, several hundred thousand Jewish homes were pillaged during the Revolution, not to speak of the women who were violated and the 300,000 children left to wander about homeless . . . the circumstance that the Bolshevist authorities discourage anti-semitism both in theory and practice does not mend matters in the least. . . .

'The very fact the Bolshevists are so deeply involved in it [the Jewish question]—as was the old régime, though in another way—may prove as fatal to *their* Government as it did to the Government of the Tsar.'

Quisling clearly sympathised with Jewish suffering in theory, as he did in practice as a Relief worker. He had nothing against the Jewish *race*. But then he reaches dangerous ground:

'There is little doubt that socialism—apart from its adherents among the Jewish intellectuals—is mainly prevalent in the short-skulled Alpine race, which includes the bulk of the lower classes in Central Europe and the majority of the Slav inhabitants of Eastern Europe. In the case of Bolshevism, we find that this revolutionary development of socialism exists as a mass movement precisely in those parts of Russia where there is most Asiatic blood in the Slav population. Bolshevism might be described as an Asiatic-Slav movement led by Jewish minds . . . Bolshevism partially runs in the blood. . . . In Western lands, on the contrary, Bolshevism is a matter of confused thinking. . . . Neither socialism nor Communism suits the Nordic temperament.'

That is to say, Communism is competitive with Nordic civilisation and the Jews, like Asiatics and other exponents of Marxism, are un-desirable *ideologically*.

Developing this theme, Quisling asserts: 'From very early times Russia has been an area where the Nordic and Asiatic mentalities have caused a struggle for mastery. The sharpest antagonisms in the world today, especially in my own country of Norway and in Germany, amount in the last resort to a duel between the Nordic-European principle and Bolshevism. . . .

'The only way to wean people from this brachiocephalic religion

95

and prevent the ultimate triumph of Marxism is by organising a comprehensive and thoroughly educative campaign. People must be made to realise that their salvation depends upon their Nordic origin and character, and upon a truly religious and responsible philosophy of life. Like every society which is struggling to surmount a great crisis they must draw upon their own natural principles and thence derive a fresh access of power.'

When Quisling wrote '*made to realise*' in 1930, I do not believe that he meant physical compulsion, although this was where the 'Nordic cult' and 'Aryanism' in fact led. Like the Hebrew prophets and Greek and Roman philosophers, he was advocating a return to the good old godly culture of yore, in preference to the disruptive and 'alien' new mode of life. The full implications of Aryanism and its logical conclusion in genocide were not understood until the end of the war, when he came to trial.

From this point in his race theory, Quisling goes on to summarise the dangers to Norway: 'The fact is that the social revolution which, for instance, the present leaders of the Norwegian Labour Party are "actively fighting for"—I quote their printed phrase—would be relatively as cruel and destructive of human life in Norway, or in other countries, as it has been in Russia. . . . Northerners should be under no delusions concerning the superior strength of their own civilisation. A strong inside current of Viking blood still runs in the veins of most of us. Although Northerners have never been prone to wanton cruelty, they have not flinched from putting out their enemies' eyes or carving blood-eagles in their backs. . . . Most people are not so civilised after all. When established traditions and customs of society are weakened or overthrown, as invariably happens in a social revolution, the low human instincts awake to life. Men use their intelligence to be more bestial then the beasts themselves.'

The salvation, he maintains, is a Corporate State: 'Far be it from me to suggest that there is necessarily better stuff in our upper classes than in the lower strata. . . . But for all that, the destruction of educated intelligence and stored-up personal culture and experience, which accompanies social revolutions, is a very serious matter. These indisputable facts regarding the effects of revolution should prove sufficient to banish all thoughts of a Communist revolution from normal minds, whether in Norway, Great Britain or elsewhere. . . . The existing [capitalist] system needs reformation—co-partnership—planned development to avoid recessions—full exploitation of natural resources—a national organ, representative of different industrial and trade union organisations, to form a unit expressing the organic development not only of rival sections but of society itself.'

I may remark that the Corporate State has worked so far, with some success as well as blemishes, in another small, proud and backward country under the aegis of another cultivated, religious and strong leader, namely Portugal under Salazar. One may not like it, but it is not an absurdity.

Approaching the end of his book, Quisling reviews foreign policy, with particular reference to Northern Europe: 'Russia has a Baltic policy, aspiring to the North Atlantic Ocean; a Black Sea policy, aspiring to the Mediterranean; an Arctic policy and a Pacific policy; and last but not least an inland policy aspiring to the Indian Ocean....

'The Northern element, which was of vital importance in the foundation of Russia, will in future play a weighty part in the development of events—though we must hope that it will not manifest itself, as it did 200 years ago, in a Great Northern War. Unfortunately there are already signs of such a possibility....

'Russia is a successor of the Eastern-Roman Empire at Constantinople. . . . This fact has permeated the whole of Russian history. . . . Russia still retains her character as a state embodying the Roman-Byzantine imperial idea and especially as the Northern patron of the Eastern Hemisphere. . . . Such then are the natural dynamic lines behind Russian foreign policy.'

Quisling then cites examples of Russian penetration in Turkey, Persia, Afghanistan, Caucasia, Outer Mongolia and China. Thus he arrived full-circle back in the North and the 'risk of a dispute between Poland and Russia', 'the tempting prospect which the Bolshevisation of Poland would offer as a move in the great game of the World Revolution'. 'The Baltic States would be the next to fall, almost automatically.' 'Estonia and North Latvia were wrested from the Swedes by Peter the Great and South Latvia and Lithuania came into Russian hands towards the end of the eighteenth century—part of ambitions to gain entrance to Europe and free passage to the sea.' 'Estonia and Latvia must be regarded as buffer states between England

97

and Russia; for England's actual frontiers are coterminous with the sea. We all know the fate of such buffer states!' 'If we include Finland, whose frontier lies thirty kilometres from Leningrad, there are no points from which a blow could be so speedily and effectively aimed at Russia.'

In short, Quisling identified precisely the spots which triggered off the Second World War—Poland, the Baltic States and Finland—and the geopolitical set-up which brought Norway into the firing-line. Few, if any, other statesmen had such foresight or the knowledge with which to arrive at it.

He goes further: 'Unsolved problems are to be found along the whole length of the new frontier-line across the Continent of Europe, from the Gulf of Finland to the Black Sea. . . . It is of vital importance for Europe that this frontier should be stabilised. . . . How far this will be possible in the long run depends to a very great extent on the relations between Poland and Germany; and these again are governed by the relations between France and Germany. In other words the issue depends upon the consolidation of Europe. . . .

'If Europe allowed the Baltic States to go, we should probably experience a repetition of the conquests of Russia under the Tsars, and the chronological order would probably be Poland followed by the Balkans and the countries of the North. . . . Finland would be seriously weakened by an Estonian Soviet Republic in the south. . . . Finland was captured from Sweden in 1808. . . . The intention was to bring about the entire destruction of Sweden's sovereignty on the eastern shores of the Baltic; to ensure the safety of St. Petersburg, the Russian capital; to augment Russian influence in the Baltic and throughout the North; and at the same time render possible further advance towards the Atlantic. Speaking generally, these conditions are as valid now as they were then.'

Quisling visualised something like the Atlantic Pact (NATO) eighteen years before events forced this alliance upon the Western world. 'A Nordic Federation,' he writes, 'between Scandinavia and Great Britain, plus Finland and Holland, and in which Germany and eventually the British Dominions and America could be included—such a federation could break the frontal onslaught of the Bolshevik combination and save European civilisation and peace for a long time to come. . . . It is natural for Scandinavia, especially Norway, to seek a

closer tie with the British Empire, since we have so much in common.'
A prophet is without honour. . . .

He adds: 'The Norwegian people in particular must learn to understand itself and its distinctive characteristics. . . . The Nordic race has been and is the most important creator of the world's civilisation, and to which both Greece and Rome as well as Europe and America owe their greatness. . . . By combining the "Nordic idea" with a religious and moral perception of the world, and attention to the requirements of modern progress, a scientific-political doctrine may be evolved. . . .

'A national renaissance in the Nordic spirit; a peaceful and just solution of the social problem, and a world-embracing co-operation between various peoples and people of Nordic sympathies to promote the world's reorganisation and peaceful development—this is not merely an anti-Bolshevist but primarily a positive policy founded upon realities, and with a strong and noble aim in view, something really worth living and dying for. Far more so than the godless chimeras of Karl Marx and Lenin.'

In that broad context the phenomenon of Nazi Germany is merely a ghastly incident. It depends how close one is in time and space to Soviet Russia how one reviews the history of the last half-century. To Quisling, who was close in both respects, Bolshevism was a greater threat than Nazism.

Quisling laid his cards on the table in 1930 and never deviated. Nobody said he was talking nonsense in 1930, when there was still time to restrain Hitler and to contain Bolshevism. If we had listened to Quisling, the Bolsheviks would not now be entrenched on the line running from Petsamo on the Norwegian frontier, through the Baltic States, Poland, East Berlin and the Balkans as far as the Adriatic (Albania) and the exit to the Mediterranean (Bulgaria). Nor would they be penetrating the Middle East as far as Egypt and East Africa, Persia and Iraq, nor yet the northern Japanese islands (Sakhalin) and South-east Asia. Quisling's misfortune was that he had too much vision and logic for his contemporaries. NATO, CENTO and SEATO bear witness to his foresight.

For all its merits, Quisling's thesis contained seeds of failure.
Unlike Finland and Sweden, Norway never quarrelled with Russia

or dreaded her. The Labour Party's affiliations with Bolshevism did not therefore seem preposterous. Norway had no great indigenous nobility and so the upper classes were less bigoted. Quisling's fulminations against socialism accordingly fell rather flat. Russia seemed a long way off and Norwegians reacted to the Bolshevist peril with British indifference.

Quisling, straight from the steppes, over-estimated his countrymen's sensitivity to the danger, partly owing to his long absence abroad, partly owing to his foreign marriage and partly to his expatriate anxiety to prove in a hurry that his country's welfare was at his heart. His perspective on Norway was faulty and this eventually led to his adoption of alien Nazi symbols under duress.

He also over-emphasised the Nordic cult. International socialism had already made too many inroads on the old 'Viking spirit', by diverting it into communal or selfish activities, for Quisling's racial theories to hold a very wide appeal.

Besides, there was never a Jewish problem in Norway and his identification of the Labour Party with Jewish international Communism or the Right with Jewish international finance seemed bizarre. His distinction between the Jewish *race* and Jewish *ideology* was too fine for average Norwegians, and—if it had any validity—it was too complicated for popular comprehension. It was assumed that he wanted pogroms, which was never true. This was most damaging to his reputation at home and eventually abroad. It antagonised many idealists who might have followed him, provoked unnecessary opposition, and in the end contributed to the atmosphere of hate that led to his execution.

Furthermore, his simultaneous attack on socialism and capitalism was too comprehensive for the tiny Norwegian nation. In discarding *both* wings of potential support, he left a rump too small to provide adequate backing for true and effective national unification. He made too many enemies. Hitler knew his people and human nature better. He absorbed the bulk of the Communist vote and did a deal with the extreme Right. Then he gave the masses what they wanted. He also used the Constitution to seize power, whereas Quisling, like Nansen, sought to float above it. Quisling was too impractical.

His timing was also unfortunate: on one level too vague and on another too provocative for Norway in 1930. He was too early in the sense that he branded his movement inadvertently with Hitler's future misdeeds, thus giving his opponents time and ammunition for a counter-attack. It was also too late in so far as the socialists were too thoroughly dug-in to be halted by mere idealism and the Right was too set in its partisan habits to co-operate with him effectively.

Quisling evidently sensed those weaknesses and was not long in trying to overcome them by more practical measures in the form of a new organisation, under his own leadership, which absorbed the Fatherland League and was called *Den Nordiske Folkereisning* (Nordic Folk-awakening).

II

Into Action

THE Central Committee of Nordic Folk-awakening, consisting of thirteen members, met on March 25, 1931, and on April 8 it appointed a directorate, including Dr. Herman Harris Aall, a philosopher and lawyer who was born in the Arctic at Varanger, near Russia, and had lived in Germany; Captain Halvor Hansson, a General Staff officer; and Halvor Egeberg, a rich financier.

On May 12, Quisling was enlisted by the new Agrarian Prime Minister, Per Ludvig Kolstad, to fill a key post—the Ministry of Defence—which had been starved by previous governments and black-guarded by the socialists, and which now assumed major importance owing to the confrontation of Hitler and Stalin. Kolstad was no innovator, but a sound and intuitive politician who had been a member of Parliament for ten years and latterly the President of one of the divisions of the *Storting*. Before that he had been head of an agricultural college. As the former paragon of the General Staff and an international expert, Quisling was obviously the man for the job. Nobody suggested that he was unbalanced. Nobody registered any astonishment that he had been preferred to Majors Otto Ruge and Carl Fleischer.

On the 13th the Central Committee of Nordic Folk-awakening met and appointed Prytz, Quisling's old friend from Russia, as leader instead of Quisling. It also stated that the programme should be continued energetically and that the movement would appear as a public organisation in due course. This clearly indicated that Quisling intended to use his position as Minister to spread his own ideology and to promote the aims of his private organisation. Evidently the Prime Minister did not object; otherwise he would not have drafted Quisling, whose views were already well known. Kolstad may even have hoped to profit from Quisling's high standing in influential business, military and intellectual circles, for the Farmers' party was only ten years old, part Liberal and part Conservative, and this was the beginning of its first and only term of office (1931-33).

The inaugural meeting of Nordic Folk-awakening was held in the Handicrafts and Industrial Union headquarters on the National Day, May 17, with thirty members present apart from Frederick Prytz, who took the chair. Prytz uttered the prophetic words: 'What we have now set in motion is the first effort in the North, so far as I know, to build up a political doctrine consciously begotten of our people's distinctions . . . as part of the great Northern folk-family. . . . Perhaps we have started a movement which will have great and unexpected consequences.'

Quisling said: 'The main object is to destroy the imported and corrupting Communist insurrectionary movement. . . . First of all it is necessary to form a new society, a new political system. The parliamentary system, with its fruitless party politics, cannot solve Norway's national problems. The movement must bring into being a *Riksting* (National Assembly) alongside the *Storting* (Parliament)—a two-chamber system.' He intended that the *Storting* should become the Upper, consultative, House, and the *Riksting* the corporative, legislative Lower House.

Quisling's government appointment was well received in the Press except by *Arbeiderbladet*, the organ of the Labour Party, which initiated the future smear that he was both a Bolshevik and a Fascist. The fact that Quisling, as Minister of Defence, was actively concerned with a movement outside the government, however, expectedly produced more violent comment from the Left.

The Communist organ, *Arbeideren*, started off with articles, inspired by editor Jakob Friis, between May 15 and 22, alleging that Quisling was a British spy and provocateur who had sought to discover the plans for resistance against a British attack on the Soviet Union. Another week onwards, on May 28, *Arbeiderbladet* broadened the attack from Quisling's personality to his movement, Nordic Folk-awakening, which was accused of seeking to end parliamentarianism. Its literature, adorned with the gold and red cross of St. Olav, was said to resemble the swastika, and its programme to be chauvinistic.

A week after the Kolstad Government had taken office, Alfred Madsen, the Labour Party leader, accused Quisling in the *Storting* of having been enthusiastic about the Soviet Union late in 1924 and claimed that he had approached not only the Labour Party but the Communists, Friis and Olav Scheflo (another editor) during January-February 1925. Now that Quisling had joined the Agrarians, he seemed to Madsen to be running in circles.

So Quisling was accused by the Left, during his first week in office, of having been simultaneously a Communist, a British agent, an anti-Communist and a Fascist! Any stick was good enough to beat the first serious challenger of the party which already scented decisive victory four years ahead.

Quisling held his fire for the time being, lest he embarrass his colleagues, and contented himself with explaining that he had merely contacted the Left in 1924-26 to warn them with first-hand evidence of the drift which Stalin was starting away from Lenin's hopeful New Economic Policy. He added that he had returned from Russia in 1930 because his work there finished when Britain resumed diplomatic relations and made it no longer necessary to look after British interests.

Afterwards, Norwegian politics gradually became war to the death.

Two days only elapsed before the most serious rising in the history of Norwegian industrial strife was staged in the heart of the Quisling country—at Menstad, near the Norsk Hydro fertiliser plant at Porsgrunn in Telemark, which was the greatest factory in the whole country. The timing and the place can hardly have been coincidental. Obviously it was aimed at placing the new Defence Minister in a predicament, which would accomplish his fall, and possibly at sparking off nation-wide disturbances, which would be the prelude to revolution on the Russian model.

On May 30 and June 2 large demonstrations were held on the ground that the management held some thirty workers to their three months' notice, loading and unloading saltpetre, during a lockout. On June 8 a thousand employees, led by sixty stormtroopers, marched on Menstad, armed with clubs, chains and hose-piping. The police were power-less to cordon them off. Many were injured on both sides and the victorious workers marched off with police caps and accoutrements on top of their Red Flag standards. In other countries such riots may have been commonplace, but in Norway they were unprecedented, and the Press voiced general alarm.

Quisling feared that the rebels would seize the arms in a neighbour-ing armoury. He sent in a company of local infantry militiamen and a few other troops, who restored order with the help of two sloops. The police were then reorganised and the Community Guard lent a hand. Society had shown that it could defend itself and Quisling became the hero of the hour—supported by the Cabinet to a man—and hailed as the one person who knew how to stand up to the Reds.

After consultation with the other bourgeois parties, with *Storting* President Hambro in the chair, a communiqué was issued on June 8, reviewing the rising. This produced a violent counter-attack by the Left. *Arbeiderbladet* alleged that 1,500 men and four warships had been sent to Menstad the previous day, 'thus confirming afresh what the Norwegian armed forces were to be used for'.

On June 15 a special messenger from the Oslo Telephone head office was sent direct to Justice Minister Asbjørn Lindboe, with a tele-gram that revealed the grave danger that Norway still faced. It was from Peter Furubotn, Leader of the Norwegian Communist Party, who was in Moscow, ordering a counter-attack by the trade unions and unemployed in the form of wider demands for increased wages, a strike among seamen, dockers, transport workers and railwaymen, also battle against strike-breakers with a view to attracting sym-pathisers, and the spreading of dissensions and the sharpening conflict, notably in Oslo and Bergen. Financial demands by the police and armed forces were advocated, as well as the organisation of protective guards for exploiting the situation, and a general strike.

After consultation with Police Chief Kristian Welhaven, it was decided to deliver the telegram to Furubotn's 'post-box' lest another version should be sent in secret, thus leaving the authorities in the dark. The Army and the Police were alerted and an anti-sabotage watch was established. Wisely, Quisling maintained his habitual silence and let bourgeois opinion coalesce behind him.

Within four weeks the troops were withdrawn and the authorities lowered their guard again. Patriots, such as Harald Franklin Knudsen, who had helped the police at Menstad, were threatened by the Labour Press and its strongmen. Legal redress was unobtainable. When the indemnification of policemen who had been injured at Menstad was proposed in Parliament, the Labour spokesman said that they should be refused compensation because they had entered into the service of capitalism. This speaker was none other than Johan Nygaardsvold, who had been in the 1928 Labour Government and was to be Prime Minister from 1935 to 1945.

Proceedings were brought against activists in the 'Battle of Menstad', but those who had instigated it were ignored. Defence counsel was the thirty-six-years-old Trygve Lie, Secretary of one of the Trade Unions which demonstrably had been receiving money from Moscow. Einar Gerhardsen, Prime Minister from 1945 with hardly a break since, organised a Workers' Legal Aid Fund to cover the expenses of Communist as well as Labour accused.

Gerhardsen was a former road-navvy. He said at this time: 'The Army is a political weapon, and if one assembles at training camps, it means the same as having joined the enemy forces. However, the training obtained in the use of weapons and in shooting can be of use to the workers in their struggles with the upper class. It is necessary to be active and start energetic Communist agitation in the military camps.'

He was a conscientious objector, who frequently chose prison instead of military service. Trygve Lie, defending him in 1927, spoke of him as 'walking in and out of prison' as a military saboteur. Once Gerhardsen was actually arrested for anti-military agitation on an Army parade ground.

In 1927 he was jailed for 120 days for having published, with two others, an inflammatory article in the Communist organ, *Red Youth*, encouraging the unemployed young people to enter shops and take food packages without paying for them. Many youngsters did so. Trygve Lie pleaded that the action was 'idealistically motivated' and therefore not punishable.

Since those days of violence, Gerhardsen has developed an ingratiating manner, frequently referring to 'my dear Norwegian people' in his speeches. But he rarely commits himself. His equivocation has latterly been illustrated by Norwegian membership of NATO and the punishment of conscientious objectors under his régime, while at the same time a pacifist exhibition, recalling his anti-military pre-war activities, has recently been allowed in the University Library.

By 1932 200,000 (40 per cent) of Norway's organised workers had been laid off. Time and again the employers reduced wages. Strikes, lock-outs and fighting broke out between strike-breakers and unionised workers. The Great Depression was in full swing. Stalin's purges and collectivisation were taking place in the Soviet Union, while Hitler had smashed organised Communism in Germany. That was the atmosphere in which Quisling, as Defence Minister, had to set about his main task—the presentation of a Defence Budget and the creation of Armed Forces bearing some relationship to the urgent need of the time.

The *Norsk Biografisk Lexicon*'s statement that 'Quisling himself took no effective measures to revive defence' is a travesty, as the records of the Quisling Trial (pp. 236-68) show. Even the *Lexicon* admits that 'His two Defence budgets were influenced by the many interests which swayed Norwegian politics in the 1930s.' Kolstad headed a minority government, which depended on the votes of other bourgeois parties, and those parties were competing with the Left for the votes of the smaller businessmen and farmers—the very people who were worst hit by ruinous prices and foreclosures. Any grandiose Defence Budget was therefore impossible politically. This dilemma reflected the very malaise in parliamentarianism which Quisling and his friends in the Fatherland League and Nordic Folk-awakening had deplored for years. He had not got a free hand, but he did his best.

Major-General Halvor Hanson of the General Staff, who was editing *Our Army* at the time, told the Court: 'It was a period of eclipse for Defence. . . . The preceding Government, under Mowinckel, proposed a figure of 32 million *kroner*, so far as I remember. . . . When Quisling took over . . . it was impossible at that time to do anything about building up any defence. There was to be disarmament. It was actually more a question of the friends of Defence doing what they could to prevent havoc, rather than anything positively constructive. I am pretty certain Quisling did what he could, as was shown then and later. Quisling's Defence Budget proposals were 3 million *kroner* higher than those of the Mowinckel Government.' The general added that there was no dissatisfaction among higher officers with Quisling as Defence Minister.

Quisling himself gave details of his proposals, which General Hanson recalled, and these were not disputed in Court (p. 238), and the *Lexicon* actually pays Quisling the backhand compliment of adding that 'The weaker Defence Budget of 1940 was based on Quisling 1931 proposals'!

General Hanson continued: 'Quisling had great respect, even devotion, for Kolstad. But Kolstad died and I understood that Quisling did not have the same feeling towards Hundseid,* who succeeded Kolstad. I formed the impression that Quisling was disappointed over the way in which matters were decided . . . and in the way that parliamentarianism worked. That was also the impression I got from Quisling's utterances at the time.'

Quisling did not let the side down. The reverse was the case. The insinuation that Quisling did not really have his heart in improved Defence or did nothing about it, while he merely used his position to strengthen his private movement or to feather his own nest, does not bear examination.

Three famous 'affairs' followed Menstad in quick succession. Each deepened Quisling's disillusionment with party politics, provoked new extremes of vituperation from the Left and kept him in the limelight.

First, there was the ancient Norwegian claim to East Greenland between parallels 71° and 75°, which was energetically publicised by the company-director and lawyer, Gustav Smedal, who on June 2 telegraphed Norwegian fishermen to land and occupy this territory. They did so, and the next day the action was brought before the International Court at The Hague by Denmark, the injured power.

This remote incident touched off the ingrained 'Nordic imperialism' in Norway and particularly stirred Quisling. His spirit was alien to the Left, who were eager to attack anything he favoured at this time, and who ridiculed him. Nor did he get the support which he expected from

* Sverre Hartmann says in *Fører uten Folk*: 'The Agrarians' chairman and parliamentary leader was considered by many to be the more gifted and able of the two [i.e. than Kolstad], with more schooling and theoretical insight. But Jens Hundseid's personality did not stamp him as a government leader. He was easily swayed by his emotions and in that respect was unstable.'

108

his own government. The Agrarian leadership was already embarrassed by Menstad and had its eye on the next election. It was not looking for more trouble, being in a tiny minority of 30 out of 150 seats in Parliament, and it therefore soft-pedalled the Greenland claim.

Captain Johannes Kristofer Tornøe of the Norwegian Army, the leading expert on his country's historical Arctic claims, is alive to tell the inside story of how East Greenland was lost. He informed me: 'The Norwegian delegation appointed to handle negotiations with Denmark knew little of the centuries-old Norwegian rights and cared less. They were Professor Halvdan Koht (Labour and future Foreign Minister), J. L. Mowinckel (Liberal and three times Prime Minister), C. J. Hambro (Conservative and future President of the *Storting*) and Kristofer Høgset (Agrarian).... In disgust I supported the Quisling movement afterwards, and during the German Occupation I passed the time by putting all the facts into book form.* We gave away increasingly valuable rights—not only as regards fishing but also in terms of civilian and military strategy, shipping rights under the ice cap in peace and war, and mineral deposits. All that went by default.'

Greenland was capped in September when the Norwegian Naval Captain, Olaf Kullmann, addressed an anti-war congress in Holland, saying: 'War has already begun. . . . So long as the Soviet invitation to disarmament is not accepted by imperialism, it is the duty of officers to be on guard against criminal governments which do not recoil from war. Should those criminals dare to go to war, officers must go on strike.'

This was taken up by the Oslo Press and Kullmann was called before his commanding admiral on his return. The same day the Labour Party called a conference at their headquarters and launched an hysterical defence of Kullmann in print—the main agitator being Martin Tranmael, one of the leaders of the Left attacks on Quisling upon his appointment as Defence Minister and during the Menstad controversy.

Quisling was again touched on the raw. He demanded not only the prosecution of Kullmann for treason but also of those whom he considered the conspirators who were behind him, notably Tranmael. A

* *Norges svalbard- og Ishavs-Undersökelser, Meddelelser No. 56. Lysstreif Over Noregsveldets Historie* (Oslo, 1944) is the standard work on this subject.

terrific controversy raged throughout the Press upon the rights and wrongs of the case, far into 1932, and again Quisling did not get the support from his own party which he expected. Premier Kolstad died in the middle of it and his successor, Hundseid, was so lukewarm that Quisling declared openly he had been 'betrayed'. However, he attracted many admirers among the frightened bourgeoisie by his firm stand against subversion and pacifism.

The sedate British view of these hectic events was presented in the Minister's Annual Report of 1931 to the Foreign Office in these terms: 'The new Cabinet took office on the May 12. . . . They were given a friendly reception by the Press, with the exception of virulent attacks on Major Quisling, the Minister of Defence, by the organs of the Labour and Communist parties. . . . Against these accusations he successfully defended himself in the *Storting*. The truth of the matter seems to be that he was impressed, whilst in Russia with Professor Nansen for famine relief, with certain aspects of the Bolshevik régime —particularly, no doubt, like Mr. Bernard Shaw later, with the features it had in common with fascism. At all events, when he returned to Norway he seems to have hoped to lead the Labour and Communist parties into paths of his own choosing: but finding them unresponsive and having, perhaps, modified his views as a result of further contact with Bolshevik Russia, he has now developed pronounced Fascist tendencies, and has carried on propaganda against Bolshevism and in favour of the "*Samfundsvern*" and the "Nordic Movement" and other similar activities.'

The Menstad, Greenland and Kullmann controversies were still going full steam on February 2, 1932—with Quisling in the forefront —when the third sensation of his stormy Ministerial career broke.

That afternoon he was having the usual Norwegian late luncheon, at the picturesque Engebrets Tavern in Oslo, with a respected old Norwegian business friend from Russia. They parted shortly before 5 p.m., and the friend has told me that Quisling was 'absolutely normal and of course quite sober, because he never drank'. Quisling then walked over to his Department to collect papers he had been studying.

The janitor let him in and gave him the key to his room. To his surprise the door was open, as was the entrance to the conference room. Both were usually shut after office hours. Inside he saw a strange portmanteau, and as he looked closer, he was attacked by an agile little man who sprang from the shadows of the conference room.

The man had a knife which Quisling parried so that it only ripped his clothing at the ribs. Next moment he was struck on the head, and pepper was thrown in his face, blinding him. Another struggle followed before Quisling lost consciousness. Forty-five minutes later he recovered, clambered into his chair and collected his thoughts. He considered sounding the alarm but decided to go straight home. In handing the key back to the janitor he turned away his face, thus hiding his expression and any scars. He picked up a taxi and arrived at his flat at 26 Erling Skjalgssongs-gate at about 6.30 p.m.—some ninety minutes after he had finished lunch.

He climbed up to the third floor and his wife noticed that his steps were slow and heavy. His first words were: 'Don't be afraid, but I have been attacked.' He then lay down on a sofa and asked for the light to be shielded from his eyes. Mrs. Quisling thought he was so pale, injured and exhausted that she called their great friend Frederik Prytz. When Prytz arrived Quisling held on to him and nearly fainted.

Doctors and the police were then called. Dr. Francis Harbitz, a Professor of Pathology, diagnosed 'typical symptoms of serious concussion' and 'a scar on the face and scalp, one centimetre broad, but quite long, probably inflicted by an oblong, blunt instrument, for example a baton'. He added that 'the lesions could scarcely have been self-inflicted'.

Professor Peter Bull pronounced: 'Without doubt a reticent and reflective man, such as Minister Quisling, will react differently from a man of impulsive nature.' Charles Bruff, a judicial medical expert, held the same opinions.

Quisling went to work for the rest of the week (Wednesday to Friday), while the investigations were concluded and the police decided what to do. On the Friday the police issued a statement, giving facts and offering a reward of 5,000 *kroner* ($700) for information leading to an arrest.

The Press accepted the official version, with the exception of the Labour organ *Arbeiderbladet*, which commented under the headline 'Highwayman film in Defence Department' that Quisling 'drove home and lay down without saying a word'. This sneer set loose an avalanche of Press speculation and the 'affair' became a 'mystery', which is still supposed to exist. Exhaustive efforts were made at Quisling's trial to prove that the incident was a fabrication, indicating that he had either invented it to make himself out a martyr to Red extremists, or that he was subject to brain storms. But the medical evidence was never shaken and remains conclusive.

Nordahl Grieg, the young poet,* after consultation with the well-known criminal psychiatrist, Dr. Johan Scharffenberg, maintained in 1936 that malaria could cause physical changes and that some such affliction had upset Quisling's balance of mind. It is true that Quisling had malaria in the Caucasus in 1923, but in the intervening seven years he had exhibited no abnormality, other than outstanding intellect and energy. Later he had no symptoms of chronic malaria and a whole panel of doctors pronounced him to be of sound mind, after painful and exhaustive probing in the middle of his trial. In the face of all the expert evidence, it is now argued that no doctors could diagnose a passing disturbance of the mind, for it has become a Norwegian act of faith to believe the worst of Quisling.

Paal Berg,† the Liberal politician from Hammerfest, has another theory. He told me: 'Quisling was having an affair with the good-looking wife of the War Office caretaker, who surprised him and threw pepper in his face. Afterwards, Quisling and his friend Captain A. F. Munthe cooked up the story of a Communist attack.' If that was so, why did the caretaker not come forward and so bring about Quisling's disgrace and downfall? Why did the police not discover this during their investigations? And what about Quisling's scars and the medical evidence? Besides, nobody who knew Quisling at all well has ever suggested that he was a womaniser. On the contrary, he was shy, diffident and distant.

A third and abstruse supposition has been produced by Sverre Hartmann, who has written a study of Quisling. He says in *Fører uten Folk* that the 'plausible explanation', the 'hypothesis' and the 'reasonable ground' behind the 'Pepper Affair' are to be found in the arrival of the German Naval Officer and newspaperman, Captain Horst Pflugk-

* Chairman of The Friends of the Soviet Union.
† Minister for Social Affairs in 1919-20, and Minister of Justice and Social Affairs in 1924-26, also a founder and chairman of the State Wine Monopoly in 1922-26. He became Chief Justice in 1929 and in 1944 co-ordinated the 'Home Front'.

Harttung, in Oslo twelve days previously. *Arbeiderbladet* had raised an outcry against his presence, alleging that he was a fascist responsible for the murder of the Communist luminaries, Karl Liebknecht and Rosa Luxemburg, in Berlin in 1919. The Ministry of Justice was accordingly urged to expel him before he could establish communication with Norwegian fascists. On January 29 a protest meeting was held at Labour headquarters, where a poem on Liebknecht was read. Next day the paper urged the Passport Police to investigate whether Minister Quisling had a finger in the pie. He and the German were said to have met in private and to have done a deal: information for cash.

Circumstantial evidence, before and after the 'Pepper Affair', has lent some credence to Labour accusations. In 1927 Pflugk-Harttung was suspected by the Swedish authorities of having bought arms on behalf of a Stockholm banker in order to fight Communists, and the Social Democrat Press raised the alarm. Nevertheless the German did not claim asylum in Oslo until three years later. Again, in 1938, just after Munich, Pflugk-Harttung was uncovered by the Danish Police as a shipping spy in Copenhagen, where he was correspondent of *Berliner Börsen-zeitung*.

Asbjørn Lindboe, Minister of Justice, affirmed that he and his Department knew of no connection between the German and Quisling. *Aftenposten*, the most responsible Norwegian daily, said that 'the Captain had nothing to do with politics', and no meeting between the two men has ever been proved.

Sverre Hartmann, however, assumes that a meeting did take place, and from this deduces that 'the action in the Defence Department may have been spontaneous, but also inspired to a certain extent from outside quarters, namely Friedrich Wollweber'. Wollweber was a sworn enemy of Pflugk-Harttung. 'In that case,' says Hartmann, 'one has a fully acceptable explanation why Quisling did not want at any price to set in motion a full enquiry after the attack. If he, for his part, did not know who attacked him, he must—with these previous negotiations with the German Naval Officer in mind—have reasoned that this was the reason for the action.'

Now I do not put anything past Ernst Friedrich Wollweber, who became East German Security Chief in 1953, when I had known him for fourteen years. When he organised sabotage in Sweden in

1940, he was known among his fellow-workers as 'Little Lenin' and 'The Walking Pancake', as he is almost a dwarf. Finns called him 'the animal nearest approaching a human being'. He is a real tough, who joined the Communists in 1918 and organised a mutiny at Kiel when he was a stoker on the cruiser *Heligoland*. During the Second World War he was chief of Russia's shipping sabotage and therefore working in the same field as Pflugk-Harttung. Afterwards he turned his skill against NATO shipping. He would have been just the man to perform or arrange a burglary of Quisling's documents which incriminated the Communist movement before they could be exposed to Pflugk-Harttung and fascist enemies.

But there is no proof that Wollweber was involved, and there is no need to invoke his sinister name to reach the obvious conclusion that Quisling was attacked in his office by Communists or their sympathisers in the Labour movement.

Norway was in an uproar, with Quisling and the Left at daggers drawn. It was known that Quisling, who had remained remarkably calm and reticent in the face of outrageous attack, was preparing a major, documented counter-attack for the occasion two months ahead when his conduct during Menstad would come under review in the *Storting*. It was also known that he had collected a dossier on the Norwegian socialist leaders' subversive activities during his residence in Russia—material which could now be supplemented by the internal security files of the Defence Ministry—and the most likely explanation of the Pepper Affair is that it was organised by left-wing opponents.

The immediate reaction of the socialist Press to news of the attack on Quisling showed how anxious the Opposition had become. They saw public opinion coalescing around him, and in his person a major obstacle on their road to power.

The big debate on the Defence Minister's conduct during the Menstad insurrection was tantamount to a vote of confidence. For once the atmosphere in the *Storting* was electric. The country sensed that its future was at stake. The Labour Party knew that its reputation and future were in the balance. The question was whether the bourgeois parties would stand by their man, Major Quisling, and that in turn depended upon his own parliamentary performance. This sorely tried newcomer also realised that he had reached a crisis. Could he carry his adopted party and the rest of the non-socialists with him, or was he to be driven out of the parliamentary fold into the untried arms of his private non-parliamentary movement?

The Labour leader, Johan Nygaardsvold, got off to a poor start in opening the debate. This former farm-hand, saw-mill and brick-factory worker from near Trondheim had received no formal education and emigrated to America, where he worked for six years as a railroad navvy. Returning to Norway in 1907, aged twenty-eight, he educated himself and entered Parliament in 1916. Within two years he was President of the *Storting*, and he became Minister of Agriculture in the eighteen-day-long Labour Government of 1928.

He said that the assault on Quisling was 'either a private brawl or else complete fiction' and doubted if the 5,000 *kroner* reward for information would ever have to be paid. On the second day Jon Sundby, the Finance Minister, found it 'rather shabby to attack a man who has been nearly smashed to pieces' in those terms, whatever one's party.

The third day, April 7, belonged to Quisling, and the House was on tenterhooks. For a year he had held his peace and, from what members knew of his oratory, he was not eloquent. Nor was he an expert parliamentarian. He had little finesse or talent for compromise, and stuck to his guns. How would he react now that he had to answer for a year of repeated crisis and vile accusations?

From the moment he ascended to make his speech from the throne of the House, there was no doubt. He banged the table before he uttered a word, and it was clear that he had decided that attack was the best means of defence. As he got into his stride, his pent-up fury and frustration took charge of him. He pointed the finger of scorn and accusation at the Labour seats and his eyes blazed. For the first time the *Storting* realised that it had a demagogue in its midst, and probably Quisling surprised himself, too. The Opposition screamed and shouted with rage and his supporters twiddled their thumbs in embarrassment. Histrionics were strange to the *Storting*. But gradually Quisling took charge and he obtained a fair hearing.

'Herr Nygaardsvold should remember there is a nemesis for those who act unlawfully, even if he believes it is against injustice,' he began. 'Herr Nygaardsvold fears the coming election. . . . From my first entry into our political life I have been made systematically and malignantly the object of attack by the revolutionaries in our country and also to some extent by their foreign associates.'

After reviewing his own career at home and abroad and rebutting the many Labour accusations against him, he continued: 'I have the greatest sympathy with trying to bring about good conditions for all citizens. . . . But, as I have written in my book, Communism as practised is *not* socialism. It is anti-social.'

Quisling then counter-attacked the Socialists on the riots: 'Herr Nygaardsvold spoke, in connection with the Menstad affair, of brain concussion. But there are two forms of concussion—one which comes from outer violence, and one which is due to the victims knocking their heads together so that right cannot be distinguished from wrong, white from black. Herr Nygaardsvold had defended events in Menstad, branding us lackeys in the service of foreign capital. But what was the Menstad affair in fact? During the disturbances in Menstad it became known that it was not some local affair but was to spread into an insurrection throughout the country. Documents have fallen into our hands from abroad which show that the movement should be extended to Oslo and Bergen. Who were those that stood behind this thing, who were instrumental in it? Yes, it was two of those who have borne witness against me, and others who style themselves honest and deserving members of society. I permit myself to regard them as bought and paid agents, as foes and enemies of our country and our people.'

Quisling went on to give details of how the Norwegian agents of international Communism had received 500,000 *kroner* ($70,000) from 'a foreign power' in 1928-29 and even more substantial sums in the current year, and how this had been going on for years previously; how 4,000 men were enlisted in Norway for a revolution, 'double as many as carried through the Russian Revolution'; and how Communist cells were established in the Armed Forces, factories and strategic outposts in the far North.

He did not openly accuse Russia, because his Ministerial position forbade that. Nor did he produce documents because, he said, he did not want to imitate the Labour Party by indulging in personalities.

Towards the end Quisling declared: 'The instruments for the defence of society must be under society's control . . . the fighting organisations of labour and capital must be replaced by unified organisations, first by united leadership of industry . . . party conflicts and industrial conflicts must be brought to an end.'

So great was his effect that for once the *Storting* nerved itself to demand documents, and it appointed a Committee to examine them.

This Committee consisted of eight members, representing all parties, and it reported on June 23. Althogether 190 documents revealing revolutionary organisation in Norway were produced by Quisling and scrutinised.

Documents 17, 61 and others revealed that Sverre Støstad, a future President of the *Storting,* had received 8,000 *kroner* ($1,120) a year from the Comintern as a member of the Scandinavian Communist Federation.

Document 18 and others revealed that the Federation's programme included the formation of cells among soldiers and sailors and the arming of workmen in order to seize control on the outbreak of revolution, also the storage of arms for this purpose.

Document 65 showed that $1\frac{1}{2}$ million *kroner* ($210,000) had been transferred from the Comintern as recently as March 8, 1932, to its cell in the Army for propaganda purposes.

Document 77 was a letter from the Commander at Vardøhus fortifications in the far North, dated June 20, 1921, regarding a Communist code, at the foot of which was written: 'Received for Grepp 5,800 *kroner*, Trygve Lie.'

Document 149 featured Oscar Torp, a future Minister of Supply, as leader of labour forces amounting to 5,000 men in Oslo and 3,000 elsewhere in the country, whose object was to take over the police and to occupy telegraph, radio, post and railway stations.

Document 150 revealed that in Trondheim the Labour Party had 2,000 armed and trained men, plus other squads detailed to arrest local leaders. In Bergen there were 1,600 stormtroopers.

Details of arms-smuggling occupied many pages.

Document 121 exposed the relationship of the Norwegian Labour Party and Comintern: 'The Party must execute orders from Moscow concerning Norwegian and Foreign Affairs. . . . In the event of Revolution a Soviet Republic is to be established in North Norway, independent of the Norwegian State. . . . The Soviet State pledges itself to support the Norwegian Revolution economically, politically and militarily.'

On the basis of such voluminous and damning evidence the *Storting* Committee found:

1. that the majority agreed that Herr Quisling had proven reasons for his declarations before the *Storting* on April 7;

2. that the Norwegian Communist Party is a direct sub-division of the Communist International Confederation (Comintern) and is managed and financed from Russia;

3. that the Norwegian Labour Party is still a revolutionary party which has not dropped all connections with Moscow.

Only the two Labour members dissented, saying: 'Minister Quisling, by his irresponsible statements and unsupported imputations, committed a gross error of judgement in his position as a member of the Government'; and further that 'the *Storting* should request the Government to insure that in future the Intelligence Service of the General Staff should cease to serve as a centre for espionage in domestic politics.'

When it came to a vote the *Storting* upheld Quisling, the Government and the Committee's Report by an overwhelming majority of 108 to 42. The bourgeois parties for once united to a man and the Socialists were isolated. This was a great parliamentary victory for Quisling—a complete vindication of his course of action—and a new peak in his status as a national figure.

In retrospect one sees that Quisling had given Norway the one chance of holding her own in the gathering storm, but it was squandered. This was the decisive moment in Norwegian history between 1905 and 1940.

If the Right had followed the logic of its vote for Quisling and had continued to stand together, the conspirators and pacifists of the Left could have been brought to book or contained. More than a feeble semblance of Defence could have been introduced. The country could have been rallied. Mentally and physically Norway could have been prepared to face its responsibilities as a sovereign state. Any invasion would then have been fraught with difficulty and Norway would have stood a chance of survival.

But logic and reason, cohesion and perseverance, are not Norwegian specialities. They like their parish pump and to do things the hard way. So they were doomed. The party politicians left themselves no choice but to cut and run in 1940. So the Norwegian people were left

to their fate. This was the treason of the Right, as well as the Left—
of the blind, opinionated and selfish individuals and groups whom
Quisling castigated.

No action was taken on the Committee's damning report. It was
June and the *Storting* went into recess. The nation once more took to
the wilds for four months. But Quisling had started something. For
many Norwegians he had become a symbol and a rallying-point—the
strong man who could stop dissension and stem the Socialist-Com-
munist wave.

Among his admirers was Johan Throne Holst, director of the great
Freia chocolate factory and president of the Norwegian Industrial
Association. He had known Prytz and Dr. Aall for two years and was
one of the backers of another patriotic circle known as *Vort Land*
(Our Country), which sprang up in the twenties about the same time
as the Fatherland League. It was a loosely knit group, mainly composed of businessmen, who met irregularly, and did not mix in party
politics. Some members belonged to the Agrarians and contributed to
the Party's funds, but *Vort Land* was essentially non-political, bourgeois
and anti-socialist—thinking roughly along the same lines as Quisling
and Nansen before him.

On October 25, 1932, Throne Holst invited Quisling to a private
meeting at home, attended by Prytz, Aall, A. F. Munthe and a young
lawyer named J. Bernard Hjorth. Holst's expression of confidence in
Quisling and the latter's reply were, according to the minutes, 'the only
bright spot' in the meeting. Aall and Hjorth outlined a scheme for a two-
chamber parliament. A boycott of the *Storting* was suggested, also the
setting up of a dictatorship—possibly under the king's leadership. The
kroner was to be halved in value and large public works begun. The
complete reorganisation of defence was also mentioned. All this
amounted to no more than an airing of minds, a debate.

Next day a general meeting of *Vort Land* was held at the home of
another businessman. Among those present, besides those from the
previous evening, were General Jens Bratlie (Conservative Prime
Minister in 1912-13), Stortingsman Østby Deglum (Chairman of the
Agrarian Party), Dean H. J. Aandstad (Chairman of The Free Worker
organisation), David Seierstad (Chairman of the Parishioners' Emergency Aid organisation), and Thorvald Aadahl (editor of *The Nation*).

Chiefs of organisations similar to *Vort Land* and Nordic Folk-awakening were also present, namely Major Hvoslef (Community Guard), Captain Fougner (Community Aid) and Joakim Lemkuhl (Fatherland League).

Thus Quisling found himself amidst a representative group of non-socialists, with active political minds, and blessed by big business.

The theme was 'the government which would be best for the country'. It was pointed out that parliamentarianism was not built into the 1814 Constitution. Hjort stressed the advantages of the Swiss cantonal system and advocated a two-chamber parliament in order to decrease the elected Storting's influence. Østby Deglum extolled the Agrarian Party and Quisling's performance, about which Bratlie agreed. Dean Aandstad also praised Quisling. Christopher Borchgrevnik, a lawyer, expressed the utmost alarm over the state of the country and apparently thought that it was too late even for Quisling to save the situation. Throne Holst apparently tried to back out.

Quisling himself was non-committal. The meeting evidently fancied his chances, but it decided on no course of action. It was just talk.

By mid-November the Socialists had recovered their nerve, in default of prosecution, and resumed their all-out attack on Quisling. *Arbeiderbladet* said on the 16th: 'Quisling must go . . . he is a dangerous man for the country and the Farmers' Party.' On the 17th it attacked 'Quisling's friends', saying that he 'consults with people outside the Government and seldom with his Ministerial colleagues. His springboard lies outside the parliamentary system.'

On the 18th he was visited by the old Nazi, Max Pferdekämper, in the Defence Ministry, who reported to Himmler, recommending that Hitler or General Ritter von Epp should get in touch with Quisling. One of Quisling's visiting cards was enclosed 'for further use', which seems an odd way of presenting oneself to the Führer of Germany. The natural interpretation of this second meeting is that the two acquaintances exchanged cards; that Quisling was receiving Pferdekämper as an act of politeness and keeping an eye on German developments; and that the visitor was instructed by Himmler, who was always interested in the 'Nordic cult', to see where Quisling now stood. Hence Pferdekämper's 'busy' dispatch. Nazi officials were always exaggerating their own importance and success in order to improve their careers or feather their nests. There is still no evidence that Quisling was in league with the Nazis, although his exasperation with Norwegian politics must by this time have evoked comparison with the futility of Kerenski, or that of the Weimar Republic.

By November 26, the immunity of the revolutionary Socialists, the unabated ferocity of their personal attacks and the impotence of his colleagues in the Agrarian Cabinet decided Quisling to bring down the Government. He wrote to Hundseid saying, 'I have come to the conclusion that the Prime Minister should resign', and attached a sixteen-page memorandum explaining why. This he circulated far and wide, outside the Party, with the obvious intention of finishing his parliamentary career and attracting followers for his own extra-parliamentary movement among the influential people who shared his disillusionment.

By the time of the Finance Debate on February 24, 1933, the Farmers' Government was doomed. Quisling used the opportunity for a memorable swan-song, and electioneering. He was glad that the Government was going. That clarified the situation and brought national unification nearer. 'What we need today', he said, 'is that once and for all we push aside party politics and adopt positive, national policies in order to build and mend our society for the good and happiness of all. . . . From now on we are going out into every nook and cranny of the land, agitating and arousing the people. We shall be coming back before very long. Though I may not return in person, my ideas will. . . .

'I will end by saying that I am no party man. I have never engaged in narrow party politics. I stand by my country. I maintain that I have both feet on Norwegian soil. There are many who share my outlook. I say again—it is a battle for an outlook on life, and victory is assured —victory will be ours sooner or later. . . .'

Thus Quisling prepared his next step. His future lay outside parliament and he never spoke there again. He appealed to what he considered the higher instincts of the Norwegian people and their Nordic traditions, over the heads of the political hucksters.

The Agrarian Government finally fell on March 3, but Quisling's bid for the leadership foundered on the 9th when Hundseid was re-elected chairman. Quisling needed a going political concern as a basis for his own movement and he continued to intrigue for the

Farmers' support for two months. On May 4, *Arbeiderbladet* decided to try and short-circuit any such possibility by a frontal attack. For the first time it used the epithet 'Nazi'. Quisling was reported to be trying to concert the Farmers' Party into a new 'National Party', with the help of Thorvald Aadahl, editor of the Party organ, *The Nation*, and to dislodge Hundseid in favour of himself. *Tidens Tegn*, which had launched Quisling into politics, was named as the new party's future organ, and Throne Holst was said to be its backer.

The timing and tactics were clever and fortunate. Quisling's overtures to the Farmers were already doomed. So he could be represented as a reject from his own party and his remaining friends might be put off by the Nazi jibe. Throne Holst was known to be lukewarm and might be embarrassed, not only personally but in his business relationships. Also, a conflict of interests between the Opposition organs, *Tidens Tegn* and *The Nation*, was ventilated. The word 'Nazi' was to assume a new notoriety the following month, when Hitler was to have his first meeting with Mussolini on June 14 and on the 30th the 'Night of the Long Knives' was to cripple the Left wing of National Socialism.

Meanwhile another loosely knit organisation was bidding for Quisling's patronage. This was the National Club, set up by businessman Walter Fürst, who arranged secret lectures on such subjects as Fascism and National Socialism at the Royal Norwegian Automobile Club during 1932-33. Fürst's object was to find an alternative to Marxism. Quisling addressed the club once. Early in 1932, Fürst had approached Quisling several times in the Defence Ministry, urging him to revive the Fatherland League, but had received no encouragement.

A member of the National Club was a newspaperman named Adolf Egeberg, Jr. He ran a sheet entitled *The Front*, which was read and supported by a group of politically-minded young men with sympathies with National Socialism, Fascists in Sweden and the Lapua Movement in Finland. He also shared Quisling's belief that the traditional parties were doomed and accordingly went to see him with the May 1 issue of his journal.

Quisling was interested and just at that moment an advertising office fell vacant at Prinsensgate 7 in the heart of Oslo. Fürst offered it to Quisling, who accepted.

That seems to be the event which precipitated Quisling into battle.

Now he had an operational base, the goodwill of a variety of sympathetic groups throughout the country, and his symbolic status. All he needed was an organisation to centralise goodwill and to promote his ideas.

The following week Fürst of the National Club and Prytz of Nordic Folk-awakening busied themselves collecting a committee for the inauguration of a new party. Quisling merely contacted Aadahl, editor of *The Nation*, to tell him of the plans afoot and to persuade him to back the new party in the forthcoming General Election.

Aadahl was the more realistic and pointed out that there could be no thought of fighting the election because there was no time to get the party going or to launch a programme. Quisling would not listen to reason, and when the preliminary committee meeting convened on May 8 he absented himself. The only result of his conference with Aadahl was their agreement that 'Nordic Folk-awakening' was an impossible title for a political party and that it should be renamed *Nasjonal Samling* (National Unification), the slogan which had been bandied about in Norway since the days of Michelsen and Nansen ten years earlier.

The meeting convened at the Palm Court of the luxurious Grand Hotel, which lies between the Italian-style *Storting* and the Palladian Royal Palace on the central Karl Johan boulevard of Oslo, was a fiasco without Quisling. Prytz promised, however, that Quisling would appear the next day, and persuaded him to do so.

Quisling sat uncomfortably in his chair and seemed unwilling to speak, and when eventually he broke his silence it was merely to reiterate his previous demands for a spiritual and religious national movement which would take account of modern science and technology. He referred specifically to catastrophic agricultural problems and to unemployment, but declined to go into details of his proposed solutions.

Prytz struck the most practical note, saying that the objective was a party fund of 500,000 *kroner* ($70,000), of which 37,000 was in the kitty. He insisted that nobody in particular stood behind the movement and that it must depend on the contributions of 'the colossal number of people who support Quisling's politics'.

Pressed for a clarification of his programme, Quisling said he had worked out different plans. One was for the merging of the two internal divisions of the *Storting* into one, or the alternation of one division into an Upper and the other into a Lower House. Fürst suggested it would be an advantage to decide on one of those alternatives immediately for the purposes of electioneering, but Quisling replied: 'No, not now.'

Further meetings were held on May 9 and 11, but no specific programme had been drawn up by the time of the inaugural General Meeting on May 16 at the Grand Hotel. Quisling intended to launch *Nasjonal Samling* with a speech at Eidsvoll, the birthplace of the 1814 Constitution, next day. But this could not be arranged. Instead he had to be content with registering *Nasjonal Samling* as a political party on May 17, of course the National Day, thus invoking patriotism in his characteristic style. Major Hvoslef of the Community Guard was General Secretary.

Considering all the anxiety, thought and discussion which had preceded the formation of some such party in Norway for a generation, it was a shaky and haphazard start—typically Norwegian.

12

Defeat

WHETHER Quisling was wise to fight his first General Election at less than six months' notice, with no party machine behind him and an undigested programme, is debatable.

Aadahl calculated that the change of party name would leave the way open for sympathetic Agrarians to co-operate. He continued to provide Quisling with a newspaper platform and so his initial opposition to participation in the election seems to have been modified.

Walter Fürst of the National Club, who had provided Quisling with an office and spoken up for a precise electioneering programme at the initial NS meetings, was also in favour of fighting the election. So was Frederik Prytz, who pointed out that Nordic Folk-awakening had been organised in three weeks and believed that they had a 'colossal' following in the country.

Major Hvoslef of the Community Guard, with its 'emergency police force' at potential trouble spots throughout the country, had also come over to the Quisling movement, and so there was a ready-made corps of local political agents available.

Quisling had therefore the elements of an organisation, a base from which to work, a newspaper and an enthusiastic following.

Besides, there was the loose allegiance of like-minded associations such as the Fatherland League and *Vort Land* which might be expected to lend a helping hand. There were the politically conscious young men of *The Front*, too. From that sort of background several personalities also emerged to support Quisling activity, for example Odd Nansen, a craggy young architect who resembled his father physically, Harald Franklin Knudsen of the great Telemark political family, and Bernard Hjorth, the handsome and rising young lawyer.

The time seemed ripe for a new force in Norwegian politics. Quisling's bitterest enemy, C. J. Hambro, the President of the *Storting* and Norwegian representative at the League of Nations since 1926, admits in *I Saw it Happen in Norway*: 'There was a feeling that political institutions and procedures had not been readjusted to meet modern conditions: sections of the Press were constantly trying to ridicule the *Storting* and the whole political system was not efficient enough. And the complex party situation called for a thorough discussion of the very principles of our parliamentary system.' He goes on to mention 'evidence of a growing realisation of the waste of energy in party strife . . . and that national politics means co-operation and co-ordination'.

Quisling was the personification of that anxiety and outlook, as he had proclaimed in his book, newspaper articles and lectures and in Parliament for three years, with no effect. He was a symbol, the attraction of putting which to the test, while his views were fresh in the public eye, was obvious. Continued vilification by the Left provided evidence that the Socialists took his challenge seriously and served as excellent propaganda for him among his potential supporters.

The electoral situation could also be interpreted in his favour. As Hambro says: 'Active political interest had never been more manifest in Norway.' Between 1930 and 1936 polling in General Elections was 76·36 to 84·02 per cent. There were six parties competing, besides half a dozen minor groups, and Quisling could legitimately expect to pick up a few seats among the 150 constituencies contested in eighteen provinces and eleven groups of towns under a system of Proportional Representation. Labour had lost twelve seats and the Conservatives had gained thirteen in the 1930 election, and so Quisling could anticipate a further swing in that direction. The abortive Labour Government's extremism in 1928 had cost the Party dear, and its subsequent behaviour had introduced no moderation.

126

Such were the auguries. But were they good enough?

As it turned out the answer was No. In retrospect, the explanations are not far to seek.

Quisling's diagnosis of the political malaise and impending disaster was too logical and downright, too daring and too 'pat', for the electorate to draw the necessary conclusions for abandoning their ingrained party allegiances and turning out to vote for him in large numbers. They sensed there was a catch in what he said.

His programme, such as it was, seemed too vague. Was NS a real 'party' or some sort of 'movement'?

The main points of his policy were laid down in his Budget speech of February 24, 1933, and were incorporated in the NS electoral manifesto. Besides an 'end of political turmoil and different parties' and 'a national government with full powers to take all necessary measures for economic and political revival', he urged (*a*) a rational and purposeful Budget, (*b*) reorganisation of financial and municipal management, (*c*) a new industrial life of internal peace but with opportunities for competition, (*d*) crash programmes to cope with the farmers' and fishermen's crisis, and (*e*) work for the workless. All this was very laudable, but it was far too imprecise to carry conviction or even to appeal to the suffering groups in the community whom he addressed specifically. The supposition is that he had not thought out the details—any more than he could enlighten Walter Fürst on a proposed reform of Parliament—and that anyway he deemed it unwise to get involved at this stage in argument with sectional interests. He virtually asked for a blank cheque, and Norwegians were too cagey for that.

The general tone of his programme was also too easily represented by his opponents as 'Fascist' and 'Nazi'. He advocated a 'corporative national state'; the leadership principle; the adoption of 'true socialism', which could have meant National Socialism; good and sound conditions of life for every Norwegian; a ban on strikes and lockouts; and the uprooting of Marxism. A small council was to advise the leader (*fører*).

What he really wanted at this stage was a national government of experts under his own guidance, which was not the same as a dictatorship. Events in Russia, Italy and Germany all pointed to the need for firmer direction of national affairs, just as bickering in the West spotlighted the infirmities of liberal democracy. He had no liaison with

127

Mussolini or Hitler at this time and his thesis was derived from traditional Norwegian modes of thought. But still he frightened the Liberal Centre, where he might have gathered supporters if he had clarified his programme and been a better tactician. Similarly, he scared the middle-of-the-road Agrarians, and his head-on attack on Premier Hundseid completed a breach which left him with little or no support within the *Storting*. So he found himself out on his own.

The hostility of the Left was axiomatic, but he might have offered a more appealing bait to the uncommitted fringe of Socialism than vague promises of work and better conditions. His programme contained no real attraction for the masses, which seems surprising in view of his own experience of Bolshevik methods. He also underestimated the efficiency of the Moscow-trained Communists and ex-Communists in the Socialist leadership. Not only did they thump the Nazi smear for all it was worth, thus stoking the fears of the Centre, but they let loose their underground stormtroopers at all Quisling's public meetings. With his inside knowledge of the Red Guards and his personal experience of violence in the Pepper Affair, one might have thought he would appoint at least a bodyguard, if not a corps of stewards; but he was fearless and felt inspired by some semi-divine blessing to save his country. He disdained precautionary measures. Consequently, he was often silenced, and the general rowdiness created by the Socialists at his meetings created a wary attitude among the populace.

As for the Right, his threat to knock socialist and capitalist heads together, in order to produce 'economic and political revival' by means of some semi-parliamentary corporative state, threatened the existing economic system, including investments, and warned off businessmen as well as reactionaries who might have supported him or thought they could use him in the same way as their counterparts in Germany adopted Hitler.

In short, Quisling left himself with an insufficiently broad base on which to operate, without plunging either to the extreme of Bolshevism or Nazism. He virtually left himself where he started, namely with an amorphous following of intellectuals, do-gooders and windbags. Politically, this was hopeless.

Personally, he was too nice for the job of national salvation which he had taken on, and he was not the stuff of which successful agitators and dictators are usually made. For a start, he was transparently honest to the point of naïvety. Catchpenny tactics never entered his calculations. He appealed strictly to logic, reason and the lessons of history, to Nordic values and spiritual instincts. By the thirties Norwegians wanted homelier politics, social benefits on the Left and profits on the Right. They were not interested in the tide of history and 'isms'. Norwegians in general did not understand what he was talking about. Many regarded him as a very clever and experienced man, possibly great, but his ideas seemed airy-fairy compared with the everyday realities of life.

Quisling had been alone too long—as a studious youth, as an independent humanitarian in Russia and as an isolated politician in the *Storting*—to get the feel of his countrymen and to come down to earth. His appreciation of the situation was horribly correct, but he lacked the necessary instinct for compromise and concerted action to put it across. What was required in Norway in the 1930s was a Stanley Baldwin—somebody to dampen political antagonism and to rebuild constructive parliamentary life. The *détente* that Baldwin provided enabled the British instinct for compromise to operate, and prepared the country to face the storm when it broke. No such man existed in Norway, with the result that the politicians were all sent packing and parliamentary life collapsed. The Norwegians were not mature. They would neither put their own house in order, nor listen to Quisling.

He estimated that he had 80,000 adult supporters in 1933, excluding thousands of immature youths. This may well have been no exaggeration, but it was another matter to bring them to the polls to vote for him. He failed. The party machines and voting habits were far too strong for him. Labour got 500,526 votes, the Conservatives 272,690, the Liberals 220,001, the Farmers 173,534 and *Nasjonal Samling* 27,847. Quisling's only consolation was that the Communists polled even less —22,000. In Oslo, his stronghold, it took 21,000 votes to win a seat and Quisling polled 5,441. In Opland Province, another of his strongholds, it took 9,000 votes for victory and he got 2,841.

Quisling and his loyal supporters were not dismayed. They reasoned that there were alibis. Their meetings had been smashed, notably at Arendal, Gjøvik, Trondheim and Bergen. They had had insufficient time to prepare for the polls. Now there were three years until the next General Election to profit from experience and to build up their support.

Accordingly, some young stalwarts, who had rallied to protect Quisling's person during the campaign, formed themselves into a *hird*, reminiscent of the old Norse King's retainers, in order to keep the 'Red Guards' at bay. Hjorth, Nansen and Knudsen were among the originators of this unofficial, defensive bodyguard, who never numbered more than 500 up to 1940 and were negligible compared with thousands of armed and disciplined stormtroopers at the disposal of the Communist and Labour Parties in the underground.

It was decided to fight the next election as a party, hoping to win enough seats in the *Storting* to attract supporters from other groups so as to earn a place in some future bourgeois coalition, or at any rate to establish a regular political platform. Quisling was not disgraced. The incoming Liberal Premier, J. W. Mowinckel of Bergen, had not got a working majority; he had voted for Quisling during the Menstad debate and had given him the following testimonial on the dissolution of Parliament: 'I believe that Quisling is an idealist. I know that he is an idealist, but I am not certain that it is advantageous for a Norwegian government to be so idealistic in these times. One and all who know what Quisling has done for humanity during his long residence in Russia cannot do otherwise than give him credit for that.' The door to the *Storting* was not for ever barred.

Quisling was scornful. He declared: 'Russia's Mowinckel, Kerenski, had his February, but he also had his October.' Sure enough, Mowinckel was ousted from office in March 1935, for the third and last time,* but not before he had banned the Community Guard and political uniforms, thus playing into the hands of the Socialist underground.

The Labour Party took control, which it has kept ever since.

Nygaardsvold, the new Premier, had said in 1932: 'In the first place we are against militarism in principle. As a party we have always stood for complete demilitarisation. . . . The main reason for military preparedness, in sum, is primarily the interest of the capitalists, that is, the making of equipment for the military and the usual speculation in that connection. . . . I will close with the thought—if we could get the *Storting* to enact a law to the effect that officers should wear striped uniforms, like those of the incarcerated criminals of yore, I am sure that militarism would soon be abolished in this country. . . . It is in the

* Disgusted with Norwegian politics, he spent his later years in America.

interests of the officers and the capitalists that we keep up this so-called defence system—as a delusion of the people in order to entice the workers and the peasants off and on to go out and kill each other. It is also for this reason that we are against, and very definitely so, the voluntary organisations which are at present being organised in this country.'

Two years earlier Trygve Lie had told the International Labour Congress: 'The working class will never rely on a random majority in its struggle. It will take possession of power by force the moment it considers itself strong enough, irrespective of a majority.'

A pamphlet, to which Lie contributed later, said: 'The working class will march forward, always forward, either through the Law or giving the Law a wide berth.'

In 1928 he had also declared: 'The workers' sports movement must train strong cadres from which it can obtain its storm columns for the revolutionary combat which is imminent. They must be imbued with implacable hatred for the bourgeois class and the bourgeois sports movement.'

As late as 1935, Gerhardsen brought out a Labour Party textbook saying: 'The Norwegian Labour Party considers one of its most important tasks to be opposition to the Defence system and to unmask its class character. By influencing youth on and off duty, the Defence system must be rendered unfit as an instrument of the ruling class in its struggle against the workers' advancement and for settling international disputes.'

The lithographer, Alfred Madsen, who became the Labour Party's parliamentary leader in 1928-31 and Minister of Social Affairs in the abortive Government of 1928, had actually been caught bringing Russian gold over the border.

These were no kid-glove Socialists, believing in 'the inevitability of gradualness', like Ramsay Macdonald, or vulgarians, like J. H. Thomas. They were deadly earnest and ruthless men schooled in the Bolshevik manner for many years. Quisling was a tyro by comparison.

He was their public enemy number one and they went for him unmercifully; but he battled on under the slogan which he was to use as his main theme right up to 1940: 'Norway neutral—Norway prepared!' During the next five years he addressed more than 500 meetings. The most savage attack was made on him in 1936 at what went down to history as the 'Gjøvik Massacre', when many were injured on both sides, the 'red' and the 'blue', as the opposing factions became known. Quisling's boldest effort was during the General Election campaign of 1936, when he challenged Labour outside their headquarters in Youngstorvet, the open place in downtown Oslo where the workers' traditional May Day rally assembled. The Labour bosses declared they would never allow Quisling to use 'their' stamping-ground, but 30,000 people in fact heard him there—the largest electioneering crowd ever collected in Norwegian annals.

His warnings of the approaching Armageddon went as unheeded as Churchill's. Each man was a 'one man opposition' in his own country. Labour in Norway was as unrepentant and guileless as Labour in England, only more extreme. It stuck to its manifesto calling on workers to 'declare a general strike, should Norway be drawn into war, and to oppose war by every means' and favouring 'the conversion of military installations and factories to civil production'.

Niggling increases in armaments were eventually voted on the eve of the Second World War, but Norway remained with virtually little more than a police force until 1940. The soporific was the League of Nations. Meanwhile such luxuries as unemployment insurance, old age pensions and holidays with full pay were introduced at the expense of elementary security. No proper balance between social justice and national survival was ever struck or even attempted. Labour simply used its five years of pre-war office to buy votes, regardless of the consequences. This was national suicide, but nobody except Quisling seemed to care.

Quisling was crying in the wilderness and out-manœuvred. Inevitably he went down to another crashing defeat in the 1936 General Election. The results were even more unfavourable than before: Labour 618,616 votes; Conservatives 329,560; Liberals 239,191; Farmers 168,038; and Nasjonal Samling 26,577. Nowhere did NS win a quarter of the votes necessary for a seat.

This time there was no excuse, and naturally there were recriminations within the movement. Odd Nansen soon quit. 'Quisling fell under the influence of undemocratic extremists . . . and frightened people off,' he told me.

Bernard Hjorth did not leave until February 1937, but for different reasons. He told me: 'Quisling was a sort of prophet, with an air of

132

mystery about him. But you can't lead by theory. There is no law-enforcement behind a political party. If people won't work for you, the machine stops. He was not a good speaker and he was very suspicious about people in his own party. For instance he suspected that I wanted to take the leadership from him. The last straw was when some nice young men—now prominent citizens—argued with him about what they should do. He banished them on the spot, instead of going through procedure, and when I protested that one shouldn't act like that, he replied, "I am the leader".

'After the 1936 Election, he would not discuss what went wrong and get our best brains together to start afresh—professors, engineers, doctors and good people in the movement. He simply cut off the head of the party. He was too wrapped up in his own philosophy and was not really of this world. He was gifted, learned and well-read and should have been a professor of mathematics.'

Despite some desertions, several thousand supporters swore a formal oath of loyalty to Quisling at the NS national rally in Oslo during the summer of 1936 and promised to give their lives in continuing the struggle under his leadership unto victory.

Dr. Halvdan Koht, the historian who was the Labour Foreign Minister from 1935 to 1940, in his Norway Neutral and Invaded, has described Quisling's followers variously as 'a hodge-podge of spiritually crippled individuals' and 'morally, if not intellectually, the scum of the nation.' He also claims that Quisling 'found his adherents mostly among the youth of the secondary schools'. Among leading supporters of Quisling at one time, however, were, in the Arts, Knut Hamsun, Norway's leading living writer and a Nobel Prizewinner; Christian Sinding, the leading composer; Henrik I. Sørensen, a leading painter; Professor Wilhelm Rasmussen, sculptor of the national monument at Eidsvoll; and the husband of Kirsten Flagstad, the leading singer. In Science there were Professor Almar Naess, who turned Einstein's Theory of Relativity into a curriculum at Princeton and is an authority on the mathematical mysteries of early Norse navigation to America; and Captain J. K. Tornøe, the other authority on the long-ships. In Applied Science there were Professor Ragnar Schanke, Director of Trondheim Technical High School, who was a radar pioneer and musician; Dr. Gulbrand Lunde, of the Hermetic Laboratory, Stavanger, a pioneer of fish-canning; Sam Eyde, creator and managing director of the largest factory, Norsk Hydro fertiliser plant; and Dietrich Hildisch, chairman of Da-No-Fa, the great margarine plant in Oslo where he made a fortune by removing the smell of whale oil, and who had served as the old Austro-Hungarian Consul-General. Other prominent business supporters were Olaf W. Fermann, President of the Red Cross; Oscar Egeberg, Sen., Chairman of the Royal Automobile Club; and Arne Bergsvik—three of the richest men in the country.

Several shipowners, among whom were Boar Stenersen and Captain K. S. Irgens, Commodore of the Norwegian-American Line, who was one of the King's bridge partners, were others. In the Services —especially in the Navy, after it had been spat upon by the mob in Skien at the time of Menstad—there were innumerable sympathisers, including the gallant Tryggve Gran, Police Chief Jonas Lie, who headed the international police force which supervised the Saar Plebiscite in 1934-35 and was the leading detective story writer in Scandinavia, and Colonel Konrad Sundlo, Quisling's only rival in brilliance on the General Staff and his predecessor as Nansen's assistant in Russia. In Sport there were Charles Hoff, the leading athlete, who set up world records in the pole vault to order, and Petter Østby, pioneer of split-cane skis and waxing, who made an international fortune from his discoveries and was married to Quisling's unpaid publicity-manager, Haldis Østby.

Probably all these distinguished people valued freedom very highly, and if the price of freedom is perpetual vigilance, Quisling must have seemed the most democratic Norwegian of his day. One of the most disturbing aspects of his tragedy is that he was the one man who was almost always right. He was the statesman who looked ahead and alerted the nation, while his opponents temporised. This is apparent from the files of *Fritt Folk* (Free People), the newspaper which he started on March 26, 1936.

In the very first issue he harped on neutrality and published an interview with Colonel Konrad Sundlo from strategic North Norway, who was at this time in close touch with Colonel Otto Ruge, Chief of the General Staff. Next day the ex-blacksmith and future Prime Minister, Oscar Torp, who was Minister of Defence, replied: 'It is too costly to increase Defence . . . The best defence we could wish would be to keep the peace.'

On March 30, Hitler's 99 per cent election victory was reported, and on the 31st *Fritt Folk* contrasted the 135 million *kroner* (some $196m.) Sweden spent on Defence with the pittance allocated in Norway. The paper added: 'The USSR is rearming on an unprecedentedly huge scale and is clearly pressing westwards. The Norwegian people are rolling towards the abyss under their present leadership.'

On June 29, *Fritt Folk* devoted a three-page spread to the theme that 'war between England and Germany is a catastrophic possibility'. Thus 'Norway can and will not march unless our freedom and frontiers are endangered. We therefore demand strong and unequivocal support for Norwegian neutrality . . . that the neutrality and freedom of the country be insured by the strengthening of our defence quickly and effectively.'

Next day Quisling addressed a large public meeting and demanded 'Nordic Defence Co-operation', which was not tried until war began in 1939, when it was too late.

Another of Quisling's incessant themes was the danger of Trotsky's presence in Norway as an exile. This bizarre and unexpected 'affair' dragged on for two years. It helps to place Quisling's whole anti-Bolshevik thesis in an international perspective.

Trotsky was admitted to Norway on June 18, 1935, at the invitation of Olav Scheflo, the Communist parliamentarian. The Agrarians protested, and after a *Storting* debate the Labour Government pledged Trotsky to abstain from Norwegian politics. *Arbeiderbladet* said: 'The Norwegian people feel honoured by Trotsky's presence'; and Martin Tranmael, the Labour Party founder, sent personal greetings. The Government also asked newspaperman Konrad Knudsen to accommodate Trotsky, which he did at his home in Vexhall, thirty miles north of Oslo.

Trygve Lie, Minister of Justice, paid a formal visit and remarked that Trotsky had participated in negotiating the Norwegian Labour Party's entry into the Comintern in 1921. Lie also asked him to pledge himself against 'hostility towards any friendly government'. No guard was imposed on Trotsky and visitors from all over the world came to see him.

On September 19, Trotsky entered Oslo Municipal Hospital with fever and was in bed most of the time until Christmas. (Quisling maintained that Trotsky was shamming and carrying on political activity.) Then he went with the Knudsens and some youths into the wilds to convalesce. In the state trial of Radek and Pyatakov in Moscow a year later, Trotsky was accused by Andrei Vyshinsky, the Prosecutor-General, of having used the circumstances of his convalescence to receive Pyatakov secretly. This was admitted by Pyatakov but denied by Trotsky.

During the next six months Trotsky completed his book, *The Revolution Betrayed*, at Vexhall.

It was not left only to Quisling to attack Trotsky; *Arbeideren*, the Communist organ which echoed the Soviet Legation, attacked him for using Norway 'as a base for terroristic activities directed against the Soviet Union and its leaders'. Labour rejected the allegations, but imposed a watch on him and deported his secretary. Foreign Minister Koht said later: 'We knew, of course, that Trotsky continued to write his commentaries.'

On August 4, Trotsky and the Knudsens left for an island holiday in South Norway, and that night Quisling's followers broke into his house. Although the Knudsen children raised the alarm, the intruders departed with some typescript which Quisling claimed was evidence of Trotsky's political activity contrary to the conditions of his residence. (Trotsky's main archives were in a bank.)

A week later, Trygve Lie sent the Chief of the Norwegian Criminal Police in a light aeroplane to the island to interrogate Trotsky for the purposes of the forthcoming trial of Quisling's men. Next morning the radio announced that Zinoviev, Kamenev and fourteen others would stand trial in the USSR for treason, with Trotsky named as the chief abettor. Amazed, Trotsky rushed back to Vexhall and told the Press: 'Stalin's allegations are the greatest forgery in the world's political history.' He also denied that he had any connection with the USSR while he was in Norway. *Arbeiderbladet* quoted him and stated, 'the Moscow allegations are false'.

But on August 26, Trygve Lie robbed Trotsky of his freedom, demanding he should refrain from 'interfering directly or indirectly, orally or in writing, in political questions current in other countries'.

The Soviet envoy repeated a demand for Trotsky's expulsion on August 29, insisting that he was using Norway as 'a base for conspiracy'. Koht says, 'My colleagues in the Government were afraid of economic reprisals.'

Isaac Deutscher's biography of Trotsky, *Volume III, The Prophet Outcast*,* is the leading independent source. Deutscher remarks about this affair: 'The Ministers were afraid of a break with Russia and losing the election over this issue.'

'The Government became more and more terrified to see their Lilliputian interests and reputations involved in a contest with giants,' Deutscher continues, 'and they cursed the hour when they had allowed this man-mountain to come to their country.'

On August 28, Quisling's men pleaded that they had exposed Trotsky's 'disloyal' behaviour. Trotsky agreed that he had corresponded with comrades abroad, offering them political guidance, and criticised foreign governments, although this had no bearing on the case; whereupon the Judge said Trotsky had violated the terms of asylum on his own showing.

Lie demanded again that Trotsky should agree not to engage in any political activity, to reside where he was told by the Government, to limit his writing to uncontroversial subjects and to submit to censorship! Twenty years later eye-witnesses of the scene remembered the flashes of scorn in Trotsky's eyes and the thunder of his voice as he refused to comply. Did Trygve Lie believe himself so powerful as to obtain from him what Stalin could never obtain? How dare the Government base the charge against him on a document supplied by Nazi burglars? Were they allowing a gang of Hitler's stooges to determine their conduct?

Deutscher writes: 'Here Trotsky raised his voice so that it resounded through the halls and corridors of the Ministry: "This is your first act of surrender to Nazism in your own country. You will pay for this . . . The day is near when the Nazis will drive you from your country." '

Four years later Koht recalled Trotsky's words as the King and Government waited for a boat to take them to exile in England. He remarked: 'We had brushed his words aside. Such things had seemed to us utterly impossible.'†

On December 12, Lie visited Trotsky in internment and was told: 'Your Government has all the vices of a bourgeois government without any of its virtues.'

Trotsky then quoted Dr. Stockman from Ibsen's *Enemy of the People*:

* Oxford University Press.

† It is said that King Haakon reminded Trygve Lie of 'Trotsky's curse'.

'We shall yet see whether meanness and cowardice are strong enough to close the mouth of a free and honest man.'

When Lie offered to shake hands in a last farewell, Trotsky refused.

A week later the Police Chief, Jonas Lie, escorted Trotsky to a tanker, chartered by Trygve Lie at Government expense, to take Trotsky to Mexico, where he was done to death with an ice-axe by Stalin's agent, Mornard Jacques ('Jacson') on August 21, 1940.

The Norwegians did not react to Quisling's warnings about the Norwegian Government of 'all the vices'. In the October 1937 municipal elections *Nasjonal Samling* got only 0·15 per cent of the vote in rural areas, and the party was almost wiped out in the towns, where the percentage was only 0·06.

'The results were not good for *NS*,' Quisling admitted. 'Failure was due to desertions following setbacks at the *Storting* Elections in 1936. The electorate has chosen Marxism and Mammon. But we will continue the fight. We shall do our duty. Our cause will win in the end.'

What did he mean by 'our duty'?

The answer will be found in his conduct during the Second World War, which he had so exactly predicted and which was shortly to break out.

13

Peace and War

ALTHOUGH Quisling had polled less than 30,000 votes in the General Elections of 1933 and 1936 and had slumped again in the 1937 Municipal Elections, he was not downhearted. In 1938 he judged that time and world events were on his side. 'Over the entire world, nationalism is on the march forward,' he wrote in his newspaper *Fritt Folk*. 'Fate has determined its final victory.'

In this mood of optimism he still hoped that the Norwegian people would see sense, and he looked forward to another General Election in 1939. But he had another shock coming. On April 22, 1938, the Labour Government passed a law extending the mandate for the *Storting* by another year, to 1940. This was in flat contradiction to the Fundamental Act of May 17, 1814, which clearly defined the Norwegian Constitution and was to be invoked by Quisling's enemies constantly from 1940 to 1945. Paragraph 71 laid down that *Stortings* should be triennial. Paragraph 112 stipulated that any change in the Constitution had to be introduced by one *Storting* and approved by another, thus giving the electorate a chance to express its view before the amendment could come into force.

If the Constitution meant anything, the 1938 Act was illegal and the *Storting* elected in 1936 was defunct from January, 1940, onwards— as Quisling maintained. It represented, he said, a 'fraud' and a 'coup d'état'. The action spotlighted the Labour declaration that they would 'always march forward, either through the Law or giving the Law a wide berth'. This Labour trick, designed to tighten their grip on office and to stifle opposition, naturally coloured Quisling's future behaviour.

The Defence situation was equally depressing. Premier Nygaardsvold stated in 1937: 'The Government has based its defence policies on the building up of the nation economically, socially, materially—not militarily.' From 1935 to 1940 he followed this policy consistently and blatantly to the disadvantage of the already derisory Armed Forces.* Nygaardsvold's first Defence Minister, Oscar Torp (the future Premier), had been sentenced to five months' imprisonment for inciting troops against their officers. Alfred Monsen, who succeeded Torp, told the Labour Party: 'It has always been our programme to render the Defence of the bourgeois parties unfit for use.' He also urged the workers at Horten naval yard to rebel against their officers and superiors.

In 1938 the few increases made in Defence expenditure were negligible, and, like the appointment in December, 1939, of a 'salon soldier', Colonel Birger Ljungberg, to succeed Monsen, was a sop to the critics. Ljungberg, who was pro-Socialist and married to a Lady-in-Waiting to Queen Maud, was appointed on the recommendation of Monsen, who had to quit because of ill health.

Nor were the opposition more Defence-minded. The outgoing Liberal Premier, J. W. Mowinckel, told the *Storting* in 1939: 'People seem to believe it is our common interest to re-arm. But I do not allow myself to be disturbed by this agitation. My confidence in the might of guns is not great. If war breaks out, I take it as granted that the first thing to do is to increase our foodstocks as long as there is a chance to do so. This is a policy of preparedness. It will probably not arouse the same cheap enthusiasm which stirs people when there is talk of guns. My desire is that all the forces for Good shall serve to shield our cherished Liberty.'

Nor yet were the Conservatives realistic. C. J. Hambro calmly wrote after the German Invasion: 'Norway had no standing Army, but Article 109 of the 1814 Constitution obliged all to serve as Territorials. Training was very short: in the first year forty-eight days until 1934, then sixty days, later seventy-two days and in 1940 eighty-four days. Afterwards it was thirty days for three years. But "regimented

* In the issue of *Fritt Folk* dated December 18, 1937, Colonel Konrad Sundlo, the Narvik Commander, wrote: 'The Norwegian Air Force is a museum piece.'

training" was cut for "social purposes". The period was insufficient: but there was a strong current of anti-militarism in Norway until the Second World War. . . . There was a complete lack of tanks, anti-tank guns, and little anti-aircraft artillery. There were no military secrets.' Yet he and his friends did nothing about it.

Quisling was a voice crying in the wilderness, more isolated even than Churchill in England at this time.

Here are some pertinent comments by Quisling which appeared in *Fritt Folk:*

March 26. 'Norway is heading for war. She has had four years to set her Defence in order: since it became clear which way Europe was going. . . . But our country and our people are still wholly unprepared materially and morally. . . . If Norway is not to be driven into war and chaos, party politics must be stopped.'

April 2. 'We demand neutrality—an honourable and strong neutrality.'

August 27. 'Norway must leave the League of Nations and strengthen her own defence of the country's neutrality and national interests.'

October 1 (at the time of Munich). 'Norway is being drawn into war. . . . Europe stands on the edge of the greatest tragedy in human history. A new war could defeat our whole civilisation. . . . Our country's neutrality has been abandoned. We are bound by the League of Nations to the united front on which the Soviet Union stands. . . . Our Defence is undermined and totally unprepared militarily, civilly and morally to meet the demands of modern war.'

November 5. 'Norway was so very near to war. . . . Russia intended to take the Aaland Isles [Finnish territory, off Sweden]. . . . Our defences must be strengthened.'

So, by 1939, we find Quisling despairing of his Government, his people and the Western Democracies, and frantically searching for a Norwegian way out of the gathering storm.

The popular theory is that he planned to deliver Norway to Hitler long before 1939 and actively set about doing so after Munich in September–October, 1938.

Is that true?

The complicated evidence behind Quisling's alleged Nazi plot must be examined thoroughly.

As we have seen, his original political philosophy was documented in his book *Russia and Ourselves* in 1929-30. He was motivated initially by the paramount need, as he saw it, to hold Russia at bay. 'There are two great commandments,' he wrote, 'in the law which governs human actions. First, self-assertion: the development of our innate powers and capacities. Secondly, mutual responsibility and love of one's neighbour. The first is more in accordance with human nature. The second is more difficult and is apt to lead to discrepancies between precept and practice. Nationalism and Fascism use the candid language of egotism. Socialism and Communism inscribe the Christian virtues on their banners but worship utilitarianism in their hearts, and are prone to hypocrisy.' A plague on both their houses! Hence his preference for a corporative state which would marry the virtues of both systems.

From that framework, Quisling's foreign policy followed: 'Unsolved problems are to be found along the whole length of the new frontier-line across the Continent of Europe, from the Gulf of Finland to the Black Sea. . . . It is of vital importance for Europe that this frontier should be stabilised. . . . How far this will be possible in the long run depends to a very great extent on the relations between Poland and Germany; and these are governed by the relations between France and Germany. In other words the issue depends upon the consolidation of Europe.'

Having diagnosed the basic European problem, Quisling first set out to be a unifying factor in the West and only when events frustrated his efforts did he choose what he considered to be the lesser of two evils for Norway—an accommodation with Nazism in preference to any truck with Bolshevism.

It can be argued that the choice was fundamentally a practical matter (not a moral issue), dictated by circumstances (not ideology). For instance the five Northern Countries each accepted the facts according to their own lights. Finland, with historical and frontier grievances against Russia, chose Germany. Sweden, having no frontier quarrel with Russia (only traditional hostility), chose armed neutrality. Denmark, which knew that it could not be defended from any quarter, was forced to acquiesce in a German occupation, and (except for a marginal resistance) enjoyed a profitable war. Iceland, similarly placed to Denmark, acquiesced first in a profitable British, and later in an always cultivated. Until the last moment, when Hitler made an honest woman of pinheaded, bosomy and adoring Eva Braun, Hitler treated women with contempt, whereas Quisling always treated women with respect, compassion and intelligence. The Party uniforms, which Quisling adopted during the Occupation in order to keep up with the German Joneses, did not go down well in shirtsleeves Norway and therefore his embellishments had none of the glamour of such signs of rank in regimented Germany. Indeed he and his followers looked out-of-place and ridiculous outside Nazi circles at home.

Nor did Quisling possess Hitler's advantage in having risen from the ranks, of being an underdog who reached the top, of belonging to the common people. Quisling sprang from the officer and gentleman caste, and he spoke above the heads of ordinary folk, and in fact of most people of his own station, too. As his one-time collaborator, rival and enemy, J. Bernard Hjort—the leading Norwegian defence lawyer—told me: 'Quisling was gifted and in some ways an idealist. But he was not very sensible. He was logical and rational, and he believed that other people were, too. In that way he was very different from Hitler. He should have been a professor of mathematics.'

What, then, was Quisling's uncanny attraction?

Everybody speaks of his kindness, helpfulness and consideration for others, which are endearing in any country and particularly in rough-and-ready Norway.

For instance, Mrs. Mollö Christensen, who ran the Chancery in the Norwegian Legation in Helsinki when he was Military Attaché, and shared with him a gift for science and languages, told me: 'I was not very clever at my job because I had been trained as a chemist and a linguist, and I had got it because I was related to Minister Urbye by marriage. But Quisling helped me. He was a very quiet, good and clever man, and we answered letters in no time. I had known him in my teens, when he was a lieutenant, and made the red and gold banner of St. Olav for him, at his request, for Christmas.' She added: 'There was no romance. He was rather too fat. But I must say he was always very smart and courteous. In ceremonial uniform he looked impressive. He did not like diplomatic parties, but he went to them conscientiously and, curiously, he was a success. He knew the answer to everything and people found this was entertaining, although he was not *spirituel*.'

Quisling was pleasant-looking in a strong, manly sort of way, and he had that sudden childlike smile which suddenly lit up his solemn manner and captivated people. To lonely and insecure women he must have seemed solid and reliable. There was his fitness and stamina to admire as well, developed and tempered by hiking, hunting and exploring the wilds of Norway and unimpaired by either smoke or drink.

Above all there was his monumental reserve, which suggested mysterious, hidden depths of character and strength—an impression confirmed by his record, by his encyclopaedic knowledge when he talked, and by his deep insight on the rare occasions when he opened his heart and mind to friends. Thus he appealed to clever, public-spirited and 'blue stocking' women through their minds. His innate bashfulness offset his air of superiority and prevented him from being a bore. His aloofness was a challenge to women, who were attracted by the very fact that he seemed so hard to get. Hence he was surrounded by serious, active-minded women all his life.

A Mrs. Cappelen remembers driving with him and his publicity manager, Halldis Neegaard-Østbye, before the war for eight hours, and picnicking on the way. 'Quisling never said a word all the time and when we sat down to eat he stayed yards away from us, wrapped in thought. It was fascinating', she told me, 'one felt that he was solving some profound problem or originating some great new idea.'

He, too, was attracted by high-minded women, among whom he sought an ideal—some almost abstract goddess of the virtues which had been inculcated in his highbrow home and which he sought to emulate. In Court he quite seriously cited Olav Tryggvason and St. Olav, Oliver Cromwell and even Jesus Christ as his forerunners. Among women, his formidable, strait-laced and ambitious mother represented perfection to him, and he instinctively sought a woman in her mould to be his wife. Einar Østvedt, the authority on Ibsen, who was tutored by Quisling's father at Skien and used Vidkun's private, self-made Latin primer ('Clear and concise as one would expect from such a first-class brain'), told me: 'Quisling was "broken" when he buried his mother at Gjerpen in 1940. He worshipped her.' This is another good mark from an unexpected quarter, for Østvedt did two years' hard labour in the Arctic during the Occupation.

By nature Quisling was a hero-worshipper. Conversely, he demanded admiration. Likewise he craved to find an object for his affection and to be loved in return. There was his mother. Then came the Norse heroes; then Nansen and Hitler. As recompense he expected the adulation of Norway, humanity and the world. Born into the greatest turmoil in history and self-indoctrinated with the past, he sought to be not only a servant of events but an arbiter—to obey the signs of the times and to weave them into his own pattern.

No ordinary mate could fit into such a majestic concept. There had to be a mutual admiration society of two paragons, or nothing. So it was not until 1923, when he was thirty-six, that Quisling found his soul mate. She was twenty-three: a dazzling, raven-haired beauty from the minor aristocracy of Russia, born in Kiev on October 12, 1900, of well-to-do parents settled in Kharkov, and an only child. In fair-haired Scandinavia she might have been taken for a Jewess—and some-times was—but he claimed that she was of 'ancient Nordic extraction' when he celebrated his twenty-fifth anniversary of becoming a student. She fitted in with one of his favourite historical themes—that Russia was originally a Nordic country, settled by Vikings from the Swedish coastal district of Roslagen. Hence the very name 'Russia', which has its counterpart in the Finnish for Sweden—*Ruotsi*, the land of the 'rowers' down the Neva and the Volga to Nijni Novgorod, their capital. Symbolically he thus imagined himself reuniting Russia with its roots and defying what he regarded as the inferior and alien Slavs who had undermined the true Nordic destiny of the country for a thousand years.

A fantasy? Well, the Great Finland (*Fennia*) Movement, which sprang out of Lapua, wallowed in the same mystique and aspired to be reunited with kinsmen in the Kola Peninsula, Karelia, the Leningrad hinterland, out to the Urals and down to the ethnically Finnish belt of forest as far as Smolensk. Only the stern hand of Mannerheim restrained the victorious Finnish Army from pursuing this dream in 1941.

When the Army recaptured Viipuri, capital of Finnish Karelia, in August, 1941, the Corporation declared: 'All Karelia's railways lead to Viipuri and the port will always be important. As Viipuri is now getting Karelia and Aunus as a hinterland, its importance is even greater. A project is on foot to build a canal from the Gulf of Finland to Lake Ladoga so that the Neva will only be the Neva and Leningrad will become an ordinary fishing village.'*

* Stockholm's *Tidningen* Helsinki correspondent on August 31, 1941.

Kuvalehti, the leading Finnish weekly, stated on October 11, 1941: 'It is to Finland's advantage that Russia ceases to exist and that Russia be replaced by several second-class states built on a national basis. . . . Russia is now heading for destruction and Germany intends to wipe her out and remove all threats to Europe. Finland must help in this whenever possible and our geographical position enables us to help in blocking Russia's breathing-holes. In our own interests we intend to co-operate until Russia is finally destroyed and to take for ourselves compensation for a thousand years' suffering. . . .

'It is in our interest that the Russian fleet and its bases be destroyed; that the entire Leningrad area be demilitarised; that Leningrad ceases to exist as an industrial or commercial city and as a metropolis; that all chances of recovery be withheld from it by isolating it from its hinterland and finally that Finland's traffic along the Neva be taken into account. . . . Finland's future Eastern frontier must be pushed back and made the shortest possible. It must run from Lake Ladoga, along the River Svir, through Lake Onega to the White Sea.'

The Conservative *Uusi Suomi* stated on August 21, 1941: 'It is a question of time before Europe, Asia and North Africa form the new area under Hitler's leadership. If Britain still resists, Hitler must perhaps even conquer India. Germany is reserving an important position for Finland in the New Europe as the outermost bastion against the East. Hitler as a real statesman realises that Finland therefore requires a bigger basis and different frontiers and Finland is going to become greater, richer and more powerful.'

Norway, too, has her imperialists, notably those activists who backed a movement to occupy Eastern Greenland, also 'a wide scattering of people motivated by strong nationalism—under a sort of Old Hebrew delusion that God had given Norway to the Norwegians [those of and for the traditional culture]. Among them were found military officers, educators and government officials, theologians, writers and small farmers. In the roster of their names we find "the best families" in the country.'*

Those imperialists believed that the Germans would help them to get the lands in 'the western sea' back again—an objective which has not yet been abandoned by Norwegians with a similar historical

* The Norwegian-born Professor Lynder L. Unstad in *Susquehanna University Studies*, May 1959.

even more profitable American, occupation. In all those countries, the rigour of the grim choice has been recognised with realism and magnanimity. Norway, having no historical or frontier quarrel with Russia, chose Britain and eventually the Russo-Western Alliance.

So one embarks on the detail of how Quisling eventually found himself in the German camp and asks whether he was exceptionally culpable, if at all.

We have previously noted that his first Nazi contact was Hitler's old crony, Max Pferdekämper, in Oslo in 1929 and 1932. Another two years probably passed before he was found in Nazi company again. According to Sverre Hartmann, writing in the Norwegian magazine *Aktuell* (March 21, 1964), Quisling met Dr. George Liebbrandt in 1934 when he visited Berlin for the first time and discussed the possibilities of co-operation in a crusade against Bolshevism. Afterwards Quisling was formally introduced to Alfred Rosenberg, the official Nazi philosopher who ended the war as Minister for the Occupied Territories in the East. Liebbrandt was head of the Eastern Department of *Aussen Politisches Amt der NSDAP* (APA)—the Nazi Party's Office for Foreign Affairs, run by Rosenberg.

Professor Skodvin says that Quisling's Nazi contact in 1934 was Thilo von Trotha, who had organised the APA Northern Department for Rosenberg in 1933 and attended meetings of *Nasjonal Samling* in Trondheim and Stiklestad. Skodvin admits that 'nothing lasting came of this contact'.

The *Norsk Biografisk Lexicon* seems to confirm this view by stating that Quisling's contact—incidentally his first, according to this source —with Nazis was during a visit to the leader of the Nordic Department of NSDAP's 'foreign policy office'—presumably Trotha—in 1934. The *Lexicon* adds that this was apparently the only contact until 1936.

William Shirer says in *The Rise and Fall of the Third Reich** that Rosenberg kept in touch with Quisling from 1933, but he also asserts that Quisling appropriated the ideology and tactics of the Nazis when *Nasjonal Samling* was founded in the same year, whereas the most reliable local sources seem to indicate that all Quisling was doing was to take an intelligent interest in National Socialism rather than model his movement on it.

* Simon and Schuster

What Quisling did have in mind in 1934 was an end of the destructive multiple-party system and the formation of a national government—an idea with an ultra-respectable Norwegian history, going back to the time when Hitler was still a corporal. Any resemblance to Fascism or National Socialism was accidental.

Quisling was a stickler for the sacroscanct Norwegian Constitution of 1814 and the fact that Hitler, too, used the Weimar Constitution to achieve power is one of the accidental similarities; and the fact that Quisling first appealed to the Norwegian Constitution in 1934 in order to by-pass the parties—contemporaneously with Hitler's legitimate success in Germany—was also fortuitous and due to internal causes, not to foreign inspiration.

In June, 1934, Quisling wrote in vain an open letter to the 'officers of state' demanding that the Labour Party should be expelled from Parliament unless they renounced their revolutionary programme—thus paving the way for the national government which he advocated and hoped to lead.

Another two years passed before there is a record of his meeting another Nazi and meanwhile the international situation had changed dramatically for the worse. Mussolini entered the Abyssinian capital on May 2, 1936; the League of Nations capitulated and called off sanctions against Italy on July 4; Franco staged his military revolt on July 16; the Rome-Berlin Axis was forged on October 24.

Quisling warned Oslo: 'There is a growing possibility of a general war and Labour foreign policy is dragging Norway into it'; but the Socialists continued to mock his 'Hitler imitation procedures' and disregarded his comments on the 'enormous development of air armadas'.

Thus Norwegian politics became more embittered and hopeless, as danger mounted, and Quisling resumed his effort to find some constitutional way round the suicidal parliamentary system. Time was running out. He could not hope to win a parliamentary majority or even a place in a friendly coalition in order to put across his policy of armed neutrality and, as he believed, save the country.

In the time available, his last hope seemed to be his old friend, King Haakon. Quisling therefore addressed an open letter to the monarch on August 20, 1936, exercising the right and duty of every Norwegian citizen to do so (Article 100 of the Constitution), and requesting him to recall Parliament as Article 69 prescribes in 'extraordinary cases':

'A stop must be put to this dangerous situation where the government of this country is in the hands of Trotsky's Norwegian followers and the leaders of the now completely exposed and compromised so-called Labour Government. . . . This must be removed and replaced by a constitutional national government in accordance with Article 12 of the Constitution which vests in the King the right of choosing his own government. . . . We have no confidence in the present *Storting*. . . . The bourgeois majority of the *Storting* has itself become associated in guilt in this matter by letting the Marxist government into power and tolerating the permission given to Trotsky to stay here.'

King Haakon simply passed this letter to Trygve Lie, the Minister of Justice, who had brought Trotsky to Norway.

The *Norsk Biografisk Lexicon* records that Quisling again called on Rosenberg in 1936 and that 'according to German sources, a lasting contact began'—the insinuation being that Quisling now entered into a conspiracy with the Nazis. But no details are supplied, and the indefatigable Sverre Hartmann has apparently failed to ferret out any direct contact between Quisling and Nazi officials in 1936-37.

Professor Skodvin says of 1936-37: 'All in all, *Nasjonal Samling* did not achieve any special position among the other small groups and outright political sects which at that time had a more or less casual connection with Germany. . . . The German Legation in Oslo had not much use for Quisling. On the contrary, the Legation reckoned many of Quisling's "renegades" to be far from useful friends of Germany.' Baron Ernst von Weizsäcker, Secretary of State in the German Foreign Office, who had been Minister in Oslo, shared the Legation's opinion of Quisling.

The reliable evidence suggests that Quisling must be acquitted of conspiracy. His interest in National Socialism was still academic and he was not even invited, along with many prominent pro-German Norwegians, to the Berlin Olympic Games in 1936—Goebbels's masterpiece in showmanship which was meant to fool the world into imagining that Germans were 'sporting', peaceful and manly Aryans.

A plot does not begin to thicken until just before Christmas, 1938, when Dr. Herman Harris Aall went to Dresden to see Albert Viljam Hagelin, a Norwegian businessman who had lived in Germany for twenty years.

Aall was a Doctor of Law and Philosophy and a scientist, who for many years had lived in Germany. The particular bee in his bonnet was 'the freedom of the seas', which prejudiced him against 'British world domination' and in favour of the Germans. He was not a Nazi. He had his own ideology, which he called 'social-individualism', 'controlled individualism' or sometimes a 'cultural catechism'. This had something in common with Quisling's 1930 thesis of the two great laws governing human actions, self-assertion and mutual responsibility, and the necessity for marrying them, thereby leading to the corporative state. Two scholarly minds thought alike, which is doubtless how Aall came into prominence in Nordic Folk-awakening.

Quisling's first-hand knowledge of Germany was superficial, and Aall was therefore useful to him. The hate and fear which the two men had in common was Bolshevism. Like most enthusiasts for the 'Nordic cult', Aall was a 'Norwegian imperialist', dreaming of supremacy in the 'Western Sea' and a reassertion of Norwegian Viking rights in Greenland. He hero-worshipped Quisling, who did not get much admiration in the late thirties and appreciated what little came his way. Aall looked upon him as a kindred spirit and a vehicle for promoting his own ideas.

That was why Aall went to see Hagelin, who was no ideologist but had a lot of money—a million *kroner*, he told the Court at Quisling's trial. Hagelin seems to have thrown in his lot with the Germans for business reasons. He had suffered enough in his adopted country as a youth in the First World War, and in the event of a new war had in mind the possibility of returning to his native land, which he hardly knew and hoped would remain neutral, or, if the worst came to the worst, side with Germany. Hence his interest in Quisling, whom he had met casually in Oslo in 1936. Hagelin had noticed similarities between *Nasjonal Samling* and National Socialism during the Election campaign and visualised Quisling as the up-and-coming Norwegian who might help him to build up a new business if he returned home.

Hagelin was born in Bergen in 1888, the son of a small silversmith and a Swedish-Jewish mother. As a young boy he had a good voice and such an amusing manner that he was invited by the patricians of Bergen to sing at parties, and one of them thought so highly of his talent that the lad was sent to Germany to train as a professional vocalist; but he was not successful. He made his money, mostly in coffee, during the First World War, when he settled in Dresden.

By the thirties he had become a respected citizen, an associate of the leading Scandinavian businessmen in Germany and influential Nazis. He was a brother-in-law of Captain K. S. Irgens, by the latter's third marriage, and while they were in Italy together met Hermann Göring's brother, Eugene, a civil engineer and director of the Hamburg shipyards. As Commodore of the young Norwegian-American Line, Irgens often visited Hamburg to check construction, and through Eugene Göring got to know the mighty Hermann. Now Hermann Göring had been a Swedish Airlines pilot after the First World War and had married a Swedish beauty, Carin von Kantzow (née Baroness Fock). The Görings, Irgenses and Hagelins thus formed a cosy group with Scandinavian connections.

Hagelin was not the man to ignore such precious connections—Irgens played bridge with King Haakon—and doubtless Göring appreciated the possibilities, too. Through the Görings, Hagelin got to know Dr. Max Winkler, the 'grey eminence of German finance' throughout the Weimar and Nazi periods, who—unlike Dr. Hjalmar Schacht—shunned the limelight. He was born in Denmark and had first worked in Graudenz, in the East Prussian area which was ceded to Poland at Versailles, thus acquiring the expatriate passion which distinguishes so many characters, German and Norwegian, in this story. It was Winkler who handled the secret finances of the Nazis' manifold subversive activities abroad.

In this capacity he knew Ellef Ringnes, the old Austrian Consul in Oslo—a Norwegian who was the local representative of the great German film company, UFA. By 1937, Ringnes and his Norwegian associates were trying to buy *Tidens Tegn*, with a view to converting it into an organ of German propaganda. Winkler was to arrange the finances of this deal.

Joseph Goebbels also had a finger in this pie. Frank Züchner, a German newspaperman in Oslo, who had kept the German Minister, Dr. Heinrich Sahm, informed about the Norwegian-Danish dispute over Greenland in 1931, had a brother as head of the Nordic Department of the Nazi Propaganda Ministry. And it was Frank Züchner who served as go-between for Ringnes in his work for Goebbels in Norway.

Another deal which Ringnes was hatching with Goebbels and Winkler by 1938 was the purchase of the Kino Palace—the only cinema

in Oslo outside the hands of the Labour-controlled Municipal Council
—where he planned to show Nazi propaganda films.

Hagelin must have known of the proposed deals over *Tidens Tegn*
and the Kino Palace by the time Aall came to see him at Christmas,
1938. Aall probably had an inkling that something of the sort was in the
wind and this may have been why he singled out Hagelin for a visit at
this juncture, hoping to raise funds for *Nasjonal Samling*.

It appears that Quisling knew nothing of such financial intrigues.
That is the conviction of Olaf W. Fermann, a rich Norwegian
businessman,* who lived in Germany at this time and knew all the
principals concerned. In a letter of April 4, 1959, he says: 'As regards
Quisling, I think we must sooner or later inform the public of all we
know. I have myself taken part in some of his life. Professor Aall made
contact with Hagelin in Dresden and informed me that Hagelin had
substantial means for financing *Fritt Folk*. At a meeting in Dresden I
lunched with Hagelin and formed the impression that he was some
sort of actor and in reality very little of a businessman. I am a businessman myself and so I could form some conclusions about his affairs—
mostly coffee—and I was able to orientate myself about these through
his connections. . . . Hagelin's connections went through Hamburg—
new building for the Norwegian-American Line—Irgens's inspection
of progress in building—Göring's brother, who was a Director of
Deutsche Wherf—Winkler. . . .' Details of the newspaper and cinema
deals follow, and Fermann concludes: 'Ringnes wanted to show
German propaganda films as a *quid pro quo* for the money which he gave
Quisling for *Fritt Folk*. Through Goebbels, Ringnes got refunded what
he gave for *Fritt Folk*. Quisling did not know where the money came
from, beyond Ringnes.'

This last sentence is significant. It tallies with the fact that Quisling
never bothered about finance and was accustomed to anonymous wind-
falls falling out of the blue into *Nasjonal Samling*'s kitty from rich
supporters who did not dare to be identified with such an outspoken
anti-Government movement. Indeed, some of his meetings in Telemark
during the 1936 Election campaign were financed by Harald Franklin

* Fermann became President of the Norwegian Red Cross and as such
accompanied Himmler to Poland. Being married to a beautiful White Russian,
he was anti-Bolshevik. After the war he was jailed for membership of *NS* and
mulcted. He now lives in exile in Switzerland.

Knudsen's gambling. Knudsen used to go to the businessmen's club in Skien to raise the expenses for travelling and meeting-halls by his skill at cards, and Quisling used to say: 'You know I disapprove of games of chance. But I hope you won!' The worst that can be said of Quisling's reaction to Aall's fund-raising is that he did not enquire too closely about the source and turned a blind eye to the obvious Nazi trail behind it. At any rate the initiative was not Quisling's and the evidence does not add up to a conspiracy by him with the Germans at this stage.

Solid support from ostensibly Norwegian sources in Germany eventually encouraged Quisling further to explore the financial possibilities there. On April 12, 1939, less than a month after the German Army had poured into Bohemia-Moravia, thereby destroying the Munich settlement, Quisling wrote to Aall in Berlin saying that Hitler's *nordpolitik* might decide his own destiny, and on the 19th he wrote a six-page letter to Hagelin, whom he had only met once—in Oslo in 1936—saying that he wanted introductions to the German authorities, and describing his own career. Obviously he was trying to impress Hagelin and the 'German authorities', for he went into extraordinary detail, including his representation of no less than thirteen countries' diplomatic interests in Russia (among them the United States, Holland, Switzerland, Spain, Serbia and Rumania) and reporting on Norwegian timber interests in Russia.

This self-advertisement at once suggests that he was still little known to the Nazis. The enumeration of the foreign countries that he had served indicates that he was anxious to dispel any notion in Germany that he was irrevocably committed to Britain or actually a British agent. The fact that he specified the German authorities and not the Germanophile Norwegians, who were now financing him, furthermore implies that he had guessed that the money received from Ringnes for *Fritt Folk* was at least partly Nazi. If that is so, then Quisling's approach, through Aall and Hagelin, marks a definite departure in his career—his first constructive move, made on his own initiative, to seek Nazi aid.

On April 20, Hitler's fiftieth birthday, Quisling was not among the half-dozen Norwegian guests invited to the celebrations in Berlin, again suggesting that the Norwegian *fører* was either still held in little esteem by the National Socialists or else was only slightly known to

149

them. Quisling had to content himself with cabling congratulations. The invited Norwegians were Aall and Ringnes; the writer, Victor Mogens, who now chaired the rump of the Fatherland League; Fritjof Heyerdahl, Siemens's representative; Thorvald Halvorsen, the ship-owner; and General Kristian Laake, the Commander-in-Chief, who was to stand by Quisling, as far as he was able, at the latter's trial.

At a party given the following day by Ribbentrop for Hitler's military and civilian guests from abroad, Aall met Captain Walther de Laporte, who invited him a few days later to meet his superior, Dr. Theodor Gottlieb von Hippel.

Hippel was now forty-nine, a typical Prussian, the great-great-grandson of a former Minister of the same name, who owned the castle of Leistenau in West Prussia and had taken a hand in issuing an appeal to the German people when Napoleon loomed up in 1813. His grandfather owned Hohenstein Castle in East Prussia near the Tannenberg battlefield of the First World War. In 1908 young Hippel went to Africa to work on a German plantation, and when war broke out became a volunteer under General Paul von Lettow-Vorbeck, thus learning irregular warfare. Later he was interned by the British in India, in company with the celebrated German guerilla organiser, Wasmuss. Afterwards he took a doctorate in sociology and political science at Tübingen University and joined a bank that handled American post-war credits. Thus he became interested in agriculture, like his forefathers, and took up the threads of his pre-war career, but with a fresh slant.

In 1923 he began to work out ideas for a new form of society and five years later began campaigning for what he called 'controlled individualism' or 'social-individualism'. Among his adherents was Colonel Schubert, who had accompanied Lenin in the notorious closed train from Germany, via Sweden, to join the 1917 Revolution in St. Petersburg, and had later become Military Attaché in Moscow. 'Social-individualism' was a sort of ideal, biblical communism, and was visualised by its founders as the German alternative to Communism. Hippel received some support from the Berlin authorities and claimed to have 600 families organised in a settlement at Spandau and another 1,500 elsewhere.

By 1933, Walter Darré, the Nazi Minister of Agriculture, and Alfred Rosenberg were enthusing over 'social-individualism', but in the end Darré vetoed it as smacking of 'collectivisation'. Hippel was suspected of Communism, and in 1935 decided to take refuge in Kärnten, Austria, in order to continue his work. As he was about to leave, the Chief of Staff of the Berlin military garrison persuaded him to abandon politics and to serve under the Berlin Commander, General Erwin von Witzleben, later to become world-famous as one of the would-be assassins of Adolf Hitler on July 20, 1944.

In October 1937, Hippel was transferred to the head office of German Military Intelligence under Admiral Walther Wilhelm Canaris, another dedicated anti-Bolshevik and celebrated anti-Nazi, who secretly filled his office with Hitler's enemies.

In the autumn of 1938, Hippel reviewed *Abwehr* policy with his chief, Colonel Hans Piekenbrock, in the Espionage Department, and maintained that they were at a disadvantage against the British Secret Service, which employed civilians and did not regard Intelligence as primarily a military matter, and that the strength of Soviet Intelligence was Communist ideology and the avenues of information it opened up. In short the *Abwehr* needed constructive ideas—for example a ration-alisation of society in the fields of industry, agriculture and community life on the basis of co-partnership between capital and labour.

Admiral Canaris thought there was some merit in this idea as a means of gathering information, of founding an alternative to National Socialism and of winning cells of friendship for Germany abroad, should Germany lose another war. Accordingly Hippel was trans-ferred to work under Colonel August Groskurth, whose right-hand man was Colonel Hans Oster, one of the main leaders of the military opposition to Hitler, in *Abwehr* Department II.

It was at this time that Hippel was introduced by Captain de Laporte to Dr. Aall. They invited Aall to take charge of an international 'peace' and 'social' movement along novel, idealistic lines. The movement was said to be in funds, thanks to a foundation established by a phil-anthropic French tobacco manufacturer.

It was suggested that the movement should have its headquarters in a neutral country, such as Switzerland or Sweden, and Aall was recommended by Hippel to go into the whole matter more closely with de Laporte, the ideological expert. They were to use discretion, since the movement did not exactly match the ideas officially in vogue in Germany at the time. The world needed fresh inspiration.

At first sight this looked like a clumsy Nazi attempt to lure more foreigners into their toils, sparing their more patriotic feelings, and to establish another subversive centre abroad. Actually Aall had stumbled into an anti-Nazi movement!

After further discussion, Aall drew up a memorandum, as a joint basis for action, and proposed to invite Quisling to Berlin in order to persuade him to propagate the new gospel in Norway and the North.

None of them could have known the perils in which they were becoming involved. The slightest whisper of the anti-Hitler plot would have been fatal. They were simply to be unwitting German stooges, assisting in what they were led to believe was an idealistic movement working on parallel lines with National Socialism, against Bolshevism.

Aall obviously imagined that he had found influential German support for spreading the ideas which he and Quisling had been advocating in Nordic Folk-awakening and *Nasjonal Samling*. Hagelin was brought in by Aall as a well-connected businessman who had already proved his good faith by raising money for *Fritt Folk* through Ringnes and the Göring clique in the background.

So it happened that Quisling, who previously had been merely paddling, took his first plunge into German waters.

On June 6, 1939, Quisling cabled Aall in Berlin saying: 'Arriving Thursday the eighth *Stettiner Bahnhof* 18.13 for about five six days.' Aall immediately telegraphed Hagelin: 'Friend coming Thursday evening.' Dr. von Hippel and de Laporte were also alerted.

Thus Quisling unwittingly sealed his fate as surely as had Hitler sealed his own twelve weeks earlier, when his invasion of Czechoslovakia presaged world war, as the world sensed and realists knew. The next step was Poland.

'Irregular warfare' or the 'fifth column', which had proved so useful in the recent past, now assumed fresh importance. Hippel, de Laporte and their superiors, the specialists in military penetration of Hitler's intended victims, found themselves in a key role.

The circumstances at last rendered Quisling worthy of consideration in Nazi circles, for Poland was a Baltic power and Scandinavia could not be expected to remain indifferent to German expansion along the northern shore, let alone domination of these hitherto fairly shared waters. Quisling was to be used to placate Scandinavian opinion and to build up pro-German sentiments.

So much he must have expected and been prepared to do, in exchange for increased help for his own movement. He could not have known, however, that he would be groomed as an instrument for some form of German *coup* in Scandinavia at an unspecified date, and that the intention of his hosts was to use him in a worldwide pro-German but anti-Nazi plot. As Harald Franklin Knudsen says: 'They must have been "playing a part" with Quisling.' In retrospect that is a sound appreciation.

As an expert on Bolshevik and Norwegian Communist conspiracy, a luminary of the Norwegian General Staff and a former Defence Minister, Quisling must have suspected something fishy when he attended his first conference with the Germans at Sybelstrasse 40, Berlin, on June 9.

The night before, on arrival, Aall had shown him and Hagelin a contract recently signed by himself (as Dr. Alvaz), de Laporte (as Dr. de la Roche) and Hippel (as Dr. von Hohenstein), establishing a centre in Malmö, South Sweden, for developing the 'social-individualist' movement.

Aall was to take up residence in Malmö, and similar movements in other parts of the world★ were to be merged in this centre, among them Dr. Hans Keller's *Bund der Völker*, which had its official office in Pall Mall, London, but was actually headquartered at 137 Kurfürstendam, Berlin.

Quisling, Aall explained, was to have the use of the Malmö centre for spreading the *Nasjonal Samling* 'Nordic' and 'corporative' ideology, but he was not to be responsible in any way for expenses. These were looked after. Until August 15, Malmö would be subsidised to the tune of $11,000, and as the organisation expanded would be primed with another $11,000 so as to form a sort of 'foundation'. In principle, this money was to be regarded as a 'loan'—the implication being that it should be repaid if ever the movement achieved power.

The Sybelstrasse rendezvous—one tiny room, ostensibly the office

★ The *Abwehr* Department II had corresponding organisations in most countries where there were restless minorities, and the plan was to centralise them in neutral Sweden.

of Dr. Schafferdt & Co., Import & Export, which was decked with Rumanian posters and looked like a combined travel bureau and business agency—could hardly have been more conspiratorial. Quisling must have wondered where he had landed on this fateful day in his life, but he was not to know that Hippel's colleague, Dr. Fritz Schafferdt, only used the place occasionally and was really providing cover for General von Witzleben and other anti-Nazi conspirators.

Hagelin introduced Quisling to Hippel, the only German present, and the two Norwegians leaped at the overnight proposals when they were recapitulated. In addition to the use of the Malmö centre, Quisling was to get $5,900 for the extension of his work in Norway: again in the form of a loan. Another contract was signed.

The proceedings lasted several hours and were continued for several hours more on the following day, June 10. These were what Quisling at his trial termed 'private scientific discussions'. He was in his element, theorising on trends in history and exploring solutions to all the problems of mankind. 'Social-individualism' was just the sort of ideology to fit into his life's work on 'Universalism', which he had discussed *ad infinitum* with his cronies in Russia and Norway for twenty years and was to leave as his memorial (yet unpublished). Quisling, Aall, and Hippel all had their pet theories, and their speculations could have continued indefinitely had not Quisling arranged to address a Nordic gathering at Kolding in South Jutland and to attend a conference of the *Nordische Gesellschaft* (Northern Association) at Lübeck. Both appointments were independent of his activities in Berlin.

In Lübeck he had his first chance of talking at length to Rosenberg. One evening, after the formal proceedings, Quisling aired his views freely on power politics and the great Germanic and Nordic future. In Rosenberg he found a ready listener.

This meeting marked a turning-point in Quisling's life and in the modern history of Norway.

Quisling could not possibly have believed Rosenberg's theory, inherited from the Dutchman, Hermann Wirth, that all human culture is the product of a single Aryan race, originating in North America and sweeping over Europe via Greenland, Iceland and Ireland. The starting-point of the Nordic cult in Norway did not go back to pre-history and Quisling was too intelligent, too well-

informed, and insufficiently fanatical to swallow Rosenberg's un-
scientific claptrap. By 1939 it was already clear to what ghastly extremes the 'Aryan myth' was leading.

Of this Quisling was aware. The most foolish thing he ever did was
to have any truck with Rosenberg, the arch-priest of racialism, or
later to propagate the absurd and brutal 'Aryan myth' in any shape or
form. This caused him incalculable harm, and has never been forgiven
—rightly.

There are many explanations and extenuations for his acquiescence
in Nazi racialism, but there is no justification.

Obviously he did not favour extermination of non-Aryans. He
admired the Russians and had saved hundreds of thousands of them
and their neighbours, irrespective of race or religion, at the risk of his
own life. In *Fritt Folk* (November 19, 1938) he actually wrote: 'The
only solution to the problem of the Jews is that they must have their
own state.'

Then why did he have truck with Rosenberg and later acquiesce
in the deportation of 782 Jews, only 22 of whom returned to Norway?

The answers are that in the first place he sympathised with Rosenberg's belief in the superiority of the Germanic and Nordic peoples;
secondly, he realised in mid-1939 that only a miracle could prevent
the Germans overrunning Europe in another war and he therefore
seized upon Rosenberg, his first important Nazi contact, in the hope
that he could influence the Party hierarchy in favour of Norway;
thirdly, during the German Occupation, he believed that the only
chance of preventing the Germans from turning Norway into a
Protectorate (like Poland, Bohemia or Holland, under Gauleiters)
was for him, as Minister-President, to accept what he regarded as the
subsidiary evils in order to secure his overriding objective, an independent Norway within the Great Germanic Community.

If Hitler had won the war, as Quisling expected until 1942, or had
obtained a negotiated peace, as Quisling anticipated until almost the
end, collaboration would have obtained results. Norway was Hitler's
main experiment in the creation of a 'New Order'. Quisling might
have been forgiven and even become a national hero. But Germany
surrendered unconditionally. Quisling perished in the vengeance, and
for this fate his miscalculations on the crucial issue of race were largely
responsible. He allowed himself to appear to be a cruel and evil man,

which he was not. Having supped with the devil, he found that his spoon was not long enough.

This is the main indictment of Vidkun Quisling. The rest of his theories and actions were logical, often enlightened and always aimed, rightly or wrongly, at the salvation of his country. He should have relegated the time-honoured Norwegian version of the 'Nordic cult' to its proper, innocuous place—nostalgia. Instead he attempted to make the dream walk roughshod over common sense and humanity, and to become an instrument of high policy. This was madness. This was Peer Gyntism in the extreme. This was fatal.

Another key character in the drama that unfolded when Quisling took the lead in Norway in April 1940, was Hans Wilhelm Scheidt, thirty-year-old, Moscow-born head of the Northern Department of Rosenberg's APA, who had succeeded Dr. Liebbrandt. Scheidt was a bright and personable enthusiast over Norway, where he later married an Oslo girl of good family and had already met Quisling during the holiday season of 1938-39. They were introduced by a language teacher named Günther Kern, who was regarded as 'unreliable' by the German Legation, after a political discussion in the Old Hall of Oslo University in January.

By then Scheidt had already made Norway 'his pigeon' in APA, and naturally he sought out Quisling, the champion of the 'Nordic cult', who bore Norse names, looked Norse and was a Norseman. There were not too many such real Nordic types in APA, or indeed at the top of the Nazi hierarchy, and the capture of Quisling would lend a cachet to the Aryan cause.*

Scheidt's interest in Norway can be traced to Hagelin, who

---

* In APA Rosenberg (from Estonia), his staff-chief, Arno Schickedanz (from South-West Africa), Scheidt (from Russia), and his predecessor, Liebbrandt (from the Ukraine) were all of doubtful origin. In *NSDAP* Hitler (from Austria), Göring (son of a Governor of South-West Africa), Rudolf Hess (born in Cairo), Darré (from Argentina), Ernst Bohle, leader of the Germans living abroad (from Britain) and Schacht (from Denmark) all had expatriate backgrounds. Likewise a number of the leading characters in the Quisling drama—Quisling himself (twelve years in Russia), Hagelin (twenty years in Germany), Prytz (half a lifetime in Russia) and Aall (resident in Germany)—not to mention King Haakon (a Dane), Premier Nygaardsvold (six years in America) and C. J. Hambro (many years in Geneva with the League of Nations). Perhaps this explains some of the virulence.

lived near a branch of the Scheidt family in Dresden. Hans Wilhelm was their nephew, and he became on such affectionate terms with the Norwegian that he addressed him as 'Uncle Viljam'. Scheidt lapped up what Hagelin told him about Quisling and soon acquired an unbounded admiration for the man and his works.

Hagelin had prepared the ground thoroughly for Quisling's first long talk with Rosenberg. On May 18, Hagelin had written a six-page letter direct to Göring, extolling the Norwegian *fører*'s Nordic merits, and requested a $6\frac{1}{2}$ million *Reichsmarks* subsidy for Quisling either to convert *Fritt Folk* into a daily or to bring out a large twelve-page Sunday edition. Thus the Göring clique was forewarned of further requests for money for Quisling, which was to be sought through Rosenberg at Lübeck.

Quisling must have been briefed on the bare fact that Aall and Hagelin were seeking financial aid for him through their Nazi contacts, but there is no evidence that he was enlightened on the intricate and high-level footing of his friends' plan. What Quisling wanted was to impress Hitler's 'philosopher' and so to secure introductions to other Nazi leaders, if possible to Hitler himself.

He certainly did his stuff, expanding, as he had been doing at home for ten years, on the destiny of the Germanic peoples, the necessity for them to unite against the Bolsheviks, the impossibility of small nations keeping out of another World War, the dangers of Russian and British intervention in Scandinavia, and his own mission in Norway, and so on.

Rosenberg, primed by Scheidt with exaggerated versions of Quisling's importance at home, was impressed. With the Polish invasion impending and the Baltic thus implicated, the contact with Quisling was a feather in APA's cap. Rosenberg immediately dashed off memoranda on Quisling to Hitler, Göring and Ribbentrop—the latter, primed by Weizsäcker and the Oslo Legation, having so far displayed no interest at all in *Nasjonal Samling*.

The memorandum for Hitler was sent to Hans Lammers, Secretary of State at the Reich Chancellery, 'for the attention of the *Führer*', who for the time being ignored the document, perhaps because Rosenberg's verbosity was notorious. But at least Quisling was now on Hitler's files!

Four tangible results emerged from Lübeck. First, Dr. Winkler provided another advance to Quisling for *Fritt Folk*, although further sums were delayed by the Polish Campaign on September 1—despite entreaties by Rosenberg for regular payments.

Secondly, twenty-five trainees from *Nasjonal Samling* were invited for fourteen days at Germany's expense to the *NSDAP* Foreign School in Berlin and to see the Reich in all its might. This visit has been represented as the foundation of a fifth column, intended to seize strategic points in a Norwegian *coup d'état*, but as it turned out, the trip could hardly have been more innocent. Indoctrination was minimal and most of the programme was sightseeing. Rolf Fuglesang, the *NS* General-Secretary, was in charge, and he has protested that there was no military or subversive training at all, unless a brief inspection of *SA* (Brownshirt) Headquarters, near Berlin, could be interpreted as such. As Fuglesang said at his trial, '*Nasjonal Samling* was a national movement and we did not regard Nazism as something for export'.

Thirdly, Quisling and Hagelin were introduced to Paul Körner, Göring's Cabinet Secretary, with whom there was further talk of a Germanic Union against Bolshevism, the economic situation of Norway, and—according to Scheidt—some mention of air strategy.

Fourthly, Scheidt was soon sent 'on holiday' to Norway by Rosenberg in order to check on Quisling's position there. On July 15 Scheidt reported to Rosenberg in writing that in the event of a Russo-German war (the Molotov-Ribbentrop Pact was only two months ahead!), Marxist circles in Norway would cede the North to the Soviet Union and convert the South into a Soviet Republic. The military consequences were obvious. This unreliable information was almost exactly a copy of a letter that Hagelin had sent to Scheidt three days earlier! His report would be pathetic had the outbreak of the Russo-Finnish War just over four months later not given his observations a spurious importance in Berlin and been instrumental in triggering off Quisling's forthcoming visit to Hitler, thus helping to precipitate Quisling's initiative on April 9, 1940.

Also in July 1939, Aall, Hippel and de Laporte met to discuss 'special military units' for helping the 'leaders' in different countries to gain power. Hans Clausen Korff, an expert on Danish border affairs, was consulted, and in November, Fritz Clausen, who led the equivalent of Quisling's movement in Denmark, was invited, with seven followers, to discuss details in Berlin. This was a precaution in case the occupation of Denmark should be ordered by Hitler, and one of the paradoxical anti-Nazi moves of the military opposition. As regards Norway, it was decided that a 'revolution in feeling' had to be created and that Quisling was a suitable instrument, although he was admittedly not bound up with National Socialism. Korff has since said that Hippel was considering a coup in Norway, but that the preparations were to be kept on a civilian basis for the present. That was as far as the conspiracy got in Scandinavia.

Thus we find Quisling far out of his depth on the eve of the Second World War, in a whirlpool of intrigue, with hardly an inkling of where the ripples led. He was certainly sailing close to the wind, but was something of an innocent abroad. In his own mind he doubtless preserved his integrity, but his subsequent prosecutors took the view that he was already compromised. The argument will never be settled.

14

Ragnarokk*

EVENTS raced towards the catastrophe Quisling had long predicted. In April, 1939, at which time the author arrived to open a Press Department in the British Legation in Helsinki, to serve Finland, Estonia, Latvia and Lithuania, Anglo-Russian flirtations began in Moscow. On June 14, as Quisling returned to Norway from his fateful meetings in Berlin and Lübeck, William Strang, Neville Chamberlain's Foreign Office adviser on Eastern Europe, who had participated in the Munich surrender, arrived in the Soviet capital and held eleven meetings with Vyacheslav M. Molotov, the second man in Russia. Although these meetings were abortive, an Anglo-French military mission reached Moscow on August 11. Quisling's worst fears were confirmed. The capitalistic Powers were seeking to line up with the arch-enemy, Bolshevism. 'Will Bolshevism take Norway from the West?', he had written in Fritt Folk as recently as March 18. 'The Comintern is working against the North from America and England.'

The terrible prospect emerged of Norway being destroyed in cross-fire between Russia (from the North), England (from the West) and Germany (from the South). Fortunately, in Quisling's judgement, the subsequent military talks broke down on the old, basic difficulty of Poland and the Baltic States, the crucial points which he had identified

* In Nordic mythology the final catastrophe in which the worlds of men and gods go under.

Vidkun Quisling and his wife, Maria, in their home.

Maria Quisling and, *below*, her husband Vidkun, when, in 1936, he was 49 years of age.

Two informal photographs taken
of Vidkun Quisling in 1941.

The first German troops entering Oslo on April 9th, 1940. *Below:* Quisling's friend, H. Franklin Knudsen, welcomes him on his return from Berlin, August, 1940.

Quisling, *left,* with Adolph Hitler in the Reich Chancellery, Berlin, in February, 1942. The figure in the center is Albert Viljam Hagelin.

Quisling speaks in 1942 against a background of Nasjonal Samling red and gold St. Olaf banners. *Below,* he reviews a parade in honor of his birthday, July 18, 1942 at Gimle, Norway.

Quisling in the dock at his state trial, 1945.

Above: Quisling at Akershus Prison in 1945. *Right:* Akershus Castle, where Quisling was imprisoned in its tower during his trial. *Below:* Where Quisling was shot at 2:40 a.m. on October 24th, 1945, on the grounds of Akershus Prison.

in 1929. Britain and France jibbed at giving Russia a free hand in these areas.

It is to be doubted in fact whether Britain pursued its negotiations with the Soviet Union other than faint-heartedly. Like Quisling, the British Government felt fundamentally that a pact with the Russians would be a misalliance, and that Russia was the ultimate danger. There is evidence that, like Quisling also, the British authorities would have preferred an Anglo-German anti-Bolshevik rapprochement. In *The Origins of the Second World War** A. J. P. Taylor says bluntly that a 'peaceful settlement with Hitler, at the price of considerable concessions, was always the avowed aim of British policy' and gives details of a proposed Anglo-German treaty of non-aggression. This was in the form of a memorandum from Sir Horace Wilson† to a German representative which, like many compromising documents from official Norwegian archives, is missing from British records.‡

It is abundantly clear that Chamberlain was prepared to go a long way towards some such 'Great Germanic Community' as Quisling had long advocated. In a different form, he had in mind something not unlike the NATO of today.

Who, then, has the right to blame Quisling for seeking out Hitler and trying to save Norway in 1939-40 from the Nazi-Bolshevik tug-of-war at the crossroads of Northern Europe? Who is to blame him for doing his best to avert disaster before it started, to arrest it while there was still time, and later to cut losses? Quisling was not a cynic. He was consistent. He never wavered from his premise that Bolshevism was the supreme enemy and he acted throughout accordingly. Who is now to say that he was wrong in principle?

Following the breakdown of negotiations with Britain and France, the *volte-face* in the shape of the Nazi-Soviet Pact came about. This did not worry Quisling, who almost alone among world political figures anticipated the collapse of this alliance.

Quisling's view of events can be found in the first issue of *Fritt Folk* in 1940 (January 6): 'From April 14 to mid-August (five months), England (and France) were negotiating in Moscow to draw the USSR

---

* Atheneum Publishers.

† Chamberlain's confidential adviser, who also participated in Munich.

‡ Equally compromising documents have disappeared from official Norwegian archives, much to Quisling's detriment.

into a war-coalition against Germany, after giving Poland a blank cheque against Germany . . . But our "democracy" in Norway could or would not see the danger to our country. . . . We in *Nasjonal Samling* alone sought to make our people understand . . . that Scandinavia was destined for a leading role, like Czechoslovakia, as a bridge and base for the anti-German war coalition. . . . That means that the North, especially Norway, would immediately be a firing-range for total war by land, sea and air between England and Russia from the West and East and Germany from the South—war, chaos and Communism.

'From that unspeakable catastrophe Hitler and Germany truly saved us—not for the sake of our blue eyes, but for his own vital interests in shutting out the Soviet Empire by means of the Russian-German Pact signed in Moscow on August 23, twelve days before England and France declared war on Germany and let loose the world war demon.

'It seems beyond our café strategists to see that the Russo-German Pact does not make Germany more Bolshevik than the Anglo-French-Soviet Pact would have made England Communist.'

Not only did Quisling anticipate the collapse of the Russo-German alliance, which surprised even Stalin, but he actually looked forward to German military aid for the North against Russia. The Nazi-Soviet alignment, automatically placing Nordic Germany in a position of custodian for Nordic Norway, merely deflected temporarily the danger that Norway would become a battlefield between an East-West alliance and Germany.

Quisling read the signs of the times and his original thesis had to be modified. By the autumn of 1939 there was no longer much hope of Britain and Germany uniting in any Great Germanic Community to hold Russia at bay. The anti-Bolshevik leaders were at daggers drawn. The stark choice for Norway, as he saw it, was between Britain and Germany. Every prospect of keeping out of either camp was remote. This was the dilemma which brought him on his exploratory visit to Berlin and Lübeck in June 1939, and which was to bring him face to face with Adolf Hitler in December.

In the interval, everything conspired to disillusion Quisling with Great Britain, his first love, and to throw him into the arms of Nazi Germany.

The duplicity of the British, in his view, matched that of the Russians in the Anglo-French negotiations in Moscow in April–August and undermined his faith in the integrity, brains and determination of the very people whom he and Nansen had most admired.

It seemed impossible in any case to place too much faith in the British. Poland lasted only sixteen days before she was re-partitioned between Russia and Germany—without England or France firing a shot on her behalf. Coming swiftly on top of the *Anschluss*, the disappearance of Czechoslovakia, and a long succession of Anglo-French humiliations at the hands of Adolf Hitler, this blitzkrieg confirmed Quisling's disillusionment with the Western Powers.

It seemed to Quisling also that only Germany could halt Russian imperialism. The Baltic States, Poland up to the threshold of Warsaw and the Vistula, the Bukovina and Bessarabia were all absorbed swiftly into the Bolshevik empire. Bolshevism had taken a huge stride into Central Europe and along the Baltic coast, as Quisling had always feared. Paradoxically, however, although Germany was largely responsible for this advance, it was obvious to Quisling that Hitler would not tolerate this new obstacle to his *lebensraum* in the Baltic, the Ukrainian granary and the Caucasian oilfields indefinitely. A clash must come.

The 'final solution' of the Jewish problem was not ordered into effect until mid-1941, although pogroms were carried out in Germany before the war and anti-Semitism was an integral part of Nazism. Quisling could not have anticipated the later atrocities which liquidated at least 5 million people in German Occupied Europe and directly enslaved $7\frac{1}{2}$ million others. The New Order or Nazi Gangster Empire had yet to take shape and Quisling was as ignorant of the ghastly future as the rest of the world. He was no more guilty than Chamberlain, Daladier or Stalin in seeking out Hitler at this period. Like the Zionists themselves, he advocated a 'national home' for the Jews. Although he was aware of the Jewish problem in Germany, there was no obvious cause for his conscience to hold him back at this time.

On September 28, the day after gallant Warsaw fell, Ribbentrop and Molotov signed a resounding declaration of peace. It included the words: 'Should, however, the efforts of the two governments remain fruitless, this would demonstrate the fact that England and France are responsible for the continuation of the war.'

Two days previously, Birger Dahlerus, the indefatigable Swedish businessman, who had been in the thick of the Polish crisis in Berlin and London, understood from Sir George Ogilvie-Forbes, the Counsellor of the former British Embassy in Berlin, who was now in Oslo, that the British Government might not be averse to seeking peace, although only of course on certain terms.

'They can have it in two weeks,' Hitler told Dahlerus, and on October 6 made one of his longest speeches to this effect:

'I have always expressed to France my desire to bury for ever our ancient enmity and bring together these two nations, both of which have such glorious pasts. . . .

'I have devoted no less effort to the achievement of Anglo-German understanding. . . . I believe even today that there can only be real peace in Europe and throughout the world if Germany and England come to an understanding. . . .

'Why should this war in the West be fought? For the restoration of Poland. . . . It would be senseless to annihilate millions in order to reconstruct a state which at its very birth was termed an abortion by all those of non-Polish extraction.'

Instead Hitler proposed a conference of the leading European nations, yet took the precaution of preparing an assault on the West. This was Quisling's cue.

If Dahlerus and Axel Wenner-Gren* of Sweden could gain the ear of Hitler and Chamberlain, why not Vidkun Quisling of Norway? If war eventually came between Germany and Russia, or if it really flared up between Germany and the Western Powers, Norway would be more exposed than Sweden. Now was the time to act. Public declarations in Germany and Russia demanded peace, and by all accounts the German people expected it. The Anglo-French inactivity on the placid Western Front provided obvious evidence of the reluctance or immediate inability of the Western Powers to extend the struggle. Winter was drawing nigh and hostilities were unlikely therefore to be resumed on a large scale for some months. There still seemed to be a chance of preventing general war on the Continent, and Norway being dragged into it.

Accordingly, Quisling cabled Chamberlain through the British Legation. He had no mandate for doing so, but he reasoned that he had

* Wenner-Gren was also in touch with President Roosevelt.

other qualifications. He was the friend and successor of the great Anglophile, Fridtjof Nansen, whose name was still something to conjure with in London. He held a British Order for looking after British diplomatic interests in Soviet Russia. His prophetic views in *Russia and Ourselves* had been published in London, where he had several eminent acquaintances.

Perhaps a Norwegian voice would help in some small way to buttress Chamberlain's inclination for a peaceful settlement with Germany. It was worth trying. If it came off, his own soul-destroying choice—England or Germany?—would be postponed.

Quisling must have known he was at the final parting of his way when on October 11 he wrote:

'Having been charged with the care of British interests in Russia in 1927-29, I venture to address myself to Your Excellency and know that I am speaking the thought of almost all in the Northern Countries when I state that the fratricidal war between Britain and Germany, with Bolshevism as *tertius gaudens*, is felt particularly tragic in our countries which are so close to Britain and Germany.

'We were deeply impressed by your declaration of September 30, 1938, concerning Anglo-German relations and their vital importance to the peaceful development of Europe, and we are convinced that today the question is how to save European civilisation through peace with Germany in the spirit of your declaration.

'The only positive way of realising this is fusion of the British, French and German interests into a European Confederation on the initiative of Great Britain, with the object of creating a community of interests beneficial to all parties.

'Under these circumstances and in view of the suffering which the war is causing all the neutral Northern Countries, I respectfully appeal to your immense authority and responsibility and beg to suggest that the British Government should—in accordance with the tested methods of federation in America, South Africa and Australia—invite every European state to elect ten representatives to a congress charged with the task of preparing a constitution for a Commonwealth of European Nations, to be submitted to a plebiscite in each state for acceptance or rejection. You are the only statesman who in the present crisis can restore Europe to peace and reason.'

This initiative has been represented as camouflage for Quisling's approach to Germany, or as Utopian, but Hitler and Stalin genuinely wanted a *détente* for digesting their gains, Chamberlain's Britain was hardly beginning to steel itself, and France was rotting behind the Maginot Line; so that an effort of this sort need not necessarily have been wasted.

On October 21 the British Legation informed Quisling that it was 'desired by the Prime Minister to acknowledge with thanks the receipt of his telegram of the 11th instant with kindly reference to Mr. Chamberlain's declaration of September 30'. So his appeal remained unheeded.

But Quisling was stubborn. Perhaps there was one last hope.

He thereupon composed a draft Armistice for submission to the German authorities. It read:

'1. Cessation of hostilities, subject to ten days' notice of any resumption.

2. Great Britain and France to guarantee that their dependencies and allies observe the ceasefire.

3. Plenipotentiaries of the parties concerned to meet for peace negotiations.

4. Basis for negotiations:

(*a*) Peace without annexations or indemnities and co-operation in a peaceful union in the common cause of humanity—a public declaration of the principles whereon international and social life should be based.

(*b*) As a proof of sincerity, Germany would agree to re-establish the naval agreement with Great Britain and acknowledge the inviolability of the British and French Empires, also the inviolability of countries situated between those empires, namely Holland, Belgium, Luxemburg and Switzerland.

(*c*) Also as proof of sincerity, Britain and France would declare the Treaty of Versailles null and void.

Alternative A. Agree to restore to Germany the former German colonies held as Mandates of the League of Nations.

Alternative B. Germany to waive all claims to her former Colonies in exchange for concessions there, freedom of Germans to trade there, or something similar.

(*d*) Britain and France to acknowledge a new Polish National State with frontiers to be agreed between Germany and Poland.

(*e*) Bohemia and Moravia to obtain complete sovereignty over their own national institutions and to be acknowledged as a Czechoslovakian National State, allied to the German Empire.

(*f*) After the conclusion of peace, the three powers to agree on a clear programme of disarmament.

166

(*g*) Complete freedom of the seas for all powers to be established by a new judicial system.

(*h*) International arrangements and regulations of the Jewish problem.

(*i*) Lowering of tariffs and, if possible, a customs union of the three empires, open to others.

(*j*) Co-operation on Exchange problems so as to keep currencies stable in relation to the value of goods and services and the placing of the requisite capital at the disposal of industry in order to prevent unemployment with a view of forming a total foreign Exchange union, open to others.

(*k*) Freedom of movement for labour between the countries concerned.

(*l*) The tri-partite treaty to be extended, with the consent of the three contracting parties, to comprise other European states and the British Dominions with a view to the federalisation of Europe.

(*m*) A congress of ten representatives per European nation to frame a constitution for a Federal Europe which is to be submitted to a plebiscite in each nation.

(*n*) Britain and France to quit the League and, after the conclusion of peace, the three parties to invite the Great Powers to discuss a new pact for a League of Nations, omitting all obligations which practical experience has proved to be unserviceable (e.g. Articles 10 and 16—Sanctions) and preventing the League from becoming a universal league of peace among the peoples.

5. The present Armistice Agreement to come into effect on signature.'

This document became known as Quisling's 'Europa Pact', which went through various adaptations, as the situation changed, and was promoted by him until as late as 1944. Twenty-five copies of one of the later editions were printed in Norway, but not one was produced in his defence at his trial, although it would have helped to prove his consistency and idealism.

Another six weeks and a fleeting outside chance of peace had passed. On November 30, the Red Army marched across the Finnish border and Helsinki was bombed. War had come to the North. The Bolsheviks had come to stake their claims, exactly as Quisling had predicted. The British and French accelerated their own plans for staking a claim on the North. The Germans did likewise.

Four months later, on April 9, 1940, British, French, Free Polish and German forces converged on Norway simultaneously. The North was caught in the crossfire of Russia, Britain and France, and Germany, again exactly as Quisling had prophesied.

There was only one thing left to do by November 30—to go to the

167

heart of the matter, to tackle if possible the single individual who had provoked this upheaval, Adolf Hitler, the mightiest man in Europe. When, therefore, on December 2 Quisling received an invitation and the fare from Dr. Aall to visit him and Professor Stangeland,* there can be no doubt that he expected to meet Rosenberg again, and through him some more authoritative members of the Nazi hierarchy. He took with him his 'Europa Pact'.

---

* Charles Stangeland was an American who shared a Berlin flat with Aall and was also a 'Social-individualist'.

The most famous of all Quisling cartoons:
In audience with Hitler
'I am Quisling.'
'And your *name?*'

15

The Point of No Return

UNLESS one accepts the concept of 'The North' as a reality —as one does the much more disparate British Commonwealth—Quisling's mission to Hitler in mid-December, 1939, following the Russian attack on Finland, is incomprehensible.

This concept is not one even which all 'Northerners' accept. Ninetenths of the inhabitants of Finland are not Scandinavians. Their language is supposed to be the most difficult in Europe, with sixteen cases, and is not understood by their neighbours. Few Scandinavians ever visit Finland and what they know of the Finns is tainted by ancient myths. The Finnish and Lappish blood, which is plentiful down to central Sweden and Norway, is resented as diminishing the purity of the Scandinavian race. Yet Finland is very much a part of the North—bilingual, heavily weighted at the top in commerce, industry, culture and the Armed Forces by people of Swedish descent. The history of Finland is bound up with Sweden's long struggle, going back to Peter the Great, to hold Russia at arm's length.

In fact, as Quisling knew, Finland was the connecting link between the Polish and Norwegian campaigns.

On December 9—the very day he left for Berlin—*Fritt Folk* said: 'The Bolsheviks' attack on Finland and the nature of the sly and cynical brutality with which it was made have rightly shaken Europe, and especially the North. Norwegians can now see for themselves. . . .

Europe must at once wake up and understand that it is from the East that civilisation is threatened and that it is against Bolshevism —not against Germany—that the civilised world must rally. . . . Let Finland's brave fight for her freedom and independence, her very national existence, be an example to us.' There can be no doubt what was uppermost in Quisling's mind, but his trip to Germany was exploratory and no arrangement seems to have been made in advance for him to meet Hitler. Certainly his visit was no part of a deep-laid plot.

This is what Quisling stated in writing under arrest on June 21 and August 7, 1945:

'After the Polish War the time had come to try negotiations between Germany and Great Britain. Peace and understanding between them was—as is well known—a major point in our policy. With Mr. Prytz, who had many good connections in England, we resolved to make an effort there. . . . In the telegram [to Chamberlain], I stressed that war between Germany and Great Britain gave us the utmost anxiety in the Northern Countries.

'At the beginning of December 1939, I had a chance to go to Germany. The direct reason was a private request by Dr. Aall, who was living with the Norwegian-American Professor Stangeland, to visit him in order to discuss a scientific work. It had nothing to do with this case.

'Through Reichsminister Rosenberg, I then had an audience with Hitler. It was the first time I met him. However, I formed the impression that he at once felt strong personal sympathy for me. Our conversation may be summarised thus—

'I mentioned peace and Hitler then, as was his wont, lectured me at length on Anglo-German relations. He explained vehemently that emotion as well as reason made him fervently desire understanding and co-operation with Great Britain. He thought he had made all possible concessions. But now he felt bitter. . . . Events must run their course, but in due course he would revert to the subject. This happened, as known, in the summer of 1940, but proved a failure.

'He also discussed Norwegian and North European affairs. He was aware of our endeavours to keep Norway out of the war and emphasised strongly that Germany's interests were best served by the Scandinavian States, especially Norway, remaining neutral. . . . Hitler emphasised that Germany had no interest whatever in interfering in Norway so long as she vindicated her neutrality.

'Otherwise Germany would have to intervene, because if Great Britain tried to establish herself in Norway, it would be a crucial threat to Germany and Hitler would do everything in his power to prevent it. Germany would then have to occupy Denmark, too. Against Norway he would pit everything necessary to break any resistance, regardless of how many divisions were required—six, ten, twelve or sixteen.... If required, Germany would then occupy Sweden as well. Germany had air supremacy and such military forces that there could be no doubt of the results. Hitler shuddered to think of the fate of Norway and the North if events evolved in that way.

'This was exactly what I had foreseen for years and had preached to my countrymen in numerous articles and speeches. It was however important for me to get it confirmed at first hand. There was no doubt about his being in deadly earnest.

'Hitler also asked about our movement (*Nasjonal Samling*). I told him about it and the struggle I had been carrying on in Norway. He asked what chance there was of our taking over the Government and whether it were possible for us to get some men into the Government. I replied that I did not think this was possible for the time being but that the number of our sympathisers was growing; that the war might develop so as to make it possible and even desirable. Hitler said he would hail it with delight, because Germany was first and foremost interested in the neutrality of Norway . . .

'I took the liberty of also mentioning the Finnish question. Hitler said that he considered Poland herself was responsible for the dreadful fate of her Eastern provinces and that he had no sympathy for Finland after the ingratitude she had shown Germany for assistance in 1918. I objected that this did not apply to the whole Finnish people—that Finland was Nordic, a bulwark of the North—and that the Finnish people undoubtedly deserved and were fit to live in independence.

'I therefore asked him earnestly to devote all his influence towards bringing about a fair Russo-Finnish settlement—Germany and Russia then being on the same side. Later I got two influential Germans to make the same representations.

'I must presume that this intervention in favour of Finland contributed significantly to a fair termination of the 1939-40 Winter War, which was of vital importance to the peace and security of Norway.

'This was my first and only meeting with Hitler before April 9, 1940 (Invasion Day). To report to the (Norwegian) authorities about the German view of Norway's neutrality seemed to me a matter of no importance. Indeed, I had stressed, without intermission, and continued to stress the dangers of the situation. However, no one would listen to me. In any case the Government should have been well aware of the German view through its Ambassador in Berlin, the Foreign Office and the German Ambassador.'

Obviously it was useless for Quisling to go to the Labour Government, which hated, distrusted and feared him, and had branded him as a 'Nazi' for years. The Government was adamantly opposed to realistic defence measures and was already spreading the falsehood that Quisling exaggerated the German danger so as to afford the Western Powers an excuse for intervention and thus justify German retaliation! Any disclosure of his meeting with Hitler would have produced further accusations of his being 'Nazi' and reduced any influence he might have brought to bear. Nor was it any use Quisling going to his friends and former colleagues in the High Command, who should have been as well aware of the dangers as he himself. These men were hamstrung by the Government, and powerless.

Perhaps Quisling might have gone to King Haakon. There were many objections to such a course. The King had twice refused to intervene in defence of the Constitution at Quisling's request, and had also countenanced the extension of the life of the current parliament. The certainty was that he would simply have to pass on any information imparted by Quisling to the defeatist Government, in accordance with the Constitution, and that the result would be nil. The King did not enjoy, at the time, the widespread popularity that he was to win during the war, and he was in no position to issue a proclamation of warning to the people on his own initiative and over the head of the Government. He would have been strongly reproached in public for unwarranted interference—as he was more than once in Council with his Ministers—and would thus have diminished any influence that he might later need to exercise. At least, however, had Quisling gone to the King, he would have put himself all right, for the record. Instead, true to his secretive nature, he remained silent. Even his intimate friends, such as Harald Franklin Knudsen, and the General-Secretary of *NS*, Rolf Fuglesang, and his Staff Chief, Orvar Saether, were not informed.

It is perhaps not surprising therefore that he has been accused of having persuaded Hitler to invade Norway, of betraying Norwegian military secrets, of providing a fifth column to facilitate a German invasion, of offering to stage a *coup d'état* in concert with a German invasion, of having a puppet government in cold storage, and of having been primed on German invasion plans. Some of those terrible charges are fantastic and highly improbable in the light of the evidence, but Quisling's secrecy is partly to blame.

Was his meeting with Hitler treason? An indictment against him in 1945 was that he 'discussed with the German authorities the question of a German Occupation of Norway and the incorporation of the North in a Great Germanic form of government under German leadership. During these discussions, he offered guidance and advice with a view to such a German Occupation.'

It is necessary further to consider at some length his prison statement of August 7. 'Great Nordic Co-operation ought, in my judgement,' he said, 'to be based on Great Britain and Scandinavia, and into this co-operation Germany would be drawn, in the end, away from any connection with Bolshevism. Thus peace in Europe would be secured, the further spread of Bolshevism prevented and at the same time a Franco-German understanding would be sought in order that the Continent might be pacified.*

'This line of foreign policy I explained in my book, *Russia and Ourselves* (1930); it constituted the basis of the movement *Nordiske Folkereisning* (Nordic Folk-awakening). I also formed a separate organisation exclusively for this purpose: *Det Stornordiske Fredssamband* (Great Nordic League of Peace) and corresponded with a series of persons, especially in England, about this matter. . . .

'Now war had after all broken out again between Germany and Britain. However, it was at a preliminary stage in the autumn of 1939. There ought therefore to have been a chance of a peaceful arrangement before Europe was laid waste. Anyway this was the only chance of preventing Norway and perhaps the whole North from being

---

* It is interesting in this context to compare the present status of the German Federal Republic and the *rapprochement* that began between de Gaulle and Adenauer.

173

drawn into the war. It was this work of peace which engrossed me in 1939-40: in a discreet manner. That is why, in the autumn of 1939, I contacted the British Prime Minister, and why, in December, I called on Hitler and presented my plans* to him. . . . It was my plan to rouse popular opinion . . . and to get the Norwegian Government to raise the issue with the other Scandinavian Governments and thus to obtain joint Scandinavian action.

'I outlined to Hitler how I envisaged this co-operation between Norway (Scandinavia) and Germany, with the agreement of Great Britain. I of course had to present the matter on this basis, which, incidentally, despite the Moscow (Nazi-Soviet) Pact, conforms to the development that took place.†

'My aforesaid plan might, in my opinion, have changed the whole Norwegian attitude of mind and prevented the whole North being drawn into war, if we had had sufficient time. . . .

'I wish to interject that most people seem to be labouring under the delusion that if the Germans had *not* come to Norway on April 9, Norway could have passed the next five years peacefully, as if nothing had happened. The fact is that the Anglo-French action in Norway was already mooted and if the German Occupation had not taken place on April 9, something very much worse would have happened. . . . The German Occupation actually averted a far worse catastrophe. It guaranteed Norway against the East and saved the country from being destroyed as a war theatre of the Great Powers. One must imagine how it would have been if the British and French had, as planned, occupied the country and Germany had staked her whole offensive power on ejecting them, while Russia charged into the North. . . .

'During all this there was no question of any German Occupation of Norway, certainly not of my giving any guidance and advice with a view to such an occupation. Hitler was, however, emphatically clear that if Norway did not vindicate her neutrality *vis-à-vis* Great Britain, Germany would attack with all her power.

'One may take it for granted that the German authorities themselves knew best how to carry out such a counter-action and that they were

* The 'Europa Pact'

† i.e. the various forms of Norwegian Government during the Occupation, which never degenerated into a Protectorate on the Polish model.

not willing to discuss it with a foreigner whom they were meeting for the first time—particularly not one, like myself, who had so much to do with Great Britain.'

Quisling continued: 'Germany probably had plans for every eventuality . . . there would be nothing remarkable about this. Even we, in Norway, had plans for various alternatives—at any rate in my time. But that Hitler first and foremost wanted Norway to vindicate her neutrality was my distinct and indubitable impression.

'That there was any question of bringing Norway under foreign domination I formally deny.

'It was not until the summer of 1940 that schemes cropped up in Germany which gave the words "Great Germany" quite another meaning: schemes which I did my best to counteract and eventually got consigned to oblivion.

'Had I favoured bringing Norway under German domination, I should presumably not have tried indefatigably to counteract German domination during the five-year occupation, certainly not after we (NS) came to power in September, 1940. In fact we fought with all means to restore the full liberty and independence of Norway. . . .

'Had I favoured the Germans coming to Norway, NS would not have opposed the Anglo-French plan to intervene in Finland in 1939-40 as strongly as we did. We would have joined the general chorus about help for Finland because this accorded with our known attitude. Transit (for the Anglo-French) would have proved the surest way of bringing the Germans Northwards. . . . Because Russia was then allied with Germany, we opposed this: we wanted to *prevent* an "April 9" and what it might lead to. Personally I supported Finnish interests privately, that is to say in my intervention with Hitler.

'I intended to raise the question of Germany relieving hard-pressed Finland by an action in the East because Finland's position was hopeless and sooner or later, I believed, Germany would come to blows with Russia. German action would bring great advantages to Germany and rouse such sympathy in the other Nordic nations that the North would join Germany, not militarily, but in its attitude. So long as Germany remained on the defensive on the Western Front, relations with the Western Powers would probably not have been exacerbated. Simultaneously, plans for their intervention (via Norway) would have been dropped.

175

'However, I gained the impression in Berlin that such a proposal would have been inexpedient: the agreement with Russia was regarded as a great diplomatic victory* and a great military respite for operations on the Western Front. I contented myself with asking Hitler's help towards a fair Russo-Finnish settlement.

'Actually, one might believe that I had more reason for bringing the British here (to Norway), instead of the Germans. . . . However, I considered that we should remain *Norwegian* and have neither British nor Germans here. Therefore I fought for years before the war, until April 9, with my entire Party, to defend Norway's neutrality. We carried out the most intensive and comprehensive agitation and educational work ever attempted in this country.

'It is quite preposterous to believe it was I who caused the German action against Norway on April 9: a very risky act of war for which Germany gradually detached several hundred thousand men and considerable supplies from the principal war theatre and tied them down for the duration. There they actually served as a strong defence of Norwegian neutrality. . . .

'The real fact of the matter is that Germany acted entirely on her own initiative. . . . When the Western Powers violated Norway's neutrality and the Norwegian Government demonstrated that it could not vindicate its neutrality, Germany found that she had to intervene . . . as Hitler plainly enough explained to me. Should the occasion arise, they intended to do this with all their means. This historical fact stands firm and there is no getting round it.

'The Germans occupied Norway and were not brought here by some "quisling" or other, for the simple reason that the responsible leaders of our country betrayed their duty and did not observe the obligations of our neutrality. Thereby they exposed Germany's war interests to serious injury and brought the Germans to the country.

'Saying that there were no preparations for such a situation (by Norway) is the strongest self-indictment of a government which based the security of the country on "a prudent foreign policy". The excuse is false because there was no lack of warnings and intimations,

* The Moscow Pact was Ribbentrop's pride and joy. Thus Quisling's scepticism over the Pact was anathema to Ribbentrop, which helps to explain the antipathy of the German Foreign Office to Quisling's ambitions in Norway later.

not least my own. The Norwegian authorities are therefore the really guilty ones beyond doubt: they and no one else. This is the basis of the whole matter. From this basis everything follows.'

This explains the attempts ever since to make Quisling the scapegoat for the deficiencies of a government and a nation.

Quisling concluded with this footnote:

'Before April 9 our movement (NS) had *no* connection with German National Socialism. There was in Norway a separate Norwegian National Socialist Party. We had for years been advocating better relations with Germany, but our connections were no stronger than with other Scandinavian countries and England. There was absolutely no fifth column activity by *Nasjonal Samling*. What [subversion] there was, was the work of Bolsheviks. On April 9, *NS* was suddenly drawn into events, not as a German fifth column but as a consequence of our national policy for the past ten years.'

A vast Norwegian literature, filling half a room in Oslo University Library, has accumulated during the last quarter of a century, seeking to prove that Quisling went very much further with the Nazis than his two statements (above) indicate. The case against him has been summarised in the *Norsk Biografisk Lexicon*, which says that he went to Berlin early in December, 1939, and, together with Hagelin, was met by Rosenberg and Admiral Raeder, who obtained two interviews for him with Hitler between December 14 and 18. Quisling's idea was to mediate between the Great Powers, but he quickly realised that this would not get him a hearing. He then described Norway's strategic position, stressed the danger of British action, and hinted that his small but dependable following might assume power when the *Storting*'s 'legal' term expired on January 11, 1940. He asked for German military aid, and for a subsidy. Hitler was evasive, but promised financial help, and immediately ordered the planning of an armed attack on Norway —as the Navy had advocated for two months. Quisling's visit certainly led to the attack being decided upon at that moment.

Quisling, so this version goes, got his money through Hagelin, enabling him to establish a new headquarters, engage new staff and publish *Fritt Folk* daily instead of weekly. Quisling's suggestion of a *coup d'état* was not pursued. The generals planned a military operation, and obtained from Quisling information about Norway's military condition and advice on how the operation could best be carried out.

This is a particularly tendentious summary. The gravamen of its case against Quisling is that he suggested a *coup d'état*, and that he gave the Nazis military information about Norway. This latter charge is patently absurd. The pitiful condition of Norwegian defence was a matter of public record, and Hitler's commanders had nothing to learn from Quisling about the country's derisory Defence system.

As to his 'small but dependable following possibly assuming power', at the time, by the most optimistic calculations Quisling had 25,000 voters and 80,000 sympathisers scattered over a vast country. He had at the most 500 *Hird* (bodyguards), un-uniformed, untrained and unpaid—only twenty-five of whom had taken part in a fortnight's 'course' in Germany. He had one daily paper, tottering on the verge of bankruptcy to the extent that it had to be subsidised by wealthy Norwegian sympathisers at home and abroad, and to some extent by the Rosenberg and Göring cliques. Quisling also had the general sympathy of the microscopic Norwegian Armed Forces, including the leading commanders, who were grateful for his efforts as Defence Minister and shared his views on the appalling dangers to which the pacifist Labour Government had laid the country wide open. But he must have known that not one of them was a traitor, as indeed events proved—not even the much-libelled Colonel Konrad Sundlo, Commander at Narvik when the Germans crashed in, who has been exonerated from any dereliction of duty.

It is inconceivable that this small and penurious *Nasjonal Samling* movement could have staged a *coup d'état* or that Quisling could have believed in the possibility. His timetable in Berlin in any case just did not allow for his masterminding such a difficult task as a *coup d'état*:

December 10 (Sunday). Quisling arrived in Berlin at 8 p.m. to stay with Professors Aall and Stangeland.

December 11. Rosenberg reported in the morning to Hitler that Quisling had arrived and had a talk with the Norwegian, whom he had previously met three times—only once at any length. At noon Rosenberg arranged for Quisling to meet Grand-Admiral Erich Raeder, Commander-in-Chief of the German Navy,* which would play the main part in any action against Norway.

* Personally, I am doubtful if Rosenberg was actually responsible for Quisling meeting Raeder, and thus Hitler, in the first place. It is far more probable that Raeder knew all about Quisling and may even have met him long before Rosenberg ever came into the picture. Raeder had good Norwegian friends, loved Norway and knew it well, and must have known about Quisling before

December 12. Raeder discussed Quisling with Major-General Wilhelm Keitel, Chief of Staff of the High Command of the Armed Forces (*OKW—Oberkommando der Wehrmacht*) and General Alfred Jodl, Chief of Operations of the *OKW*. In the evening Hitler consulted Rosenberg about Quisling.

December 13. Rosenberg wrote to Raeder saying that Hitler was about to meet Quisling.

December 14. Raeder and Rosenberg consulted about Quisling.

December 15. Hitler, with Keitel in attendance, received Quisling and Hagelin. Hans-Wilhelm Scheidt, head of Rosenberg's Northern Department, held a watching brief for his chief, who was in bed with an old leg injury.

December 16. Quisling conferred with Corvette-Captain K. J. von Püttkamer and Walter Hewel, who held ambassadorial rank in the German Foreign Office.

December 17. Quisling, Hagelin and Scheidt were received by Hitler for one hour.

December 18. The trio met Hewel and Colonel Rudolf Schmundt. (Rosenberg's Chief of Staff, Schickendanz, kept Hitler's Chancellery Chief, von Lammers, informed.)

December 20. The trio took leave of Rosenberg—Quisling bound for Oslo, Hagelin staying in Germany.

Thus Quisling's only military contacts in Germany were his meeting with Raeder on December 11, one long meeting with Hitler and Keitel on December 15 and an hour with Hitler on December 17, plus a meeting with each of the two junior officers, Püttkamer and Schmundt.

Quisling had no further contact with any leading Nazi official or senior German officer again until after the invasion in April, four months later. Young Scheidt, who followed Quisling to Norway on

Hagelin and Scheidt introduced him to Rosenberg. What Raeder may have done was to contact Quisling through official Nazi channels, namely through the Rosenberg organisation. This procedure would have had the advantage of dissociating the German Admiralty from any untoward consequences of a visit by Quisling to Hitler while still providing the Navy with a claim to any credit for the introduction and at the same time providing a scapegoat for any blame in the event of Norwegian operations going wrong. Blame was what Quisling got in the end and this is what makes Raeder's later 'evidence' against him unreliable. However, I have followed the conventional theory in my text, because I have no proof—only a strong hunch based partly on the known antipathy between the two men—that Rosenberg's supposed influence on Raeder was imaginary. If my hunch is right, it upsets the whole theory of a prolonged conspiracy by Rosenberg and Quisling.

December 24 and remained until January 2, had nothing to do with the *Wehrmacht* and merely held a watching brief for Rosenberg in Norway. He was small fry and Quisling's only liaison with Nazi officialdom.

There is not known to have been any verbatim report of any of Quisling's conversations in Berlin. He understood and spoke German very imperfectly, so there may well have been misunderstandings on both sides.

In fact most of the German leaders, civil and military, who were involved in the invasion had a vested interest in building up Quisling in their own minds and on paper before the action took place and still more so for using him as a scapegoat afterwards for the muddle and losses with which it was carried out. This applies particularly to Raeder, whose Navy was permanently crippled in Norway, and to the German generals charged with running the Occupation.

The contemporary and retrospective comments of Rosenberg, Scheidt and Schickendanz of APA and Raeder, Keitel, Jodl and other commanders involved in the Norwegian invasion are therefore hardly worth the paper they were written on. Keitel and Jodl were hanged and Raeder was condemned to twenty years' imprisonment as war criminals at Nuremberg on October 16, 1946. Their depositions about Quisling's alleged participation in a *coup* against Norway were therefore made under duress and are even less trustworthy than their wartime memoranda. Their lives were at stake.

That such 'evidence' should have been admitted at Quisling's trial, let alone taken at its face value, without Quisling being given the chance of cross-examining his German accusers face to face in Court, is a disgrace to Western jurisprudence.

The most damaging document was found in Rosenberg's archives as the Quisling trial was opening. It is headed 'The Political Preparations for the Action in Norway', and dated June 15, 1940—in other words two months *after* the invasion of Norway, when a new situation had arisen from which Rosenberg hoped to profit. So unfortunate was the effect of this memorandum that it is worth listing the allegations it made about Quisling, and commenting on them:

NSDAP's Foreign Affairs Dept. (Rosenberg's APA) had already been in touch with the leader of *Nasjonal Samling*, Vidkun Quisling, for several years.

Thus Rosenberg at once claims Quisling as his man. Several years is a misrepresentation at least as far as Rosenberg himself was concerned.

He (Quisling) pointed out Norway's geopolitical significance in the Scandinavian sphere and all the advantages which would belong to the power that controlled the Norwegian coast in the event of a conflict between the Greater German Reich and Great Britain.

Such an advantage was always self-evident and its mention so early in this memorandum is designed to put the matter on a geopolitical level, which was Rosenberg's speciality and the only reason for his inclusion in the Nazi hierarchy.

As he no longer believed it possible for small states to remain neutral in the event of a conflict, as they had done in the 1914 World War, but was convinced that the states would by one means or another be dragged into the conflict, he requested—anticipating the intentions of Greater Germany—backing for his party and press in Norway.

There is nothing unusual or illegal about a party accepting foreign subsidies. The Norwegian Labour Party had been doing so for a generation. Anyway, Quisling's policy was 'armed neutrality' and it was in order to propagate it that he accepted German funds. As for anticipating intentions, Quisling expected the Great Powers to race for the North from three directions. He was not preoccupied with Hitler's intentions, as his cable to Chamberlain and his overtures to Hitler for intervention with Stalin on behalf of Finland prove.

Rosenberg instructed Amtsleiter Scheidt to arrange a visit by Quisling and his representative Hagelin, to Secretary of State Körner in anticipation that General Field-Marshal Göring would be particularly interested in the matter from the point of view of air strategy.

What on earth could Quisling, who was no aviator and had rarely been in the air, tell one of the world's great fighter-pilots, the creator of the Luftwaffe?

Quisling had enquired as to the possibility of a short suitable training for responsible (NS) party functionaries, specially chosen by himself. Reichsleiter Rosenberg had given permission for this and in August (1939) a fourteen-day course was arranged for twenty-five.

Again note Rosenberg's self-advertisement. There is no independent evidence that Quisling made the request. Anyway, the twenty-five had no subversive or military training.

In September Dr. Winkler announced that he had been instructed by General Field-Marshal Göring, through Secretary of State Körner, to handle the financial side of the request which Quisling had already put forward. As a result of the outbreak of war and the newly launched Polish campaign, the settlement was delayed.

Note the implication that Göring had let the side down and penny-pinched Rosenberg's Norwegian protégé, thus contributing to the mess now existing in Norway and to the frustration of Rosenberg's brilliant plans for Quisling.

At the same time the Russian activity which was becoming evident in the

Baltic region increased political tension in Norway. On this Quisling kept the office (APA) informed through his representative in Germany . . .

Scandinavia was in an uproar! Not only had Russia seized the Baltic States, but was openly turning the heat on Finland. What new could Quisling possibly report on tension?

The possibility that Great Britain might consider an occupation of Norway and perhaps Sweden, too, in order to complete the blockade of Greater Germany in the North Sea and especially to set up convenient air bases against Germany, began to appear under the cloak of unselfish aid for Finland—the object also being to draw the Northern Countries into a military conflict with Germany. Through his representative in Germany, Quisling informed the office (APA) of those new possibilities.

Rosenberg must have known or guessed that Britain and Germany had been planning intervention in Norway since the start of the war. The world-wide outcry against the Russian attack on Finland, coupled with demands from statesmen, newspapers and the public for aid for Finland, alerted everybody to the new possibilities. Any information from Quisling would have been a glimpse of the obvious.

The ever more noticeable activity of the Allies in Norway led Quisling to go to Germany once more to give verbal expression to his anxiety. He was received by Reichsleiter Rosenberg early in December. . . .

The ineffable Rosenberg on the ball again!

Quisling saw it as his duty, supported by a small but determined minority, to bind Norway's fate with that of Germany, the new centre of power for a Nordic-Germanic Union.

This in fact means no more than that Quisling sought a dignified place for Norway in a 'Germanic Union' in the event of Hitler winning the war, as he had proclaimed for ten years. He always assumed that Britain would also be a member. Norway was not at war at the time and such a speculation was then neither senseless, nor unpatriotic, since Quisling and a great many other statesmen were to believe up to the following March that a peace, giving Germany predominance in Central Europe and the Baltic, could be arranged. Rosenberg twists Quisling's position to suit his own ideology and his Nazi colleagues' ambitions.

His (Quisling's) representative in Germany, Hagelin, had also arranged a conference between Quisling and Admiral Raeder. . . . In a report to the Führer, Reichsleiter Rosenberg once more led the subject round to Norway . . . Because of his (Rosenberg's) conference with Quisling, and at his request, Admiral Raeder was also summoned to the Führer.

Thus Rosenberg hogs any credit not only for Raeder meeting Quisling and acquiring prestige and backing for his naval plans, but also for the Führer having the opportunity of meeting the Norwegian!

The Führer emphasised several times that the complete neutrality of Norway and the whole of Scandinavia would please him most. . . . But if enemy preparations were made to extend the war with the object of further

182

encircling the Greater German Reich, then he (Hitler) would naturally feel obliged to arm himself against such an eventuality.

This confirms Quisling's own story.

To counter increasing enemy propaganda the Führer promised Quisling financial backing for his movement, which was based on the Greater German ideal.

The inclusion of England and other 'Germanic' peoples in Quisling's plan is, of course, omitted.

The military side of the matter was taken over by the military Sonderstab, who gave Quisling special tasks and asked for his opinions.

Quisling certainly gave his opinion of Norway's strategic situation to Hitler, Raeder, Keitel, Jodl, Püttkamer and Schmundt. Such generalisations are common between visiting statesmen and their hosts in the Armed Forces. But since there were no military secrets, as all authorities agree, there can have been no treasonable revelations by Quisling. As for special tasks, Quisling was never brought into the military preparations against Norway or enlightened about them, as is now admitted by most informed persons, even in Norway.

The political side was taken over by Reichsleiter Rosenberg.

Actually he and Quisling were never again consulted and the civilian aspects of the occupation were handled primarily by the OKW.

Financial transactions are under the control of the Foreign Ministry, in which connection the Foreign Minister (Ribbentrop) was to be kept informed.

Ribbentrop was not informed and was only briefed on the invasion of Norway at the last moment. He was fanatically opposed to Quisling's belief in the ephemeral nature of the Nazi-Soviet Pact, and his Ministry and the Oslo Legation were thoroughly sceptical of Quisling's potentiality.

In January (1940) a conference was held between Reichsleiter Rosenberg and Foreign Minister von Ribbentrop at which it was arranged that an amount of 200,000 Gold Marks in currency should immediately be earmarked as backing for Quisling.

No such princely sum ever reached Quisling.

Quisling sharpened the tone of the messages sent through his representative in Germany, Hagelin, on the possibility of an active attack on Norway by the Western Powers with the tolerance of the Norwegian Government. . . . These opinions were in direct contradiction to the views of the German Legation in Oslo. . . . Hagelin, of whom nobody in Norway knew that he was on the most intimate terms with Quisling, was particularly fortunate to gain a foothold in Nygaardsvold Government circles and to hear the undisguised opinions of members of the government who were like a sworn company of Norwegian-Anglophiles.

Hagelin was not Quisling's representative, nor was he on intimate terms with Quisling, who got rid of him soon after Hagelin's influential friend, Göring, fell from grace after the Battle of Britain. Meanwhile Hagelin's intimate knowledge of

Germany and his contacts were useful, and Quisling used them. He did not realise for some time that Hagelin was using him. Quisling and Hagelin had only casual contact after their December meetings with Hitler. The emphasis on the manifest English danger was Hagelin's hobbyhorse.

These commercial transactions (the delivery of coal and sugar to Norway through Hagelin) were to be handled in a camouflaged form, either through a newly established company here in Germany or through specially chosen firms in existence, while Hagelin made his appearance in Norway as the [bona fide] contractor.... At the same time the coal transport would probably serve to find a way over the technical difficulties of launching a pro-German political action by Quisling in Oslo. Quisling intended to send a number of specially chosen and particularly reliable people to Germany to receive short military training here in a completely secret camp. Then, as locally known people and good linguists, they were to be put under a special German command which could travel to Oslo by the coal ships and carry out a political *coup.* Quisling's idea was thus to secure the leading political opponents in Norway, including the King, in order to frustrate any military resistance.

Against a hostile army, police and population, is it conceivable that Quisling would have suggested such a naïve plan?

In February this year (1940), Reichsleiter Rosenberg, after a conference with General Field-Marshal Göring, informed Wohlthat, Ministerial Director of the Four Year Plan, about sending coal to Hagelin in Norway. Further details were drafted in conference between Wohlthat, Staff-Chief Schickendanz and Hagelin. When no further instructions were received from the General Field-Marshal, Foreign Minister von Ribbentrop declared in conference with Reichsleiter Rosenberg that he was prepared to make the delivery through his own channels.

Thus Rosenberg again slights Göring, whose Scandinavian connections he envied, and asserts his own imaginary superiority over Ribbentrop.

At this conference [with Ribbentrop] ... it was agreed that for the next three months from March 15 $28,000 monthly should be paid to Quisling as backing for his work, and should be handed over through liaison-officer Scheidt.

No such sum was ever handed to Quisling.

Regular conferences between the King, the Commanding Admiral, War Minister Ljungberg, newly appointed at the special request of London, and the Crown Prince (Olav), were taking place regularly. A person who was close both to the King and the Commanding Admiral, told Hagelin that an action by England was unavoidable, as England knew she could only win the war by holding the central Norwegian coast. This was probably the most important report which Hagelin had delivered and Reichsleiter Rosenberg handed it over to the Führer immediately.

Rosenberg's sense of values is extraordinary. This information probably came from Hagelin, and it is unlikely that the person who divulged this glimpse of the obvious was Quisling. Note that Rosenberg did not know the correct rank or even the Service of the War Minister, Colonel Ljungberg!

Hagelin was instructed in Berlin by Colonel Schmundt to arrange a meeting between Quisling and a colonel from the German General Staff in a neutral country as soon as possible. This conference took place in Copenhagen early in April.

Quisling met Colonel Hans Piekenbrock in the Hotel d'Angleterre, Copenhagen, on April 3, 1940—five days before the German invasion, but there is no evidence that Quisling was then informed of the impending action, nor was Piekenbrock called at Quisling's trial to support such an implication. Quisling himself did not bother to mention it, let alone try to explain it away. Clearly he was kept completely in the dark about German preparations, as more reliable German records show and as events on April 9 confirmed. Quisling merely went to Denmark to see if he could find out more than in Norway about what was happening across the Skaggerak.

After the successful performance of the military occupation of Norway, the Führer sent for Reichsleiter Rosenberg. He (Hitler) . . . revealed to Reichsleiter Rosenberg that he had taken this most audacious step, which was now reaching its happy conclusion, on the basis of the repeated warnings from Quisling which had been delivered by Reichsleiter Rosenberg.

Reading the full document, it becomes so obvious that Rosenberg was only blowing his own trumpet—and incidentally trying to score off his rival, Ribbentrop—that his revelations and allegations are thoroughly suspect. Nevertheless they were pounced upon by the prosecution at Quisling's trial at a stage when it was being conceded reluctantly that a pre-war conspiracy charge would not stand up.

The Rosenberg memorandum was just what the authorities wanted in order to avenge themselves against their arch-enemy, who had for so long exposed them, and who now became the scapegoat for their astonishing sins of omission and commission during the past fifteen years or more. It was also what the populace wanted, screaming for blood and threatening riots if Quisling were not condemned to death. They conveniently forgot that they had had an easier war and a weaker resistance movement than any occupied territory except Denmark and the Channel Isles.

The climate was against Quisling, and consciously or unconsciously, the Supreme Court bowed to these pressures. Whatever his judges may have decided about his conduct after the occupation, they could hardly have convicted him of betraying his country before April 9, 1940, but for Rosenberg's incredible distortions.

16

Two-way Stretch

IT is idle to argue whether Britain or Germany was the more to blame for the invasion of Norway. If anything, the onus is on the British, who provoked it, beyond recall, by the seizure of the German ship *Altmark* in Norwegian territorial waters on February 16.

The invasion was deplorable but inevitable, once Britain and Germany had made up their minds to fight the war to a finish. The existence of two rival Great Powers was at stake on this Norwegian issue.

Norway was caught in a two-way stretch, as she should have realised from past history and the obvious circumstances of the current situation. She could have satisfied Britain and Germany by taking proper precautions to honour her neutrality, on which her policy was based, but she neglected to do so and abused her responsibilities to both powers. Thus she paid the inevitable penalty of becoming a battlefield between them.

The myth of a brutal Germany, helped by Quisling, attacking an innocent Norway and an altruistic Britain rushing to the rescue does not bear examination.

As T. K. Derry rightly says in *The Campaign in Norway,* the semi-official history, the German plan *Weserübung* (for the invasion) can be traced back to controversies regarding German naval strategy in the

First World War, in which the views of Vice-Admiral Wolfgang Wegener played a leading part. 'His book *Die Seestrategie des Weltkrieg*, published in 1929, was well known in Great Britain and America and even in Norway. . . . It is even alleged that Hitler treated Wegener's writings as his "naval bible". Grand-Admiral Raeder, the earliest advocate among German war leaders of aggression against Norway, first laid the matter before the Führer on October 10, 1939.'

Derry says that Raeder again raised the matter almost two months later, and goes on: 'At this juncture the strategic was fortified by the political argument, when Vidkun Quisling, the leader of the tiny National Union Party in Norway, was brought before Hitler by Raeder and Rosenberg, the expert on Nazism for export. . . . This caused the operation, as conceived and authorised by Hitler, to be based on the two alternative hypotheses: that it might be carried out by peaceful methods . . . on the invitation of a Norwegian government, real or sham, or by an invasion without such pretext.'

Quisling in fact disabused Hitler of any such fifth column expectations, fostered by Rosenberg, and thereupon the idea was dropped.

Derry then makes a very serious charge against Quisling: 'German confidence in Quisling's proposals was so small that he was not informed of the German military plans in time for him to take any advance measures of co-operation before the landings; the German military authorities let him into the secret at Copenhagen on April 4, only five days before the invasion, when he provided some mistaken intelligence about the gun defences of Narvik in return (Col. Olof Sundell's *9th April*, p. 106). Nevertheless, he has double importance in relation to *Weserübung*, because he held out the prospect of co-operation by treacherous Norwegians, which made the plan seem less foolhardy, and because he directly influenced Hitler to favour such a plan by his allegations that the British intervention in Norway was imminent.'

This view from an influential source must be respected, but in the light of more up-to-date information it does not appear to be supported by the evidence. Quisling was not informed of the invasion plans because he was not involved. He took no advance measures because there were none he could take and none were expected of him. Why the Germans should let him into such perilous secrets five days before the invasion, having kept him at arm's length for four months, when one whisper by Quisling to his English friends would have wrecked the whole operation—and indeed his interest might well have been to wreck it in order to keep Norway neutral—is unexplained. Quisling visited Colonel Piekenbrock in Copenhagen because Northern waters were just becoming ice-free and navigable, thus rendering the expected race for Norway imminent. He was completely in the dark, and was anxious for any inkling of what would happen. There is of course every reason to suppose that he guessed what was inevitable, and the mystery is why the Norwegian Government appeared so ignorant.

Professor Skodvin has a credible account of how German plans developed after mid-December. He says Berlin was the scene of a tug-of-war between the political and military planners. *OKW* worked on Raeder's B-plan (the military), which Hitler went into realistically, showing no interest in the ephemeral, political A-plan because he 'did not take Rosenberg seriously'. After the *Altmark* episode, Rosenberg submitted another report from Scheidt, who had been in Norway another month, but 'Hitler was by now concentrating exclusively on military action'.

On March 5, a fresh note from Rosenberg reached Hitler, apparently inspired by Hagelin, but 'the political plans were now dead' and 'Rosenberg's behaviour was unrealistic to the point of fantasy'. He and his APA apparently never made an analysis of the politics or the political climate in Norway and only looked for arguments which would support their own preconceived course of action. Everything which did not fit the picture was 'British propaganda'. Scheidt's view of Norwegian politics was simply that official Norway was England's willing and helpless tool and that anything appearing to the contrary was camouflage. 'He was intent on building himself up as the German expert on Norway.'

Professor Skodvin is equally emphatic that the German Foreign Office was not involved in any political plot against Norway and actually opposed Rosenberg's manœuvres.

Nor did Quisling cut any ice at the German Legation in Oslo. He had met the new German Minister, Dr. Curt Brauer, on November 27, at a book exhibition shortly after the latter had arrived at his post, and remarked that Germany could not expect much help from Russia, which was borne out by the Soviet invasion of Finland three days later.

Otherwise Quisling's only contact was an historian, Dr. Ulrich Noack, with whom he aired his well-known geopolitical theories.

Noack informed the German Foreign Office after the outbreak of the Finnish Winter War that Quisling had said that Germany would now have to attack Russia in the spring and had indicated on a map how this could be done, militarily and administratively.

These two theorists appear to have met three or four times during the first eight days in December, culminating in Noack helping Quisling to formulate his thoughts in German and to present them to the Wilhelmstrasse.

Noack gave Quisling letters of introduction to Professor Fritz Becker and the information chief, Gesandter Altenburg, in the Foreign Office, the day before Quisling was due to visit Germany. Noack actually telephoned both contacts, trying to make appointments for Quisling to see them, but there was no interest. Noack made no impression on Werner von Grundler, chief of the Foreign Office Northern Department, and was told to steer clear of politics—presumably on the advice of Minister Brauer, who reported he was 'naïve'.

The interest of these minor activities is that they show Quisling was operating on a low level, that his thoughts were centred on Finland, not subversion, and that he was preoccupied with promoting his anti-Bolshevik thesis in more receptive quarters than at Rosenberg's APA. Had he been less naïve himself, Quisling might have realised that Noack would get him nowhere in the Wilhelmstrasse. As Skodvin says: 'Ribbentrop was sticking to his Russo-German Pact. . . . The Foreign Office took all the more exception to Quisling when it saw that he was embroiled—through Rosenberg and Raeder —with affairs in which it had no say.'

On December 16 von Weizsäcker rang Brauer for more information on Quisling, NS and Hagelin—especially on contacts Quisling might have with Britain. Brauer mentioned that Quisling visualised British participation in 'Germanic Co-operation'. Weizsäcker, who had been envoy in Oslo, also told Ribbentrop that it was pointless to hold serious political discussions with Quisling. In the new year, Brauer himself was called to the Wilhelmstrasse to report on Quisling, Hagelin and Scheidt's activities in Norway. A report on them was handed by Lammers to Hitler, who said he was doubtful if such intermediaries in Norway could keep their counsel—the strongest possible indication that Quisling was never involved in any invasion plans.

After Scheidt had returned to Norway on January 20, 1940, Minister Brauer sent a supplementary report to the Wilhelmstrasse minimising the young man's theory that Quisling held influence over Norwegian officers and emphasising that Germany could only expect help in Norway from the Nygaardsvold Government.

Any collusion between Quisling and the German Legation or Wilhelmstrasse can be ruled out of consideration, but this antipathy between *Nasjonal Samling* and its German champions on the one hand and Ribbentrop and the Legation on the other is important. It came to a head on invasion day and did as much as anything to ditch Quisling's intervention.

Thus we find three key groups of Germans at loggerheads on April 9—Rosenberg, representing the Nazi Party; the *Wehrmacht*, headed by Raeder; and Ribbentrop's more or less conventional Foreign Office —with Hitler, the master of them all, holding their fate (and Quisling's) in his hands. This confusion was typical of the Greater Germany and it bedevilled the Norwegian situation from start to finish. Quisling was an enlightened statesman, but when it came to finding his way through this Nazi political jungle he was like one of the babes in the wood.

Meanwhile, what were the British doing? Called to the Admiralty again on September 3, 1939, Winston Churchill sought earnestly for means of attacking Germany on the seas. 'First and foremost,' he has written, 'gleamed the Baltic', the command of which carried with it possibly decisive gains. 'Scandinavia, freed from the menace of German invasion, would thereby naturally be drawn into our system of war trade, if not indeed into actual co-belligerency.' In other words, in Britain's interest Churchill hoped to involve the neutral Northern countries in the war.

All the resentment felt against the Soviet Government because of the Ribbentrop-Molotov Pact was inflamed by the Russo-Finnish Winter War. Anger at this fresh example of bullying was mingled with scorn for the inefficiency of the Red Army and admiration for the gallant Finns. With the desire to help the Finns, Churchill explains 'the iron-ore port of Narvik with its railroad over the mountains to the Swedish mines acquired a new sentimental if not strategic significance. . . . I welcomed this new and favourable breeze as a means of achieving the major strategic advantage of cutting off the vital iron-ore supplies of Germany.'

By January, 1940, a recruiting office had been opened in London for British volunteers for Finland, who arrived in Narvik the following month. Rallies were being held all over the country to raise Red Cross aid. Scores of British and French aircraft were arriving in North Finland—in un-numbered packing cases and of unknown vintage! On February 5, the Supreme War Council met in Paris and approved plans for preparing three or four divisions to aid Finland and for persuading Norway and Sweden to allow the passage of supplies. Naturally Norway and Sweden refused to help. The War Council, deciding that the destruction of Finland would be disastrous, formed a plan to replace the volunteers with thirty to forty thousand trained men who were to go to Finland via Narvik.

On his fourth day at the Admiralty, five months earlier, Churchill had asked that a plan for forcing a passage into the Baltic should be prepared by the Naval Staff. If practical, it was to be carried out no later than the following March, with the object of isolating Germany from Scandinavia and intercepting the supplies of iron ore, food and other goods important to the German economy.

Thus, from the start, we find Britain and France planning to interrupt Norway's legitimate foreign trade, the legitimate passage of foreign ships through her territorial waters, to infringe her neutrality and plunge her and her neighbours into destruction—exactly as Quisling had forecast. The pressure from Germany on the one hand and Britain on the other could end only in disaster for Norway, whose fate was decided with the inevitability of a Greek tragedy.

In the First World War the British and American governments had had no scruples about mining the 'Leads', as the sheltered Norwegian territorial waters were called. The great Northern Barrage, which consisted of 181,000 mines and cost £20 million to lay from Scotland to Norway in 1917-18, could not have been fully effective if German commerce and U-boats had only to slip unmolested round its end. The Allied Governments had therefore put the strongest pressure on Norway to close it themselves, which the Norwegian Government eventually did in September 1918.

Twenty-one years later, on September 19, this precedent having

191

been brought to notice, Churchill instructed the First Sea Lord to take all steps to prepare to lay a similar barrage.

On October 3, Grand-Admiral Raeder, at the head of German naval policy, raised with Hitler the question of Norwegian bases for the first time.

Diplomatically Britain and Germany pursued the same line. Dr. Heinrich Sahm, German Minister in Oslo, affirmed on September 3: 'The German Government has, in accordance with the existing friendly relations between Germany and Norway, resolved under no circumstances to encroach on the integrity and inviolability of Norway, and to respect Norwegian territory. . . . Naturally it expects that Norway should maintain indisputable neutrality vis-à-vis Germany and will not tolerate any breach of Norwegian neutrality by another state.'

Cecil Dormer, British Minister, affirmed on September 23: 'In order to avoid misunderstandings, I have the honour to declare, on the orders of my Government, that Norway's neutrality will of course be respected by Great Britain as long as it is respected by Germany.'

The timing of this statement will be noted, as also will the fact that both governments inserted the reservation regarding breaches of Norwegian neutrality, thereby placing a tremendous onus firmly on the Norwegian Government, which had early warning of its responsibilities. The US Ambassador, Mrs. Harriman, recounts in her *Mission to the North*: 'In October, about the time we were in Bergen, a number of British destroyers were sighted skirting the West Coast in territorial waters. Norwegian ships drew alongside and kept edging the visitors towards open sea. The British officer in command called out to the Norwegian commander, as they separated, "All right, but mind you give my love to my cousin, the Crown Prince of Norway." It must have been Captain Lord Louis Mountbatten.'

Real or arguable breaches of neutrality by Britain or Germany accumulated.

Foreign Minister Koht records in *Norway Neutral and Divided*: 'It was at least possible to place on record [nine] cases of evident violation of international law on the part of Germany—wilful sinking of ships without any warning at all or without any attempt to rescue the crew, or sinking of ships bound for neutral ports, e.g. Norway. Such cases became frequent from the middle of January, and the Norwegian Government sent protests to Berlin with judicial evidence. But no answer was received. . . . Other questions regarding the neutrality of Norway arose almost every day. . . . Almost weekly, foreign 'planes were observed inside Norwegian territory.'

In November 1939, came the *City of Flint* affair. This American ship, carrying a cargo for Britain, was captured as a prize by the Germans and taken towards Germany along the Norwegian coast, where she stopped at Haugesund on the 3rd, thus saddling Norway with the right and duty to lay hands upon her. The German officers and crew were interned, and the vessel was allowed on her way, after 'violent menaces' from Berlin. Later the Germans were allowed home, whereas they should have been interned for the duration of the war or awaited an exchange.

Far more serious was the *Altmark* affair of February 16, 1940, although Koht claims that 'the true importance was grossly exaggerated'. After the pocket-battleship *Admiral Graf Spee* had been blown up by her commander in the River Plate on December 17, her 12,000-ton supply ship, which was registered as a warship, was traced off Trondheim on February 15. She was believed to have some 300 British Merchant Navy prisoners on board, and the destroyers *Ivanhoe* and *Intrepid* were instructed by the Admiralty to board her, but she refused to stop and their efforts were frustrated by the Norwegian Navy.

The *Altmark* then entered Jössing Fjord and Captain Philip Vian of H.M.S. *Cossack*, acting on Admiralty instructions, with the agreement of the Foreign Office, demanded from the Norwegian torpedo-boat *Kjell* that the British prisoners be handed over to him. The Norwegians 'refused to co-operate and remained passive'.* Vian thereupon laid the *Cossack* alongside the *Altmark* and boarded her in old style. 299 prisoners were discovered in the holds. The cry of the *Cossack*'s boarding party 'The Navy is here!' rang throughout Britain.

The rights and wrongs can be argued indefinitely. Churchill maintained that the essential point was that British prisoners were found on board. 'Every allowance must be made for the behaviour of the Norwegian Government, which was of course quivering under the German terror. . . .' Neville Chamberlain told Parliament: 'The Norwegian Government see no objection to the use of Norwegian territorial waters for hundreds of miles by a German warship. . . .

* Captain S. W. Roskill in *War at Sea,1939-45* (His Majesty's Stationery Office).

Such a doctrine is at variance with International Law as His Majesty's Government understands it. It would in their view legalise the abuse by German warships of neutral waters and create a position which His Majesty's Government could in no circumstances accept.'

Koht had this to say: 'As the ship had to be acknowledged as a warship, the Norwegian authorities had no right to search it. By an unfortunate misunderstanding the British authorities imagined that the ship had been taken into the port of Bergen and searched there in such a superficial way that the prisoners on board were not detected; in fact, it had only touched the outskirts of the large Bergen area, and it was never searched. . . . In the night of February 16, *Altmark* was boarded. . . . Two small Norwegian torpedo-boats were on the spot, but, in the face of the overwhelming British superiority, they could do no more than protest. . . . The First Lord of the Admiralty, Mr. Winston Churchill, had given special instructions to send out so large a fleet to capture *Altmark* as to make it impossible to accuse Norway of any kind of negligence.

'Evidently the Norwegian Government was by duty bound to protest with the greatest energy against a warlike action performed inside the national frontiers. Finally an agreement was reached upon all the chief and even the minor facts in question, and from the start the British Government declared themselves willing to admit that they had committed a technical violation of Norwegian neutrality and territory. They even expressed their regret. . . . [By April 1] it was already evident that the *Altmark* affair had not created a lasting antagonism between Great Britain and Norway nor led to serious consequences for the conduct of subsequent policy. It was an episode, sensational, but not of far-reaching influence.'

This rosy view seems rather naïve, for the *Altmark* incident was the parting of the way for Britain, Germany and Norway.

It demonstrated that Britain's assurance of September 23 meant what it said—that infringements of Norwegian neutrality by Germany would not be tolerated. It illustrated the impunity with which the Royal Navy could enter Norwegian territorial waters. It also touched off a wave of jingoism in England, which indicated that the nation would back the public outcry for armed intervention in Finland, via Norway and Sweden, which the Government was secretly plotting.

It proved the inability and unwillingness of Norway to protect her vaunted neutrality, which was the basis of her foreign policy and the condition of British and German forbearance towards her.

It was also decisive in Germany. At Keitel's suggestion, on February 20 Hitler urgently summoned General Nikolaus von Falkenhorst* to Berlin from his command of an Army Corps at Coblenz. 'The incident of the *Altmark* no doubt gave spur to action,' says Churchill.

Said Hitler: 'The occupation of Norway by the British would be a strategic turning movement which would lead them into the Baltic, where we have neither troops nor coastal fortifications. The success which we have gained in the east and which we are going to win in the west would be annihilated because the enemy would finish in a position to advance on Berlin and to break the backbone of our two fronts. In the second and third place the conquest of Norway will ensure the liberty of movement of our Fleet in the Bay of Wilhelmshaven, and will protect our imports of Swedish ore. . . . I appoint you to command the expedition.'

The timing and circumstances of Falkenhorst's appointment strongly imply that this date, February 20, was when Hitler finally decided to go ahead with *Weserübung*, although this will always be debated. Churchill puts it at December 14, when Hitler decided to see Quisling, but this seems too early, since Germany's vital interests were in Norwegian neutrality until this lapsed over the *Altmark* and produced Britain's drastic reaction.

There is no point in labouring the moral issue. Technically, all the countries involved, whether from the highest motives or otherwise, were at fault. The whole Norwegian story in relationship to Quisling and the issues at home and abroad in which he found himself at the centre, is about a ruthless, merciless and naked struggle for power at all levels. Quisling was wrong over several aspects of this fight to a finish, but no more so than were his friends or enemies. Exceptional circumstances demanded exceptional measures, and there was no legality left for anybody.

---

* He had taken part in the German intervention in the Finnish Civil War in 1918. Thus he was contemporary with Quisling in Finland. He was from an old Silesian military family named Jastrzembski, which sounded Slavic, and he changed to Falkenhorst ('falcon's eyrie'). This may have appealed to Hitler, who did not hitherto know him. It may also have contributed to Falkenhorst's rivalry with Quisling as a 'Nordic' expert.

Churchill recognised this when he minuted: 'The final tribunal is our conscience. We are fighting to re-establish the reign of law and to protect the liberties of small countries. Our defeat would mean an age of barbaric violence . . . we have a right, and indeed are bound in duty, to abrogate for a space some of the conventions of the very laws we seek to consolidate. . . . The letter of the law must not in supreme emergency obstruct those who are charged with its protection and enforcement. . . . Humanity, rather than legality, must be our guide.'

Quisling at least had the foresight to anticipate the inevitability of Norway's involvement in the struggle. The astonishing thing is that, despite the proven defeatism and pacifism of the Norwegian Government, it could apparently remain oblivious to these mighty developments on its doorstep.

The great Soviet offensive on Finland opened on the Karelian Isthmus on February 1, and within a fortnight the so-called 'Mannerheim Line' was breached. By March, Mannerheim's defence system was disorganised. He had been making secret overtures to the Russians since January, but now things were desperate and rumours of capitulation were rife. A top-secret personal telegram from Chamberlain to Mannerheim, promising massive aid in men and material, had gone astray between London and the British Legation wireless receiver in the forest, and Mannerheim sent a secret peace delegation to Moscow—not knowing that Britain and France were in earnest. (By such miracles do we survive. Otherwise Britain and France would in all probability have found themselves at war with Russia as well as Germany, and gone under.) Mercifully for all concerned, Mannerheim made peace with Russia on March 12, on harsher terms than could have been obtained before the invasion, but Finland survived, unlike the Baltic States, as an independent country—thanks to foresight and guts.

That is widely supposed to have been the end of British designs on the North until the German invasion of Norway, ordered by Hitler on April 2, sailed forth on the 7th and entered Norwegian territorial waters at 11 p.m. on the 8th.

The popular legend has taken hold that an altruistic Anglo-French force rushed to rescue innocent little Norway from brutal and unprovoked Nazi aggression. Quisling, the alleged conspirator in this atrocity, saboteur and puppet-elect, has of course come in for his full share of abuse and become the major figure in the legend, because a traitor is rightly considered to be exceptionally vile.

The legend is false, however; Quisling had no part in the invasion at any stage; and as to unprovoked aggression, the Norwegian Government had already proved incapable of honouring the foundation of its foreign policy, its duty to the belligerents and the first interest of the Norwegian people—namely the maintenance of strict neutrality. That omission alone gave Britain and Germany the right in international law to take the necessary measures to protect their vital interests, namely to use force, if necessary.

How could Germany in any case have ignored the public statements of the British and French leaders, their press and their peoples' demands regarding an intervention in Finland, which could go only through Norway, Petsamo being in Soviet hands? Germany could not have been ignorant of the massive troop movements, the embarkations and disembarkations, the flood of diplomatic messages, the scurrying of secret agents, the arrival of arms, and the transit through Narvik of British volunteers for Finland.

Was Germany to accept that the Finnish peace of March 12 marked the end of the advanced British and French preparations for intervention through Scandinavia; that the assembled Anglo-French forces would all be disbanded; that aid for Finland was the genuine Allied motive and not a blind for severing Germany from her naval and mineral lifeline; that the Allies would abandon their historical and topical objectives; that the French would prefer to fight another war on their own soil, rather than in the North? Hitler would have been irresponsible as well as naïve if he had entertained any such illusions.

What exactly the Allies were up to is even today not entirely clear. The official records, the memoirs and histories are confusing and much has been written to sustain the legend of injured innocence. It is attractive to portray the self-styled idealism of the victors in contrast to the alleged crimes of the losers, but in truth the issues were not so black and white.

The defeat of Finland was fatal to the Daladier Government in France. Churchill welcomed the appointment of the new French Premier, Paul Reynaud, since they had been in agreement over Munich. The new French Ministers came to London for a Supreme War Council a week after Daladier's fall, and Reynaud was quick to agree that cutting off supplies of Swedish iron ore from Germany would be fatal to the German output of iron and steel. It was agreed to lay mines in Norwegian territorial waters and obstruct ore exports from Luleå to Germany. It was also agreed, in Churchill's words, that 'a British brigade and a French contingent should be sent to Narvik to clear the port and advance to the Swedish frontier. Other forces should be dispatched to Stavanger, Bergen, and Trondheim, in order to deny these bases to the enemy.'

In plain language, Britain and France decided to occupy Norway before the German invasion sailed, and were only prevented from doing so because the Germans won the race.

When a German squadron was sighted steering in the direction of Trondheim on the forenoon of April 8, Allied troops were already embarked themselves for Trondheim, as also for Bergen and Stavanger. A sabotage group drawn from all three services was established at the British Consulate in Stavanger, under Colonel Malcolm Munthe, in order to seize the only airport where fighter-aircraft could then operate between Britain and Norway (presumably with Norwegian connivance), and Flying-Officer Willard Whitney Straight of 601 Squadron was embarked on HMS *Devonshire* in Scotland to reinforce the group. Admiral Lord Mountevans hoisted his flag on the cruiser HMS *Aurora* on April 4th and, says his biographer Reginald Pound, 'on April 9th he was ordered to haul down his flag. As the mountains of Norway showed through the dawn mist of the morning of April 10th he went down to his cabin and cried'. Our forces were disembarked, and the scheme to occupy Narvik was similarly abandoned. The Allies had been pipped at the post.

The whole myth of unprovoked aggression by Germany should be abandoned. It is incredible, and does grievous injustice to the 'quislings' who are quite wrongly alleged to have engineered the German Occupation. There is no truth in this sinister legend.

This falsification of history has served also to excuse the Chamberlain Government from monumental political and military blunders in the North in 1939-40, and at the same time to divert part of the blame from the Norwegian Government, which provoked both Allied and German invasions by their own incompetence, if not by their actual abandonment of neutrality and their connivance at the prepared Allied intervention.

17

Abhorred Vacuum

BY the afternoon of April 9, 1940, the worst had happened to Norway, as Quisling had long prophesied in books, newspapers and speeches and to patriotic societies, alone in the wilderness of Norwegian party politics. Little Norway had become the battlefield of the Great Powers. The Bolshevik Army had advanced across Finland and was poised, victorious, on the Norwegian frontier. Britain had mined Norwegian territorial waters and had declared her intention of defending the barrage by force. The Germans were already in possession of Oslo, the capital and predominant city, besides every key naval base and aerodrome from Narvik southwards.

The manner in which the Norwegian authorities reacted before, during and immediately after the event explains Quisling's historic initiative that evening.

Apart from the temptation and danger of Norway's exposed position to the embattled nations around her, and the constant belligerent activity on her threshold, the Norwegians had ample warning of a British and/or German invasion in April, with the added risk of Russia joining the fray to protect her strategic interests in north Norway.

As the US Ambassador, Mrs. Harriman, says: 'There were plenty of people who, in memoir fashion, could repeat the remarks of German officers who would say, "the mistake of the last war was that the High Command did not take Norway at once and use it as a base to break the blockade"! The Norwegian policy did not start with that in mind.'

Koht admits that the Norwegian Legation in Berlin reported on April 5 that a German fleet had been ordered against Norway, but he was 'sceptical' and felt the country was 'reasonably well guarded'. This tip, as Koht does not say in his book, came from Ulrich Stang,* First Secretary in the Legation, who was warned by the Dutch Military Attaché, Col. J. G. Sass, at meetings in the Adlon Hotel between April 2 and 4. Sass, in turn, had been warned by none other than Colonel (later Major-General) Hans Oster, chief assistant to Admiral Canaris in the *Abwehr* (the High Command's Intelligence Service), both of whom were by this time conspiring against Hitler. Nobody was to know, outside the *Abwehr*, of Oster's motives, but he was nevertheless a source of staggering importance.

Koht recalls that he did not take alarm because the Navy was patrolling Oslo Fjord from Horten, its chief naval base; because coastal forts were manned; artillery was installed at specific points; local troops were mobilised from Narvik to Kirkenes; and around Kristiansand and Stavanger in the far south special units were under arms. 'Until just before the invasion there seemed to be no need for a general mobilisation. There was good reason to believe the country was comparatively well protected against aggression from the south. As to the western and northern parts of the country, it might be thought that the British fleet, operating in the North Sea and even farther North, would be able to prevent any attack coming from Germany.'

Such was the policy of 'unarmed neutrality', which on Koht's admission was not neutrality at all. As for being 'comparatively well protected', the available Norwegian forces were of course insignificant and antiquated.

To understand how any Minister of the Crown could be so deceived, one has only to read Mrs. Harriman's description of him: 'Veritably Norwegian in his sense of a single standard. He wanted to know what was right and then to do it. To rationalise evil was to him to double the evil. Long Professor of History at Oslo University, he had piercing brown eyes, grey hair and grey moustache. Twenty-five thousand

---

* Stang's adherence to NS was widely known at this time and was not held against him by the Norwegian Foreign Office, and his warning is corroborative evidence that Quisling and his followers were patriotic.

volumes lay on his dining-room floor, across which guests picked their way carefully.' He was just not a realist.

He even recalls that the 'Germans themselves gave a kind of warning in the way peculiar to them'. On April 5 the German Minister, Dr. Curt Brauer, invited Norwegian Ministers and General Staff Officers to see a 'peace film'. It was a formal affair and the guests, including 'all the bureau chiefs' of the Government departments and high-ranking officers, according to Mrs. Harriman, were treated to a 'horror film'. This was a documentary of the bombing of Warsaw. Naturally the company was alarmed, as was obviously intended. Explained Brauer: 'These pictures are peace propaganda. They proved to all witnesses what happens to a country that resists National-Socialist attempts to defend it from England.'

On April 8, between 4.30 and 5 a.m., four British destroyers laid three minefields without warning and apparently without detection off the entrance to West Fjord, the channel for Narvik iron ore. At 5 a.m. the news was broadcast from London, also without warning to the Norwegian Government. At 5.30 a.m. Sir Cecil Dormer, the British Minister, handed a note to Koht stating that the Allies felt entitled to take appropriate action to prevent Germany from obtaining through Norway resources vital to her prosecution of the war, the justification being 'lawful retaliation for deliberate German violations of international law and international rights'. The note also stipulated that if Norway tried to remove the mines, Britain would stop the clearance by force. Exactly twenty-four hours later Brauer was to get Koht out of bed again and use the same language.

Later on April 8 the Norwegian Government demanded that Britain remove the mines within forty-eight hours, or the Norwegian Navy would do so, which would have meant war, since Britain had already stated that she would intervene. This was therefore no more than a paper protest, as Quisling justly pointed out in due course.

Whether or not the Norwegians carried out their idle threat against Britain, the Germans could not be expected to sit back and watch. They were bound to try to remove the mines, which implied hostilities against Norway if she resisted.

Either way Norway was bound to be embattled. This suited England, as Churchill obviously calculated. If Norway forgot her retaliatory threat and helped to defend the minefield, she would become a British ally. If Norway stuck to her guns and collaborated with Germany in sweeping the minefield, Britain would have a pretext for occupying the country. The loser in either case would be Norway.

When it came down to hard assessment of which ghastly alternative Norway would choose, the betting was heavily on Norway forgetting her scruples and siding with Britain. But in fact Norway adopted neither course, and simply did absolutely nothing, as anybody who knew that dreamy country might have expected.

Norway's pigeons had at last come home to roost. Even at this eleventh hour the Norwegian Government could not face stark reality and the consequences of its long and feckless policy. Perhaps, at dawn on April 8, there was still a remote chance of forestalling a German invasion by inviting in the assembled Anglo-French forces, but this departure was never even considered.

The Norwegian Right was as inactive as the Left. The dominant figure on the Right, Carl Joachim Hambro, had for many years been President of the *Storting* and as such second in precedence to the King; he was President of the League of Nations in December 1939, when Russia was excluded from the League. 'Carl Hambro,' says Mrs. Harriman, 'was a man of Europe and of the world as well as Norway, a worker for the League of Nations, aware of religious developments throughout the world, for a time a pillar of the Buchman Movement, since he saw in it a way of orientation to modern living.' He was also a loyal member of the distinguished banking family, who came to London from Denmark in the first half of the nineteenth century and founded one of the largest merchant banking businesses in the world.

A man of such international connections was hardly one to fight for a strong independent Norway. He regarded *Nasjonal Samling* as a dangerous movement and had actually stated that Quisling and his programme constituted a case for medical investigation.

He and Koht agree that almost the whole of April 8 was occupied with discussion of the British minelaying, as though there was no danger of the British seizing the bases they had sought or of the Germans intervening forcibly.

At 9 a.m. the Chief of the General Staff, Colonel Rasmus L. Hatledal, contacted the Defence Minister, Colonel Ljungberg, proposing mobilisation, but he could get no decision.

Yet from 10 a.m., according to Derry, 'messages began to flow in from Sweden and Denmark reporting the enormous procession of German ships northwards through the Great Belt and the Kattegat'. What was the Norwegian Navy doing? Certainly it was never sent to sea to investigate.

At noon the Polish submarine *Orzel* torpedoed the German transport *Rio de Janeiro* off Kristiansand in the south. German soldiers were rescued by a Norwegian destroyer and fishing boats. The survivors stated that they were on their way to Bergen 'to protect it against the Allies'. News reached the Norwegian Admiralty at 3 p.m., and was reported in the Oslo afternoon newspapers. It was dismissed as 'a strange story' by Koht, who continued to protest to Britain about the minelaying. Hambro surmised from this 'astounding story' that it was 'rather amusing evidence of the willingness of the German people to believe anything'.

Also at noon, the Commander-in-Chief, General Kristian Laake, and Colonel Hatledal called on Ljungberg, again proposing mobilisation, but were informed that the Defence Ministry could not raise more than two battalions.

By 5.15 p.m. the Divisional Commander at Kristiansand, General Liljedahl, had reported to Oslo that German troops had been landed at Lillesand from the torpedoed *Rio de Janeiro* and very shortly he confirmed that she was 'indubitably military in character'.

'The ominous portent of this story did not strike the members of the *Storting*,' says Hambro, when it assembled at 5.15 to approve the minelaying protest to London.

The Kristiansand reports were relayed to London, and, as the *Stortingsmen* were assembling, the Norwegian Legation in London telephoned that a German attack on Narvik was anticipated from 10 p.m. onwards. A telegram documenting the British Admiralty's information followed very shortly.

'Still more disquieting' was Koht's reaction. 'When the Government was able to meet in the evening . . . it was decided to call to arms the battalions that could be mobilised easily on the east side of Oslo Fjord . . . the west side seemed sufficiently protected. . . . A general mobilisation, it was stated, would take three days to become effective.'

Actually only two battalions were called up and the General Staff Officers were told to go home!

At 9.15 p.m. 'the decisions were adopted', says Koht. Exactly what this means is unclear. General mobilisation was certainly not announced at that time in any form, and there is little evidence of any serious last-minute action.

At 11.6 p.m. the Norwegian patrol-boat *Pol III* challenged German ships entering the mouth of Oslo Fjord. The challenge was ignored, and the Commander gallantly rammed a German torpedo-boat and went to the bottom—one of the isolated redeeming acts. At once the Chief of Naval Staff reported that German warships were passing Ferder, the island marking the limit of territorial waters, but still the Government took no action.

At about this hour King Haakon and the General Staff were breaking up after a lecture on 'Gastronomy in Ancient Rome'. As he left, he remarked: 'What a lot of food! I shall have an awful night.'

Just before 12.30 a.m. on April 9 an air alarm sounded and Koht says: 'Most people thought as I did, that this was just a test signal . . . but the sirens continued and I began to suspect the danger was serious.'

After some difficulty on the telephone, because the operators were in shelters, he managed to get through to the Foreign Office at 12.45 a.m. and was told that coastal forts inside the Oslo Fjord, at Bolaerne and Rauer, had opened fire on foreign warships, which were able to enter the fjord because a British Naval Attaché had requested on April 8 that no mines should be laid there! To let the British in?

Suddenly, says Koht, 'it flashed upon me that the Germans were making a dash to capture Oslo'.

He could not get a taxi to return to the Foreign Office, with his pyjamas and toothbrush, because of the air alarm. He stumbled through the blackout and reached his desk at about 1 a.m. By 1.30 a.m. the entire Government had managed to reach the Foreign Office and, according to Koht, 'they were informed that it was impossible to determine the nationality of the warships entering Oslo Fjord owing to the darkness. . . . We followed their advance from hour to hour until they were quite near to the chief fortress, Oscarsborg.'

The Government frittered away two hours before it could steel itself to reach even a half-hearted decision on mobilisation.

'We were determined at least to put up all possible resistance,' says Koht, 'and the first thing decided at the Government meeting was the full mobilisation of the Army . . . orders to that effect were given straight away to the military commands, and from these they were sent out by telegraph and telephone to all parts of the country.' As Derry points out however: 'Even then the Government's decision was for a partial and unproclaimed mobilisation—the call-up to be by post, with Thursday, the 11th, as the first day on which troops were to present themselves.' Certainly the Press and Radio were not used.

Nothing more was heard of mobilisation for another crucial four hours when the Government abandoned Oslo to its own devices and the Germans. As Derry says, in 'a chance interview with the Foreign Minister at 7.30 a.m. he spoke of general mobilisation, but when those concerned presented themselves they found they were not expected'. Any orders that may have reached commanders were meaningless. No amount of pretence can show that Norway was ever mobilised or on a war footing until Germany declared war after the British had returned a fortnight later.

The whole mobilisation story was a near-invention. It could never have amounted to more than a lame political gesture and was denounced by the General Staff at the earliest opportunity. The only importance it ever had was as an instrument for impugning Quisling. He sensibly adopted the same line as the General Staff. At no time did the government or the King ever order Norwegians to *fight*, although they frequently exhorted the country to 'continue the struggle' or to 'be Norwegian', and the like.

At 2.06 a.m. 'we were told that foreign warships were steaming in past the outer forts of Bergen and it was stated with certainty that the ships were German', as Koht puts it. In fact the Norwegian Admiralty had reported an actual attack on Bergen.

This marks the first moment when the Foreign Minister admits that he and the Government knew that a German invasion was in progress —the implication being that it was then too late to mobilise and that therefore the authorities were guiltless.

Surely the Government *must* have been hoping against hope that the intruders were British, and in fact have been expecting the British to forestall the Germans all along? Surely that was the basis of the policy of 'unarmed neutrality'? If so, the pretence of real neutrality is a sham.

At 2.35 a.m. Koht telephoned Cecil Dormer, exclaiming 'So now we are at war!'—a tell-tale phrase, obviously designed to provoke the British Minister into some statement of solidarity and common defence measures with the country which up to a few hours previously had

205

been protesting to Britain. Dormer however brushed aside Koht's naïve assertions that 'Oslo defences were strong enough for the Government to remain there'.

That was Koht's ghastly moment of truth—the collapse of half a lifetime of muddled thinking and self-deception, which had brought his country and its irresponsible people to calamity in a friendless and predatory world. 'We were all profoundly struck,' he records, 'by the terrible fact before us; Little Norway attacked without warning by a Great Power. Our peaceful country suddenly at war!'

Hambro saw the dilemma thus: 'What we are witnessing today is not a fight for a place in the sun or political supremacy in Europe and on the seven seas. . . . It is a war between two different codes of honour. . . . The whole structure of Christian civilisation is threatened by waves of moral leprosy, far more destructive than waves of bombers.'

In that case what was Norway doing, pretending to be neutral, with her foreign policy as a 'national affair' on neither one side nor the other? Norway was embroiled in a struggle for power, and not in a philosophical discussion. However, this argument served to excuse himself, the government and the Norwegian people from the responsibility which they had so grievously failed to discharge. It served also to smear Quisling, who had alone seen the situation clearly.

At 3.20 a.m. it was reported that two warships had passed the Agdanes Forts and were steaming into Trondheim Fjord.

At 5.20 a.m. according to Koht's calculations, or between 4.30 and 5 a.m. according to Hambro, who was not present, Koht received the German Minister, who handed him a nineteen-page document, which contained the crucial words: 'The German Government therewith takes over the protection of the Kingdom of Norway during this war . . . to defend peace in Norway against an Anglo-French attack and to safeguard it indefinitely. . . . It is therefore in no hostile spirit that German troops enter Norwegian territory. The German High Command does not intend to use points occupied by German troops as bases for operations in the fight against England unless it is compelled by British and French measures to do so. The sole aim of the German military operations is to protect the North against the intended occupation of bases in Norway by Anglo-French forces. The German Government are convinced that in taking this action they are at the same time serving the interests of Norway. For the protection afforded by the German forces represents the only guarantee that the Scandinavian peoples can have that their countries will not even yet, in the course of this war, be made a battlefield.'

Brauer spoke of the terrible consequences to Norway of a 'foolish resistance'. Practical requirements were the surrender of all military establishments—the Norwegian troops to keep their arms if they co-operated—and all communications and information services.

'I had no doubt that to comply with this demand would mean war with Great Britain,' says Koht. 'I remembered very well that, in September, the British Minister had said to me on behalf of his Government that Great Britain would regard an attack on Norway as an attack on herself. . . . We had no wish to see it [the British offer] transferred into a treaty. I was conscious that nevertheless help would come.'

Cannot Quisling be excused for believing, after that statement, that there was an understanding somewhere along the line between the British and Norwegian authorities?

Hambro had been awakened at 1 a.m. Unlike Koht, he now acted realistically. At 1.30 a.m. he telephoned *Morgenbladet*, of which he had been editor during 1913-20 and was still Chairman. He also telephoned the Norwegian Telegram Bureau, the news agency of which he was ex-Chairman, but it was impossible to get through until 2 a.m. because 'the whole staff had been in the air-raid shelter'—before a bomb had been dropped! Between 2 and 2.15 a.m. he contacted the Prime Minister and the Foreign Office, at which time, as he puts it, he reflected: 'Our Army was not mobilised. We were absolutely un-prepared to meet the attack.'

This was his terrible awakening—the exposure of his faith in the League of Nations, and of his 'national affair', which had passed for a foreign policy. It was also an exposure of Moral Rearmament's theory that 'morals' exert influence in power politics. Quisling's policy of the last ten years was now seen to have its point, whereas his own life's work was collapsing around him.

'The only thing to do was to move out of Oslo,' he records. There was no pretence of offering resistance, of calling out the troops to fight. No call was put through to London to seek immediate help, nor at the time had British help been offered. Nobody was left behind with any authority to protect the nation in its hour of deadly need. Not a word was said over the radio to the baffled population. No guidance appeared in the newspapers. No arrangements were made for carrying on the public services. No effort was made to extract some crumbs of relief from a hopeless situation by leaving somebody behind to argue with the Germans.

Hambro rounded up the King and Royal Family, the entire Government, the entire General Staff and all but four of the 150 Members of Parliament, and bundled them into the wilderness—to Hamar, the nineteenth city, if such it can be called, in Norway, which was actually a small country town of 10,200 inhabitants—thus following the instinct of every Norwegian to 'get away from it all'. At 11.10 p.m. on April 10, the King in Council at last spoke over the feeble Hamar Radio and reached a fraction of the Norwegian population. Even then he did not mention *fighting* the Germans.

What many might regard as a dereliction of duty has since been represented as an act of statesmanship. Says Hambro: 'If the King and the Royal Family, the Government and Parliament should be taken by surprise, Norway would not only be at the mercy of the Germans but would cease to be a sovereign state with an independent government . . . Hamar, 100 miles inland from Oslo, seemed the only reasonable place for the *Storting* to meet. It is a great centre for communications . . . and if the worst should happen, from Hamar several roads led into Sweden.'

Norway was of course already at the mercy of the Germans, as their occupation of all key places, the failure properly to mobilise the Norwegian Forces, the omission to order a fight, the flight of all the authorities and the absence of any guidance to the nation proved.

Hambro's reference to several roads leading into Sweden is highly significant, for in fact the King and Royal Family, Hambro himself and other members of the government, as well as thousands of panic-stricken Norwegians, proceeded there within a few days. His insistence on Hamar's good communications and accessibility to Sweden indicates that he had flight into Sweden in the forefront of his mind. Notably, no suggestion of fighting the Germans from Hamar occurs in his recollections of this historical decision to flee Oslo.

Quisling and others assumed, in the absence of information to the contrary, that the authorities were Sweden-bound, and he can be excused for thinking that they had left the country in the lurch. To him this seemed an act of abnegation almost unparalleled in modern history.

From 7.30 a.m. on April 9, 1940, when all the Norwegian authorities from the King downwards fled helter-skelter,* the official Norwegian Government had no more than a marginal and distant nuisance value for the Germans for the next five years.

Quisling—like the Germans—stepped into a vacuum.

II

There is no dispute as to the German plan for Norway. It was to occupy bases in the interest of German security and supplies of iron ore. This necessitated control of communications, and involved censorship. Only token resistance was expected from the Armed Forces, the King and the existing government. Surprise was the keynote and the Allies were not expected to interfere. An overwhelming force was deployed.

The plan assumed the presence of a King and government who would acquiesce to *force majeure*, and no arrangements were made in case they vanished. Any fleeting idea of installing a puppet pro-German government had been abandoned in December, when Quisling disabused Hitler of Rosenberg's proposition to this effect. Neither Quisling nor any other Norwegian was intended, earmarked or nominated for the role of puppet. Only the ignorant, or the prejudiced, can maintain the contrary in the light of present evidence, and no serious Norwegian historian now believes otherwise.

Essentially the plan was the same as that Britain would have had to operate if she had invaded Norway—with the difference that the Germans' prime object was defensive. Hitler was preparing the invasion of the West, and the last thing he wanted was a major

---

* Koht has an interesting note on the flight: 'Thanks to the well-considered plans of the chief archivist of the Foreign Office, it proved possible to remove the most important secret papers of this office, filling three lorries. Nobody could take along more of his private property than he could carry in a suitcase; in fact that was all they had during all the following months.' So at least someone had had the foresight to anticipate the possibility of the need for evacuation. How odd then that the Foreign Minister was taken so completely by surprise. It should be noted too that Oscar Torp, the Finance Minister, managed to smuggle the Gold Reserve to England.

campaign in the North, on his exposed flank. It was not until March 3 that *Weserübung* was given priority over an attack on the West.

The British intention was to force Norway and Sweden on to the Allied side, to deprive Germany of the Leads and iron ore, and to use the North as a general battlefield instead of Flanders, thus outflanking Germany and exposing her lightly guarded rear. This strongly appealed to the French, who jibbed at any such mildly offensive action as 'Royal Marine' (dropping fluvial mines in the Rhine) which would have involved the possibility of retaliation.

The Germans tried in vain to impress on Norway that, looked at dispassionately, a German occupation was preferable to an Anglo-French one. Hitler understood his 'Nordic' Norwegians, however, less well even than did the British. The betting was on the Norwegians having to bow to force, but they nonplussed the Germans as much as they did the British.

Norwegians are unaccountable. The only certainty is that they will not be pushed around by friend or foe, British, German, Scandinavian or NATO. Motivated more by emotion than reason, they will always try to avoid facts. They will in any case always do things differently from anybody else, and will never admit they are wrong. This national characteristic lies at the root of the national tragedy. It may have a certain charm and grandeur, and may even produce results on occasion; but it involves a haphazard attitude towards the affairs of a nation.

This Norwegian irrationality saved the German invasion at noon on April 8, when nobody in Oslo believed that the German troops rescued from the torpedoed transport, *Rio de Janeiro*, were, as was claimed, on the way to 'save' Norway from the Allies. Likewise there was no accounting for the fantastic initiative of two elderly and obscure Norwegian junior officers who sent the flagship of the invasion force to the bottom, with most of its complement and all the occupation documents, thus retarding the subjection of Oslo by from six to ten hours.

It is one of the most amazing stories of the Second World War, and curiously has never been fully described. The sinking of the flagship gave the Norwegian authorities an unpredictable opportunity of stemming the invasion, or at any rate of exploiting the Germans' predicament, but nobody was at hand to seize it. The authorities had given themselves no chance of utilising the unexpected that always happens in war. Incredibly the hero of the sinking was subsequently treated by the Norwegian authorities as a traitor, and died in obscurity in 1959, aged 74!

The episode also dispels the common illusion that the German invasion was an invincible masterstroke in conception and execution. It was nothing of the sort. The British and German invasion plans were both monumental muddles, comparable with the inefficiency of the Norwegians' own precautions.

Weserübung was strictly a High Command operation, under the military and political control of Falkenhorst, in view of his Finnish Civil War background. He remained at headquarters in Hamburg, in touch with Berlin by courier and telephone, and with Norway by the Legation radio and telephone—a precarious line of communication.

His field commander was General Erwin von Engelbrecht—another good old 'Nordic' or 'Angle' name—on board the brand-new, 10,000-ton heavy cruiser, *Blücher*, with Rear-Admiral Oskar Kunmetz, commanding the invasion squadron. This flagship was supposed to reach the quayside at the vast, rectangular red-brick City Hall in Oslo not later than 4 a.m.—an hour and three-quarters after the Legation staff had assembled in readiness to co-operate in taking over the capital.

No arrangements were made in case Engelbrecht failed to show up. Then the *Blücher* went down. Its fate was the first major surprise of the day, in turn producing the second—the sudden emergence of Quisling. The two events together have coloured Norwegian history ever since.

Another immediate consequence was that Curt Brauer suddenly found he had to act on his own. Engelbrecht had not appeared by 5 a.m., when the Minister had to present the German terms to Foreign Minister Koht, and he had no alternative instructions in case the invasion was delayed. So now there was a German vacuum and Brauer, a true bureaucrat, stuck to his outdated brief, hoping for the best, encouraged by exhilarating news from other ports and gunfire down Oslo Fjord.

Brauer was unprepared by nationality, training and temperament for such an emergency. The invasion was not in accordance with his own concept of Norway's standing, which he believed was as genuinely neutral as could be expected. This view was shared by Ribbentrop,

Baron von Weizsäcker ('the brains of the Foreign Office' and ex-Minister in Oslo) and Werner von Grundler, head of the Northern Department, all of whom cold-shouldered the intervention from the start and especially Rosenberg's interference in it.

Political aspects of the invasion were not documented until February 26. Hitler did not give the North priority over the West until March 3 and *Weserübung* was not stationed at the ready until March 26. Ribbentrop was only informed of zero hour on April 2, the day Hitler set the operation in motion. Nobody thus had proper time to thrash out the political problems. On the same day Brauer was simply handed the terms he was to present to Koht, and told to put himself at the disposal of the High Command. Ribbentrop otherwise wiped his hands of the whole operation, which explains his uncontrolled fury when the loss of the *Blücher* and Quisling's intervention suddenly brought the Foreign Office into the forefront of the picture on April 9.

Later on April 2, Brauer had a word with Falkenhorst, but was not informed of zero hour. His only instructions from the High Command were to keep a watch on the King lest he should escape and form an alternative government. Brauer was given no agents, however, to apprehend the monarch, and, when the time came to seize him, Engelbrecht was not at hand. Brauer in any case had no time to improvise a kidnapping. He was only briefed on zero hour by Lieutenant-Colonel Pohlman late on the night of April 8, five hours before Engelbrecht was due in Oslo. Nor yet was there anybody in the Legation on whom he could rely to help him. Only the Naval and Air Attachés knew that an invasion was planned and neither of them knew when, until the legation briefing at 2.45 a.m. Most important, he lacked the support of an organised fifth column.

Hitler, Keitel and Falkenhorst were so confident of their own daring that they anticipated no surprises. They foresaw a 'friendly occupation' and a 'peaceful solution'. Troops at all levels were briefed accordingly, and pains were taken to include in the attack as many Norwegian-speaking men as possible. The Army only sought to be 'correct'. It expected to function 'in agreement with the Royal Norwegian Government'.

Any fighting was expected to be over quickly and then the High Command would hand over political matters to Minister Brauer. The situation in Norway would return to normal, except that Germany's military and industrial interests would be safeguarded by the *Wehrmacht* on the spot.

No allowance was made for a long hiatus between the occupation and a return to normalcy. It was not deemed necessary to go into details of the re-adjustment until the military first phase was completed and the situation clarified. What would happen if there were no swift clarification was not considered.

It was of course recognised that complete Norwegian co-operation could not be expected. Some functionaries in the government administration, public services and utilities, the police and even in the *Storting* might prove recalcitrant. There was also the danger of espionage, sabotage and insurrection, organised by Allied agents and their Norwegian associates. The only practical step adopted therefore was to embark a large administrative and security force on the *Blücher* in case of unpleasant emergencies. All of them went down with their documents, the blueprint for the occupation, when the flagship was sunk. So neither the High Command, when at last its members arrived, nor Brauer, on the spot, knew what they were supposed to do in such a crisis. Poor Brauer found himself filling a vacuum, like Quisling, and within a fortnight he was dismissed and sent to the front. Between them, these two men, who had done more than anybody to avoid war, were made everybody's scapegoats.

By 7.30 a.m. the Germans were therefore in as big a fix as the Norwegian Government. They were out on a limb, having delivered an ultimatum with nothing to back it up—no troops, no fifth column and only a few prestige bombers overhead. (Göring was not one of the principals in this operation, which was against his pro-Scandinavian inclinations, and he was reserving his Luftwaffe for the West.)

If the Norwegians had placed Brauer under house arrest, mobilised all available men in Oslo, blocked the airport, told the supernumerary population over the radio at 6 a.m. to take to their beloved log-cabins, the government might at least have bargained or even earned Allied aid. They would anyway have saved their dignity. But Norwegians do not think like that. As it turned out, not a bomb was ever dropped, not a shot was ever fired and not a German soldier was seen in Oslo for another eight hours!

In this context, it is interesting to note the details of what one Norwegian with an ounce of guts actually managed to do.

From 1930 to 1940 Lieutenant August Bonsak had been an artillery instructor. From March 1940, he was second in command of three 1892 Krupp 25cm. guns at Oscarsborg, the Crimean War fortress, fifteen miles down the fjord from Oslo, on which Koht 'pinned hopes'. One of these guns was affectionately known as 'Moses', having fallen into the sea when it was hoisted into position in 1900. Its fellows were therefore known as 'Aaron' and 'Joshua'.

On April 1, fifty of the seventy-strong garrison were posted elsewhere, and six days later were replaced by twenty-five raw recruits. Next day, when Britain mined Norwegian waters, the commandant, Colonel Birger Eriksen, telephoned Bonsak to 'fire as soon as there is something to fire at', but stipulated that the alarm should not be sounded by a trumpeter 'so as not to frighten the recruits'.

Bonsak showed them how the museum-pieces worked. That night he placed Ensign Høye in charge of range-finding and of the telephone to Captain Sødem, the commanding officer; Sergeant Raekken, in charge of 'Moses'; Sergeant Strøm in charge of 'Aaron'; and himself at 'Joshua'—none of them being trained gunners, except himself.

At approximately 3 a.m. a dark shadow appeared in the range-finder at 1,400 metres which Bonsak cross-checked. Then he sprang to 'Moses', aimed and fired a 345-kilogram shell, which hit the deck of the oncoming warship. He next sprang to 'Aaron', fired and hit the vessel amidships at the waterline. There was then a terrific explosion and a blinding flash that lit up the countryside.

The brand-new *Blücher*, flagship of the German invasion, was doomed: all 10,000 tons of her, 1,600 men, including the administrative staff for the occupation, and the whole timing of *Weserübung*.

Commodore-Captain Anders Anderssen, aged 61 and retired, who had shown up at Oscarsborg the day before to 'do his bit', finished her off. Not for nothing was he widely known as 'The Finger', because he could pull up his whole weight on one finger. What is more his aim was unerring. He fired one 150-kilogram torpedo (Model 15) at the blazing hulk, and down she went. (Luckily the 100-kilogram model had been replaced the previous year, otherwise the *Blücher*'s armour would not have been penetrated.)

This was a mighty naval victory—the outstanding triumph achieved by Norwegian forces, under their own command, during the entire war.

One would have thought that Bonsak would become a national hero. We are dealing, however, with Norway, the land of dreams. After the war, instead of compensation for the loss of all his personal belongings under German counter-fire, Bonsak was forbidden to wear Norwegian uniform. He was also condemned, for 'economic treason', because after the Norwegian capitulation he worked—in common with 146,000 other Norwegians—as a labourer for the Germans. He happened to be a member of *Nasjonal Samling*, and had committed the unforgivable Norwegian sin of doing the right thing in the right way and exposing the ineptitude of his superiors.

The Germans were more generous. When Bonsak was working at a camp at Ørland, the commander called him in to meet a visiting general, saying: 'May I present the Norwegian lieutenant who cost Germany 165 million golden Reichmarks—and our proud ship *Blücher!*'

The Norwegians imprisoned him, took away his pension and allowed him to die in poverty and disgrace—the one man who might have saved the day, if anybody in the government had had the vision and courage to follow up his feat.

He was the second man who made sense on April 9. The first was Ulrich Stang, who had given the hottest invasion tip. Yet both were so-called 'Nazis'! The third man was Vidkun Quisling.

III

By 7.30 a.m. on April 9, 1940, there was no effective government in Norway. Twelve hours later, at 7.32 p.m., Quisling went on the air and assumed the position of Prime Minister. The case against him stands or falls on what happened during those twelve vital hours.

If Vidkun Quisling was not a Nazi, not a conspirator against his own country, not a German puppet and not a party to the German invasion, why did he suddenly step into the breach? This is the central question of the Quisling controversy, for if he was not a traitor when he broadcast, he was never guilty of high treason.

If he did not commit high treason on April 9, the rest of his career is only an epilogue. His subsequent mistakes, compromises, errors of judgement and acts of weakness were open to censure, but not to a charge of treason.

His actions in the days immediately before April 9 have, therefore, to be examined closely.

To begin with, he had been laid up for two months with a kidney complaint, contracted long before in Russia, which greatly increased his weight and would have landed most men, with weaker physique and less determination, in bed. He had, therefore, been less active than usual. What kept him going was growing anxiety about his country's predicament. However, he was well enough to travel to Copenhagen on April 3 and to take the greatest decision of his life on the 9th, so there is no pleading illness in extenuation of any mistakes he made, and he never did so himself. It can be said that he was slightly below par, which is a consideration because the relationship between health and judgement is often underrated.

On March 22, Dr. Aall and Walther de Laporte visited Oslo. Quisling was not to know that the object of de Laporte and the *Abwehr* and its influential, far-flung backers in the *Wehrmacht*, big business and intellectual circles, was anti-Hitler and that they were using *Nasjonal Samling* to build up goodwill for Germany against the day when Hitler was assassinated or Germany had lost the war.

De Laporte had several talks with Quisling at NS headquarters in Rådhusgate 17, circulating around what Quisling would do in the event of a *British* invasion. Presumably Quisling would have opposed such an invasion, as his supposedly neutral government was in duty bound to do also. The details of these conversations are unknown, but there is no reason to believe that they were subversive.

Hardly had de Laporte left Quisling when Rosenberg's young representative in Norway, Hans Wilhelm Scheidt, accompanied by the German Naval Attaché, Corvette-Captain Richard Schreiber, contacted him. Scheidt was jealous of his contact with Quisling, and had actually protested in Berlin about the *Abwehr*'s 'interference'. Thus we find two more German departments at loggerheads over Norway —Military Intelligence and Rosenberg's APA—providing additional evidence that there was no comprehensive or master German plot, and that the invasion was strictly a military operation.

Scheidt and Schreiber discussed with Quisling the possibilities of a *German* invasion, which had not yet been decided upon, far less ordered into battle. Zero hour was therefore undecided and unknown to these three men, or to anybody else. Their discussions must there-

216

fore have been as theoretical as Quisling's talks with de Laporte about a problematical British invasion. Presumably Quisling agreed that a German invasion would come as a surprise and result in the capture of the King and government, for without surprise it could not have been carried out at all in the face of pro-British sentiments and the prospect of British interference by force of arms.

The only extraordinary aspect of these advance discussions about the two alternatives is that the Norwegian Government and General Staff were not considering the same matters at the same time.

Scheidt and Schreiber, who were as anxious as Quisling to know the future, recommended him to see Colonel Hans Piekenbrock, Chief of *Abwehr* I in Copenhagen, which explains his visit to Denmark on April 3. In the course of the journey he must have seen that the ice in the Great Belt was about to break up, thus making a German invasion possible. Actually, it broke on the 5th, after an exceptionally hard winter, and this alone was enough to alert any military man of intelligence. Piekenbrock must have known of Quisling through *Abwehr*, so it would have been natural for the two soldiers to discuss defence problems, although, as far as the German was concerned, Quisling was only involved ideologically with *Abwehr*.

It must be regarded as highly unlikely that Piekenbrock, an experienced spy, would have committed an appalling indiscretion and divulged the current top secret of the war to a foreigner, and a stranger at that. Even Ribbentrop and Brauer only heard of zero hour twenty-four hours before the event. Why should Quisling, who was summarily jettisoned from the plot in December, following his own advice to Hitler, suddenly be let into the secret now? The theory that Quisling was ordered by de Laporte, Scheidt and Schreiber to Copenhagen for a final briefing on the invasion and his own allotted part in it is too far-fetched and improbable to be entertained any longer.

Quisling arrived back in Oslo just in time for his party's General Meeting on April 7, attended by the NS Council and county leaders —about thirty-five persons. Much of his speech dealt with supply problems in a war, in case the North became isolated, and he said that he had discussed this with his opposite number, Fritz Clausen, in Denmark. A joint meeting was arranged for Aalborg in the summer, and there was no mention of imminent war. The leaders dispersed far and wide. Even had Quisling known about the German invasion, there would not have been time during the meeting on the afternoon of April 7 to organise a coup. He simply had not got the men for such an operation, supposing even that he had ever entertained such an idea. His *Hird* still numbered under 500 and they were untrained, un-uniformed and virtually unarmed—capable of preserving some sort of order at a political meeting, in default of the police, and no more.

The whole allegation, supported by a number of commentators, is a case of the pot calling the kettle black. It was the Norwegian Labour and Communist Parties which had a widespread underground army of Red Guards, trained, armed and well placed in public utilities. Had they been alerted by the government, the German invasion might have been prevented, in conjunction with the Norwegian Armed Forces.

Once again we find Quisling hoist with the petard of his opponents. It was not until 8 a.m. on April 10 that about 200 unarmed *Hird* showed up in driblets outside the *Storting*, with no duties assigned to them. Nor has a single case of treachery been proved among Quisling's friends and admirers in the Armed Forces.

One confused Captain K, who is alive, actually went to the *NS* office on April 10 to ask what he should do. Quisling told him to report back to the fugitive General Staff. The captain did so, and was promptly arrested! That is the nearest that any member of the Armed Forces came to defection—for the simple reason that *NS* was not a subversive movement. Would the Norwegian Government otherwise have appointed Ulrich Stang, a known member of the party, to be Coun-sellor in the Berlin Legation? Nor was *NS* a pro-German espionage organisation. Members had express instructions from Quisling *not* to pass on classified information to him, and to perform their state duties honourably.

What convinced Quisling that a German invasion was as good as certain within the next few hours was the British mine-laying opera-tion, which took place after his leaders had dispersed. He realised that the Germans were bound to retaliate.

NS members have ever since maintained that Foreign Minister Koht was actually informed of the British action in advance, but was too perplexed to tell his own Prime Minister, Johan Nygaardsvold, but this is not confirmed by Sir Cecil Dormer, the British Minister in Oslo, nor by Koht himself. Assuming that this belief was unjustified, it nevertheless existed, and was an important factor, rightly or wrongly, in the dénouement on April 9.

Quisling's position was made clear in his newspaper. On March 30 he declared in *Fritt Folk*: 'Norway rejects an alliance with Sweden, Finland and Britain because it would turn the North into a battlefield and soon merge with the continental conflict. . . . According to Chamberlain's own reckoning 100,000 men of the Western Alliance were ready to intervene in the North. . . . That would provoke a combined Russo-German counter-intervention. . . . Norway can be defended against a British intervention or blockade, but not against a German attack, still less against a Russo-German attack. . . . Our politicians are therefore pursuing a suicidal "Polish" policy. . . . Norway's and the North's vital interest is therefore the same as Germany's: neutrality, economically and militarily. . . . Nor can we ignore an Anglo-Russian agreement at the expense of Scandinavia. . . . A strong Germany will never permit Russian supremacy in Northern Scandinavia. . . . There must be immediately *i*) national revival *ii*) agreement with Germany *iii*) a breach with pro-British neutrality.'

On April 8 he proclaimed: 'Countrymen! Now see where the party politicians and their misrule have brought Norway. These people have led our land to the abyss. They must not have occasion to play out their hand further and to deliver Norway to England and France in order to save their own skins. This desperate policy will lead Norway to share the fate of Poland.

'The Nygaardsvold Government and the other politicians, notably Hambro and Mowinckel, must be retired immediately from further dealing with the direction of the realm.

'*Nasjonal Samling* is the only movement which can rescue Norway's freedom and independence in the major crisis ahead. It is therefore our national duty and right to claim governmental powers.

'Countrymen! Understand that you now face the decisive choice— the greatest and possibly the last. It now concerns nothing less than our existence as individuals and as a nation.

'Do your duty and report yourselves for service in the national movement. Norway must without delay get herself an able national government which can protect the Norwegian people's independence and safety.

'Oslo, 8-4-40. For *Nasjonal Samling* (*NS*). Vidkun Quisling.'

Ever since, the government has maintained that Quisling had a 'lust for power' and was 'seizing his opportunity' in collusion with the Germans. There is a far more natural explanation. Quisling was suggesting that, as the only person who had the foresight to anticipate events, he and his supporters should be entrusted to lead a national government—shorn of the politicians, whose dangerous incompetence was by now manifest. Sensing that the German invasion was imminent, he now dropped his proposal of March 30 for 'agreement with Germany', and urged the formation of a government that could speak for the nation and cope with the terrible unknown which obviously lay immediately ahead.

Quisling hoped that the nation would rally to him, the prophet who had been proved right—as England put aside recriminations and rallied to prophetic Churchill, and as France (twice) rallied to another voice crying in the wilderness, de Gaulle.

The Norwegian people did not respond. Perhaps he should have been more magnanimous in his proclamation, and let bygones be bygones, if the nation was to rally in unison. The abuse and violence to which he had been subjected for so long, however, had entered into his soul, and he allowed his bile to creep into his text. The initial references to the politicians' misrule and the 'abyss' were tactless and divisive mistakes in psychology. They antagonised not only men with whom he sought to work in the national interest but a population which was as yet unadjusted to reality. It was expecting too much of a constitutional monarch, for all his latent power, to retire all his Ministers, and to call Quisling into office to save the country single-handed. Quisling, in his indignation, overplayed his hand—an error of judgement which he might have been statesman enough to have foreseen and avoided had he been fully fit.

He should have couched his appeal on a higher and more dignified level. His failure to appreciate the acrimonious tone of his proclamation perhaps did more than anything else to ruin his cause and his case. It deprived him of a fair chance of rescuing the country which he so dearly loved and sought to serve. This was an unnecessary and misguided mishap, but in itself it was very far removed from high treason.

On the night of April 7-8, while the British were minelaying and the Germans were advancing, Quisling attended a party for four at the Astoria Hotel in Oslo where his family friend, Harald Franklin

Knudsen, was celebrating his thirty-fifth birthday. During the course of the evening Knudsen remarked that the war had ruined his shipping business, and Quisling suggested that he should come round to his office the following morning at 10 a.m. to discuss the possibility of a salaried appointment on *Fritt Folk*.

By then the minelaying was public knowledge and the German advance was rumoured. Quisling told Knudsen: 'We must reckon that Norway will become a war theatre in a few hours. Tell your father and get him home to Telemark before the rail services are interrupted.' Thereupon Knudsen was appointed Quisling's secretary-adjutant, in which capacity he had often served without payment before. He was to await instructions by telephone.

On April 8, the government organ *Arbeiderbladet* stated: 'The situation is once more exceedingly serious for our people and our country. Make no mistake about that. It is, however, at such times that the great point is to keep cool.' The newspaper's foreign editor commented: 'Probably Germany will demand that Norway removes the mines and provides a free passage through her territorial waters. This we shall of course endeavour to do by diplomatic means. There can, however, be no question of any military action.

'The question then is whether the Germans themselves will take action. . . . It would be an unheard-of thing for the Germans to resort to military operations against Norway for something for which we are not responsible. . . . It is however not certain that Germany will take such steps. . . . If she forces Norway into war, there is a danger of Sweden becoming involved. There is therefore every reason for the Norwegian people to envisage calmly the further development of this critical situation.'

This was the most authoritative advice that the nation received, on that day, apart from Quisling's proclamation.

In extra evening newspapers came the news of the sinking of the *Rio de Janeiro*. It became clear to Knudsen that the situation was very serious and he hurried to see Quisling at home. In fact Quisling was walking in nearby Frogner Park. While awaiting his return, Knudsen talked with Maria Quisling and Mrs. Haldis Neegaard-Østbye, wife of Norway's world-famous pioneer of ski equipment and technique, who was Quisling's unpaid publicity manager. She had hurried to the flat for the same reason as Knudsen.

Both agreed that the Norwegian authorities might vent their wrath on the man who had exposed them, and that for his own safety, and for the sake of the country, which might now depend on him, Quisling should take cover. At first he refused. Knudsen then made a personal appeal. Quisling left the room, and after five minutes' consultation with Maria, returned with a small suitcase and an overcoat.

As Mrs. Østbye drove the two men off in her car, a police car hurtled round the corner, whether with the object of arresting Quisling they did not know. Taking a roundabout route to throw off pursuers, they made for the Astoria Hotel, but on the way Knudsen remembered an advertisement saying the Continental was the only hotel in town with bomb-proof cellars, and it was next door to the underground.

At the Continental, Knudsen asked Quisling to walk up one floor to a small breakfast room, so as to avoid the desk, carrying his own baggage. The chances were that the room would be empty, and so it was. Meanwhile, Knudsen checked into a single room with the hall porter, whom he knew well, and rejoined Quisling. Then Knudsen told him to take the lift to the bedroom from the first floor, while he himself ran down to the lift on the ground floor, so that the staff would see him go upstairs alone. The manœuvre was successful. Nobody, except Knudsen, knew that Quisling was in the Continental—not even Mrs. Østbye for certain.

Maria had implored Knudsen to look after her husband because his kidney trouble had produced a high fever, and she had said what he should eat. So Knudsen insisted on his chief taking the only bed in the room, while he himself slept fully dressed on the divan.

At about 8 a.m. the following morning, according to Knudsen, there was a knock on the door. He opened it cautiously to find in the corridor a pale young man, about 30, in a grey suit, a darker grey overcoat and a black velour hat, who bowed and asked in German: 'Am I speaking to Mr. Franklin Knudsen? My name is Hans Wilhelm Scheidt. May I ask if you know where I can find Major Quisling? I know him from Berlin.'

Knudsen replied as well as he could in German that he had no idea where Quisling was. Scheidt then produced a diplomatic passport and Knudsen accepted his identity, but he did not want to disclose Quisling's presence and suggested that Scheidt should try the flat. Scheidt replied that he had already done so and had been told that Quisling was with Knudsen. Still pleading ignorance, Knudsen then withdrew and consulted Quisling, who said that he seemed to remember someone called Scheidt from Berlin, but that he had nothing to say to him at the time.

A moment later, Scheidt rang through, saying that he was going up to a room above and that there was something he wanted to speak to Knudsen about. Knudsen then went upstairs, where Scheidt introduced him to a rather elderly man called Hagelin who was dashing back and forth in pyjamas, speaking in a mixture of German and Norwegian. Hagelin's wife and sister-in-law were in an adjoining room.

Hagelin insisted that Knudsen knew where Quisling was because, he said, they had been seen together the night before. A little later Knudsen left, promising to try to find Quisling.

At 10 a.m., after Knudsen had returned from buying some food, cigarettes and two watches—for he and Quisling had left their watches behind in their hurry—Quisling agreed to see Hagelin at 11 o'clock, whereupon Knudsen engaged an adjoining sitting-room for receiving the visitors.

During the hour to spare, Knudsen went into the city centre to find out more of what was happening. Some people remained calm, but there was also wild panic. Notices appeared dismissing employees from their jobs. Newspapers said Bergen, Trondheim and Narvik were taken. The Government and *Storting* was reported to have left for Hamar, and all the authorities had disappeared except for the police. It was reported that the Germans were just outside Oslo, which was to be evacuated on orders of the Civil Defence Chief. Most of *Aftenposten*, the largest morning paper, was filled with the *Rio de Janeiro* incident and the protest to Britain. There was not a word from the King or government, nor an editorial on the invasion. No guidance was provided, except to evacuate the capital.

Such was the picture of the situation facing Quisling at 11 a.m. on April 9. He knew little more than the rest of the nation. He had not been in contact with a German for six days—since April 3 in Copenhagen. It was now too late to stave off an occupation by agreement, too late to fight, too late to talk, too late to create a real national government from the rump of a purged parliament. Perhaps something could still be saved from the wreck of Norwegian policy. Somebody had to act, and act quickly. Was this his hour—the hour of which his mother had dreamed, when he, like St. Olav, would save his country?

Such was his frame of mind when he met Viljan Hagelin and Hans Wilhelm Scheidt in an upstairs sitting-room at the Continental, at their request, while German bombers droned over the capital and the mystified population fled.

Scheidt had learnt from his friend Corvette-Captain Richard Schreiber, the German Naval Attaché in Oslo, that a German invasion was planned. Schreiber had been in Falkenhorst's staff room in February, but neither he nor, consequently, Scheidt, knew when the invasion was to occur until the Legation staff were briefed by Minister Brauer on April 8. Scheidt, not being directly under Brauer's orders, was not present at the briefing, but Schreiber immediately rushed to let him into the secret. Schreiber and Scheidt were of one mind with regard to Quisling's potentiality, in opposition to the views of Ribbentrop and therefore Brauer.

At dawn the two men drove together in Schreiber's car to the City Hall quayside to await General von Engelbrecht on the *Blücher*. When the ship failed to appear, they drove to the Nautical College at Ekeberg, on a hill overlooking the harbour. At 7 a.m., with still no news of the flagship, they drove away, Schreiber intending to see what was happening at Fornebu Airport, where at least there was some sign of action. In fact Norway's only modern fighters, 19 Curtis Pursuits, lay unpacked in their crates from America, and of nine Gloucester Gladiators only seven were serviceable. These, however, brought down three Heinkels and two Messerschmitts—another rare redeeming action, in which civilian fliers played the major part.

On the way through Oslo Schreiber dropped Scheidt at the Continental, where Hagelin always stayed. It was alleged at Hagelin's trial that he and Scheidt went down to the harbour together to have another look for the *Blücher*, but this seems unlikely since Hagelin was still in pyjamas when Knudsen saw him later.

Neither Scheidt nor Hagelin was briefed in any detail on *Weserübung*, militarily or politically, and they could not therefore have told Quisling very much that he had not guessed. When they met Quisling at the hotel, Scheidt and Hagelin were both excited and voluble. Scheidt, who spoke adequate Norwegian, stressed how total the occupation was—as far north as Narvik—and claimed that the British had been repelled from the West Coast by the Luftwaffe, and that Germany had already taken over 'the defence of Norwegian neutrality'. The only problems were the apparent loss of the *Blücher* and the possibility that the fugitive Norwegian Government might organise guerilla warfare. Both men emphasised the terrible consequences that the Norwegians would bring on their own heads at the hands of the Germans if guerillas went into action. Could Quisling not do something to prevent such a catastrophe? Quisling made no reply, and the two men left.

Quisling then took Knudsen on a short tour of investigation in the centre of the city. There was a run on the banks. They saw a two-line reference in *Aftenposten*, buried beneath the fold, to Foreign Minister Koht having mentioned a 'general mobilisation order' as the authorities disappeared by special train to Hamar. There was not a word more on this crucial subject, and the Armed Forces, such as they were, had to guess what to do on the basis of this passing reference in a newspaper that did not reach the provinces in peacetime, let alone war, until the night or next day. Even if these two lines had been noticed and interpreted in a positive sense, general mobilisation could not have been achieved at the best of times in under three days. The 'order' was therefore nothing short of suicide in so far as scattered and lightly armed or unarmed men obeyed this whisper to their patriotism.

Major Quisling, the brilliant Staff Officer and former Defence Minister, could not help being profoundly shocked by this half-hearted attempt of the government to shelter behind the bodies of the very people whom it had not only left defenceless but actually exhorted not to bear arms—up to the last moment. The opportunity for resistance had been allowed to pass, as was proved by the fall of all key bases, the severance from Allied aid and the flight of King and government.

At noon a single lorry, containing a platoon of some twenty German soldiers, drove up to the National Theatre, opposite the Continental Hotel, with their rifles slung over their backs to show the gaping populace that no harm was meant. An old woman spat at one soldier, who wiped his face and smiled. The men formed up and marched up to the mounted police, whom the German sergeant in charge saluted. The constable in charge dismounted and shook hands with the sergeant.

Thus a capital city of nearly half a million inhabitants surrendered without a shot—with a handshake!

Noon, April 9, 1940, was Norway's hour of utter shame and supreme peril, from which the government had run away. This must have been the moment when Quisling, who had stood his ground, first realised clearly that he would have to act.

About an hour later Quisling was again contacted by Scheidt. They exchanged a few words, and Quisling invited Scheidt to accompany him to the Defence Ministry, on the assumption that Scheidt would be his protection in case the *Wehrmacht* moved in. However, a Norwegian guard was still posted outside. Inside, the abandoned junior officers and staff recognised their former Defence Minister and saluted. They were mystified by their complete lack of orders and were obviously glad to see Quisling. All agreed that it would be insanity to offer resistance, without previous mobilisation—except possibly in the remote North. Quisling told the staff to put away documents and then left with Scheidt and Knudsen to see what was happening at Akershus Fortress, the complex of buildings overlooking Oslo Harbour.

Outside they met a high-ranking German Army officer, who was soaking wet and turned out to be General von Engelbrecht himself. He claimed to have swum ashore from the *Blücher*, although how he could have done this in full uniform, through icy water and over a distance of some 1,500 yards, is hard to imagine. The extraordinary circumstances in which he now found himself in Oslo have never been properly explained. It appears that both he and Rear-Admiral Kunmetz had been taken prisoner for a time, but exactly how they secured their release is uncertain.

At any rate, Quisling extracted a promise from him that the Germans would not occupy the Defence Ministry. On the way back to the Continental, Quisling crosschecked that the Ministry was still in Norwegian hands and that the staff had put away documents, as he had asked. In fact, a Norwegian soldier still stood guard outside, but inside the Germans had stationed their own watch.

Quisling next telephoned to various military establishments to find out how the land lay. Most of the connections were broken, but he succeeded in getting through to Colonel Hans Hiorth, commanding at Elverum, which is fifteen miles beyond Hamar and thirty miles from

Sweden. Some confusion exists about the exact time of the call and much has been made of this, but it is really immaterial. King Haakon and members of his government were actually on their way east or were about to take off in the direction of Sweden when he and Hiorth conversed. Quisling did not know this, but he was entitled to assume that, the worst having happened, the authorities would abandon Norway physically.

Hiorth did not make a note of this important conversation until May 3. On oath in 1945, he was confused. Under cross-examination by the prosecution, he said that Quisling had telephoned between 5 and 6 p.m. as Prime Minister, asking him to 'arrest' the 'Marxist government' if they should try and cross into Sweden, and holding him 'personally responsible'. Cross-examined by the defence, Hiorth said there was 'no talk of arresting the King'.

Clearly Hiorth's memory was at fault, because Quisling had not assumed the role of Prime Minister by 6 p.m. If he was inaccurate on this major point, how can his recollection, however sincere, or exact words, long after their utterance, be trusted? Possibly Hiorth read into his evidence, subconsciously, words that were later attributed to Quisling by his enemies.

It seems most likely that Quisling telephoned Elverum at the same time as he was calling other defence establishments, namely between 5 and 6 p.m., as Hiorth said, asking him to 'try to stop the government going over to Sweden', as Quisling claimed. It really seems most unlikely that he can have expected an obscure regimental commander to arrest the government, let alone the King, on the strength of a telephone call and at a moment's notice.

The insinuations made by the government against Quisling in connection with this confused conversation are against the weight of probability. The real importance of the call may equally well have been that Quisling showed that he still wanted the King and government to rally round in order to save something from the wreck. At any rate, Hiorth disposed on oath of the allegation that Quisling ordered him to abandon mobilisation. On the contrary Quisling said that he supported mobilisation for defence, but not for suicidal offence against an overwhelming enemy.

During the late afternoon, NS leaders from Oslo and some from the south-east saw Quisling at the Continental. Now that the authorities had departed without trying to arrest him, there was no longer any need to keep his presence there secret. They reported that the Government and *Storting* were moving east, presumably to Sweden; that the population and scattered military units were confused and nervous because no directions had been received; that mighty German forces and armaments were being landed, such as Norway had never seen before, and that the *Storting* building was occupied by several thousand German troops.

Schreiber then arrived and said that the sinking of the *Blücher* had shocked and angered the High Command because they had been instructed that the occupation was to be bloodless, if possible. Now there were isolated forts still firing—notably Bolaerne on the Outer Oslo Fjord—and Engelbrecht was threatening to destroy it. Could Quisling not do something to avoid German retaliation?

Quisling then paid a second call on the Defence Ministry, this time to contact Bolaerne, but he could not get through, so he went to the Norwegian Broadcasting Station, in the same block as the Continental, meaning to address the fort and advise it to cease fire in its own interest and that of the Norwegian population at large. Paradoxically, the broadcasting station was occupied by the Germans, who refused him admittance.

By this time it must have been clear to him that he could not achieve very much as a private citizen.

Some time after 5 p.m., Hagelin and Scheidt again called in a very excited condition. According to Knudsen, who heard part of the conversation: 'It was sensational enough. Scheidt said that *Nasjonal Samling* must take over the Government as this was Norway's only hope. . . . The Germans were furious over the sinking of the *Blücher* and were preparing to crush all further resistance ruthlessly. It was only Hitler's orders that had so far stopped the *Luftwaffe* from going into full-scale action. At any moment he might issue fresh orders. . . . Scheidt said that he had direct information from Berlin that Hitler would regard with favour any government formed by Quisling. . . . Germany only wanted to protect her vital interests against British violations of neutrality, and this was Norway's obvious interest, too.'

Quisling then crossed his Rubicon.

The meeting had lasted more than an hour. He sat down at his desk in the Continental, took off his jacket and, as he began to work, told Knudsen to arrange for him to speak over the radio. Knudsen asked Scheidt to contact Minister Brauer in order to get permission from the Germans for Quisling to use the air.

At 7 p.m. Scheidt returned, giving the impression that time had been allocated. Actually Brauer and Colonel Pohlman, representing Falkenhorst, had just told Scheidt that there was no place for Quisling in the German plans!

Quisling, Scheidt, Hagelin and Knudsen then walked round the building to the radio station, where they were blocked by German guards. Scheidt bluffed a way in, saying that he represented the German Legation and showing what purported to be identification papers to that effect. He then bluffed the Director of Broadcasting, Egil Sundt, and the Programme Chief, Olav Midthun, by the same means.

Thus, at 7.32 p.m., Quisling found himself before the microphone, speaking to the nation and the world. He said: 'Norwegian men and women! England has violated the neutrality of Norway by laying mines in Norwegian territorial waters, without meeting more than flimsy protests by the Nygaardsvold Government. The German Government has offered the Norwegian Government its help, accompanied by a solemn assurance respecting our national independence and Norwegian lives and property.

'In reply to this offer of a solution to the untenable situation in which our country finds itself, the Nygaardsvold Government has carried out general mobilisation and given aimless orders to all Norwegian military forces to oppose German help by armed force.

'The Government itself has fled, after thus recklessly wagering the fate of the country and its inhabitants.

'Under these circumstances, it is the duty and right of the *Nasjonal Samling* movement to assume the powers of government, in order to vindicate the vital interests of the Norwegian people and the safety and independence of Norway. By virtue of the circumstances and of the national aims of our movement, we alone can accomplish this and thereby save the country from the desperate situation brought upon our people by the party politicians.

'The Nygaardsvold Government has withdrawn. The national government has assumed power, with Vidkun Quisling as its head and as Minister of Foreign Affairs with the other following Ministers:

1. Professor Birger Meidell, Labour.
2. Police Chief Jonas Lie, Justice.
3. Dr. Gulbrand Lunde, Social Affairs.
4. Director Albert V. Hagelin, Trade and Supply.
5. Architect T. Hustad, Agriculture.
6. Estate-owner F. Prytz, Finance.
7. Major R. Hvoslef, Defence.
8. Professor Ragnar Skancke, Church and Education.

'All Norwegians are hereby called upon to keep the peace of the Realm and to preserve their presence of mind in this difficult situation. By united exertions and the goodwill of all, we shall bring Norway free and safe through this serious crisis.

'I add that resistance is not merely useless in the situation which has developed but directly synonymous with criminal destruction of life and property. Every official and every municipal employee—notably all officers of the country, in the Army, Navy, Coast Artillery and Air Force—is in duty bound to obey orders from the new National Government.

'Any deviation from this will involve the utmost personal responsibility on the part of the offender and will be proceeded against according to the principles of Justice and with the same consideration towards all citizens.'

With those depressing words, scrawled on hotel notepaper with many corrections, Vidkun Quisling passed into history, transformed the Norwegian situation and condemned himself to death. The words must of course be read in their historical context, and the reader will perhaps be able to judge whether these were appropriate words in the exceptional circumstances of the time.

It will be noted that Quisling did not proclaim himself to be Chief of State, thereby usurping the position of the King.

The essence of his bid was to provide a provisional Norwegian government, totally independent of German authority. He had been in the forefront of politics for ten years, supported by many of the most respected people in Norway, notably Skancke and Lunde, whom he included in his Cabinet with six other people well known in political, business or intellectual circles. His proclamation was unpremeditated and dictated by the immediate crisis during the latter part of April 9. When Knudsen tried to shake hands with him in the broadcasting studio, saying 'This is an historic occasion. I am speaking to the new Prime Minister', Quisling replied: 'It's not a position to aspire to. Let's hope the Germans and our people understand our objectives. I shall be called the big traitor. I don't want to involve you.'

Quisling must have known that he had undertaken a thankless task.

18

Six-day Wonder

QUISLING'S initiative changed the whole situation.
His German detractor, Brauer, suddenly found that he
had a new Prime Minister on his hands in Oslo. Was he to
deal with this figure who had always sought a reasonable understanding with Germany and had powerful connections there, or to
stick to his Wilhelmstrasse policy and seek out the King and nominal
government in the wilderness?

The President of the *Storting*, Carl Hambro, who was hand in
glove with Johan Nygaardsvold's Labour Government, suddenly
found that their arch-enemy, the rejected prophet Quisling, proposed
to do what they should have done in the morning, namely try to
save something from the wreck, stop the senseless skirmishing and
protect the population—in other words face the music and argue with
the conqueror. They now had a serious rival—and, they quickly
realised, a potential scapegoat.

The King suddenly found himself in a constitutional and political
situation that he was not well fitted to face either by temperament or
experience. Thirty-five years earlier he had restored the ancient
Norwegian monarchy by plebiscite and could thus speak for the nation
in theory. On the other hand he had sworn to obey the 1814 Constitution, which stipulated that he ruled 'in Council', namely through
the Cabinet. This Council was two contradictory and complementary

232

things—the expression of the people's will through parliamentary elections, yet simultaneously the creature of the monarch, who in Norway (unlike in Britain) selects Cabinet Ministers and presides over Cabinet meetings. King Haakon therefore had power, and with it a choice of action whether to support Quisling or Nygaardsvold.

Hitler, too, was suddenly presented with an unexpected choice between Quisling, with whom he had agreed in conversation four months earlier on the priority of the Bolshevik menace, the merits of the Nordic race and the advantages of Norwegian neutrality, and the King in Council, with whom he had reckoned his commander, General Nikolaus von Falkenhorst, would be dealing, only to find that they had taken to the woods.

The British of course could hardly deal with Quisling in the existing circumstances, and Chamberlain in the House of Commons had in any case committed himself to the supposedly viable Norwegian Government on the afternoon of April 9, before Quisling had emerged. Besides, the British and Norwegian Royal Houses were allied by marriage, the British people and their authorities held a naïve belief in Norwegian solidarity and the Norwegian people were supposedly pro-British. Quisling provided the perfect scapegoat. The Foreign Office had only to look in its files to find that he had been reported by the Oslo Legation as a 'fascist' since 1931, and of course he had since openly opposed a British occupation. Quisling thus provided Britain with the 'moral' excuse for further machinations against Norway, without which the British people will not fight unless they are actually hit.

Although he was still installed in two rooms on the fourth floor of the Continental Hotel, Quisling presented a dignified front. Brauer telephoned immediately after the radio proclamation and asked Quisling to come and see him. Instead, Quisling told Knudsen to reply: 'Tell him to come and see me here, if he wants to meet the Prime Minister.' Brauer arrived soon after, thus recognising Quisling's position for the first time and demonstrating that Quisling was no German stooge.

Brauer was in the unenviable position of needing to know what backing Quisling had, before telephoning Ribbentrop in a situation in which all his superiors, from Hitler downwards, had blundered.

Obviously, Quisling's arrangements were perfunctory, since he had

233

no working arrangement with the Germans and had had less than half a working day to prepare his bid for power. Of his eight named Ministers, only three were in Oslo—Hagelin; Tormud Hustad, the Farmers' Party expert on housing; and Birger Meidell (Labour), the leading actuarial professor and brother of a cellulose magnate. Jonas Lie, the police chief, who had made a name for himself in the Saar and was a popular writer, was a thousand miles away in Finnmark. Gulbrand Lunde, the famous chemist who had removed the smell from herrings and pioneered the margarine industry, was at his laboratories in Stavanger. Prytz was on his estate near Trondheim. Ragnar Schanke, the radar pioneer, was at his job as Director of Trondheim Technical High School. Major Ragnvald Hvoslef, commanding officer at Gardemoen Barracks and dynamo of the various patriotic societies which merged into *Nasjonal Samling*, was across the water in Finland.

All, except Hagelin, were surprised by Quisling's initiative. Lie was not even a member of *NS*. Prytz heard the news from his maid. Lunde ignored the summons and buried himself in his laboratory.

As Quisling saw the situation, somebody had to speak for Norway at this hour, to try to maintain the vestiges of independence, to stop futile bloodshed and to arrange supplies for the stranded population, none of which essentials was being performed by the official government. It was also important to try if possible to prevent the Germans from applying 'frightfulness' on the Polish pattern. Hence it was necessary for Quisling to have a least a façade of good men behind him. Brauer, Falkenhorst and Hitler could not otherwise be expected to take him seriously.

Inevitably Oslo and Hamar jumped to the conclusion that the new government had been carefully nurtured by Quisling in collusion with the Nazis, but this was not so. It was not in any case intended to supplant the King, as Quisling explained to him through a respected non-*NS* emissary next day. It was a provisional government, intended to hold the fort in this hour of need, to give the King an opportunity to return to his post and form a legal, representative government—not necessarily containing Quisling or his supporters—which could deal with the all-powerful occupants of the country.

Pending some sign of life from the King and his government,

Quisling's task was to hold the Germans to their promises, as expressed by Brauer verbally and in writing on behalf of Berlin, namely to respect the 'territorial integrity' and 'political independence' of Norway and not to interfere with the internal functions of the King and government, except in military, quasi-military and diplomatic matters. The Germans were committed to serious limitations on their freedom of action, but since the King and government were incommunicado, there was nobody at hand to hold the Germans to their word, or to stop the guerillas who were giving the Germans a pretext for going back on their undertakings.

Brauer now faced a situation in which the man he had discounted was acting as Premier, while Nygaardsvold, in whom he had committed his faith, had disappeared from the scene. The German Minister had been palpably wrong, and had misled Ribbentrop. Naturally he was perplexed and harassed.

At 10.55 a.m. Ribbentrop had sent a most urgent telegram: 'You will at once impress on the Government that Norwegian resistance is completely senseless.' All Brauer had been able to do was to appeal at noon through W. M. Johannessen, the staff director in the thinly populated Norwegian Foreign Office, for a 'peaceful solution'. He had been promised an answer from the fugitive Norwegian Government late that night or early the following morning.

In the interval Quisling had come forward to offer an alternative government, accessible and realistic!

Immediately after seeing Quisling, Brauer contacted Ribbentrop, who telephoned Hitler on another line while Brauer waited.

Hitler said that things had gone well in Norway, that there was no political hurry, but that Germany must stick by Quisling ('Why not Quisling?')—ample evidence that Quisling was correct in claiming that Hitler seemed 'sympathetic' to him when they met. There was to be no question of dealing with the Nygaardsvold Government. Brauer was to seek an audience with the King and to do everything possible to persuade him to return to Oslo. It was also to be an irreversible condition that Quisling should be Prime Minister. Hitler would not listen to Brauer's objections, via Ribbentrop, that Quisling had little value and that the King, as a constitutional monarch, had to act through his ministers. This was not peacetime. The King had to act to save his throne and his dynasty.

This was a somersault by Hitler, an entirely new directive for Falkenhorst and Brauer and an astonishing victory for Quisling. He was now exactly where he wanted to be—Prime Minister of Norway, supported by Hitler and in a greatly reinforced position to bid for the King's support in holding the Germans to their promises. If only the King would co-operate, Norway could be saved from the worst.

Incidentally, it was an even more astonishing victory for young Scheidt, who had broken all Hitler's instructions and was now confirmed as virtually a political wizard. Brauer immediately appointed him to act as liaison between the Legation and Quisling. Thus Quisling was established in Oslo as the *de facto* premier, with the active goodwill of the conquerors.

Certainly it was Scheidt who informed Quisling of Hitler's blessing. For Quisling was soon at his desk, drafting a long cable to the Führer. He interrupted this to walk across the central park to the *Storting* building, and ask the German commander to remove his men as soon as possible. This was done, and the parliament thus returned to Norwegian sovereignty. A bust of Hitler, replacing a First World War seamen's memorial, was also removed.

Back at the Continental, Quisling found that 110 men of the King's Guard, commanded by Colonel Graf Wang, were moving in, the Germans having occupied the Royal Palace. They had been left behind by the King and now acted as a bodyguard for the new Prime Minister. They were billeted in the hotel conference hall, and a few stood guard at the front door.

Quisling then returned to his desk, continuing his telegram to Hitler, which Knudsen typed out with two fingers on a machine borrowed from the reception desk. The full text has been lost, but Knudsen remembers that it referred to Scheidt's intervention during the afternoon, bringing Hitler's blessing. It also referred to Quisling's reliance on the Führer's promise to spare Norway the horrors of war. Quisling added that he now considered Norway's neutrality to be re-established and that he had formed a government to safeguard the peace and integrity of the country.

This message was never in fact sent. Scheidt raised so many objections that draft after draft was abandoned, until finally it was reduced to 'general terms' and dispatched. Knudsen says this was the moment that Quisling realised that Scheidt had 'imposed upon him'.

As this hectic evening wore on, the German Legation demanded that the 1,052 Norwegian merchants ships, amounting to about 4 million tons, which were outside the blockade, should be ordered to neutral ports. Quisling had no time to handle this awkward matter and delegated the task to Knudsen, a shipping man, who then contacted his old friend, the President of the Shipowners' Association. Since the bulk of the Norwegian mercantile marine had been chartered to Britain and the West since the autumn at highly profitable rates and with ample insurance against losses, there was no prospect of the shipowners acquiescing in the German demand; nor had any Norwegian government the power to compel them to do so. Naturally the shipowners refused to comply.

There was, however, another consideration. Upwards of a million tons of Norwegian shipping lay in home waters. If the demand was not sent out, the Germans would have a pretext for commandeering those vessels. Accordingly, Quisling decided on a ruse. The order should be given to the shipowners, well knowing they would not obey it or that it would be rendered ineffectual by the Allies. In fact the order was never relayed abroad, although the German Press Attaché, von Tangens, inserted a story in the newspapers to the contrary—thus doing Quisling considerable harm, despite the fact that he had managed to keep the home vessels under their lawful ownership.

The telephone rang incessantly and there were dozens of callers, but at 2 a.m. Knudsen persuaded Quisling, who still had a high fever, to go to bed and stay there for at least three hours. However, at 3 a.m., Schreiber and three other German naval officers called, telling Knudsen that some small Norwegian ships off the south-east coast were firing on German transports. Falkenhorst had ordered his Air Force against them. Schreiber burst into tears and presented an order of capitulation, which he asked Quisling to broadcast. It was couched in Prussian terms, which Knudsen transformed into less offensive language, but Quisling refused to interfere in military details and referred the officers to his earlier proclamation.

By 6 a.m. Quisling was up again, fever-stricken but optimistic. At breakfast it was decided to restrict the number of visitors, and he went to his desk. Then General von Engelbrecht arrived with his staff, to take over the Continental, but Quisling refused to move out. Engelbrecht threatened to arrest him, but this had no effect. However, a long feud between Quisling and Engelbrecht had begun, and Quisling established his position *vis-à-vis* the *Wehrmacht*.

Next he returned to the *Storting*, where the Norwegian flag again flew over parliament, and he now established his office there, supplemented by a small secretariat. He continued to sleep at the Continental. His first duty was to try to restore normal life and supplies. Food was running out. Banks were closed. Wages were interrupted. Chaos reigned, and there was still no word from the vanished authorities. Quisling therefore arranged a series of meetings with leading businessmen and representative bodies of trade, industry and public life. He stressed the futility of resistance and the desire of his new National Government to arrange minimum interference by the Germans with internal affairs. He hoped it would be possible to arrange with Hitler for his recognition of Norwegian neutrality except in so far as it was necessary for the Germans to occupy bases against further Allied aggression. It would not be in Germany's interest to detach a huge army for the occupation of the whole country, nor to attempt its Nazification. Quisling also stressed that he had no personal plans and merely sought to establish an operative Norwegian government so as to deprive the Germans of any pretext for breaking their promises and establishing a military dictatorship.

Industrialists were chilly, but otherwise Quisling received support. He was especially pleased with the backing of the acting management of the Trade Unions, because he had long been abused as an enemy of the workers. He asked them to keep their organisations intact and assured them of his help in restoring production and distribution. The management then issued a declaration on their own initiative explaining that their organisations must now be 'adjusted to the new conditions' and they 'agreed to the request that every man and woman should remain at their posts and do their duty—not only employees but people in responsible positions'.

The Press also promised support and without compulsion loyally printed all that Quisling stated. For instance, Editor Nesse of *Aftenposten*, who had long opposed Quisling, changed his mind and wrote that there was now only one course—that which Quisling's Government had made possible. In 1948 he still held to the same line. He wrote a leading article, saying 'let us shake hands . . . because we can all make mistakes'; then cancerous, he committed suicide in the hospital.

Aftenposten furthermore enclosed Quisling's newspaper, *Fritt Folk*, within its own folds, thus providing a much wider circulation than would otherwise have been possible through his normal outlets. Today *Aftenposten* claims that it was 'requisitioned', but Quisling wielded no such power on April 10. *NS* survivors today maintain that *Aftenposten* obliged 'for profit,' and it certainly insisted on daily down payments in advance before performing this service. The deal was negotiated by Jon Tronsen, State Economic Chief of *NS*.

Quisling also appointed a young *NS* man in the Foreign Office as censor at the Norwegian News Agency (*NTB*), to whom the Press as a whole were to refer—thus forestalling the Germans and asserting Norwegian authority instead of the enemy surveillance which Brauer had prescribed in his original terms to Koht.

The Germans, counting on negotiations, had not interfered with the Foreign Office, which Quisling also visited in the morning with Knudsen. Two guards at first barred his way, but he expostulated that he was Prime Minister and Foreign Minister, whereupon a blushing corporal admitted him. Afterwards he complimented the guards for trying to carry out their mistaken orders and promised that he would recommend them to their superiors. 'You are the only men I have found doing their duty since I took over the government,' he said.

Inside he told the skeleton staff, headed by Bureau Chief Francis Irgens and Staff Director W. M. Johannessen, that they could choose whether to remain at their posts and swear loyalty to him, or depart. After half an hour they returned from private conference together and backed him. Thus he established his authority over the Foreign Service, again forestalling the Germans.

Thereupon the Foreign Office notified all Norwegian diplomatic missions abroad that the Nygaardsvold Government was superseded and that the new Quisling Government had taken over.

After about an hour in the Foreign Office, Quisling came out of *Viktoria Terrasen* to find total panic in Oslo Centre. The scene had been peaceful enough when he went in. Now the population was flee-ing *en masse* by every possible means of conveyance, including carts and barrows. Amazed, Quisling asked a police constable what had occurred and was informed that the Oslo Police Chief, Kristian Wel-haven, had ordered immediate evacuation because notice had been given that British warships were in the Fjord and would shell the capital at 12 noon sharp. Police were hurrying the seething traffic along, and ever since this has been known as 'panic day'. More than half the population fled and ten thousand spent the next twenty-four hours in the freezing open air.

The police said that the threat of bombardment had come over the British and Swedish wireless, but this has never been confirmed. Welhaven, who had been allocated a six-man German bodyguard, had been ordered to ensure that there were no anti-German demonstrations up to 10 p.m. on April 9, so as to preserve an atmosphere in which negotiation was possible. In fact he had actually sent mounted police to escort the airborne German troops from Fornebu into Oslo, complete with brass-band! The 'quislings' have always maintained that he was a German agent, but there is no proof of that allegation. However, the false rumour that created panic appears to have originated with his City Police.

Lest the Germans should intervene and usurp the functions of the State Police, using the dislocation of communications as an excuse, Quisling immediately telephoned *Wehrmacht* headquarters and arranged for reassurances to be broadcast. He also obtained German approval for him to punish the culprits. He then drove to the Ministry of Justice, where the Permanent Secretary, Carl Platou, signed a warrant suspending Welhaven—a document which was quoted in post-war treason investigations, but from which Platou's signature is missing and has apparently been clipped off!

Some time during these breakneck efforts to keep Oslo functioning and to stall the Germans, Quisling heard that the King and the Nygaardsvold government were still on Norwegian soil. At once he sought to contact the King. An ideal emissary was at hand—Hagelin's brother-in-law, a friend of the King and widely popular in Norway's distinguished seafaring fraternity. This was Captain Kjeld Stub Irgens, Commodore of the Norwegian-American Line. In the early afternoon Quisling and Irgens sat down quietly together in the Continental and worked out overtures to King Haakon—a delicate task because they had to make an explicit proposition yet one so phrased as not to antagonise the Germans should it be rejected.

This document has been lost, but Knudsen says that the key part of the message, which Irgens eventually delivered, was as follows: 'The Quisling Government requests the King and the Royal House to return to Oslo. Quisling himself will adopt a loyal attitude towards His Majesty and suggests that an arrangement should be reached in Norway similar to the one prevailing in Denmark'—where King Haakon's brother, King Christian, still ruled and stood his ground.

The sincerity of this approach was underlined three days later, after Quisling had made two more attempts to reach an agreement with King Haakon. He told the assembled Press: 'I have no interest in opposing the Royal House. The King had previous notice of my position *vis-à-vis* himself and the illegal [Labour] government. Personally, I am interested in reaching an agreement, because I set great store by the Royal House. I consider it to be an advantage to have a dynasty.'

Asked if he would have formed a government had the Labour Government not fled, Quisling replied: 'Of course not.'

He added in writing on April 18: 'I at once sent a reliable and prominent man, who is politically neutral and free, in order to persuade the King to return. We considered it to be our supreme duty to prevent useless bloodshed and the unavailing sacrifice of our gallant countrymen. We implored the King to help in this respect by returning to the capital, so that the country might return to normal. For my part I averred that I would do *everything* to reach an agreement.

'I made it plain that our aim was not dictatorship and not a German replica, but a national and free Norway with the Royal House at the apex.'

If only Quisling had sought to contact the King before assuming office, the legality of his position might not later have been challenged.

One must sympathise with the sixty-seven-year-old monarch in this supreme test. He had taken no important decision since he had insisted on a plebiscite before his accession thirty-five years earlier. Since then he had been a mere figurehead, a grotesque six-feet-six, usually clad in an Edwardian dark suit, butterfly collar and elastic-sided or button boots, his bald and thickly bespectacled head crowned with an absurdly small bowler. The first of his dynasty, he enjoyed no terrific popularity. The dominant Labour movement was vaguely republican, most of his ministers openly and passionately so. He was addicted to silly jokes and extravagant gestures with his long prehensile arms, and he infuriated the grim Labour leaders. His nautical language shocked the prim and proper.

His bright, gay and intelligent wife, Queen Maud, had been dead

241

three years. Although he was a jealous man, she had kept him in touch with reality, restrained his quick temper and produced an harmonious atmosphere at Court. Since her influence was removed, King Haakon had become a confirmed misogynist, a lonely widower, surrounded by elderly cronies. His public duties were few and when he presided at Cabinet meetings, he acted only as a rubber stamp. Unlike his rival, King Gustaf of Sweden, who was senior, richer and even taller, King Haakon did not demand inconvenient documents or take any constructive interest in the administration. When he tried, he was rebuked, so that his very real constitutional powers had in practice lapsed. He was a simple man of narrow views, and he had little bent for statesmanship or personal initiative.

His greatest asset was Crown Prince Olav, then aged thirty-seven, married to the Swedish Princess Märtha,* a well-connected and charming woman, by whom he had three small children, Ragnhild (10), Astrid (8) and Harald (3). Olav looked and acted Norwegian, excelled at the Norwegian manias, skiing and sailing, and spoke the language with gusto. By no means an intellectual, he was a very normal, healthy man, and has always been popular. He was the real man of the Royal House and he came out of the ensuing difficulties with high credit.

King Haakon and the Royal Family did not reach the Høsbjør Tourist Hotel, Hamar, until about 11 a.m. on April 9, owing to air alarms. Premier Nygaardsvold reached there at 10.15 a.m. by car with his family, and was 'sadly shaken'; he retired for an hour's rest. Later Hambro discussed the situation with Nygaardsvold, who, very properly, said that he and his government would take full responsibility for the catastrophe and resign, to make room for an all-party government. 'It is impossible to change governments now that all communications are upset. A change would create confusion,' said Hambro, who went to the King, who had not hitherto been consulted. Hambro shortly came away from this audience with the King's word that he was 'convinced that Norway would win neither security nor peace by complying with German demands'.

At 12.30 p.m., 145 of the 150 Members of Parliament assembled

---

* Märtha, aged thirty-nine, was niece of all three Northern monarchs and sister of ill-fated Queen Astrid of Belgium, as well as King Haakon's daughter-in-law.

242

in the hotel, and Hambro 'obtained the unanimous approval of the *Storting* for the request that the government should not resign. Instead, it was resolved that the government should be supplemented by representatives of the parties in Opposition.'* King Haakon and the Crown Prince agreed. Ivar Lykke(Conservative ex-Premier), Johan W. Mowinckel (Liberal ex-Premier), and Jon Sundby (the Farmers' ex-Finance Minister, in the absence of his leader, Jens Hundseid) were then co-opted. All three were bitter opponents of Quisling.

At about the time when the State Police were escorting the Germans into Oslo, Hambro 'strongly advised in favour of adhering firmly to the decision for national resistance embodied in the answer which the government had given to the German Minister', thereby cutting the ground from under negotiations. Not the slightest effort had been made to check conditions in Oslo, or to contact the two men who might help there, Minister Brauer and Vidkun Quisling.

Instead, the government decided belatedly to plunge the country into a 'national resistance'. Earlier such a course might have succeeded, at least enabling the Allies to come to Norway's defence; but what earthly chance had Norway at this late time, when the Germans had already achieved their initial objective? The pursuit of a policy of resistance would simply have gambled the country on a dubious Allied victory at some distant and unspecified future, thus condemning Norway, heedlessly, to comprehensive occupation, widespread destruction and unrelieved persecution.

Perhaps sensing this, second thoughts seemed to prevail in the early afternoon, when members of the government discussed the situation informally with other *Stortingsmen*. 'Opinions were somewhat divergent,' Koht records, 'but the view prevailed that the Minister (Brauer) would be willing to compromise on his original terms.' New negotiations were then proposed by wire, and at about the time when Quisling was making his historic broadcast, a second meeting of the *Storting* took place in the hotel to rubber-stamp the Government's later decision to negotiate.

Almost at once it was reported that German troops were within ten miles of Hamar, approaching in four big Schoeyen buses.

Hambro jumped on a newspaper van. Justice Minister Terje Wold had just time to telephone Police Chief Welhaven, ordering the arrest

* Koht.

243

of Quisling. Defence Minister Ljungberg announced that hopes of resistance were 'not encouraging'. Colonel Otto Ruge, ex-Chief of Staff, bravely rushed forth with a handful of raw Territorials, who had not yet been taught to fire machine-guns, towards the approaching Germans. By 8 p.m., everyone except Ruge, including the King, had disappeared in the direction of Elverum and Sweden.

King Haakon and his Cabinet now split up for the first time, and the process of disintegration quickened. The government, *Stortings-men* and Hambro trudged from their vehicles through the inky blackness of the night and deep white snow into Elverum Secondary School, where they held their last meeting for five years.

'On the motion of President Hambro,' Koht records, 'the *Storting* unanimously adopted the proposal to give the government all-embracing authority to guard the vital interests of the kingdom, and on behalf of the *Storting*, to take all measures that might be found necessary for the security and the future of the country, such authority to be valid until the government and the Presidential Board agreed to call the *Storting* to session again.' Full powers were also accorded to the King, should be be obliged to absent himself from Norway for more than the statutory six-month limitation.

The government exercised no practical authority outside a radius of a few miles, and no vote was ever taken on this so-called 'motion' that provided the legal basis of the government in exile. 'It was decided', is all that *All for Norway*, published by the Norwegian Government, says.

The already illegally prolonged parliament thus perpetuated itself indefinitely, without debate, without a vote, and without giving the electorate a chance of expressing an opinion on the plight in which the politicians had landed it. 'Full powers' for the government were simply enunciated by Hambro, who later evolved the extraordinary theory that 'one *Storting* continues until another is elected'. This is not only constitutional nonsense but an abrogation of any parliamentary system practised in a Western democracy. However, it had the desired effect of enabling the government and *Storting* to judge its own case and to fix the judicial enquiry which eventually let them off with a reprimand.

Exceptional circumstance may excuse unconstitutional behaviour, but what is objectionable is that these 'full powers' of doubtful legality should have been used subsequently to bring unnecessary misery upon the Norwegian population and to punish the so-called 'quislings' who tried to do their duty in the face of the enemy.

The last act of the supine *Storting* was to burst into the National Anthem, 'Yes, we love with fond devotion, This the land that looms rugged, storm-scarred o'er the ocean'. Then it dispersed, never to function again for what Norwegians call 'the long years'.

Hambro followed the Royal Family and Nygaardsvold to Nybergsund in Trysil, twenty miles from Sweden, but got stuck in the snow; he was dug out by British Legation staff, who were somehow keeping up with the exodus, and he only reached his group at midnight. He found King Haakon, the Crown Prince, Court Chamberlain Wedel, Nygaardsvold and Trygve Lie (Minister of Supply) in the sitting-room of the tiny post office.

Nygaardsvold was in bed, but Hambro roused him and told him that 'the burden of government cannot now be lifted from your shoulders'. Flight into neutral Sweden was suggested, and Hambro proposed going there right away in the hope of buying Swedish materials, though how they could have helped at that stage is unclear. A more important consideration may have been that he had 'some notions of a joint Northern policy and joint Nordic interests' (which had been advocated as a policy for years by *Nasjonal Samling*!).

Crown Prince Olav then spoke up like a man. He said he had no intention of entering Sweden, thus embarrassing the Swedish Government and probably precipitating the surrender of Norway. He wanted to go north to Rena and Rendal in Central Norway to organise guerilla warfare and to share the fate of the people. He was overruled however, and it was decided that Hambro would accompany Princess Märtha and the three children into Sweden the following morning on his way to Stockholm.

At about 5.30 a.m., the King and Hambro were awoken by the Finnish Military Attaché—not, one notices, by their own people—to hear surprisingly that the Germans had been repulsed outside Hamar. What had happened was that Captain Spiller, the German Air Attaché, had taken leave of the High Command to try to waylay the King. It was his men—about 100 in number—who had frightened the Norwegian authorities out of Hamar. His buses were too broad, however, to cross the bridge at Minnesund, so the troops transferred to smaller

245

vehicles. They encountered Ruge's scratch force at Midtskogen at 1.30 a.m., and amazingly the Germans were badly shot up by the raw Norwegian machine-gunners. Spiller himself was mortally wounded.

This was actually the first resistance made under the aegis of the Nygaardsvold Government—a mere skirmish, but enough to earn Ruge the High Command within twenty-four hours! It demonstrates what the Norwegians could have achieved in Oslo if the government had given a lead. Having been roused, Hambro departed unshaven with Märtha and the children for Sälen Tourist Hotel, thirty miles inside Sweden among the well-patronised skiing slopes. He himself reached Stockholm by 10 p.m. The second man of Norway was no longer in the country.

Meantime Minister Brauer, who was now faced with the problem of two Norwegian governments, was continuing to follow up his initiative in contacting, unknown to Quisling, the Nygaardsvold authorities: Koht and three negotiators had in fact remained in Elverum with a view to meeting Brauer, the decision to reopen negotiations having been taken. Following Spiller's repulse, Koht was prepared to go to Oslo, but Brauer now suggested that he should meet the King alone in Elverum. The King thereupon drove back to Elverum to meet Brauer at 1 p.m. on April 10.

Before the meeting, the military leaders were consulted about the possibilities of resistance. The Defence Minister, Colonel Birger Ljungberg, the Commander-in-Chief, General Kristian Laake, the Chief of Staff, Colonel Rasmus L. Hatledal, and Colonel Ruge were unanimous in declaring that resistance was 'hopeless.' Laake had a nervous breakdown and resigned. Hatledal, who was suffering from a painful illness and had been shouted down by the King for suggesting general mobilisation on April 4, also resigned, but promised to continue until the 14th. Ruge, who at the time was Inspector General of Infantry, pointed out that without fortifications, with no organised army and interrupted communications, the Armed Forces were a 'rabble'.

Thus the leading military men of Norway, all of whom supported Quisling's defence policy and spoke up for him in 1945, came to precisely his conclusion. 'Such happenings are comprehensible in an army that had never known war,' was Koht's heartless comment! The Foreign Minister's delegation was 'not in very high spirits' when it met Brauer at 3 p.m., two hours late. Brauer would have nothing to do with the delegation, but he allowed Koht to sit in with himself and the King.

Brauer then said that he could have nothing more to do with the Nygaardsvold-Koht Government. He demanded a government in which Germany could have confidence and said that he was authorised (by Hitler on the telephone) to ask the King to appoint as his councillors the Cabinet now in power in Oslo under the leadership of Major Quisling.

The opportunity was now presented to co-opt Quisling and to form a real national government, as Quisling had always advocated and now sought. Koht decided that he must leave the decision to the King. 'I only took part when King Haakon wished me to do so,' he records. 'I endeavoured to leave the King a free hand.'

At last King Haakon was really and truly out on his own. As Koht says, it was 'difficult for the King to find words'. Fatally, the King hedged. He pleaded that 'he could not appoint a Prime Minister who had not the confidence of the people', although legally in fact he could have appointed anybody he chose. He said that he would have to consult his government.

He then had a quick conference with Koht and the three negotiators who were outside the room. Mowinckel has recorded that the King was deeply moved and in tears, and was naturally aware of the misfortune and the horrors with which the Germans threatened the Norwegian people. . . . The government would have to take its decision without considering his person. 'If the government came to the conclusion that the interests of the country necessitated submission to the German demands, he personally would not support the appointment of the Quisling Government, and would be forced to abdicate.'

It was arranged that Koht would remain in Elverum, while the King drove back to Nybergsund, thus gaining time to collect his wits. There was little doubt that his resistance to Quisling would be supported by Nygaardsvold's Cabinet and stiffened by Dormer, the British Ambassador.

Koht sat down quietly in the school to draft a proclamation while he awaited the official reply from the King in Council, upon receipt of which he had arranged to telephone Brauer at Eidsvoll, the home of the Constitution.

The King told his government at Nybergsund: 'This is the first time I have expressed myself on a subject before it has been discussed by you. I have spoken to the Crown Prince and if the Government decided that it was necessary to accept Quisling, I should abdicate on behalf of myself and my House.' This news was telephoned to Koht at Elverum, who relayed it to Brauer at Eidsvoll. 'We shall stand firm,' Koht said.

The King had thus thrown away his chance to unite the country for the duration of the German Occupation and to be a rallying point for his subjects, like his brother, King Christian in Denmark, who ruled without a slur on his name, putting no smear on his people and causing them infinitely less misery than faced the Norwegians.

Hamar and Vigra (Aalesund) radio stations then broadcast to a small fraction of the Norwegian people a proclamation in the name of Premier Nygaardsvold and King Haakon. No lead was given to the country, but only vague advice such as 'the Norwegian nation will use all its energies to restore liberty and independence' and 'the government . . . exhorts the whole Norwegian nation to cling fast to the Norwegian heritage of liberty'. This was typical of the government's equivocal tactic throughout the war, always evading the crucial point, whether to fight or not to fight.

Quisling's emissary, Captain Irgens, designated as 'Acting Chief of the Defence Ministry', did not manage to find and contact the King in Nybergsund until 7 a.m. on Thursday, April 11. Government accounts pass over this meeting in a line or two. Irgens took notes of the conversation, but these have disappeared like so many key documents that might have helped to rectify Quisling's image. However, Knudsen was present in Quisling's *Storting* office when Irgens returned empty-handed at 3 p.m. 'Irgens was weeping,' Knudsen says, 'and he sobbed that the King could hardly speak for weeping.' For what it is worth, Rosenberg's diary confirms this reaction. The entry of April 13 says that the King was shocked when Irgens described the situation in Oslo, and the King is reported to have remarked: 'If only I had known all this beforehand! But now I have taken my decision and this has been made public.'

Quisling was angry and disappointed when Irgens reported failure. He ordered him to return to the King, but without result because by then the war had reached Eastern Norway and the Nygaardsvold government had disintegrated, either in headlong flight or Swedish exile. Quisling also tried to reach the king through Colonel Johan L'Orange who had no success either. An attempt was also made to speak to Crown Princess Märtha, who was now in the Royal Palace in Stockholm but the Court Chamberlain refused to let her take the call.

Having failed to get Hitler by telephone early in the morning, Quisling tried again at 5 p.m., but Hitler passed the call to Ribbentrop, who in turn relayed it to Walter Hewel, the Foreign Office representative at Falkenhorst's headquarters in Hamburg. True to form, Hitler was sitting on the fence, waiting to see what his executives in Germany and Norway reported. Criticisms of Quisling were reaching his ears from all the interested parties who had an axe to grind, the Foreign Office, *Wehrmacht* and Rosenberg—all putting the blame on Quisling for their own failures. Consequently Hewel was non-committal and Quisling sensed that Hitler was retracting the support that he had so suddenly provided a few hours previously.

He therefore sent Hagelin to Berlin. Through Scheidt's influence, Schreiber put a Naval Staff plane at Hagelin's disposal, and by 9 p.m. Hagelin was in the German capital. He was able to arrange with Rosenberg's Staff Chief, Schikendanz, to see Ribbentrop and Hitler the following day. On this meeting Quisling pinned his hopes of overcoming opposition from the German Foreign Office and High Command.

On the radio he broadcast that he sought to work 'within the framework of the Constitution' and 'in collaboration with the Royal House'. At a Press conference he outlined his well-known plans for a 'corporative state', which were naturally interpreted by his rivals and enemies as a threat to their interests and as 'Nazi'. They were his answer to the factions which had brought Norway to disaster, and his prescription for national unity. All the time his representatives were moving into government offices, thus establishing Norwegian control. The German Legation was addressing him as 'Prime Minister' and, for the first time, as 'Minister-President', the title he was to bear officially from February 1942 until May 1945.

During this hectic April 12, while Quisling was battling to contact both the King and Hitler, German aircraft strafed the area where the King was wandering. This has been represented as an unwarranted

249

attack on non-military targets, but even if there were good military reasons for the bombing, Quisling was in no way responsible. King Haakon and Prince Olav, the remaining members of the Cabinet and a few staff fled seven miles north to Innbygda village. There the only question was whether to go to Sweden, or west to Lillehammer, the ski resort on the Oslo-Trondheim Railway, where Ruge, the new Commander-in-Chief, was supposed to be setting up headquarters for guerilla warfare and possibly to receive Allied aid.

Olav refused adamantly to join his family in Sweden. He insisted on sharing the fate of the Norwegian people. For the time being he prevailed and the little column of cars set out for Lillehammer after dark.

Nygaardsvold and some of his Cabinet managed to get through via Elverum, which was now in flames, and Rena. The King's party was stopped at Rena by a report that the Germans were in or near Nybergsund and Elverum, twenty miles away. They then turned back and drove sixty miles north-west to Drevsjø on the Swedish frontier.

After a sleepless night, they reached the frontier early on April 13. There, says the official government account,* 'it was proposed that the King should rest for a day or two on the Swedish side of the border'. The King crossed into Sweden as Quisling had predicted.

It is known that Koht telephoned Stockholm, presumably to request permission for King Haakon's presence in Sweden, but it is not known for certain how long a stay was requested. It is also a matter of speculation why two Ministers travelled to Sweden 'to try and solve certain problems' when Hambro was already there. Certainly, nobody Swedish or Norwegian is likely to reveal the truth while the protagonists are still alive.

In Stockholm the information in Court and diplomatic circles at the time was that King Haakon had personally telephoned to King Gustaf for permission to stay as long as necessary on Swedish soil; that Gustaf had flatly refused; and that the two men had exchanged such rough words that a lasting feud was started between them. The information that King Haakon was also furious that the Swedish Minister did not accompany him on his flight was common property. From this impression it was widely deduced that Haakon had been

* *All for Norway* (Dent), published on behalf of the Royal Norwegian Government.

refused permission to establish a government in exile in Sweden because it would have endangered Swedish neutrality.★

Elaborate pains have been taken by the Norwegian authorities to minimise the incident. *All for Norway* says: 'Just as the King's car was about to leave, a report was received saying that a large number of German planes were on their way to Drevsjø. People had not yet learnt to recognise the difference between transport planes and bombers, and everybody assumed that this was a new attempt at murdering the King. The King and his company therefore crossed the frontier into Sweden and went about 500 yards into Swedish territory. About twenty minutes later the danger was reported to be over and the cars set their course through Trysil again.' Koht says that the king 'on this occasion stayed for about half an hour on Swedish soil', and US Ambassador Mrs. Harriman, who was at Nybergsund immediately after the bombing which drove the Royal Party over the border, goes so far as to say: 'His Majesty never crossed the border,' and it is difficult to find a Norwegian who believes that he did.

The information in Stockholm was that King Haakon spent 'at least three hours in Sweden' before he was sent packing. In any case there is little doubt that he was in Sweden for a short time and that he would have remained there had it been possible.†

★ Early in 1944, when King Haakon received me alone in audience in London, I had astonishing confirmation of his bitterness towards King Gustaf. By this time some 75,000 Norwegians had found refuge in Sweden and the Swedes were inundating Norway with food and medical supplies, so that King Haakon might by then well have forgiven the Swedes for their treatment of him; but he waved his long arms furiously to emphasise his disgust with King Gustaf, whom he three times called a 'shit'—strong language even from a man renowned for his tongue, particularly from one monarch about another, in the presence of a stranger and newspapermen.

† The following is a summary of the first section of the Swedish White Paper (April 17, 1948) on the Norwegian Government Outside Norway 1940-43.

This section dealt with the Norwegian Authorities on Swedish Territory, April 1940:

'Prime Minister Nygaardsvold, on April 9, at the session of the *Storting* in Elverum, pointed out that efforts ought to be made toward maintaining the "name of government", even though the Norwegian Government might have to "go into Sweden". During the next two days the Government discussed the question of taking refuge in Sweden. After the bombing of Nybergsund, where they were staying, the King and Cabinet decided on the evening of April 11 to

He now tried to reach Gudbrandsdalen, where he might find protection with Ruge's guerillas around Lillehammer and perhaps with advance British troops, supposing the Allies returned, althought there was little hope of that immediately. If the worst came to the worst, he might get through to Romsdal, one of the only two areas in all Norway where Ruge said, according to Hambro, that 'a fairly regular mobilisation could be carried out': the other was Voss, near Bergen. This was also the right direction for rescue by the Royal Navy.

King Haakon, Prince Olav, an adjutant, Trygve Lie and Terje Wold set out in two small private cars via Rena, halfway to Lillehammer, where they abandoned the search for Ruge and turned north. They then pressed on up the Glomma River, via Koppang, and reached Renadalen at 3 a.m. on April 13, when they rested briefly until dawn.

leave for Lillehammer in several automobile groups. The group with the King, the Crown Prince, Foreign Minister Koht and other members of the Government departed, became separated from the others and, on the morning of April 12, reached the Customs Station of Lillebo, close to the Swedish frontier. From there Koht telephoned Mr. Günther, the Swedish Foreign Minister, asking whether King Haakon "might stay in Sweden and leave the country whenever he wished, or whether he would be interned".

'At 11.50 a.m. the same day, the Swedish Government's reply arrived, declaring that the King of Norway and his entourage could of course enter Sweden, but no pledge could be given as to internment.

'Later in the day—at 1.30 p.m.—the Swedish Foreign Office sent Koht another communication by which the King and his entourage were welcomed to Sweden; it was emphasised, at the same time, however, that according to international law, the functions of government could not be exercised from foreign territory, and that the Swedish Government would not give any advance guarantees regarding a possible return.

'On the same day the King and his entourage entered Swedish territory at the frontier station of Flötningen; the hour cannot be specified beyond the fact that the arrival took place after the receipt of the first of the two communications above. After staying about half an hour on Swedish territory, the King returned to Norway.

'Mr. Koht and two other members of the Norwegian Cabinet, Mr. Torp and Mr. Hjelmtveit, on April 12, were at Sarna, and on April 13 at Sälen (Sweden). After Koht had granted a newspaper interview at Sälen, Günther made the urgent request that they should not make any public statements, and reminded them that the Norwegian Government could not be permitted to exercise any governmental powers from Sweden.

'The next day, April 14, the three above-mentioned members of the Norwegian Cabinet left Sälen, Koht and Torp returning to Norway.'

252

Thus the four key Norwegians outside Oslo—King Haakon, Hambro, Nygaardsvold and Ruge—had lost touch.

The two cars continued north to Tynset, then west via Alvdal and Foldalen to the Oslo-Trondheim Railway at Hjerkin, which they reached at 6 p.m., having spent hours sheltering in the forest from aeroplanes and digging the royal car out of the deep snow when it ran off the road.

The Germans controlled the Trondheim end of the railway, but did not board the train, which was under Norwegian control from Støren southwards. Soon after 7 p.m. the train arrived going south. One of the Ministers happened to know the guard, and the royal party, dressed up in strange hats and dark glasses, bundled into the mail van. Soon after midnight they crept out of hiding and alighted at Otta— in Gudbrandsdalen at last, but fifty miles from Ruge's guerillas. A bed was found for the King in a boarding house, where he was able to rest properly and change clothes for the first time in four days: a refugee in his own country.

From April 9 to 23, when he quit Gudbrandsdalen, Koht admits that 'the king had no fixed stay anywhere, and for the most part had been cut off from communication even with the parts of Norway that were not occupied by the enemy, and still more with foreign countries'. His government had clearly ceased to function.

On April 14 Nygaardsvold arrived from Løsjaverk, and the King sent out a proclamation: 'The position is that I cannot tell you where I, the Crown Prince and the government are staying in Norway.' Eventually this news spread and created deep depression.

At about the same time, Hambro reported amazingly from Stockholm that Bergen and Trondheim had been recaptured, whereas in fact General Steffens was in full retreat from Bergen and, as he later wrote: 'With German warships in Trondheim harbour and the aerodrome lost, no resistance could be made in the town.'

Hambro's false report encouraged the belief elsewhere that Norway was waging regular warfare, and deceived the Allies at a vital moment when they were debating how to help.

Also on April 14, German paratroops descended around Dombås, a tiny ski centre at the Trondheim-Aandalsnes rail junction, thus cutting off the royal party from the coast and the world, at a time when the Allies were desperately trying to find and rescue the King. Whitney

Straight of 601 Squadron was one of two people sent to contact King Haakon. He landed secretly with an advance British naval party at Aandalsnes on April 16 and ran the gauntlet of the enemy paratroopers to discover the King at Otta and inform him of the Anglo-French intervention which was then starting.

Simultaneously, Lord Mountevans was sent from Stockholm by Churchill 'to stiffen the Norwegian government'. He followed a zigzagging course of several hundred miles in pursuit of the King and 'heard much discouraging news of the Norwegian resistance'. He was also confronted by resentments 'as strong against the British for letting the country be ravaged as against the Germans for doing it'— an amazing unsolicited testimonial for Quisling's policy of neutrality. Eventually he ran the King to earth at Vaagaa, where the monarch had found refuge in a cottage. He secured an undertaking from the King and his Ministers that they would 'fight on, although it was not really their war and had been forced upon them'. Mountevans had been famous in Norway since the Scott Antarctic Expedition, and his second wife was a Norwegian beauty. He was therefore fanatically pro-Norwegian and hardly the man to form an objective view of the military situation.

That was on April 22, and that night Haakon, Olav, an adjutant, Nygaardsvold, Trygve Lie and Terje Wold moved fifty miles nearer the west coast to Stuguflaaten Tourist Hotel, high up in the majestic Romsdal Mountains. There, says *All for Norway*, 'the most important of the government meetings were held', albeit only three Cabinet Ministers were present, and all Labour members too! The 'decisions' are reported to have concerned military administration (which was practically non-existent); civil administration (now almost entirely in the hands of the Germans and supporters—Quisling having in the meantime been outmanœuvred); the mercantile marine (working largely for Britain on charter for six months); the Bank of Norway (with its gold reserve now careering about in trucks or small boats); and the State Broadcasting System (now German-controlled).

The king and government then threw themselves on the mercy of the British Navy at Molde during the night of April 22-23. They stayed in the outskirts until the 30th, when the destroyer HMS *Glasgow* took them to Tromsö on the Arctic Ocean. Two days previously, the King and his advisers had actually had the nerve according to *All for Norway*, to 'protest' against the proposed British evacuation although Molde was admittedly 'a sea of fire'.

Things were more comfortable in Tromsö, 'the stepping stone to the North Pole'. On this fringe of civilisation the King and the remnants of his Cabinet were joined by the unfortunate Ruge, who was now saddled with the command of all the 'armed forces', virtually replacing Ljungberg. They had nothing to do. According to Hambro, who had returned from Sweden: 'Night and day we listened to the London, French and Swedish radio.' Mr. Oxholm, the Danish Minister, who was one of the five envoys to follow the King all the way, said afterwards: 'There was very little to do up there.' Mrs. Harriman added: 'I dare say I was more real use in staying by the relief work for refugees in Stockholm.'

King Haakon and the Crown Prince were actually not in Tromsö town (population 10,800) but fifty miles away, near GHQ, in a small bungalow in Maalselvdalen. The Cabinet met in the Tromsö creamery, Storsteinness. Nevertheless the pretence of governing went on. In this make-believe world, miles from anywhere, the King broadcast. On May 7 he said: 'We still hold strong positions in the North and with the help that is now planned we shall continue the reconquest of Norway.' On National Day, May 17, he added: 'We can still call the North of Norway ours. This part of the country, which for years past has not perhaps been noticed as it deserved, has given evidence during these days of the ability and dignity to represent a free and independent Norway. . . . To all compatriots in occupied areas, I would express the hope that they may not lose heart and that we may succeed . . . in regaining their liberty.' The Crown Prince indulged in no such equivocation. He broadcast straight out: 'The outlook seems dark to many of us, but in spite of everything we shall stick to the belief that the final victory will be for right.' On May 23, King Haakon said on the air: 'Many nations are fighting here . . . Comrades-in-arms of all nations fighting at the front in Norway, continue to be stubborn and strong in your conviction that the final victory will be for the good cause.'

On June 1, the King was informed of the final Allied evacuation of Norway—from Narvik, where the Germans had been pressed back through the iron-ore railway to the Swedish frontier on May 29. As we now know, Hitler had panicked, and if his High Command had obeyed him, they would have pulled out, leaving this hub of the North in Allied and Norwegian hands, so that with a little Norwegian preparation and effort, the government's preposterous gamble might actually have come off!

For Germany and the Allies, however, Norway was a sideshow. Apart from a dozen isolated acts of heroism, she had done nothing to justify further Allied sacrifice and she was now abandoned appropriately to her own devices.

Crown Prince Olav for the second time insisted on facing the music and staying to share his people's fate, but again the politicians overruled him. Had he remained, the whole nation would surely have rallied to him. Ruge was allowed to stay behind.

The King and Cabinet left for Britain on June 7 from Tromsö aboard HMS *Devonshire*. Said the King's proclamation: 'The King and government . . . are leaving the country. However, they do not at the same time give up the fight for regaining the independence of Norway. On the contrary, they intend to keep it up from outside the frontiers. . . . We are united in urging the Norwegian people to keep up courage in the face of all oppressions and trials. We feel confident that no Norwegian will betray the cause of liberty. . . . We are determined to give all our strength, our lives and all we have, to fight for Norway.'

Publication of the proclamation was postponed until June 9, when HMS *Devonshire* neared Scotland, 'in order,' says Koht, 'to give General Ruge time to prepare the demobilisation of the Army. He himself had asked to be the man who was to negotiate the capitulation* with the Germans and the capitulation was signed on June 10.'

The capitulation—the terms of which were not published until November 1947—only came to light during one of the 92,000 cases brought against 'quislings' on the basic charge that they were assisting the enemy. There was, however, in law no such enemy. The government had concluded a formal armistice with the

---

* The 'Final Armistice' of June 10, 1940, was signed in Trondheim by Colonel Buschenhagen for the German General Staff and by Lieutenant-Colonel R. Roscher Nielsen of the Norwegian General Staff, who was 'sent down from the North for this purpose', says the Defence Ministry's Historical Section. General Dietl (Germany) and Lieutenant Colonel Harald Wrede Holm (Norway) signed likewise for the Narvik area at Spionkop on the same day.

Germans, although they continued from London to urge sabotage and resistance.

The fact is that the capitulation order was given, signed, concluded and carried out on the Norwegian government's instructions, drawn up with the King in Council. Thus the Germans acquired a legal status in Norway, and the war between the two countries, which had been declared unilaterally by Germany on April 26, ceased. As the Cabinet decided in the presence of the King and recorded on June 7: 'It will be hopeless for Norway to continue the war. The king approved the report.'

Articles 43 and 52 of the Hague Convention lay down that an Occupying Power acquires all the administrative authority normally belonging to the government of the country. The latter cannot therefore legally oblige the population to act against the Occupant's orders, so long as these are confined to recognised judicial limits— basically anything covering the Occupant's security, which may stretch over a wide field. Consequently, Norwegians could not later be held responsible legally for obeying the Germans' reasonable instructions and disobeying the exiled government.

A wide degree of practical collaboration with the Occupant is inevitable if life is to carry on at all and this happened in every occupied country, whether under the Allies or the Axis. This is no crime in international law. The capitulation of June 10 is therefore vital to the whole Quisling controversy. If Norway capitulated, and Quisling did no more than was reasonable in the circumstances, there was no case against him.

After the war, the government sought at first to disown the signatures beneath its capitulation order, but photostats proved that the order had indeed been given. The next step was to deny the legality of such an order on the ground that only the King has authority to sign such a document, and that his signature did not appear on it—despite the fact that it was drawn up with the King in Council!

The fact of the capitulation and the falsity of the position adopted by the 'London Government' are still not widely known in Norway. In any case, for the next five years the exiled authorities played only a peripheral role in Norwegian affairs. The real struggle for power was inside Norway—a long, inglorious triangular fight between Quisling and the Germans with interlopers playing off one against the other until they threw in their lot with the exiles towards the end, when a Western victory seemed probable.

Quisling's attempts to influence Hitler had been as unsuccessful as his attempts to contact the King, and in fact on April 15 he had fallen from grace.

19

Down and Up

N O clearer proof can be adduced that Quisling was not in a conspiracy with Hitler than the fact that he was forced temporarily from office on April 15, at which time he looked like a six-day wonder.

First, his independence and neutralist activities did not endear him to the Germans. He failed to contact the German Legation before assuming power; he disobeyed General von Engelbrecht's orders; he asserted Norwegian authority over institutions such as the *Storting*, the Foreign Office and the Diplomatic Service; and he effectively sabotaged German orders to the Norwegian Mercantile Marine. Above all, he failed to recall the King to duty in Oslo. He had not proved to be a German puppet. His support from intellectuals, Trade Unions and other public bodies, the Press and some members of his own government was insufficient to give him a convincing air of authority. The doubt began to arise whether his organisation was viable.

Second, there was axe-grinding German criticism. Hitler held Quisling responsible for misinformation about the Norwegian batteries at Bolaerne and Oscarsborg, which had made the invasion look silly and caused delay and losses, thus reflecting on the High Command. As early as April 10, Falkenhorst had set such criticism in motion in a conversation with Minister Brauer. Taking their line from

their Commander-in-Chief, Falkenhorst, Lieutenant-Colonel Pohlman (the High Command's representative at the Legation) reported
that Quisling had caused bad blood and this stirred Norwegians to
fight, and General Bruno Uthman (German Military Attaché) reported that Quisling's was a 'gangster government' and that he was
a 'criminal'.

Ribbentrop and his closest advisers on Norway, including Minister
Brauer, had always decried Quisling and were therefore humiliated
when Hitler adopted Scheidt's policy following Quisling's coup on
April 9.

The High Command and the Foreign Office represented powerful
opposition to Quisling at Hitler's court, and their influence was far
stronger than that of Rosenberg at a time when Quisling did not look
like the man who would succeed in re-establishing law and order in
Norway.

Third, there was an avalanche of anti-Quisling Press reports,
cleverly inspired by the escaping Norwegian authorities and their
supporters in Sweden, and elsewhere. Quisling was far too slow to realise
the disastrous impact of one-sided Press criticism on his reputation at
home and abroad, which did him as much harm in Germany as among
the Allies and neutrals. He had a competent staff on *Fritt Folk* and
control of the Norwegian News Agency, besides his assumed powers
of censorship, and yet he let slip the chance of properly putting his case.

Fourth, the overriding German consideration was the prospect of
Allied re-intervention and the possibility of a prolonged campaign in
the North, which would sidetrack Hitler's main purpose, the conquest
of the West. It was therefore urgent for Hitler to establish a reliable
administration in Norway (of any sort), which could cope with the
expected emergency. He had to obtain quick results and could not
afford the time to tinker with a politically naïve rival ideologist.

Fifth, there were intrigues by a curious pro-German and pro-British
assortment of notables in Oslo with the aim of filling the vacuum with
an alternative to Quisling, fostered by Falkenhorst and Brauer, and
offering Hitler a solution to the problems he had created by suddenly
sponsoring Quisling on the night of April 9.

An awkward decision awaited Hitler therefore when Quisling's
representative, Hagelin, arrived in Berlin to try to secure a prolongation of the Quisling régime, backed by the High Command and the

Wilhelmstrasse on Hitler's orders. Any such arrangement implied Hitler's sympathy with Quisling's (and Rosenberg's) 'Nordic' ideas, which would have made a show of Norwegian sovereignty and independence possible, thus justifying the existence of a *Nasjonal Samling* government. Ideology was less important at the time, however, than security, and Quisling had ceased therefore to matter much in Berlin.

Hagelin's mission was doomed. Had Quisling tackled Hitler again personally, as he did with some success later, he might have succeeded where Hagelin failed, but he could not risk leaving Oslo. His purpose was to keep the Norwegian flag flying, and he feared that in his absence the Germans would have it down. There was in any case nobody of sufficient stature to stand in for him temporarily. He had many good men behind him, but they were too inexperienced. Besides, he had to watch the intrigues going on around him.

Hagelin was not the man to carry conviction with Hitler. He could thump tables, bluff and cajole most people, but Hitler, the master psychologist and showman, was beyond him. They knew each other from the two December meetings, but Hagelin had the wrong connections—Rosenberg, who cut no ice, Göring, who was out of the Norwegian affair, and Winkler, the financier, whereas he needed the ear of the all-important High Command or the Foreign Office.

First Hagelin saw Rosenberg and then Ribbentrop, but he got nowhere with them. Hitler gave him three hours of his time, from 11.15 a.m. to 2.15 p.m. No detailed record of this meeting has come to light, but we know that Hitler went into a long monologue, with many side issues. The meeting was interrupted by the arrival of the Norwegian Minister in Berlin, Arne Scheel, and Hagelin had to leave the room. Hitler proposed writing to King Haakon, again suggesting a friendly agreement on the Danish model as the only means to avoid total destruction, but later he changed his mind about the chances of influencing the monarch. It is clear that Hitler had not abandoned all hope of negotiations and was still looking for some form of realistic government in Norway.

Ribbentrop, after consulting Hagelin, Scheel and Walter Hewel (his liaison with Hitler and *Weserübung* headquarters), suggested to Hitler that Theodor Habicht, a Wilhemstrasse Under-Secretary, should be sent to Oslo to 'investigate'. Habicht had been a Nazi since

1925, a driving force in the Austrian Anschluss and in constant friction with Rosenberg. He was a trusted and experienced Nazi tough, with no experience of the North, and therefore on all counts an ideal man from Ribbentrop's viewpoint, to give Hitler a cold, objective appreciation of the confusion in Oslo.

Hitler agreed to Habicht's mission. What exact instructions Habicht had we do not know, but it seems safe to assume that he was intended to play Ribbentrop's game, in other words to replace Quisling with some more manageable figure. The official briefing included the improvement of German propaganda in Norway with the help of Quisling, but Quisling—and Brauer—had every reason to suspect that they were being supplanted.

At any rate Hagelin's mission failed. The best Quisling could hope was to be sustained in some marginal capacity or to be held in reserve. His bid to be a buffer between Germany and Norway had failed, as had all his preceding policies in turn—a Great German Union against Bolshevism; armed neutrality; an understanding with Germany; and a realistic settlement between King Haakon and Adolf Hitler.

Now his nightmare seemed as if it must come to pass: the North could hardly help becoming the battlefield of the Great Powers. His Norwegian enemies in Oslo were mustering against him and contacting the Germans behind his back. He had to think again.

Police Chief Kristian Welhaven had managed to defy Quisling's order for his arrest. With a six-man German bodyguard supplied by the Army, he was also well enough protected to ignore Quisling's command to come to see him, but he was not sure enough of himself to try to carry out the telephoned orders of Justice Minister Wold to arrest Quisling. Instead he went to Minister Brauer at the German Legation, thus giving Quisling strong reasons for supposing that Welhaven was acting on instructions from Wold to make overtures to the enemy. Quisling promptly summoned Carl Bernard Askvig, Police Chief of Aker (an extension of Oslo), and proposed that jurisdiction for Aker and Oslo should be combined, thus supplanting Welhaven. Askvig pleaded 'administrative difficulties'.

Thus Quisling was not supported by the Norwegian police, and his obstinacy towards the Germans alarmed prominent German residents in Norway so much that they began to seek means of replacing him. Active among them was Wolfgang Geldmacher, who was married to a Norwegian and had access to the Legation. There he learned that Quisling was not welcomed by the German authorities, and he passed this information to his friend, Johs Rivertz, who in turn related it to his father, a Supreme Court judge, whence it reached the ears of Chief Justice Paal Berg, the former Liberal Cabinet Minister.

Johs Rivertz next approached Dr. Ulrich Noack, the German writer, who was loosely attached to the Legation but was not popular with Brauer. Noack then expressed his apprehensions of Quisling to Fritjof Heyerdahl, a director of Siemens, who joined with another leading businessman, Gunnar Schelderup, to express disapproval of Quisling to Minister Brauer.

Within hours of that visit, Brauer was contacted in a similar sense by Rivertz, Geldmacher and Noack at the request of certain members of the Supreme Court whom they had sought out. Simultaneously, Pastor Günther of the German Lutheran Church in Oslo telephoned Bishop Eivind Berggrav, the Norwegian Primate, and arranged to meet him the following day, April 12. Berggrav then pointed out that 'we have not installed Quisling, nor have we accepted his government'.

It was clear to Brauer therefore that there was substantial opposition to Quisling outside the Nygaardsvold Government circles, and that there was a nucleus of influential people willing to set up an alternative régime. In fact, during the night of April 12-13 Berg and Rivertz sat up debating constitutional law and drafting the articles of a novel body which they proposed to create. Rivertz suggested it should be called 'State Council', but this sounded too obviously a usurpation for Berg, who changed it to 'Council for the Civil Administration of the Occupied Territories'.

Next morning, Brauer told Quisling's opponents in Oslo to hold their hand while he telephoned Ribbentrop to say that a 'number of good Norwegians had applied to him to remove Quisling' and that 'concrete proposals' were prepared.

Berg was preparing to go to the King, while Heyerdahl and Gunnar Schelderup sought a free passage for him from the German authorities. Ferdinand Schelderup and a number of other High Court judges suggested that the 'Administrative Council' might perhaps become a real government, in association with a peace treaty and some fresh arrangement over which Brauer would preside.

Habicht then arrived from Berlin, having seen Hitler the day before. He followed Ribbentrop's fanatically anti-Quisling line unreservedly and immediately made common cause with Brauer, whose original anti-Quisling appreciation had now been confirmed by a trusted *NSDAP* official, by the Wilhelmstrasse, and, apparently, by Hitler himself.

Within an hour the Supreme Court's proposals for a Norwegian 'civil administration' were telegraphed to Ribbentrop, and here a major misunderstanding arose. The Norwegian word 'administration' was rendered into German as 'government'. Argument continues to this day about who was to blame. Everybody was under pressure and there was room for genuine misunderstanding. Perhaps too there was room for much wilful thinking on both sides.

By the evening it was decided to send Bishop Berggrav as well as Paal Berg to the King, and their Army safe-conducts were awaited anxiously by Habicht and Brauer, who were frantically trying to trace the King. Then Haakon broadcast that he could not divulge his whereabouts, and the whole plan stalled.

So far, the Supreme Court, Hitler, Ribbentrop, Habicht and Brauer had all been working on the assumption that the King in Council would at least give them a hearing.

Habicht and Brauer were now committed at the highest level in Berlin to a 'government', so they had no alternative but to press on regardless, hoping for the best.

Berg and the Supreme Court, however, had a free choice. Were they, too, to press on, regardless of the King, or were they to pull out of the whole enterprise now that they could not contact him? Unlike Quisling up to date, they chose to ignore the King. True, the King in Council had virtually contracted out of business, and by persevering with the 'Administrative Council' without his assent, the Supreme Court tacitly admitted, even at this early stage, that the monarchy was in abeyance. For allegedly doing likewise, Quisling was shot.

Next day (April 14) Brauer was assured by Ribbentrop on the telephone that the new arrangement was desired by Germany, if necessary without the King's assent. The Second Battle of Narvik had started overnight. The Germans had been driven by the Allies into the tunnels towards Sweden, and Hitler was deciding to pull out to Trondheim. A stable government south of Narvik had become a matter of military importance, as well as political convenience.

In the forenoon, Habicht and Brauer visited Falkenhorst and Engelbrecht and everybody was delighted to hear that Quisling had been condemned by Berlin. The generals agreed that he was useless, and from their point of view this was true. He refused to collaborate with them!

At 1 p.m., Habicht saw Berg, after Brauer had paved the way, and the Chief Justice confirmed that he would still continue with the 'Administrative Council', supplanting Quisling. Berg undertook to brief his fellow judges on the text of his proposals and Habicht took Brauer to the Continental to tell Quisling that he was dismissed.

Naturally Quisling, supported by Hagelin, opposed the change vehemently. It was a 'tumultuous meeting', according to Knudsen. Quisling was shocked and angered at the very idea, as he saw it, of Norwegians taking office as German appointees, in contrast with his own government, which was in no way beholden to the conquerors. It was clear from the new Narvik battle that Norway was in danger of being transformed into a major battlefield. The only course for any Norwegian administration in Oslo was to reaffirm neutrality and independence from the forthcoming struggle, thus sparing the population from futile devastation. The 'Administrative Council' was bound to lead the Norwegians into danger. Thus Quisling's new policy was evolved and soon took shape under the slogan 'Let the nation have peace'.

Next, Berg and Brauer went to inform Falkenhorst of the proposed membership of the new régime. Ribbentrop's office was also informed by telephone. Hewel, who took the call, introduced one important new development. On Hitler's instructions, Quisling was to be accorded 'an honourable position' and 'held in reserve'.

Now Quisling and Hagelin returned to the fray. They demanded to see Brauer at the Legation, where Quisling was informed that he would be 'responsible for demobilisation'. He asked for time to consider this, and also asked that Hagelin should be appointed his representative in Berlin, but nothing came of this. Although Hitler held Quisling in reserve, the Germans had made up their minds. Berg was already being referred to as 'the representative of the King' and as 'representing sovereignty in Occupied Territory'.

Police Chief Welhaven then reappeared at German GHQ with a

list of names of Norwegians suitable for the new régime. While Falkenhorst was scrutinising them, Welhaven was called to the German Legation to meet Berg. These two men had turned out to be the main Norwegian architects of the 'Administrative Council'. Brauer informed them that he 'could not wait for the royal assent', for at 9 p.m. an attempt had been made to blow up Lysaker Railway Bridge, on the main line from Oslo southwards—an incident that stressed the urgency from the German viewpoint for a docile régime.

Next day (April 15) Bishop Berggrav went far into the forests surrounding Oslo, supported by a German bodyguard, and exhorted guerillas to lay down their arms because they were merely *francs tireurs*.* For saying the same thing in different words over the radio, Quisling was executed.

Chief Justice Berg telephoned to the Norwegian Legation in Stockholm, saying: 'The Supreme Court has considered it necessary to be instrumental in the formation of a Council of Administration to carry on the civilian administration in the occupied areas . . . confident that the King of Norway, under the present extraordinary circumstances, will approve.'

These 'extraordinary circumstances', were precisely what Quisling pleaded as justification for his own action, and there can be no better confirmation of the 'power vacuum' than this assessment at the highest Norwegian judicial level. The legality of the Supreme Court's decision to set up an administration is highly questionable, despite the ponderous special-pleading that goes on indefinitely. The plain fact is that the Supreme Court acted on April 15, 1940, as illegally or otherwise as had Vidkun Quisling on April 9, 1940, no more and no less. Both pleaded 'extraordinary circumstances' and an 'emergency'. The important difference between the Supreme Court and Quisling was that the former eventually backed the ultimate winners of the Second World War, whereas Quisling backed the losers.

At 5 p.m. on April 15 the Administrative Council was proclaimed by Berg from Oslo Science Academy. Half an hour later Brauer was

---

* He afterwards said on the radio: 'Civilians who involve themselves in war by sabotage or the like commit direct crime against their fellow citizens. . . . Civilians must never carry weapons. By the laws of war they may be executed. I have consulted the Supreme Court. We are unanimous that this should be announced over the radio.'

referring to it in a cable to Berlin as a 'government'—and to Quisling as 'retiring Minister-President'.

Quisling was present in the broadcasting studio when the Supreme Court's creation was proclaimed: Knudsen, who was present, reports that the new Council's Chairman tried to help Quisling with his coat, but 'Quisling snatched his overcoat away and said, "No, Mr. Christensen, that I will not allow. For thirty years you have been acting the patriot and as my friend in the Defence Association. Now you have taken over the government of Norway on German terms, which I have rejected with contempt. You have made yourself a vile hostage to the *Wehrmacht*. You will be forced to join in plundering the people, and, when that is finished, your new taskmasters will throw you out. It will be richly deserved."'

Quisling at once dissociated himself officially from the Administrative Council. At a farewell meeting with thirty of his colleagues at his *Storting* office, he informed them that he had been superseded because, as Demobilisation Chief, he had been unwilling to guarantee that guerilla warfare against the invaders would cease, whereas this was the condition on which the Supreme Court's 'Administrative Council' had been accepted by Berlin.*

The following day *Fritt Folk* stated: 'We have taken a step backwards, but we shall soon take two steps forward.'

The calibre of the Administrative Council was inferior to that of the Quisling Cabinet. Chairman Ingolf C. Christensen was a civil servant and former Conservative *Stortingsman*, now Governor of Oslo and a grey figure with nothing like Quisling's intellect and international experience. Judge Ole F. Harbek was an ex-Permanent Under-Secretary in the Ministry of Justice. J. Bache-Wiig was from the Ministry of Supply. Andreas Diesen was a state doctor. R. J. Mork was a lecturer at the Ministry of Agriculture. Dr. Didrik A. Seip, Rector of Oslo University, who on this very day had headed a public appeal for law, order and an end to resistance,† was a brother-in-law

---

* Affidavit by Tormud Hustad, Quisling's Minister of Agriculture, who was present.

† His appeal and that of Bishop Berggrav were actually made, with the approval of the Supreme Court, *after the Allies had made some show of coming to the rescue* (at Narvik and Aandalsnes) and on the eve of supporting action at Namsos!

of Bishop Berggrav. Among 180 appellants were 8 other professors, 15 lawyers, 8 clergy, 46 business executives, 34 trade union officials and 12 representatives of posts, telegraph and telephones. Gunnar Jahn, Director of Statistics and a former Finance Minister, was the best of an average lot.

Five representative bodies proclaimed support for the Council. The Norwegian Banking Association (Bank Chairman Sandberg and Director Torsteinson); the Norwegian Trade Association (Directors Erling Steen and Paul Frank); the Norwegian Industries Association (Managing-Director Horn and Director Vogt); the Norwegian Farmers Party (Lecturer R. Mork); the Norwegian Shipowners' Association (Owner Bjørn Hansen and Directors Klaveness and Kaare Schøning); the Labour Trade Unions Organisation (Elias Volan, Albin Raaen, Nicolas Ness and Dagfin Beck). Their appeal was undersigned by Albert Kvaal, Managing-Director of the Oslo Electrical Industries.

Almost everybody left in Norwegian civic life could now be accused of usurping the authority of the King in Council and following Quisling's policy of peaceful co-existence with the conquerors —the only difference between the 'quislings' and the 'administrators' being that Quisling sought to operate in his own right, whereas the latter were beholden to the Germans. Paradoxically it is Quisling who is now regarded in Norway as a German stooge.

The new régime made no attempt to make use of Quisling's services or those of his supporters. Nevertheless Berg made the following statement about Quisling, in the light of which it is difficult to understand how later he could have charged Quisling with high treason: 'After the Nygaardsvold Government left Oslo, there was no longer any representative of the executive authority left in the capital of Norway. In this connection, so fraught with destiny for our country and its people, Mr. Quisling placed himself at the disposal of the nation with a view to assisting in the avoidance of bloodshed in the Occupied Territories and in maintaining peace and order. By resigning, he has once more proved his sense of responsibility and his patriotism. I therefore thank Mr. Quisling for his declaration by which the arrangements of the Supreme Court of Justice have been made possible.'

In his diary, which was produced in Court in 1945, Berg also recorded: 'I said [to Brauer] that personally I was of the opinion that

Quisling acted in good faith, subjectively—that he really believed he
had been guarding the interests of his country in doing what he had
done, and that I could therefore make a declaration to that effect as it
was my personal opinion.'

German aircraft dropped 200,000 Oslo newspapers and six million
leaflets to explain the new Berg régime. The press statement following
Berg's proclamation referred five times to the Administrative Council
as a 'government', and the Germans genuinely believed, rightly or
wrongly, that this was what they had got. There appears to be no
record of Berg seeking to correct this impression before Brauer
departed enthusiastically for Berlin next day (April 16).

However, the situation was to change dramatically because of the
attitude of the King. Berg's messages, via Stockholm, took time to
find their way to the monarch. Among them, according to Hambro,
was a request that the Crown Prince should broadcast to the people,
asking them to remain calm and 'to abstain from acts of sabotage and
violence'.

On April 19 King Haakon replied: 'The authority of the Administrative Council in important matters is dependent on a foreign power
and is not exercised on behalf of myself or the Government of Norway. And so I must reserve for myself and the Norwegian Government full liberty as to the decisions taken by the Council.' The Crown
Prince could not broadcast because he had 'no access to senders'. In
any case the King continued: 'Nobody can expect that I or the Crown
Prince should admonish the people to obey the Germans' orders.'

Thus the King gave Berg the same treatment that he had given to
Quisling, making no distinction between them.

His rejection of the 'administration' on April 19 acted like a bomb
in Berlin. Suddenly Hitler, Ribbentrop, Habicht and Brauer realised
that they had not got a 'government' at all. They were frantic. Narvik
looked lost. The British had landed forty-eight hours previously in
Aandalsnes on the Romsdal Fjord, south of Trondheim. Advance
British troops had reached Lillehammer. More British forces were
approaching Namsos, north of Trondheim, where they were to land
next day. A big campaign in the North looked unavoidable. The
conquest of the West might have to be postponed.

This was a major crisis and Hitler acted when it came to this point
with his usual ruthlessness. He now saw the essentials clearly. No more

269

experimenting with puppet governments could be countenanced.

Norway was now to become a Reichscommissariat—the next lowest status in the Greater Reich to a Protectorate, such as Hitler imposed on 'racially backward' (Slav) Poland and Czechoslovakia. The nominal difference perhaps connoted some surviving remnant of respect for a 'Nordic' Norway, but the prospect for Norway was horrifying.

Hitler appointed the forty-one-year-old Gauleiter of Essen, Josef Terboven, to be Reichscommissar in Norway. The summons to Terboven came without warning through Martin Bormann's Party Chancellery, but the Gauleiter was Göring's nominee—a typical product of the Nazi system and chosen from the inner circle for his utter loyalty to the *Führer*, *NSDAP* and the Field-Marshal in that order. His qualifications were his ability, brutality and reliance on the proven methods by which the Nazis had fought their way to power. Rosenberg was not consulted, nor was Terboven sponsored by Keitel or Jodl, who were now in disgrace over Narvik, or by Ribbentrop, who was made a scapegoat for diplomatic failure in Norway. Terboven had direct access to Hitler and brooked no interference.

In the First World War he was a gunner, later a flier—hence his original contact with Göring—and had finished as a Lieutenant. He was awarded the Iron Cross. He could not settle down at Freiburg and Munich Universities, and had joined *NSDAP* at an early date. Back in Essen, his birthplace, as a bank clerk in 1923, he led the street-fighting, and by 1927 had become one of the leading Nazis in the Ruhr. By 1933 he was Gauleiter in Essen and next year he played a prominent role in the purge of Ernst Röhm's Brownshirts.

His reliability then brought him to the top—to membership of the Reichstag and the Over-Presidency of the Rhine Province in 1935, when he formed an admiration for Jonas Lie, the Norwegian policeman-author on the International Police Force during the Saar Plebiscite. This connection had far-reaching consequences.

Next came membership of the Prussian Parliament, whereby he renewed his contact with Göring, who was becoming industrial dictator of Germany. Two-thirds of Germany's iron ore was shipped from Swedish and Norwegian ports and this factor doubtless gave Terboven some insight into the importance of the North.

In appearance he looked like the mean and discontented bank clerk he had been, which not even his splendid uniforms and insignia could disguise. He was a little man with an inverted inferiority complex, who quarrelled with everybody—notably the Gauleiters of North Westphalia and Düsseldorf. To cover up his deficiencies he acted like a despot. He was the last man to carry out his brief from Hitler 'to win over the Norwegians', but he was admirably equipped to exercise his reserve powers of 'life and death'.

With him he took a huge staff to knock Norway into shape at all levels: Dr. Hans Dellbrügge and Karl Eugen Dellenbusch from the Reich Ministry of the Interior; SS Obergruppenführer Fritz Wietzel, Member of the Prussian Parliament and Düsseldorf police chief, who was a friend; Wietzel's assistants, Police Major-General Riege and Police Lieutenant-Colonel Abraham; Carl Otte, an economist from Hamburg; George Wilhelm Müller, aged thirty-one, of Hamburg, representing Propaganda Minister Josef Goebbels; Paul Wegener, also aged thirty-one, who was to be Terboven's deputy.

On April 20, when Terboven's instructions were signed, the inner circle gathered to see him off: Göring, Himmler, Bormann and Hans von Lammers (Chief of the Reich Chancellery), with Keitel added to give the High Command's formal approval.

Clearly there was to be 'no nonsense' in Norway, but the emphasis on the Nazi Party role in Terboven's appointment indicates that the pill contained in the Reichscommissariat was to be sugared with respect, as far as possible, for Norway's 'Nordic' background. An experiment was to be made in the export of Nazi 'Aryan' policy to a non-German-speaking country. This is where Quisling came in, for Terboven was instructed to 'co-operate' with him.

Terboven's subsequent behaviour in Norway shows that he took the ideological side of his assignment very lightly. He viewed himself primarily as an administrator. Winning over Norwegians or co-operating with Quisling played little part in his calculations. Could he have applied a Polish solution to Norway's tiny population, by fully utilising his powers of life and death, the problem could have been ended abruptly, but Norway was 'Aryan' and could not be treated like 'inferior' Slavs or Jews, and Quisling, as champion of the 'Nordic' cult in Norway, could not entirely be ignored.

Thus there was conflict between Terboven and Quisling from the

271

beginning of the Reichscommissariat to the end. The propaganda picture of Quisling always slavishly making himself the instrument of Nazi persecution or allowing himself to be used, simply out of a lust for power, is as false as the rest of the Norwegian legend. He described the occupation as 'the worst years of my life'. Perhaps his most important function was to have prevented a logical and easy solution on the Polish pattern. That would have been the end of Norway, which would have been crippled for ever, like Estonia, Latvia and Lithuania, with their comparably small populations. For their escape the Norwegians owe Quisling a tremendous debt of gratitude.

Quisling stuck stubbornly to his post as a self-appointed barrier between Terboven and the people, sacrificing the shadow of collaboration for the substance of small mercies, thus earning the enmity of both sides. He found himself between the devil and the deep blue sea. Terboven withheld any real power with which Quisling might have helped Norway in obvious ways and thus earned kudos for himself among his own people. The King and the Norwegian London Government, who could never regard Quisling as saviour of his country, made him the scapegoat for the multiple injuries inflicted on Norwegians *by the Germans*. Norwegian propaganda from London was as much directed with an eye on the post-war future as on the pressing task of winning the war.

In the new circumstances facing Norway, Quisling to some extent made his peace with the Administrative Council group. Already, before the arrival in Norway of Terboven, much of Quisling's work was undone. Government offices closed and were taken over by the Germans. The Norwegian flag came down from the *Storting*, and the Germans moved into the building. Norwegian administrative bodies, notably those concerned with finance, economics, production and price stabilisation, were carefully controlled by the Germans, as were the Norwegian State Police. The Bank of Norway was forced to open a German account for 13 milliard *kroner* ($140 million). A German censorship was imposed. German troops bought goods with the backing of confiscated currency.

Quisling moved back from the Continental Hotel to his wife and their flat, but he took a drawing-room for conferences in the Grand Hotel, where Knudsen, Hagelin and Scheidt were now staying.

Scheidt's continued presence in Norway confirmed Hitler's surviving interest in his 'Nordic' policy, and indicated that Rosenberg still clung to the fringe of power. Brauer was less fortunate. Hitler banished him to the front as a common soldier and he was reported after the war as a member of the Organisation Troika in Moscow—the Recruiting Inspectorate for fellow-travellers. Habicht was later banished to the Eastern Front when winter stalemate was reached at the end of 1941. Quisling's other German friend, the Naval Attaché Schreiber, survived, however, in Norway, thanks to the influence of Raeder.

The demobilisation duties wished on Quisling by Brauer and Berg evaporated, since Norway now became the scene of full-scale war. Terboven and the Administrative Council were in control of the home front, and Quisling was merely an observer of the disasters which he had predicted and sought to avoid by timely precautions. This book is therefore no place for a detailed account of the campaign, which has been adequately described from the British viewpoint by Bernard Ash in his *Norway 1940*.* Its only importance in the Quisling story is the confirmation it affords of his prophecies of futile resistance and needless suffering which led to his condemnation of the King and his government for their ill-conceived war-mongering.

The central question about the Norwegian campaign is this: If the Allies could not easily occupy Norway in the Germans' absence, how could they expect to do so in the Germans' presence? Temporary success there was, but even Narvik town was not captured until the night of May 27-28, and the order for evacuation followed on June 1. As Admiral of the Fleet, the Earl of Cork and Orrery,† who commanded the naval force that was part of a combined expedition to Narvik, says: 'I formed the opinion that the position in Norway had never really been understood.' Perhaps this is because only Quisling had been talking sense, and no one would listen to him.

General Adrian Carton de Wiart, V.C., who was in command of the Central Norwegian Expeditionary Force, recalled‡ that 'we did not seem set for victory from the start' and that the local population 'lived in deadly terror of our arrival'. He wired the War Office that he was 'quite incapable of advancing on Trondheim', only to receive the reply 'that for political reasons they would be glad if I

* Cassell.   † *My Naval Life* (Hutchinson).
‡ *Happy Odyssey* (Cape).

273

would maintain my positions'. His A.D.C., Colonel Peter Fleming, reported after a trip to the War Office: 'You can really do what you like for they don't know what they want done.'

Now for the bill gratuitously wished on to Norway and her population of just under 3 million people.

In 1940 the following towns were among the places heavily bombed: Elverum, Molde, Kristiansand (North), Steinkjaer, Namsos, Aandalsnes, Bodø, and Narvik. Before the end of the war the disastrous policies of the London Government had invoked nationwide devastation at the hands of the Germans.

The following figures are taken from *Reconstruction in Norway*, published by the Housing Directorate, Oslo, in the spring of 1947: In Finnmark and North Troms, the Arctic provinces comprising a fifth of the country and containing 75,000 inhabitants before the war, destruction included: 12,000 dwellings, of which 6,000 were farms; 500 factories; 20 churches, 15 parsonages and 150 schools; 21 medical institutions with 578 beds; 11 telegraph stations and 20,000 telegraph poles; 12 large telephone stations; 350 bridges; 180 lighthouses; 118 small power stations; 350 fishing-smacks with tackle to the value of 20m. *kroner* ($2.8m.) and thousands of smaller boats. In Finnmark alone 24,000 persons escaped deportation by hiding in caves or mines. Outside North Troms and Finnmark 3,952 dwellings, 8,230 flats and 1,238 other buildings were destroyed. The value of buildings destroyed in the two northern provinces was 160 m. *kroner* ($22.4m.) and in the South 360 m. *kroner* ($50.4m.). In Bergen, and Kristiansand N., the cost was $5.6m. or more, in Oslo, Bodø, Herøya-Eidanger and Narvik-Bjerknes-Ankenes more than $2.8m. These figures do not include movables, requisitioned houses, quays, bridges, roads and railways damaged by the Germans.

Direct Occupation costs amounted to 4,328 m. *kroner* in 1940 and settled down to a mean 1,465 m. *kroner* over the following years—that is about $616m. as a direct result of British intervention and afterwards about $210m. a year.

The Central Statistical Office estimated that the total reduction of national wealth amounted to 19 per cent of the pre-1939 figure, represented by drafts on capital to the value of 4,000 m. *kroner* ($560m.) and 1,870 m. *kroner* in war damage ($262m.)—a profound dislocation of the economy.

In comparison with neutral Sweden, twice-ravaged Finland and gently occupied Denmark, Norway suffered out of all proportion. That is what Quisling meant by the danger of Norway becoming the battlefield of the Great Powers, yet, despite his repeated warnings and his practical efforts between April 9 and 15, 1940, to avert catastrophe, he is blamed for most of the consequences.

If the British intervention had helped Norway in any respect or shortened the war by a day, one might argue that Quisling was mistaken, even a traitor, but the Allies never had a serious hope of permanent success from start to finish, as the senior British commanders confess, nor was there any co-operation worth mentioning on the Norwegian side.

The government in exile did everything they could to blacken Quisling's name, but they were not a united group. Koht started criticising the British on arrival at Rotherhithe, and took no further part of importance in the government for the duration. Trygve Lie, who was soon to call Churchill 'a mere journalist', was similarly out of favour. Soon the government raised its own rate of pay and re-treated into a country mansion. From 1941 onwards it passed laws to enable them to act against the 'quislings', their political opponents, with a show of legality in the event of an Allied victory. All these laws were retroactive in flat contradiction of Article 97 of the Constitution and have since been declared invalid in his book *Landsvik* by Professor Jon Skeie, Norway's greatest lawyer.

The most remarkable act was the 'bigamy law' introduced by the present Chief Justice of the Supreme Court, Terje Wold. This permitted Norwegians in the British Armed Forces or in the Norwegian Mercantile Marine, which was also under British orders, to ignore their marriages at home and to marry their British girl friends.

The exile government had no military control over the Norwegian volunteers in the British Armed Forces and, indeed, were not even consulted by the British prior to actions on Norwegian territory, such as Spitsbergen and the Lofoten Islands.

Back in Norway, where Quisling was out of office, Terboven extracted an oath of loyalty from the members of the Administrative Council on his arrival, and persecution began. In early May discrimination against Norwegian Jews began with confiscation of their radio sets. Within a fortnight the Councillors were put under Terboven's direct control and ordered not to act without his permission. According to Koht: 'The Gestapo were busy everywhere, listening to what people were talking about and arresting suspects. German military courts sentenced Norwegian citizens to penalties for insulting Germans. . . . Newspapers were only allowed to appear on condition that what they wrote conformed to the desires of the German masters. They were forbidden to report German losses or British victories, and they must not dare to criticise the German authorities. . . . Papers which disobeyed were suspended. . . . In the first days of June detailed rules for the Press were issued by the German High Command. . . . Foreign news had to be commented upon in a German spirit. Speeches of the King or members of the government must not be reported. . . . Regarding economic problems, nothing must be printed but reports of progress. . . . It was particularly pointed out to the editors that it was their task not only to give news, but also to lead public opinion, and so they would have to work actively for the German ideas.' In addition, schools were requisitioned and education suffered. Any youth harming a Norwegian girl for going with a German soldier would be punished.

The tasks of the Administrative Council were performed by County Governors (*Fylkes-Männer*) all over the country, thus compromising thousands of minor officials. Realising the doubtful legality of those manifold activities, representatives of all the parties presented a plan to transform the Administrative Council into a State Council (*Riksråd*), composed of the existing Councillors, together with representatives of Labour and North Norway.

Rivertz had conceived the idea for the 'State Council' and his ideas had been watered down by Berg on the night of April 12-13 because they appeared to usurp the Royal Prerogative. Naturally the Germans, who believed all along that the Administrative Council was meant to be a government, now assumed that the State Council gambit was a revival of the original plan to side-track the King.

Accordingly, on June 13, Terboven presented a German demand that the Norwegian Parliament should be convened in Eidsvoll, the home of the Constitution, and that Members should there repeal the Nygaardsvold Government's 'full powers', depose King Haakon and the Royal House, and dismiss the exiled Cabinet. In their place there should be established a Norwegian State Council with authority in all internal questions, finance, economy, administration, police, culture and social life. The Administrative Council should be dissolved because in theory it represented the King's Government and was, anyway, an emergency institution.

In return for this move, Reichscommissar Terboven would in due course be replaced by an 'Extraordinary Commissar of the Führer', and the scope of the German Civil Service and Police would be diminished.

If the Norwegians refused, the Germans would establish a Government of Commissars, Germans would be put in full charge of every branch of the Norwegian Administration, and Norwegian men would become liable for military service or forced labour in Germany.

At this critical stage, the Presidential Board of the *Storting** (with a substitute for Hambro) took the lead in negotiations, as representatives of the *Storting*. They worked not only in conjunction with the Administrative Council—notably with the Chairman, Ingolf Christensen, Governor of Oslo—but with elected representatives of the leading political parties (including Labour) and with the Chairman of the Trade Union Congress. Chief Justice Berg of the Supreme Court and Bishop Berggrav, the Primate, were also consulted.

A committee representing the above acquiesced in the German demands other than the dismissal of the exiled King and his Cabinet. The Supreme Court refused to tamper with the Constitution to that extent.

The proviso was rejected by the Germans on June 15 and the members of the Supreme Court suddenly got cold feet and withdrew. This did not deter the Presidential Board of the *Storting*, the Administrative Council, elected representatives of the political parties, and the T.U.C. Chairman from continuing negotiations with the Germans. Additional members of parliament came from their constituencies to have their say in the proceedings, and delegates from the Producers' Association (representing most sides of industry and commerce) joined in.

Terboven's spokesman, Hans Delbrügge, warned that failure to acquiesce would result in a Government of Commissars that would 'rush at you like bulls', and that 'later we will put a Norwegian Government into power, but it will be a government that you will not want to see'.

* Vice-President of the *Storting* was Magnus Nilssen.

That was one side of Terboven's brief. His deputy also presented the other: 'The Führer is a friend of heroic conduct. . . . If I therefore tell him that it has been a great sacrifice for the Norwegian people to take the decision to depose the King and the government, the Norwegians would, by this sacrifice, win from him something essential. . . . A closer union with Germany is our aim. We must demand a certain heroism of those whom we shall deem our worthy associates.'

Three nights later all the Norwegian negotiators, except for those from the Supreme Court, capitulated to this mixture of threats and flattery. They agreed to send a formal request to King Haakon and his London Government to resign. In case of refusal the Presidential Board promised to vote for dethronement. This action went far further than Quisling had ever gone.

When it came to the composition of the State Council, the Germans expanded the proposed number of ministries from nine to fifteen, thus widening its net and leaving room for additional members. Only two members of the Labour Party were selected, instead of the proposed four or five. True to his brief from Hitler not completely to shut the door on Quisling, Terboven also proposed the selection of one young and inexperienced member of *Nasjonal Samling*—Axel Stang, a wealthy landowner. A more innocuous State Councillor could hardly have been chosen, which was doubtless the reason for the choice. It was probably hoped also that this action might divert Quisling from his position of rivalry. 'If you take him (Stang) we will promise you that Quisling will leave Norway for the rest of the war, to visit the Channel ports and bombed cities as our honoured guest,' Terboven informed the State Council.

At any rate, Stang was accepted, and a sixteen-member State Council was selected by the Presidential Board of the *Storting*.

Despite attempts to suggest that the struggle was still continuing inside Norway, in fact the whole country was then effectively occupied by the Germans, who ruled by right of conquest as clearly set forth in the Hague Convention. No indisputable lawful government, let alone one with any semblance of independence, existed. Resistance was notional. The bulk of the population was indifferent to policies and simply wanted to get on with their own lives as best they could, and collaboration with the Germans actually flourished on a national scale until the tide of war began to turn. In fact many Norwegians competed

278

to secure profitable contracts for well-paid work on roads, fortifications, and airfields for the *Wehrmacht*.

In rejecting the State Council by radio from London on July 8, King Haakon fell back on the argument that Norway was at war. In a passage of such complexity that it bears the hallmark of embarrassed amendments, he said:

'In the motion of the Presidential Board (of the *Storting*) it is stated that new elections for the *Storting* can only take place "after the conclusion of peace", and this statement implies that Norway cannot have peace until the war between the Great Powers has been brought to an end. With regard to this supposition, the Presidential Board is no doubt right, but then it is also evident that the proposed arrangement will not help the people of Norway to get the peace it is so strongly looking for.'

The London line, with its abstruse legal arguments, cut little ice in Norway at the time. The majority of the 130 remaining *Stortingsmen* out of 150, the Administrative Council and representatives of the leading public bodies had conspired against the arguments of the King and the exiled government and voted to depose them. Professor Worm-Muller admits: 'In June and July (1940), they (the Germans) had a chance of coming to an arrangement with us.'

Quisling, who held no office or power at that time, took no part in these negotiations. All along he had opposed the Reichscommissariat, his trump card being a common understanding with Hitler on the right of 'Nordic' Norway to hold a favoured position in the New Order as distinct from the lowly status of a 'Protectorate', which Terboven was trying, in effect, to impose.

This fine but crucial distinction was not easy for distraught Norwegians to understand during the German Occupation and is hard to appreciate twenty-five years later, when events have become telescoped and the 'quislings' and 'Nazis' have been bracketed together in a one-sided barrage of hostile propaganda. The 1940 smear still sticks today. Crimes committed by the Reichscommissariat in collusion with prominent anti-Quisling Norwegians are held against Quisling at a time when, far from collaborating with Terboven, he was refusing adamantly to sign away his freedom of action. Throughout this period Terboven was striving to oust and supplant Quisling from *Nasjonal Samling*.

Increasingly, Terboven delegated authority to Delbrügge, who had joined him from the Reich Ministry of the Interior. It was perhaps just as well for Norway that Terboven was more concerned with preparing his plans as Gauleiter-elect of Great Britain. He openly told his cronies that Norway was only a dress-rehearsal for more important duties in London.

On August 15 the Battle of Britain began. The political parties in Norway, Trade Unions and employers got together to form a common front against the Germans in case England fell. They met on the 23rd, but were forbidden by the Germans to publicise this move. On September 7, Delbrügge summoned the Presidential Board of the *Storting* to confirm its approval of the State Council plans drawn up in June. The actual inauguration had been postponed pending the planned invasion of Britain, but in the meantime the Administrative Council, the nucleus of the State Council, had been carrying on.

On the 19th the Board summoned the 130 *Stortingsmen* to Oslo to arrange final details. They were now given the choice of deciding whether the Royal House should be deposed for ever, or only until peace.

A majority of 90 agreed that the decision could be taken by a simple majority. They then voted 80 to 50 against permanent deposition, and 82 to 48 in favour of deposition for the duration. The latter vote was as follows:

	Yes	No
Conservatives	18	15
Liberals	12	8
Farmers	16	—
Labour	35	23
Christian People	—	2
Independent	1	—
	82	48

Those figures dispose effectively of the picture of Norwegians standing shoulder to shoulder behind their beloved King.

The question of the Royal House was reopened on September 16, but there was still a parliamentary majority of 68 to 61 in favour of deposition for the duration, and the Presidential Board assured the

Reichscommissariat that a 'legal' two-thirds majority could be obtained later.

On September 18, the final draft constitution for the State Council assured the Presidential Board that the new body would be 'essentially' free and more independent than the Administrative Council, although the Reichscommissariat would retain the right to intervene. However, the Reichscommissariat could not agree to the State Council becoming the 'real' head of the Norwegian administration.

Obviously Norwegians and Germans could not agree about what they had agreed, and on September 25 Terboven broadcast that a 'Commissariat Government' would replace the Administrative Council, which was abolished. The Royal House was formally deposed. Nygaardsvold and his London Government were deposed also, their 'full powers' of April 9 invalidated. The *Storting* would cease to function. A fifteen-man Government of Commissars was established.

This body was not very different from the State Council, except that now elected Norwegians had no say at all either in selecting the government of the country, or in its running.

The King and his Cabinet attacked this proposal by radio on the following day, once more appealing to Constitutional Law, which was in abeyance. The whole story of the various Norwegian governments, or attempted governments, is pathetic, and adds point to a remark later made by Hitler to Quisling that 'Terboven had received no less than twenty-three lists of Ministers at one time or another'. With a rare flash of humour, Hitler added: 'Norway could apparently supply the whole of Europe with governments.'

In all this time, Quisling had made no approach to Terboven. The Reichscommissar had summoned him on one occasion to the Bristol Hotel, intimating that the Administrative Council would be enlarged when the Allies were finally expelled and that Quisling might find a leading place in it. Since the Councillors were German appointees, Quisling was not interested, whereupon Terboven went into reverse, saying that Quisling was too compromised by the events of April 9 to be useful. Terboven thereafter sought to change the leadership of *Nasjonal Samling*. He chose his old friend from the Saar, Police Chief Jonas Lie, to replace Quisling, and early in June nominated Lie as the new *NS* chief and as Police Chief in the proposed State Council. *NS* funds were impounded.

Lie had been nominated as Minister of Justice on April 9, when Quisling hurriedly created a façade of government to face the Germans, but none of his Ministers had been consulted in advance, and Lie never assumed office. He was an NS sympathiser, but not a member of the party, and he was at the time in Finnmark, where he joined up with the Allies until they were beaten.

Fritt Folk published an account of Lie's alleged duplicity which infuriated Terboven and decided him finally to get rid of Quisling. Early in July, Quisling was enticed to Berlin on the pretext that he was entrusted with the 'honourable' task of composing a treatise on the 'unification of Scandinavia in the Greater Reich'. Although Quisling was suspicious, he took a chance, despite the advice of his friends. For two days he was accommodated in the Kaiserhof Hotel, but Terboven ensured that he could meet nobody of any influence, and so frustrated his object in agreeing to go to Germany, namely to seek Hitler's help.

Two days after his arrival, Quisling disappeared. Exactly what happened he never revealed to a soul. He was away for a month, lost to the world, and Harold Franklin Knudsen has always believed that he was under house arrest. This was the most humiliating episode in Quisling's rise to power and he always lapsed into one of his famous silences when his friends questioned him about it.

During Quisling's absence, Hagelin vehemently opposed Jonas Lie's appointment, and went so far as to bang Terboven's table and shout at the Reichscommissar. On the spur of the moment, Hagelin declared that Quisling had appointed him as deputy leader—thus ruling out Lie—and on the strength of this bluff he regained control of NS funds, which he froze pending Quisling's return. Meanwhile NS carried on by means of private contributions.

Quisling's Oslo friends comforted themselves that he must be taking a summer holiday in the wilds of Telemark, and attributed his silence to his famous reticence, but they soon became seriously worried. Knudsen consulted Dietrich Hildisch, the venerable margarine king and friend of Grand-Admiral Raeder, who had been an ordinary member of NS from its inception but held no rank. Hildisch wrote an indignant letter to Raeder, asking him to inform Hitler that Quisling had been 'kidnapped' because, as a decent Norwegian, he opposed Terboven's 'imperialism' and its 'inconsistency with German honour'. Hagelin ensured that the letter was sent through Schreiber by naval courier 'plane, so that it could not be intercepted by Terboven or the Gestapo.

For good measure Hildisch also dictated a personal letter to Terboven, saying Quisling was the only Norwegian who could protect Norwegian interests without creating Norwegian-German hatred for a thousand years. If Terboven did not reverse his anti-Quisling policy, *Nasjonal Samling* would discontinue all contact with the Reichscommissariat. Although without authority, the old man signed himself 'on behalf of *Nasjonal Samling*'.

This bluster alerted Hitler to Quisling's predicament and secured not only his immediate release but his return to Hitler's favour, as the following telegram from Hitler to Terboven showed when it was intercepted by a German friend of Hagelin: 'Minister Quisling's many years' work against World Revolution has involved myself and the German people in a debt of gratitude and honour to him which will be repaid in full to him personally as well as to the Norwegian people who produced him.'

It was suddenly clear that Quisling would soon be back in Norwegian politics. Hagelin put aside any ambitions to head *Nasjonal Samling*, and unfroze party funds. Schreiber informed him that Quisling was due back at Oslo Airport, where there was a thankful reunion, on August 20.

Quisling had spent several hours with Hitler on August 17 at the Reich Chancellery, and this changed Norwegian history.

20

Minister-President

HOW did Quisling fight back from ostracism on June 22, 1940, to an influential position on September 25?

After Hitler first seemingly withdrew his support, Rosenberg was in eclipse, and his pro-Quisling 'expert', Scheidt, was later banished to the front, as was Brauer. Ribbentrop was as hostile to Quisling as ever, and Falkenhorst and Engelbrecht, who had never had any use for him, remained his enemies. Reichscommissar Terboven patently regarded Quisling as a rival and was bent on establishing a régime of German nominees from among the remaining civic leaders in Norway. Jonas Lie was installed in the leadership of Quisling's party, *Nasjonal Samling* funds were appropriated and *Fritt Folk* was reduced to four pages. Quisling himself was spirited away to Berlin so that he could not interfere. A crescendo of misrepresentation was also loosed against him from Oslo, Stockholm and London. It looked like the end of his mission.

His advantages were few. The best was that he alone among the Norwegians had some contact with Hitler, *de facto* sovereign of Norway by right of conquest, on whose whim the nation's fate depended.

Further, through Hagelin, who had actually met Hitler three times (compared with Quisling's twice), Quisling had a line of communication to Göring, creator of the unbeaten Luftwaffe and industrial dictator of the Greater Reich, so that in certain circumstances he might

284

have obtained the ear of the second man in Germany as well as the first.

Apart from the fact that Rosenberg was, for his own reasons, so to speak on Quisling's side, Quisling had a tenuous link with Grand-Admiral Raeder, through Dietrich Hildisch and Richard Schreiber. In contrast to the generals, Raeder was pro-Norwegian. So, strangely, was Heinrich Himmler, the dreaded Gestapo chief. When Count Folke Bernadotte of the Swedish Red Cross was negotiating surrender during the last months of the war, he recorded that he gave Himmler a sixteenth-century work on Swedish runestones—by a Norwegian who worked among the prisoners of war in Germany. 'I had got the tip that Himmler was specially interested in Norwegian runestones. He was visibly moved.' Rector Seip and Bishop Berggrav, who were eventually interned and met Himmler, agreed with Bernadotte's view: 'Himmler was a very complicated person.' Rector Seip told Bernadotte: 'In some ways Himmler was an idealist with a special affection for the Northern Countries'; and when at one time Terboven ordered that Bishop Berggrav should be shot, Himmler intervened.*

Quisling had no means of knowing Himmler's 'Nordic' weakness in 1940 and there is no evidence that they ever discussed their common interest in runestones. Himmler was, however, an unseen asset to Occupied Norway, as shown by the almost exemplary behaviour of the Gestapo until 1943, when the anti-'quislings' threw away this extraordinary advantage by arguably futile acts of provocation and sabotage.

Thus we find that, despite the opposition to Quisling in Norway, three or four of the men who ran Germany had some weird but genuine regard for Norway. Quisling was the one Norwegian who could exploit this curious situation, for his political opponents in Norway never raised their sights above the dismissed bureaucrat Brauer, the incompetent Falkenhorst and Terboven.

Quisling's political chance of infiltrating himself as a buffer between Norway and her occupants, therefore, was not entirely hopeless, and he felt that he could deal with the Germans in his own right in contrast to his opponents' readiness to serve as German nominees.

The King and the elected government were in England, and almost everybody of any importance in Norway had agreed on the necessity of collaborating with the Germans, either through the Administrative

* See *Count Folke Bernadotte; his life and work* (Denison), by this author.

Council or the abortive State Council. Opposition to the Germans amounted to no more than wisecracks published in newspapers, jibes in theatres, and snide remarks.* It was generally agreed that the international future looked grim, with Versailles reversed, Germany the master of continental Europe and Britain helplessly isolated. It was not so much a question therefore of whether to collaborate as of how best in Norway's interest to conduct relations with the occupying power. Quisling felt that his way would produce better results for his people. The realistic solution from his viewpoint was to conclude an arrangement with Hitler favourable to Norway, and he clearly thought that he could obtain the best terms.

What some have called high treason can equally well be regarded as statesmanship, but in any case there was no legal obstacle to doing a deal with the Germans since they were the effective, sovereign occupants of the country and Norway had formally concluded a comprehensive Armistice on June 10, after which the two countries were no longer technically at war, and a *modus vivendi* ought by all rights to have been established in the best interests of the parties concerned.

The obvious and realistic objective was a *de jure* peace settlement, recognising the hard fact that Germany must occupy strongpoints for the duration of hostilities with Britain and that Norway had the right to run her internal affairs so far as this did not conflict with Germany's military requirements.

Norway was free to look after her own interests and under no circumstances beholden to Britain, which had provoked the German attack and then done nothing effective to hold it at bay—in fact had deserted her, without due warning, as Koht, Trygve Lie and Ruge vociferously declared.

Not only had the remaining Norwegian leaders the right to come to terms with Germany, but the duty to do so when there was no prospect within the foreseeable future of a German defeat, and the two great powers, who might have upset the New Order, the USA and USSR, wanted nothing more than to remain neutral—Russia, gorged with easy conquest, the United States cashing in as she did in the First World War and advised by Ambassador Joseph Kennedy in London that Britain was finished.

The sensible policy for little Norway was to leave the Germans in

* See Worm-Muller's *Norway Revolts against the Nazis.*

their strongpoints, from which there was no reasonable prospect of them being ejected, and to cease pointless anti-German activities, which could only bring retribution on the defenceless population without helping to change the fortunes of war.

Such a policy held out reasonable hope of German moderation in the immediate future, as expressed in Hitler's promise via Brauer to respect Norwegian 'territorial integrity' and 'national independence' and by his briefing Terboven 'to try to make friends of the Norwegians'.

What could Norway have gained by spiting the conqueror? If the Germans lost the war, Norway would be freed anyway. If Germany won, a hostile Norway would lose her 'Nordic' right to a favourable place in the New Order. There was nothing left that the pro-British faction could do to help its friends in England. The merchant navy had been chartered to Britain since the autumn, and no Norwegian resistance movement could ever hope to do more than irritate the three or four hundred thousand Germans stationed along the coast to prevent a British landing.

To have flown in the face of these facts and the Hague Convention was senseless and did the nation damage, physical and psychological, which has never been made good. It also invited the total destruction of Norway, which no authorities inside or outside the country could have prevented. Disaster was in fact only averted by a series of last-minute miracles, and by *Nasjonal Samling*.

Another factor that influenced Quisling was that he had always proclaimed the Nazi-Soviet alliance could not last. By June 1940 he was convinced (unlike Stalin up to the last moment) that war in the East was certain, and that the North and the Baltic would therefore become embattled. A deal with either Stalin or Hitler had to be prepared in theory. In practice Hitler, the occupant of Norway, was the only choice.

Although partyless, penniless and pilloried, Quisling finally reached the conclusion that he must try in Norway's interest to influence Hitler personally, and he acted with this in mind when the King finally ruled himself out of the picture by rejecting the Administrative Council's proposals on July 3. Occupied Norway was on her own and faced with three alternatives—a State Council of German nominees, a *Nasjonal Samling* government under the leadership of Jonas Lie, or direct German rule on the Polish pattern. Hence Quisling was not unwilling to take a chance by flying to Berlin on Terboven's plane during the following week—ostensibly to embark on the 'honourable task of composing a treatise on the unification of Scandinavia in the Greater Reich', but in fact to pursue his own policy.

The line Quisling proposed to adopt with Hitler, if he could reach him, is set forth in a letter dated July 10 which was found in his files after the war. Whether it was ever sent, delivered or read we do not know. It may have been merely a draft, but still it shows the way his mind was working:

'The objective in the struggle I have carried on for a number of years was a great Germanic community with Norway's voluntary affiliation . . .

'As a result of British and French encroachment, the development of the situation has proceeded quite differently. After the German *Wehrmacht*'s occupation of Oslo, I placed myself at the head of a new Norwegian Government with an inner conviction of right. At that moment I was conscious of the importance of taking this step in the interests of Norway and of the Great Germanic ideal although this was contrary to the whole tradition of the country. . . .

'I naturally expected to meet opposition on that account from all the opposing forces, from both of the former political parties, from the whole of the pro-British intelligentsia of the town and from the former government and its supporters.

'I was, and still am, convinced that a properly directed support of my person and of the movement I lead would have won over the majority of the Norwegian population. . . . Even at that time the trade unions and Farmers' Union circles approached me and offered their co-operation.

'Unfortunately the attitude taken by the German military administration and the German Minister, Dr. Brauer, prevented my action from taking effect. . . .

'The Supreme Court lacked all legal justification, but I have had unfortunately to recognise that, as a result of the attitude taken by [Brauer and Under-Secretary of State Habicht], they fell victims to the point of view of those circles which for many long years have directed their efforts against Greater Germany and against my movement.

'In consequence of these references to previously issued orders from Your Excellency, according to which I was not permitted to reply to Your Excellency direct, I then declared myself prepared to comply with their demands.

'Dr. Brauer then read out the following assurances:

1. Full integrity for me personally and for the movement I lead. This was to take the following effect: (a) adequate financial support, (b) full freedom of movement for propaganda and organisation.

2. The promise of a letter of thanks from the Foreign Minister (Ribbentrop) on behalf of the Government for my attitude during the critical days.

3. The prospect of settling the affairs of the Norwegian defence forces, which activities would give me the chance fully to influence members towards my viewpoint.

4. For me the point raised by Dr. Brauer—that I should remain in reserve for Your Excellency for future political activities—was quite decisive. . . .

'My action and attitude was used by my opponents and by British and French propaganda to brand me as a traitor to my country. I on my side intended to unmask those circles in the country who were in the service of the plutocratic forces and to show them up in their treacherous and damaging attitude towards Norway and the Greater German Reich. . . .

'I have to inform Your Excellency that not one of the assurances given me in Your Excellency's name has been carried out. . . .

'Your Excellency needs no explanation of the fact that the Administrative Council, which was set up by the pro-British circles in Norway, saw in me their biggest enemy. These people feared that through my movement they would lose their hold on the people. . . .

'The old political parties were divided against each other immediately after the occupation. Thanks to the line of action adopted by the German administration and to the Norwegian Administrative Council, who operated most dextrously, old anti-German forces have been revived. . . .

'On June 25 I was summoned to Reichscommissar Terboven. He suggested that I should resign from the leadership of the movement because my person was supposed to be preventing certain unity among Norwegians . . . I pointed out most emphatically that the reproaches brought against me were put forward by people belonging to circles in league with the Allies.

'The Reichscommissar then declared to me his intention of forming a new government in Norway. . . . He intended to see that representatives of the *Nasjonal Samling* movement were included in the government. Meanwhile, I myself was to retire. . . . The Reichscommissar would appoint those persons whom he thought suitable. . . . He could not, of course, force me to accept his suggestions, but if I declined to comply he would have started a new movement within two months. . . .

'If any opposition were encountered from my movement, it would not be tolerated, as the new government was of course pro-German. Thus my party would be put on the same footing as a sect and treated likewise. If I were prepared to accept his suggestion and temporarily to give up the leadership of the party to a deputy, he would continue to support *Nasjonal Samling*, but I myself was to accept an invitation from the German Government and go to Germany. . . . I now find myself turned out of my country in the most polite and disguised form. . . .

'I also explained to the Reichscommissar that I could not imagine that it was Your Excellency's wish to bring *Nasjonal Samling*, which had fought for years for adherence to Greater Germany, into opposition with its previous opinions, or to force my supporters into an anti-German position. That, however, would most certainly be the result of the Reichscommissar's plan. I could not believe, either, that it was Your Excellency's intention to present me with such an ultimatum.

'To this the Reichscommissar replied that Your Excellency had always accepted his suggestions. In spite of this, however, I maintained my opposition, being quite convinced that this line of action could not be consistent with Germanic loyalty. . . . I decided to yield to compulsion, but I pointed out most expressly in the conference which followed with the Reichscommissar's representatives that in the interests of both countries I most deeply regretted the course which had been decided upon. . . .

'At a conference on June 29, the Reichscommissar announced to me, before I for my part had suggested a deputy, that my deputy should be the renegade Lie, whom he at all events had selected to be Minister of Police. I found myself once again faced with a fact established by power-politics and did not attempt to hide my misgivings from the Reichscommissar with regard to the reactions within the movement. . . . In later conferences I maintained that the announcement should at least await the formation of the new government in order to prevent conflict or a serious split in the ranks of *Nasjonal Samling*, where Herr Lie had no authority at all. . . .

'I have thus tried to give Your Excellency an unvarnished picture of conditions as they have developed in Norway since April 9. . . . Personally I have no doubt that if the German administration had adopted a different attitude, the objective [of *NS*] would already have been achieved. . . . I was and am ever prepared to work in complete loyalty for the common objective of my fatherland and Greater Germany.

'The further extension of the methods which have been adopted in Norway since April 9 this year by the German functionaries, none of whom understands the special conditions in this country or the mentality of my countrymen—so strange to any non-Norwegian— will not only endanger the relations between Norway and Germany, but will also affect the attitude of all friends of the German people in the Scandinavian states.

'I therefore regard it as my duty to inform Your Excellency of the facts in the hope of an alteration in the present policy.'

It seems unlikely that this letter reached Hitler, but if it did, it had no effect. It was Hildisch's outbursts to Raeder and Terboven on August 16, against the 'kidnapping' of Quisling, which produced an audience. Unfortunately, no record has come to light of Quisling's third meeting with Hitler, on August 17 in the Reich Chancellery, but Harald Franklin Knudsen has supplied a resumé, based on Quisling's account afterwards.

The interview lasted several hours, and covered not only Norway but Europe as a whole. Quisling was tactful about Terboven, but said that the Norwegians felt that they had lost the war and were therefore reacting more strongly against Germany than would otherwise have been the case.

It transpired that Hitler had been given a misleading impression about the formation of the government on April 9, and Quisling had an opportunity of explaining the facts, as well as his own views on the question of Norwegian neutrality and the place Norway deserved in the New Europe which Hitler's victories had made possible.

Hitler listened attentively. Then he gave a thundering lecture on the Norwegians deserving nothing in view of their pro-British policy, but when he calmed down he continued with a smile: 'It is an ironic fate that I have to wage war against the two countries for which I have had the greatest sympathy all my life—England and Norway.'*

For the time being, Hitler said, he could not change the conditions of the occupation owing to the state of the war, and because Germany's prestige forbade it, but as soon as possible he would give thorough consideration to the Norwegians' craving for liberty, which, he claimed, was a genuine Germanic feeling that he could well understand.

Referring to North Norway and Russian claims to an outlet there to the open sea, Hitler said that the German troops' quick advance to the frontier had already saved this area from Bolshevism. The Norwegians ought to be grateful to him for standing as guarantor that North Norway would remain within the West European cultural sphere.

Hitler then questioned Quisling for an hour on his experiences in Russia and his long fight against Bolshevism, ending with the explicit assurance that Quisling was to be 'afforded every facility for continuing his work and for leading Norway to a free status within Germanic Europe'.

Quisling was impressed. He thought he had obtained a promise of all he wanted: an end to the Reichscommissariat and the Administrative and State Councils; another opportunity for *Nasjonal Samling* to win over the Norwegian people to a *modos vivendi* with the Occupation Forces; and a favoured place for Norway in the New Order, instead of the status of a Protectorate. For a moment peace with Germany, replacing the Armistice, must have seemed just around the corner. From being an outcast among his own people and their conquerors, Quisling had suddenly become a creative force—with the future on his side. This was not only a remarkable initial victory for his own force of character but for Norway—if only his people would see it that way.

Perhaps Quisling assumed too much, or perhaps Hitler had still not finally intended to commit himself. Next day Terboven flew to Berlin

* Hitler had visited the Norwegian fjords on a 'Strength through Joy' cruise before the war.

to hear Hitler's decision. Again there is no record, but clearly it was agreed to increase the number of NS men in the proposed State Council beyond two, for Terboven proposed additional names from this time onwards. Negotiations for a State Council continued, and no serious difficulties were placed in the way of such distinguished NS candidates as Gulbrand Lunde. The only obstacle was Terboven's insistence on Jonas Lie as Minister of Justice with control of the State Police.

Quisling took no part in the negotiations because he had no intention of being an impotent Minister under Terboven and sought to head a government that would justify Hitler in withdrawing the Reichs-commissariat and Gestapo and limiting German control to the genuine requirements of the *Wehrmacht*.

On September 7 the London blitz began and Hitler lost patience with the Oslo negotiations. On the 10th Quisling and Terboven were summoned to the Reich Chancellery. Hitler was now in favour of forgetting a State Council and appointing a Quisling Government immediately, but on second thoughts he told Terboven to draw up a list of twenty-four names, including six NS men, and to try once more for a State Council. Hitler hoped that this strengthened NS influence would in time enable Quisling to gain enough ground to take charge of the entire government.

Quisling was prepared to let his men participate, but he himself would not toe Terboven's line. For his own part, he said, he would prefer the State Council, which all leading Norwegians seemed to favour, rather than a government of Terboven's nominees.

Suddenly, on September 25, Terboven tired of the State Council and fell back on the idea of a Quisling Government, but the difficulty was that Quisling would not participate on his terms. He therefore fell back on yet another compromise, and appointed a Commissarial Government of thirteen members, eight of whom were members of *Nasjonal Samling*, nine if one includes Lie:

Captain Kjeld Irgens	Shipping
Professor Ragnar Skancke	Church and Education
Director Viljam Hagelin	Interior
Professor Birger Meidell	Social Affairs
Barrister and criminologist Sverre Riisnaes	Justice

Dr. Gulbrand Lunde	Culture
Axel Stang	Sport
Architect Tormud Hustad	Labour
Jonas Lie	Police

Four non-*NS* members were:

Civil Servant and expert on fishing Halvorsen Johannesen	Trade, Industry, Handicrafts and Fishing
Director and international trade expert Oystein Rayner	Supply
Veterinarian and big-scale farmer T. J. O. Fretheim	Agriculture
Bank Director Erling Sandberg	Finance

All thirteen, except for the curious appointment of the expatriate, Hagelin, were authorities in their fields, and three of them (Johannesen, Fretheim, Sandberg) had been proposed by the Norwegian negotiators; another three (Lunde, Stang, Lie) had proved acceptable as members of the State Council in one or other of its twenty-three variations!

It will be noticed that the Ministries of Defence and Foreign Affairs were abolished, thus emphasising the complete subservience of the Commissarial Government to Terboven, which explains Quisling's refusal to join it. Any influence which he exerted on the Commissarial Government was indirect, as the Party leader of some of its members. Thus he ceased to be a political outcast, but his personal responsibility for the decisions of the Commissarial Government was nil. He was 'held in reserve' for a transitional period during which he hoped to win enough support to form his own government and to justify the removal of the Reichscommissariat.

This government of experts was by no means a totally unacceptable government of incompetents. It was an ingenious compromise between the minimum expectations of Hitler, Terboven, Quisling and his Norwegian opponents. As such it could not last, but still it endured the quadruple strain for sixteen months.

Hitler hankered after a model Nordic state, but Norway became 'the most difficult Commissarship of the Reich', as he said in May 1942. Terboven sought to turn Norway—failing England—into his own satrapy within the New Order, but was frustrated by Hitler's competitive partiality for Quisling and by the latter's campaign to get rid of him. Quisling knew that Terboven was side-tracking Hitler's 'co-operation' order and was bent on compromising *Nasjonal Samling* with a view to suppressing it. Quisling's opponents believed that the Commissarial Government was a step towards a real *NS* régime and outdid Terboven in vilification of it.

So, although Quisling was not even a member of the government, his opponents continued to fight him instead of co-operating in wringing better terms from Hitler, and he was blamed for everything. Unscrupulous propaganda was put out in public and private throughout the country and abroad, with the immediate result that it ruined Quisling's chance of establishing his own government. His enemies played gratuitously into Terboven's hands, providing him with endless ammunition for imposing on Hitler the fallacy that Norway was seething with trouble, that Quisling was anathema to the nation and that therefore the Reichscommissariat must be prolonged. Eventually these tactics succeeded in provoking enough genuine trouble to oblige Hitler to continue the Reichscommissariat, thereby instigating the atrocities that Quisling sought to avoid by acting as a buffer.

There was a campaign of systematic misrepresentation of *Nasjonal Samling* as National Socialism, and the 'quislings' and the Germans were blanketed as 'Nazis'. This is a gross over-simplification, but it served to saddle Quisling with most of the Germans' crimes, and created such confusion that it is still difficult to apportion responsibility fairly. Volumes are needed to sift and dismantle the catalogue of 'crime' ascribed to Quisling during the sixteen months of the Commissarial Government, of which he was not even a member.

Quisling ostentatiously disassociated himself from the Commissariat from beginning to end and had no responsibility for its policy or actions, nor any indirect influence on any except the least important departments. The key departments of Police, Finance, Trade and Industry, Supply, and Agriculture were not in the hands of his supporters. Terboven tried to compromise Quisling by sending Jonas Lie to him, but Quisling kept Lie waiting nearly four hours, although an appointment had been arranged, and then dismissed him within moments.

Norway's wartime troubles were largely of her own making or invented. Nobody died of starvation, as did 16,000 in Holland during the winter of 1944-45. There were no exceptional physical hardships to face at this time, and the Germans actually supplied the vital fishing

295

fleet with oil. Thanks to German supplies, Swedish food parcels and efficient *NS* administration, Norway ended up healthier than before the Occupation. The calories available to the average Norwegian in 1942-45 were approximately 2,000 daily. Almost everybody in Norway had to collaborate with the Germans to some extent. Fortunes were made of necessity by forest owners, timbermen and building contractors, working under German aegis on barracks to replace billets and on repairs to war damage. Nearly 150,000 Norwegian labourers worked voluntarily and consistently throughout the occupation for good wages, road-making, clearing airstrips or building fortifications for the Germans. Since normal trade had been dislocated, this saved mass unemployment.

Not a stain attaches to the characters of these people, but the 'quislings', buffers to German excess, are execrated. Perhaps, unlike Bishop Berggrav and Rector Seip, they did not court a spurious martyrdom in internment, or like Chief Justice Berg, they did not organise a 'Home Front' resistance. Perhaps also they could not afford to take a detached view of the situation from the safety of Sweden and England. They were, however, the only people to attempt to stand their ground, and they might well have gained enough support to have helped form a Norwegian government independent of Terboven had their plans not been frustrated by the opposition.

On the administrative side, state and municipal, the civil servants remained almost unchanged throughout the war. Some were 'quislings', the majority were not. Blame for inefficiency during the exigencies of war must be shared between them or ascribed to the system, which is never very good at the best of times. In the provinces, *NS* Governors exercised nominal control, their main duty being to avoid friction with the Germans, and usually they were distinguished local figures. With an eye to the future, comprehensive plans were drawn up by the leading Norwegian experts for post-war reconstruction—for instance in shipping, agriculture and re-housing, all of which were eventually discarded in favour of schemes, based on second-hand, faulty information, by the London exiles.

One particular source of the opposition to Quisling was the 4,200-strong Oslo University. On the day that the Commissiarial Government was announced, the Professor of Celtic, C. Marstrander, with the approval of Rector Seip, brother-in-law of Bishop Berggrav, posted a violently anti-Quisling declaration on the university noticeboard, presenting an entirely distorted view of the situation. Inevitably the student corps seethed with unrest, and resistance was plotted in the Students' Union, which had played a prominent part in the national movement that produced the 1814 Constitution. The NS Commissar for Church and Education, Dr. Ragnar Skancke, immediately sent Quisling's student followers to reason with their fellows in an attempt to combat the agitation, and scuffles followed.

On September 30, Seip allowed Dr. Scharffenberg, the famous mental specialist and Labour publicist, to make another inflammatory declaration at the university. This gaunt idealist, whose honesty and integrity cannot be doubted, was noted for his objectivity and disregard for his former opinions. In 1905 he had been a leading Republican, so that when he now told a thousand students that they must rally round the King as the foremost champion of liberty and national freedom, his words created a tremendous impression. The result of this ill-informed patriotic meeting was predictable. The Gestapo—not Quisling or his friends in the Commissarial Government—immediately arrested Scharffenberg, together with the young President of the Student's Union and his wife, and the Union was dissolved.

The *jøssinger** maintain that Terboven contravened the laws of the country and therefore of the Hague Convention, which are always invoked when it is convenient and are otherwise ignored. Whether or not the Germans were justified in suppressing a body that threatened their security, the result was to antagonise other civic organisations throughout the country, and to produce indignation in the homes of the 4,000 students concerned, among their friends and relations, and in intellectual circles, which had hitherto been sympathetic to Quisling.

These events at Oslo University triggered off a chain reaction. They had the result of inviting persecution, fortifying Terboven's position, whittling away Hitler's goodwill and undermining the possibility of remedial action by Quisling.

It is perhaps worth looking ahead for a moment to see how the behaviour of the students produced its own reaction. At first Skancke offered the students a neutral society in place of the Union, but only one per cent joined. He also, perhaps unwisely, tried to placate

* *Jøssing* is the NS epithet for an opponent, so called after the Jøssing Fjord where Vian of the *Cossack* boarded the *Altmark*.

Terboven by purging 'dangerous' literature from the university, including the works of the Norwegian Nobel Prizewinner, Sigrid Undset, who was waging a violent anti-Nazi campaign abroad, and the works of Albert Einstein. The university authorities, not unnaturally, protested, but none of the ninety professors (only two of whom were members of NS) objected when Professor Adolf Hoel was appointed Vice-Rector by Skancke or when three violently anti-Nazi colleagues were retired in the interests of academic peace.*

On October 9, Skancke revised the university laws so as to admit professors from outside the university faculty, and the NS sympathisers Dr. Herman Harris Aall and Gudmund Schnitler were installed, increasing the NS representation to five professors out of ninety. Students were not compelled to listen to the five and in fact boycotted their lectures.

Despite these minor concessions to Terboven by Skancke to keep the university in being, Seip, and most of the students and their professors, kept up a solid resistance until September, 1941, when inevitably Seip was arrested by the Gestapo and interned with his wife in Germany. The university was then brought directly under Skancke's Commissariat for Church and Education, thereby disrupting study still further.

In order to prevent the closure of the university in the autumn of 1943, by when Quisling was Minister-President, Skancke proposed to introduce a leavening of sixteen NS students, without the usual academic qualifications, who might combat the active resistance that Chief Justice Paal Berg was by then organising. Under Berg's guidance, all the Oslo University faculties protested, whereupon the Gestapo arrested nine professors and sixty students.

Friction continued until November 28, when a clumsy attempt was made to blow up the University Hall containing Edvard Munch's celebrated frescoes. The blame was immediately put on the 'quislings' by the budding resistance movement and the Norwegian Broadcasting Service in London, although in fact the move was organised by a supporter of Berg's 'Home Front', as the actual saboteur has since confessed!

* *Et Oppgjør med Landsmenn* by Adolf Hoel (Minerva, Oslo). Hoel, like Professor Gustav Smedal, was a fervent patriot with a generation of work for Norway's East Greenland rights behind him.

The results were catastrophic. The university was closed and no less than 1,250 students were arrested by the Gestapo. Frantic efforts by Quisling, Skancke and Hoel secured the release of half of them, but 644 were sent to a concentration camp in Germany. Pro-Norwegian members of the Reichscommissariat sought to confine punishment to a 'symbolic nature', but Terboven urged Reichsleiter Martin Bormann on December 1 that he should persuade Himmler to 'make an experiment by giving 1,200 students some sort of *Waffen SS* training and then send them to the East Front to fight partisans or allocate them to one or another useful job for the service of Europe'.*
Mercifully Himmler's 'runic' susceptibilities intervened and these boys were confined in the lesser hell of a concentration camp, where they remained to the end of the war and were rescued in an emaciated condition by Count Folke Bernadotte—all except twelve who died.

The Church authorities were another major source of opposition. Of all grievances to select for quarrelling with the Germans, Primate Eivind Berggrav picked on the elimination of the prayer of intercession for the King and his house, and his Cabinet, from the Common Prayer Book. This was a completely artificial quarrel, especially from a man who had recently sought a *Wehrmacht* pass to inform the King that he had been deposed in favour of an Administrative Council! Berggrav's opposition was bound to provoke trouble for the clergy and their flock, and Terboven was driven to issue an order abolishing the professional oath of secrecy taken by Church Ministers. Nothing otherwise prevented them using their cloth as a cloak for conspiracy against the Germans and the avoidance of the Courts. The extent of the opposition also necessitated a similar restriction on lawyers, and for good measure doctors were also included. Similarly, telegraph and telephone operators were made liable to penalties for refusing information to the police.

All these precautions came within the scope of the Hague Convention, which permitted self-defence by an occupant. However, Berggrav chose to make Terboven's measures a matter of 'conscience'. In January, 1941, the Norwegian State Church reversed its undertaking of June 1940, to obey the Hague Convention, having persisted with the 'subversive' prayers. On January 15, all seven bishops

* *Samtiden*, by the German Ministerial Counsellor, Alfred Huhnhaüser.

299

widened the quarrel by demanding from Skancke a clarification of the Church's position.

Another line of attack by the bishops amounted to a direct political appeal to all the latent anti-German and anti-*NS* feeling in the country. A scuffle, at the Oslo Business College on November 30, between *NS* and non-*NS* members, when several teachers and the Director were knocked down, was cited as an example of lawlessness which the Church could not overlook. Also cited as a reason for Church intervention was an order by Hagelin's Commissariat of the Interior, on December 16, that State and Municipal employees must support *NS*. 'If such things should continue systematically,' said the bishops, 'the Church's servants would feel the lack of any basis for guiding the conscience of the people, in so far as respect and confidence in the law of the land were concerned.'

When the bishops received an 'unsatisfactory' reply to their request for 'clarification' of the Church's status, they incorporated it in a circular letter to all congregations, repeating previous charges of lawlessness and Godlessness. 'When the authorities,' they said, 'permit acts of violence and injustice and exert pressure on our souls, then the Church becomes the defender of the people's conscience. One single human soul is worth more than the entire world.'

This circular did contain a plea to the people to avoid the use of force, but this plea reads strangely in what was in effect a plain call to revolt.

Predictably, Skancke was compelled by Terboven to forbid the reading of this subversive document to congregations. Equally predictably, the ban was disobeyed. A retaliatory prayer was then composed by the Association of Ministers, which Skancke was inevitably obliged to forbid, on February 15. Protests were, however, so widespread that Skancke lifted the ban the following day in the interest of the Church itself and general peace and quiet.

The following month the bishops ordered members of the State Church, comprising 95 per cent of the population, to boycott sermons preached by *NS* clergy over the radio. Simultaneously, the Church set about systematically to indoctrinate schoolteachers, and through them their pupils, against the Germans. By the time Quisling became Minister-President in February, 1942, according to *All for Norway*: 'Between teachers and pupils had already sprung up an understanding which is not always to be found between these two groups. The teachers readily sympathised with the children when, in their youthful impulsiveness, they began to demonstrate against the attacks on persons, ideas and institutions which they considered sacred—not least the attacks on the person of the King. There were many ways in which the children could express their feelings. They could sing the Royal Anthem . . . they could go on "strike" when Quisling sympathisers were teaching. . . . They could pull down enemy placards and paint their own slogans in every conceivable place. "Long Live the King", scrawled in huge letters on walls and fences, was a sign of their activity, and their teachers supported them.'

When eventually Quisling became Minister-President, he inherited a bitter legacy. In order as he thought to combat subversion in the schools, one of his early acts was to set up a 'Teachers' Front' and to enrol pupils in *Nasjonal Samling*'s Youth Organisation. Prompted by the bishops, the teachers protested—although the maintenance of the Christian religion was a leading tenet of Quisling's programme, and it is perhaps not unappropriate to recall that both he and Skancke were profoundly religious men. The bishops thereupon resigned. The difficulties created by German billeting in schools were redoubled by the subsequent arrest of teachers and the embitterment of the educational atmosphere. On Easter Day, 1942, most of the clergy followed their bishops' lead and denounced *Nasjonal Samling*. Two days later Quisling authorised lay preachers to hold services 'when special circumstances demand it'. His anxiety to keep the Church 'in being' was further emphasised by a personal visitation to Fyredal, his childhood parish, where his log cabin was situated. A violent theological argument developed, which appears to have hinged on the responsibility of every Christian to 'bear witness' to the faith. This has since been misrepresented as an underhand attempt to expel the clergyman so that Quisling might himself grab the parsonage! Nothing ever charged against Quisling was less in character and the story may be dismissed as fiction.

Apart from Oslo University and the Church, the strongest opposition came from Berg. Terboven had stated on September 25, in establishing the Commissarial Government, that neither the Supreme Court nor any other court could question the validity of decrees made by the Reichscommissar or the Acting Ministers, since it rested with him to decide what was expedient and essential for maintaining public order and the life of the community. The Supreme Court had also ruled itself out of authority by appointing the Administrative Council and proposing the abortive State Council. Nevertheless Berg and his supporters continued to claim that it was the 'duty of the Courts to probe the validity of laws and administrative regulations. Under military occupation the Courts must, in our opinion, judge the validity of regulations decreed by the occupation power in the light of international law.'

The legality of this claim, worthy as it sounds, is highly questionable in international law. It was the basis, however, of Berg's eventual resignation, involving the entire Supreme Court, on December 12, 1940. This action has been vehemently criticised in other occupied countries, notably Holland, where conditions were infinitely worse than in Norway. It is argued that the best means of helping the population was to have kept the Supreme Court in being at least as some possible source of protection against German excess.

Deputy Judge Andreas Mohr was appointed to succeed Berg, and Riisnaes, who had studied law and criminology in Vienna and Berlin, supervised the arrangements as Minister of Justice. Berg retired from public life to co-ordinate the struggling resistance movement, which was already gaining momentum. The newspapers for example had become such a nuisance to the authorities that NS journalists were attached to newspaper offices, and late in 1940, *Arbeiderbladet*, the Labour organ, was suppressed. A number of new newspapers were started, creating the legend of a great underground free press. The first of these, *Det Fria Norge* (*Free Norway*) was launched towards the end of 1940 by a Conservative *Stortingsman*. Far the most successful was *Friheten* (*Freedom*), the Communist publication started in November, 1940, and extolling the Russian-German alliance; after Hitler's invasion of Russia, it switched, and eventually enjoyed a peak readership of 10,000. *Bulletinen*, the 'Home Front' organ, also started in November in a small way and eventually achieved a circulation of 5,000. *Fri Fagbevegelse* (*Free Workers' Movement*), the new Labour organ, started in 1941, but its circulation never exceeded 5,000. A woman's paper, *Krig og Fred* (*War and Peace*), ran to eight or twelve pages and in 1944 printed up to 6,000 copies. The Conservative organ, *Fritt Land* (*Free Country*), concentrated on news rather than views, and perhaps circulated 10,000 copies towards the end. The stencilled London news distributed 6,000 to 10,000 copies, increasing to perhaps 45,000 copies at the peak.

On May 15, 1941, forty-three national organisations addressed a letter to Terboven complaining of *Nasjonal Samling* 'terroristic activities'. Professors, judges, clergymen, teachers and doctors—the nucleus of those who supported Berg—were joined by businessmen, civil servants, municipal workers, trade unionists and other professional bodies.

Any terror did not originate with *Nasjonal Samling*, but with the Police Chief, Jonas Lie, whom Quisling did not support, the Police President Askvig (who had replaced Welhaven), and their Gestapo colleagues. The reformed Supreme Court could obstruct German 'justice', but they were ultimately powerless to baulk the Reichscommissariat. Decisions rested with People's (Military) Courts, established by Terboven, outside the jurisdiction of the Supreme Court.

One 'terroristic' incident was attributable to *NS*—the kidnapping of Dr. Gjessing, Director of the Dikemark Mental Hospital near Oslo, whose insults goaded some of the wilder *NS* youth into retaliation. This excess was out-matched by the 'Home Front's' sabotage of the State Railway archives. Thus the nation steadily split asunder, law and order deteriorated and Terboven became further entrenched.

The net result was to bring Himmler to Norway—and more misery. On June 18, Terboven summoned those representatives of the 43 protesting bodies who had not been imprisoned to the *Storting*. There he lectured them and summoned five to his table. 'You will have plenty of time to think about what you have done,' he declared, whereupon they, too, were arrested.

Hagelin, as Minister of the Interior, dissolved the scientific organisations, which had joined in the protest, and appointed *NS* Controllers to supervise the trade unions, professions and business groups.

By this time, the Communists, who provided the only efficient 'resistance', had made common cause with the *jøssinger*, and some bite was introduced into the incipient 'Home Front'. This fusion was brought about by the Russo-German war, and gave Terboven an excellent excuse for reinforcing his stranglehold on the country.

In July he declared a State of Emergency. Three to four hundred thousand German troops were by now in Norway. A new front from the Arctic to the Baltic had emerged in Finland and the possibility arose of Anglo-Russian intervention in Norway, making it important for the Germans to protect their forces against subversion. The 'Home Front's' agitation played into Terboven's hands, producing more hardship.

On February 24, two Stavanger newspapermen, Christian S. Oftedal and Fritjof Lund, had been caught spying for Britain. They and eight others were sentenced to death by a Military Court, but reprieved. On March 26 Terboven had then formalised the death penalty for a number of subversive offences. In September the time had come to put this measure into effect.

Up to the Russian War, TUC leaders had worked closely with the Reichscommissariat against *Nasjonal Samling*. Among these labour leaders were Viggo Hansteen, the TUC lawyer, who was a Moscow-trained Communist (1929-30) and an honorary Russian colonel. Quisling discussed his subversive activities with Terboven's deputy, Paul Wegener, on August 28. Then, in early September, Hansteen organised a strike at *Akers Mekaniska Verkstad*, an Oslo shipyard repairing not only German warships but Norwegian supply boats. The pretext was the workers' demand for extra milk rations.

The strike lasted two hours. Hansteen and his young assistant, Rolf Wickstrøm, were promptly arrested, tried by a Military Court and shot for sabotage, on September 10. These were the first executions under the occupation, and the Germans had no further trouble on the Norwegian industrial front for the rest of the war.

Quisling was later condemned to death for these so-called murders, which had nothing whatever to do with him. His scope for upholding Norwegian interests through his supporters in the government was limited by Terboven's grip on the Norwegian State Police. At most he had a symbolic influence, and can hardly be called into account for excesses by the Gestapo and the police, over whom he had no control.

Looking back on the Commissarial period (September 25, 1940, to February 2, 1942), one sees that it was politically disastrous for Quisling although he was not directly implicated. Hitler's failure to 'rub out' Britain began to rouse Norway from apathy and despondency. The existence of the London Government began to assume a meaning, and the blame for the occupation was successfully shifted onto the guiltless Quisling. *Jøssing* propaganda strengthened by Communist opposition after the German attack on Russia, began to take effect, and the glimmerings of resistance began to dawn—with the 'quislings' as sitting targets in preference to the mighty Germans. Terboven and the High Command began to find it easier and easier to convince Hitler that the Reichscommissariat must remain.

As the tide of war turned gradually against Germany, and when Hitler's blitzkrieg on Russia petered out in December, 1941, the German leader became less accessible to Quisling. Hitler's intuition told him, rightly, that an Anglo-Russian pincers movement on Norway was planned. Also his prestige could even less afford concessions to 'Aryan' solidarity in 1941-42 than in 1940. For these reasons, Quisling's hopes of getting rid of Terboven dwindled and Quisling's main objective receded towards the unattainable.

Thus the Commissarial period, which was expected to last a transitional six months, dragged on and on. The *NS* Commissars, whom Quisling originally regarded as temporary expedients, holding the fort while he arranged with Hitler for a free Norwegian government under his own leadership, became tarred with Terboven's brush. Quisling's great opportunity gradually faded away, due initially to hostile propaganda, later to the fortunes of war.

The whole period from April 15, 1940, to February 1, 1942, when Quisling held no office, was frustrating and damaging for him on balance. The Russian campaign in 1941 turned the North once more into a war theatre and interfered with Hitler's promise to Quisling to sign a *de jure* peace so that a national government might replace the Reichscommissariat. The stirrings of a potential 'Home Front', with the Right and Left in alliance after the attack on Russia, created enough trouble for Terboven to argue that he was indispensable, and to poison the atmosphere with reprisals. The presence of several *NS* men in the Commissarial Government laid Quisling open to misrepresentation as a collaborator and traitor.

By the time Quisling's delayed rise to Minister-President occurred early in 1942, the German atrocities and repression were well under way and their sequels were the logical results of events over which Quisling had no control.

It may be asked why Quisling did not quit when the tide of war turned against the Germans on the East Front in December, 1941, thus stimulating pro-British hopes and opinions in Norway, and dashing expectations of a peace settlement with Hitler. Apart from the fact that he was as stubborn as most Norwegians, the outcome of the war must still have seemed to him to be a matter of speculation, and it must still have been worth while to secure for Norway a favourable place in the New Order in the event of an ultimate German victory.

More important, however, he no doubt felt that someone had to serve as a buffer between the Germans and the Norwegian people. If he defaulted, there was nobody to take his place. King Haakon, Nygaardsvold, the *Storting*, the Supreme Court and the backers of the abortive State Council had all, of necessity or otherwise, abandoned the nation to Terboven's mercy. He dreaded Norway becoming a German Protectorate, and felt that he was the one hope of obtaining favourable treatment for his people.

In 1942 there was much substance in this argument; but time was against Quisling. The year 1941 slid by and the balance of power began to change, thus weakening the argument, limiting his popular appeal and playing into the hands of his Norwegian opponents. Not that his cause was lost, for the abolition of the old parties in September 1940 had given him one great tactical advantage. *Nasjonal Samling* alone survived as a legal political movement, and it seized its chance. By 1942 *NS* had certainly trebled its membership and had at least 70,000 paid-up members, apart from sympathisers and minors. Headquarters were inundated with applications. Surviving officials of the Secretariat claim as many as 100,000 members, which seems by no means improbable since almost that number of 'quisling' cases were investigated, and doubtless many more evaded detection. The party therefore looked something like the 'national unity' movement that Quisling always claimed *NS* to be. His enemies' contention that *NS* was a dirty little clique of traitors on the idiot fringe of politics is quite untenable.

The nucleus of *NS* was composed largely of idealists, but, like all political parties, it had its adventurers. As was the case later with the 'Home Front', all manner of opportunists, crooks and thugs joined the bandwagon.

This medley produced an internal crisis. Among the newcomers were German provocateurs, who sought to twist *Nasjonal Samling* into a Nazi party, and to compromise Quisling by unauthorised actions that they committed in his name. Three German officials were appointed by Terboven as 'liaison officers', actually as spies and vehicles

306

for infiltrating *NS* organisation, propaganda and the *Hird* (bodyguard).

Quisling was aware of the grave danger of *NS* becoming a Nazi party, which would have torpedoed his whole policy of creating a *Norwegian* national movement to stand up to the Germans, but he temporised. When Harald Franklin Knudsen and others in Quisling's inner circle insisted on a purge, a fierce quarrel broke out, ending in Knudsen volunteering to leave Norway and go to the East Front to fight Bolshevism. Quisling's inaction did considerable damage to the integrity of his reputation, and the purge that he eventually carried out when he became Minister-President came too late.

Nobody gave him any credit for easing out the German liaison officers, which meant an end of Terboven's efforts to capture the party and work through it. One only sees in retrospect that Quisling held to his independent Norwegian line throughout this delicate period. It did not look like that at the time, partly due to the offence that his party uniforms, which Terboven permitted from September 1940 onwards, gave to the strictly 'shirtsleeves' and unmilitary Norwegian people.

He believed that Norwegians required discipline if ever they were going to find a favourable place in any New Europe, German or otherwise, as the lamentable performance in the field in 1940 had illustrated. If the Bolshevik menace was to be kept at bay, the Labour Party's long pacifist campaign had to be counteracted. If ever Norway was effectively to practise armed neutrality, a start with at least quasi-military training had to be made. One day Norway would need new Armed Forces. Also, the Germans, civil and military, were on the spot—nearly half a million of them—all in uniforms of varying magnificence; and it was humiliating, in Quisling's estimation, to wear shirtsleeves in dealing with them. He knew that the Germans respect a uniform. In dealing with Norwegians, he reckoned that Party uniforms would single out the *NS* members as serious functionaries and command attention.

There was much substance in this theory, but it was hopelessly wrong politically and psychologically. *NS* became visually identified with the swarming Germans and the whole movement consequently acquired a 'foreign' image. It was easy for the opposition to exploit this, although basically the whole idea of the *Hird* was patriotic, idealistic and even spiritual, like its forerunners in the Sagas.

Also held against Quisling is that he wrote to Hitler's head of Chancellery, Dr. von Lammers, suggesting the recruitment of volunteers in Norway to fight alongside the German Armed Forces. This initiative has always been represented as being directed against Norway's theoretical ally, Great Britain. It was nothing of the sort, however. As we now know, the invasion of Russia was already being prepared, and Quisling was looking for Norwegians to join the impending fight against Bolshevism, although at the time the Soviet Union was an ally of the Third Reich. The Norwegian volunteers recruited by Quisling were never intended to fight against Britain, and never did so.

Quisling's prosecutors antedated the charge of enlisting men, against the 'Allies' as they put it, from June, 1941, to August, 1940, when circumstances were in reverse. Contrary to the *jøssinger*, Quisling's recruiting campaign was popular and successful, and 8,000 volunteers were apportioned to units of varying strength. The Regiment Nordland and the Norwegian Legion, the original units, included about 2,000 men each. Another 2,000 joined the Division Viking. A Police Battalion fought in Finland, Then there were the Panzer-grenadier Norwegian Regiment, the Ski Battalion and four Police Companies. Collectively they were known as 'Front Fighters'. These became the most seasoned troops Norway has ever had.

Some fought their way across Eastern Europe to and from Leningrad and Rostov-on-Don, where they formed part of the rearguard on the *Wehrmacht*'s withdrawal from the Caucasus. Fifty Front Fighters fought to the last minute at the Reich Chancellery and Deutsche Bank as the Red Army closed in on Hitler. Three of their number were killed boarding the German tank on which Martin Bormann tried to escape. Eight hundred were killed in action, and survivors held a very high percentage of German decorations for gallantry. Whatever one may think of these exploits, as these 8,000 proved, there is nothing innately wrong with Norwegians as fighting men if they are inspired, as the Front Fighters were, with an ideal such as anti-Bolshevism—and if they are led with determination, instead of being undermined by pacifism.

After the war these men might have been incorporated as a stiffening to the five new Norwegian divisions, helping to give Norway a tough and disciplined Army, instead of a parade force. In fact, they were treated as traitors, and all 7,000 survivors were imprisoned for at least three years, deprived of their civil privileges and disqualified from anything but the humblest jobs.

The controversial unit was the Germanic SS Norway force of about 1,000 men. This came under the ultimate command of Himmler, and was intended not only for fighting Bolshevism but for 'other duties within the Greater Reich'. As such it defied the whole purpose of Quisling's recruiting campaign, which was to earn respect for Norwegian manhood, to gain combat experience against Bolshevism and to supply the seasoned nucleus of a new Norwegian Army.

It looked, however, as if Quisling was persuading Norwegians to serve the Gestapo chief. Actually, the Norwegian SS were recruited by Jonas Lie, at first behind Quisling's back, later against Quisling's orders. Loyal NS members were instructed to start a whispering campaign which was partially successful, against Lie's drive, but, with the whole apparatus of the State Police and the Reichscommissariat behind him, Lie wielded great influence. Quisling showed his disgust when Himmler came to present the Norwegian SS standard. The two men exchanged not a word, but enough damage was done to smear Quisling and the genuine Front Fighters. This struggle between Lie and Quisling was one of the reasons for Terboven's despair of working through NS after 1941.

It is also falsely charged against Quisling that he was instrumental in infiltrating some 25 members of the Norwegian Legion into the State Police, thereby associating himself with 'brutalities' that these men were alleged to have committed. It is, however, significant that whereas the State Police carried out German orders from the first to the last day of the occupation, no charge was ever brought against them—presumably because they were not 'quislings'.

While on the subject of misrepresentation of Quisling during his political isolation during April 1940 to February 1942, sport is worth a mention. Sailing and winter sports are available to the whole Norwegian nation, and therefore mean more to the individual than in 'spectator' countries. For a generation the governing bodies had been divided into two groups, Marxist and bourgeois. During the period of the collaborating Administrative Council, these two groups at last united. One of the first acts of Axel Stang, the Commissarial Minister of Sport, whom the negotiators of the abortive State Council had accepted, was to announce that there would be no interference with sport. So much trouble was stirred up among students and school-children, however, that routine sports meetings became impossible. Stang therefore dissolved the governing bodies of the hitherto feuding groups and proclaimed that a properly unified central sports organisation would take charge. All sport was thenceforth to be organised 'on the principle of responsibility', that is on a non-political basis.

Even this reform has been represented as an example of 'the dictator principle' and 'Nazification'. Photographs of small sports meetings under the new régime were circulated to prove that 'nearly all active sportsmen and sportswomen simultaneously refused to be organised by a Nazified sports association', although many other unpublicised photographs prove the contrary. International competitions, including the Holmenkollen ski festival, had to be cancelled while the war was on—and Quisling was blamed for this! Yet Norway could have enjoyed a flourishing national sports life, like Sweden, where Arne Anderson and Gunder Hägg were running middle-distance world records. Dislocation was again blamed on the 'quislings', although the difficulties were manufactured by their opponents. Young sports idols had to be dragged into the controversy since the future lay with their generation and their disgruntlement helped to diminish NS popularity. Sport of course was the victim.

II

We have now covered the various stages of the Occupation controversy leading up to Quisling's second government. His first government, which lasted only six days (April 9-15, 1940) was formed in an attempt to save the vestiges of national sovereignty. It was superseded by the Administrative Council (April 15-24, 1940), which continued to function after the establishment of the Reichscommissariat (April 25, 1940-May 8, 1945) until September 25, 1940, when it in turn was succeeded by the Commissarial Government (September 25, 1940-Feb. 1, 1942). Quisling, as we have seen, refused to join, but allowed some of his leaders to participate on the expectation that the régime was to last for a transitional six months pending the formation of his own second government. The key Ministry of Police was occupied by the renegade member of the Party, Jonas Lie, and German oppression began.

The Norwegian leaders who had supported the Administrative and

State Councils eventually reversed their policy and threw in their lot with the exiled King in Council and the anti-German 'Home Front'. Their opposition provoked Terboven, and the pattern of German frightfulness set in: arrests, deportations, executions and Jewish persecution. These troubles prolonged the Reichscommissariat, and Quisling was blamed for reprisals although he was powerless. The situation deteriorated as his chances of arranging a peace treaty with Hitler grew more remote.

Quisling's rivalry with Terboven for control of Norway continued. Terboven tried to penetrate NS and use it as an instrument of the Reichscommissariat; he also provoked more 'Home Front' disturbances in order to denigrate Quisling and to justify Hitler in retaining the Reichscommissariat. In contrast, Quisling and his men in the Commissarial Government tried to reduce unpleasantness so as to justify Hitler in making the promised concessions to Norway. Quisling believed that his mere presence prevented the Reichscommissariat from becoming a Protectorate on the Polish model.

It was in these circumstances that the Second Quisling Government (February 1, 1942–May 8, 1945) came into being. As usual, the way in which this occurred is poorly documented, and to some extent we must fall back on sources that cannot be considered very reliable. On October 2, 1940, a week after he had become Minister of the Interior in the provisional Commissarial Government, Hagelin wrote to Stabsleiter Schikendanz in Rosenberg's APA and made what he called a 'very important point': 'On December 10 of this year, it will be six months that the King has been out of the country. According to the Constitution, he must either return immediately by December 10, or forfeit his throne. This is very important in the minds of the people, although he has been formally deposed by the Reichscommissar. . . . I am of the opinion that the movement for joining NS will be so rapid that it might be possible on December 10 to appoint Quisling as Chief of State (*Riksforstander*), in the same way as Horthy in Hungary . . . Quisling does not in fact desire the position of Minister-President, but would like to leave that to me, while he takes over the function of the former King as Chief of State.'

The way in which Quisling's mind was working is seen in the letter he himself wrote to Schickendanz on October 25: 'Here things are progressing not unfavourably, yet somewhat awkwardly, since NS and I are already encumbered with the full responsibility for the conduct of the government without having corresponding freedom of action, and also without even constituting a government. Moreover, there is the additional fact that four important ministries, among them Finance, Economy and Commerce, are beyond the scope of our influence.'

A memorandum, concerning 'settlement of relations between Norway and Germany', was attached. The preamble harked back to Quisling's pre-Hitler ideology: 'The goal of the New Order created between Norway and Germany is the establishment of the Greater Nordic Confederation. Norway's key position makes the settlement of the relations between Norway and Germany the very basis for the creation of such a federation. It is therefore . . . of the greatest importance to arrive as soon as possible at peace and normal relations . . . It is absolutely necessary to create a transitional order which meets with the full approval of both the Norwegian people and the other Scandinavian countries.'

Within Norway he demanded an independent Norwegian *Nasjonal Samling* Government, with himself as Chief of State; the replacement of the Reichscommissariat by a Plenipotentiary Extraordinary or 'special representative of the German Reich'; the restoration of Norwegian neutrality and its recognition by Germany, with Germany retaining the right to take necessary military measures for the duration of the war; and the immediate opening of negotiations for peace and the creation of a Pan-German Federation.

'The immediate establishment of an NS Government and of a Regency,' Quisling continued, 'is all the more necessary as NS, even today, is regarded as the decisive factor in Norway, and the Norwegian people fervently desire the withdrawal of the German civilian administration (the Reichscommissariat), which limits the full effectiveness of the National Movement.'

The main points of the proposed Federation were listed as follows:

1. Norway to remain a free, indivisible and independent State, joined with the Greater German Reich in a Pan-Nordic Federation.

2. A common foreign policy.

3. The German High Command to function as the Federal High Command; a national Norwegian Army to be established for Home Defence within the structure of the Federal Armed Forces.

4. A common federal flag; the Norwegian national and Merchant Navy flags to remain.

5. The German Chancellor to be Federal President.

6. The Federal Government to be formed by a smaller German Cabinet, reinforced by one or two Ministers from Norway and other adherents to the Federation.

7. A German Envoy in Oslo to serve as Federal Commissioner.

8. Norway to be governed by a Norwegian Regent and an independent National Government of Norwegians.

9. Norway to constitute her own Norwegian National Assembly based on the national economic and cultural life.

10. Close collaboration between *NSDAP* and *NS*.

11. Stabilisation of the Norwegian currency on the basis of the Reichsmark with Berlin as the clearing centre.

12. Gradual relaxation of customs frontiers.

13. Joint regulation of the development of inter-State traffic.

14. Reciprocal right of movement, domicile and work, but German nationals not to acquire property in Norway without permission from the Norwegian Government.

15. Norway to co-operate with other Nordic countries as far as possible without contravening the Federal Agreement.

Quisling and Hagelin were taken to Berlin on December 4 by Terboven and General von Falkenhorst. It is evident from Quisling's later correspondence with Dr. von Lammers of the Reich Chancellory that a meeting with Hitler took place on the 7th, but no documentary record of this meeting is available. Apparently Hitler again hedged in deference to Terboven's exaggeration of 'Home Front' activity and Falkenhorst's insistence on military security.

On March 10, 1941, Quisling wrote to Lammers: 'A popularly supported voluntary association (of Norway) in a Great Germanic Federation depended (in December) upon two crucial factors: first, the establishment of a close relationship of trust and confidence between the German authorities (Reichscommissariat) and me as the leader of the *Nasjonal Samling* . . . secondly, a basic willingness to enter into peace preliminaries with a Norway led by *NS*.'

Neither condition had been forthcoming, as he revealed: 'The attempt instituted by Reichscommissar Terboven after his appointment to work with the old Norwegian political parties, through the medium

313

of the Storting, towards a solution favourable to Germany ended in complete failure. At the time I repeatedly cautioned against this attempt in the light of my familiarity with Norwegian conditions and attitudes. Pursuant to the Führer's explicit decision, the *NS* was then declared to be the sole recognised political party in Norway, and last September a provisional government was established. Its term was fixed during the preliminary discussions at approximately six months (to about March 1, 1941), as was recorded in writing.'

After outlining the consolidation of his Party, Quisling continued: 'Unfortunately, the requisite condition that the German authorities adopt and pursue a clear-cut attitude with respect to *NS* in order to demonstrate to the Norwegian people, for their own benefit and in unmistakable terms, Greater Germany's intention to seek a far-reaching solution of the Norwegian problem, has not been fulfilled. What has been given to *NS* with the right hand has been taken away with the left. Otherwise the expansion of *NS* would have reached quite different proportions.'

Among 'striking vexations', Quisling pointed to German orders for a 20 per cent wage cut, which would have 'spelled the political suicide of *NS*'. All counter-arguments were unavailing, nevertheless *NS* refused to agree. 'A request like this in itself demonstrates either a wholly blind attitude on the Germans' part as regards the political objectives envisaged, or else it reveals a disguised interest on the part of certain German authorities to frustrate these objectives . . . using *NS* itself as a lever.'

He also complained that retention of the trade union leadership had roused steady opposition that made it difficult for *NS* to win the support of the working classes. Following a conference between Terboven and Tangen, the trade union leader, a communiqué by Tangen had appeared in all Norwegian newspapers, reporting complete accord between them on maintaining current policy, and the entire population, and particularly labour circles, had interpreted this as censure of *NS*. Tangen and a number of other labour leaders had also been invited by the Reichscommissariat to inspect Germany, which too could only be interpreted as favouring opponents of *NS*.

Quisling mentioned too a social gathering for the German Forces and Administration, arranged for January 24, which had been postponed to the 26th at Terboven's request. Falkenhorst had found the date unsuitable, thus dooming the carefully prepared celebration, and compromising *NS* throughout Norway. 'What particularly hurt me,' Quisling wrote, 'was to learn that Falkenhorst had time to dine in public at the Grand Hotel on the night of the party.'

Another complaint was this: 'For racial and political reasons I have advocated collaboration between Norway and Germany. . . . This concept also moved me to resolve to recruit Norwegian men for *SS-Standarte* "Nordland", a decision bitterly attacked by my enemies. The same racial philosophy was also stressed by Reichsführer-*SS* Himmler in Oslo on January 30, when "Nordland" was sworn in. How can this be reconciled with the *Wehrmacht* view that a German soldier may treat a Norwegian girl as fair game but is not permitted to marry her if she expects a child by him, as set forth in an order by General von Falkenhorst? . . . On the other hand, Norwegian men are considered worthy of acceptance into the German Army.'

Yet another example of vexation was 'the sudden Press directive changing the title "*Fører* of the *NS*" to "*Leiter* of the *NS*", even though the former has been in use for eight years. . . . These things all produce an unmistakable effect . . . namely that the German authorities, and hence Greater Germany, are not fully backing up *NS* but are using it as a means for reaching a different solution . . . that I am a traitor, betrayed by the Reich, thus suffering the fate which all such persons deserve.'

All this brought Quisling to the conclusion that *NS* expansion would be halted, whereupon there would be 'a search for other solutions . . . just as intended'—in other words that *NS* would be abandoned and the Reichscommissariat perpetuated.

Quisling also complained of German heavy industry and big German financial interests moving into Norway, displacing Norwegians and causing dissatisfaction. 'I would not have written these words . . . if I were not convinced that lack of success with *NS* in Norway would be equivalent to losing an entire military campaign in Scandinavia. . . . There would arise a power-group motivated only by resentment and envenoming the future, bearing within it the seed of its own destruction.' On that grave note he begged von Lammers to arrange for him to meet Hitler again.

January 30, 1941, had been suggested originally as the date for confirming the establishment of an 'independent, purely *NS* Government in Norway', under Quisling's leadership, it having been stipulated earlier that March 1, 1941, was to be the latest date for this departure. Quisling now suggested May 17 as an alternative. He hoped that on the Norwegian National Day, Norway's independence might be proclaimed, along with the conclusion of a preliminary peace. He hoped also that April 9, the anniversary of the occupation, might be utilised by Hitler to declare the transformation or redesignation of the office of Reichscommissar.

He advised, however, that, in that event, no big military parade should take place in Oslo before Hitler's birthday on April 20, lest the population should take it amiss, and he reaffirmed his belief in German victory. Much as he regretted the attitude of part of the Norwegian population in Svolvaer during the Anglo-Norwegian raid on the Lofoten Islands on March 4, 1941, Quisling protested against the exaggerated fear that friendliness towards Norway was of no avail. 'If a military dictatorship were now instituted, it would only make NS's popular standing more precarious, and thereby jeopardise links with Germany. What we need is not a sterner policy against the Norwegian people but a *clearer* one. . . . I can guarantee that if the Führer promises the Norwegian people a quick and honourable peace and national independence within a voluntary association with Germany, there will be a broad shift of sentiment in favour of Germany.'

The letter also documented the fact that Terboven was very far from collaborating with *Nasjonal Samling*, and showed that the situation was deteriorating so rapidly that if Quisling were to produce peace, Hitler had to honour his promises soon. Allowing for some exaggeration of his own potential and some flattery of the Germans, Quisling's assessment of the situation from his own particular viewpoint was reasonably sound.

His long speech in the Colosseum Cinema on April 9 reflected his continued belief in the policy contained in his letter. He promised that 'the coming peace means Norway will not become a Protectorate or a part of Germany'. He also looked forward to NS representing the whole Norwegian people.

Himmler spent May 22 in Oslo, launching another detachment of Front Fighters. Jonas Lie made the welcoming speech, and Quisling remained silent, thus indicating pointedly that he and the Reichscommissariat were at loggerheads.

So the strain built up until September 6, when Quisling made another major speech at the Colosseum, warning the *jøssings* that they now had their 'last chance' to 'stop playing'. Their leaders paid no heed, and Terboven clamped down with his State of Emergency on the 10th. 'Now I will bring the Norwegians to their knees,' he said to Boehm. Hansteen and Wickstrøm were executed on the 11th. 'The responsibility for this bloodshed rests solely and alone with Terboven and not with his Norwegian associates, the Ministers,' said Admiral Hermann Boehm, the German naval commander in Norway.

Protests poured into Berlin, from Quisling to Lammers, Hagelin to Rosenberg, Boehm to Raeder, stressing the urgency of a solution to the Norwegian problem if the people were not permanently to be antagonised and the security of the German Occupation forces threatened. Hitler was preoccupied with the Eastern Front, and Terboven had his way.

Incidentally, Norway was plunging into a vast financial deficit at the rate of 160m. *kroner* ($22.4m.) a month for occupation costs, including such items as 100,000 *kroner* ($14,000) for a railway saloon for Terboven and 40,000 *kroner* for an elk hunt. There was also the item of a covered tennis court for the Reichscommissar at Skaugum Palace. 'All in a poor little country with half the population of Berlin', Hagelin protested. Here was another major practical reason for concluding peace with Germany as soon as possible.

By January, 1942, Terboven came to realise that his policy of oppression and his attempt to 'use' *Nasjonal Samling* had failed. He and his German police chief, *SS*-Gruppenführer Rediess, had repeatedly tried in vain to threaten, cajole and argue Quisling into collaborating with them. The dossier from German and *NS* sources against the Reichscommissariat was piling up in Berlin when word came that Hitler was expected back from the Eastern Front to speak to the world on January 31, the ninth anniversary of his coup. At last the Norwegian problem could again be raised with him, and he would have to decide whether to honour his promises to Quisling.

Thus Hitler once again becomes the key figure. Time was no longer Terboven's ally. Anticipating that Hitler would give Quisling another chance, Terboven decided to anticipate him. At short notice, Quisling was summoned to the Reichscommissariat on January 23, 1942, and told that he would be allowed to form a government. No first-hand record of this historic conversation exists, but it has been possible to gather its gist from Quisling's report that evening to Hagelin and Schreiber, who in turn informed Boehm.

Quisling's main conditions were the replacement of the 1940 Armistice by a preliminary peace treaty; a drastic diminution of the German administrative staff; co-operation with the Germans within the framework of the 'Great Germanic' idea; and a free choice of his own Ministers.

On January 28, suggested Quisling, a preliminary peace should be concluded, and on February 1 he should assume full power as Minister-President. Terboven, however, proposed to postpone the peace date, and the consequent reduction in German personnel, until May 1. Unwisely Quisling compromised, trusting to a State visit to Hitler at the end of January to iron out the timetable.

That was a grave political mistake. What Terboven had succeeded in doing was to saddle Quisling with ostensible power without giving him peace and the liquidation of the Reichscommissariat to show for it. Thus Quisling lost the two advantages which would have delighted the nation and built up his prestige. Instead, he again laid himself wide open to the charge of being a willing German tool. In retrospect, it is clear that he was a victim of German inter-departmental intrigue, the inefficiency of the Nazi system, and the impossibility of Hitler running everything in the Greater Reich.

Before Quisling or Hagelin could reach Hitler, Terboven rushed his deputy, Wegener, to Berlin. Although once again there is no record of their conversation, it is clear from subsequent events that Wegener obtained Hitler's agreement to the compromise on the peace date, so that when Quisling eventually reached Hitler he was confronted by a *fait accompli*. The Reichscommissariat was assured of another three months' life, which gave Terboven time to sabotage the agreement into which he had entered with obvious reluctance.

Afterwards, Quisling commented naïvely: 'I thought that peace should come *before* the formation of the government. The Reichscommissariat thought it should come later and Terboven, after conferring with Hitler, informed me that the matter would be settled in the early summer, allowing us to have foreign representatives where possible and to start separate Norwegian Defence.'

The inauguration of the new National Government took place with

318

pomp and ceremony in the snow at Akershus Castle on February 1. Quisling wore his grey *Hird* uniform. The guard of honour for the new Minister-President was formed by detachments of seven famous Norwegian Army regiments, whose presence underlined the new start to be made with Defence. The Norwegian flag was hoisted again over the old fortress—likewise over the *Storting* and the palace—for the first time since Quisling's first government expired on April 15, 1940. Admiral Boehm represented the *Wehrmacht*, General von Falkenhorst being notably absent. Martin Bormann, Terboven's boss, represented Hitler. Terboven himself and his Police-General Rediess were also prominent. Besides all the members of Quisling's new government, seven provincial governors attended.

That night Mrs. Quisling gave a banquet at Villa Grandi in the seaside suburb of Bygdø, where the Norwegian ship museum (*Fram, Kon-Tiki* and a long-ship) is now situated. This spacious but vulgar mansion, built by a tycoon who had got into financial difficulties, had passed into State hands, and been completed and reconditioned as a State institution. Quisling chose it as his official residence, rather than the Royal Castle, because it committed the State to no wasteful expenditure. Gossip about Mrs. Quisling's black and green marble bathroom and other extravagances was, of course, nonsense. Quisling did allow himself the Nordic luxury of renaming the villa 'Gimle' (Home of the Gods).

Among the notable absentees at the banquet was again General von Falkenhorst, for whom General Feuerstein deputised. Otherwise the Reichscommissariat, the *Wehrmacht*, *Nasjonal Samling* and the Supreme Court were represented at the highest level. The presence of some members of the Supreme Court was noteworthy since the Court had approved the new National Government on the basis of the 1814 Constitution, which obliged it to summon a new government after four months in the absence of the monarch. Thus Quisling could claim, as he always did, that he was instated by Norwegian law and not, like previous administrations, by the Germans. Ever since April 9, this had been his condition for serving. Of course, Terboven claimed that 'Quisling stands completely under my control'—a view shared by the exiled King in Council and, eventually, by the leaders of the 'Home Front'. The argument is irrelevant, save that it helped to condemn Quisling to death. It remained to be seen whether Quisling could

function independently. The official Berlin view, according to the news agencies, was that his government was 'authoritative'.

His former office in the *Storting* was now in use by the Reichscommissariat, so he worked in those quarters in the Royal Palace which had not already been taken over by government departments. Thus arose a fantastic charge against him in 1945, that he 'took possession of objects of art and other goods belonging partly to the State and partly to the Royal Family'—including the royal teaspoons! Actually, he did no more than put some of the valuable objects into safe storage at Gimle for the duration, in order to prevent damage and pilfering, and he moved a statue of his friend, the late Queen Maud, which he erected out of harm's way at Gimle for sentimental reasons.

Nine of the Commissarial Ministers retained their posts in the National Government: Irgens (Shipping); Skancke (Church and Education); Hagelin (Interior); Riisnaes (Justice); Fretheim, who now joined NS (Agriculture), Lunde (Culture), Stang (Sport), Hustad (Labour), and Jonas Lie (Police). Notably, Hagelin was not promoted and Lie was too entrenched in Terboven's favour to be ousted.

Four important portfolios now came under Quisling's actual control, whereas his influence on the Commissarial Government had been at the most indirect in those cases where his supporters held office. Frederik Prytz became Finance Minister, with ex-Minister Sandberg as assistant. Eivind Blehr, Governor of Oslo and Aker, took on Trade, Industry, Handicrafts and Fishing, with ex-Minister Johannessen as Trade assistant and ex-Minister Ravner as Supply assistant. Thus the administration of the country was left largely in experienced hands— the exception being Prytz among the newcomers. None of the old political parties could have put up a much better team. Rolf Fuglesang, the lawyer who was General Secretary of *Nasjonal Samling*, was included to represent the Party.

Contrary to legend, Quisling was an excellent administrator—as the General Staff, Nansen, Minister Urbye and the British Government had recognised before the war. Ministers went to Quisling in a crisis and got quick decisions. For instance, when fish distribution suddenly broke down in 1944, Quisling told his Minister of Supply (Alf Whist, who succeeded Blehr) to stop all exports to Germany and to rush free herrings to the populace.

Incidentally, Whist—an American-Norwegian—was one of the few

NS men who amassed a fortune. Like Hagelin, whom Quisling dismissed in 1944, he was something of an adventurer whose earlier financial activities in France were known to Quisling. 'Whist is the best swindler in Norway,' Quisling once said, 'just the man to cheat the Germans!' Whist did just this with skill and relish, squeezing food and supplies out of the Germans in abundance, and easing shortages.*

Quisling wasted no time in propagating his views. As Bishop Berggrav said: 'He believed in his own propaganda.' Within the first week, he ordered the teachers into a single organisation to be run by Orvar Saether, himself a teacher. This was not a happy appointment, for Saether was perhaps too fanatical. He was a man who regarded an order as an order, and he lacked the broad human sympathy needed to win over the disturbed teaching world.

A National Youth Service was also started, under Stang and Fuglesang, for boys and girls between the ages of ten and eighteen, who were to be taught the patriotic and disciplined Nordic way of life, as recommended by Quisling for the past twelve years. This was tactless, for parents and children inevitably recoiled from what smacked of German National Socialism. This was a typical example of Quisling's faulty psychology.

Thirdly, Quisling announced his intention of establishing a Corporative State (*Riksstyre*).

Although he antagonised many people by his hasty actions, he was not vindictive, and did not use his power to molest his enemies. In fact he obtained an amnesty from Terboven for Norwegians arrested during the State of Emergency.

Quisling's meeting with Hitler was delayed until February 13. Hitler again procrastinated and the conversation drifted into imponderables—the current German persecution of Slavs in Eastern Europe, which Quisling said was a mistake because Poles and Ukrainians might have been attracted into the anti-Bolshevik crusade, and the post-war future of Norway, which Hitler promised would not be comparable to Bavaria or Württemburg but would have to await definition until the

* Between the wars Whist made a fortune in Marine insurance and founded the Norwegian Lloyds. He had large offices in London, Paris and New York and his Moscow office was confiscated by the Bolsheviks to become the first headquarters of the *Cheka–O.G.P.U.*

peace. However, the special status of Norway was acknowledged in principle, and Quisling regarded this as a great gain.

An immediate concession was wrung from Hitler. It was agreed that the Norwegian Shipowners' Association should resume control of its affairs. Some 50m. *kroner* ($7m.) and nearly a million tons of merchant vessels in Axis waters were restored. Dr. Neubauer, the German Supply chief, who embezzled 1½m. *kroner* ($210,000) in Norway, was removed from the Association. Plans for post-war reconstruction were worked out.

Quisling was also received by Göring and Rosenberg. Evidently he had made an impression in Berlin, and the continuation of the Reichscommissariat was not assured, as Terboven knew, having been present at the interviews with both Hitler and Göring.

Terboven wasted no time therefore in provoking serious trouble in Norway. He rushed back to Oslo, while Quisling was still in Germany. Later he seized his chance. Without consulting Quisling, he persuaded Saether to round up a thousand teachers who were resisting the new 'trade unionisation' order, and packed them off by boat to Kirkenes to work on fortifications in the Arctic. The furore throughout Norway destroyed the peaceful atmosphere on which Quisling's plan depended.

The result was that the prolongation of the Reichscommissariat was assured, and the carpet was effectively pulled from under the 'Corporative State'. Thereafter, no other groups would co-operate, after the teachers' experience, and so *Nasjonal Samling* was left as an isolated organisation with no wider backing than before.

This was a major victory for Terboven and the 'Home Front', and fatal to Quisling. Henceforth the Minister-President could merely temporise—waiting for the promised peace with Germany, which never came. Until the teachers' strike early in 1943, Quisling had a real chance to build a national movement that would bring his ideology to life and imbue *Nasjonal Samling* with real meaning. After the strike, national unity became a will-o'-the-wisp.

Stubborn as ever, Quisling comforted himself with the illusion that the Second World War would end in a compromise peace and he, too, compromised. Harald Franklin Knudsen states his dilemma thus:

'Quisling could not believe that the Western Powers would be so stupid as to open up Europe to the Russian hordes. Churchill he regarded as a practical politician. . . . That Churchill became a party

to the Bolshevisation of Eastern and Central Europe was Quisling's greatest disappointment. . . . If Hitler failed to break Bolshevism, the Western Powers still had the chance of keeping it within the old Russian boundaries. Otherwise Europe would commit suicide and Norway would enter the extreme danger zone as a neighbour of Russia.

'Quisling did not want German victory for the sake of Germany but as a necessity for the continued existence of Europe and Norway. He respected Germans for their science and culture, their industry and solidity, but he did not like them as politicians. He said, "Fortunately Hitler is not a true German. He has the imagination of an Austrian." He felt at home with Hitler, the great generals and admirals, and their broad outlook—and he never anticipated any insurmountable obstacle to a reasonable division of power within a European community of free states.'

Quisling was no match for Terboven in tactics, as witness the following extract from *Hitler's Table Talk* in May 1942:

'In Terboven I am pleased to have found a man capable of assuming control of Norway, the most difficult Commissarship of the Reich. As he himself told me this very day, if he relaxes control for a single instant, he feels as though he is on quicksands. . . . He was, for example, compelled to arrest a number of Norwegian teachers, who had seen fit to try and sabotage certain measures taken by the German High Command, and he is now employing them to build fortifications. I only regret that the traditional German benevolence on the part of the Naval authorities charged with the transportation of these people was once more carried to stupid lengths; the embarkation authorities at first refused to carry these passengers, on the grounds that sufficient lifebelts for them were not available. Surely these Norwegians would have been delighted if they had been torpedoed by their beloved British and sent to the bottom.'

Following the teachers' strike in February, 1942, passive resistance spread from one branch of organised life to another, and Quisling's measures were widely condemned as 'Nazification'. His National Government's activities, like those of its predecessors, degenerated into little more than day-to-day administration. Quisling claimed that he saved much from the Germans, but violence overshadowed everything. The tally has been exaggerated, but it was sufficient to foil Quisling and to liquidate him.

Norway's total war fatalities were 10,307 (a third of Belgium's, a fifth of France's, an eighth of Holland's and a sixtieth of Poland's, for example), excluding 270 official and unofficial post-war executions. The breakdown is:

Killed in action in 1940	850
Civilian casualties in 1940	430
Volunteers lost with the Allies (1940-45)	1,150
Merchant sailors	3,640
'Front Fighters' lost on Eastern Front	800
'Home Front' casualties	1,481
Executions	366
Died in German concentration camps	830
Norwegian Jews lost in German concentration camps	760
	10,307

Some 35,000 Norwegians in all were imprisoned during the German Occupation.

In a small country of three million people, those figures are terrible. But they are microscopic compared to, say, the Finnish war figures. Finland lost 80,000 men in battle from a population of $3\frac{1}{2}$ million. Holland alone lost 104,000 Jews. Comparatively, Norway had a very easy war.

Many factors of course contributed to the discrepancy, notably the failure of Norway to fight seriously in 1940, the weakness of the 'Home Front' and the surrender of the huge German forces in Norway without a fight. Contributory factors were undoubtedly Quisling's prevention of a Protectorate, his mediation with the Reichscommissariat on behalf of condemned Norwegians, his assistance to Jews and his final refusal to engage in civil war.

'I don't believe it does any service to the country,' he told his prosecutors, 'to turn five years of history into a criminal story.' His role during the 'frightfulness' must, however, be carefully examined.

On October 5, 1942, an arms factory was sabotaged in Trondheim and weapons for the underground movement were smuggled ashore from England. That night Gestapo agents went by the night train from

Oslo to Trondheim, without consulting either Quisling or his government. The following morning a State of Emergency was declared. Ten local leaders of cultural and business life were immediately arrested and shot—not as hostages or rebels, but 'in expiation'. Twenty-four more local inhabitants were also arrested indiscriminately, and the assumption was that they, too, would be executed. A cry went up all over Norway which reached Germany. Admiral Boehm informed Raeder, for Hitler's ear, that Terboven's action 'destroyed any further hope of co-operation with the German civil authorities'. According to Goebbels, Terboven was about to execute 300 hostages in Oslo, and was only stopped by the last-minute intervention of Hitler, who forbade his Commissar to continue his 'old methods'.

Boehm says that he and the other *Wehrmacht* leaders were taken completely by surprise, as was Quisling, who immediately conferred at length with the German commanders in order to bring pressure against an extension of the terror. Unfortunately for Quisling's reputation, the young *NS* leader in Trondheim, Henrik Rogstad, panicked and acquiesced in the executions and arrests. Grief-stricken, he later committed suicide. Thus the 'Home Front' obtained means whereby to blame what became known as the 'Trondheim massacre' on Quisling. This baseless accusation is still held against him.

He was horrified, and did his utmost to halt the terror. Furthermore, it was through his influential German friends and acquaintances, Raeder, Boehm, K. J. Püttkamer (now a Rear-Admiral at Hitler's Headquarters) and Rudolf Schmundt (now a Major-General and also at Hitler's HQ) that Hitler was persuaded to restrain Terboven. Were it not for Quisling's contact with Hitler and his entourage, hundreds more innocent Norwegians would undoubtedly have been butchered —and in all probability Norway would have degenerated into the Protectorate that Quisling so dreaded.

Admiral Boehm says that Terboven deliberately sabotaged Quisling and made difficulties for him among his own people, the real object being, in short, that 'he wanted to be Gauleiter of Norway', having been dashed in his hopes of becoming Gauleiter of Britain. Püttkamer wrote to Boehm on October 31, saying that Hitler had admitted that 'Boehm was right', but at the same time Hitler found fresh excuses for retaining Terboven—including the unlikely possibility of 'Sweden taking Norway in the rear'.

Quisling's contact with Hitler undoubtedly prevented the Trond-heim treatment being meted out to all Norway, and persecution was less in evidence during the next few months. Instead, Terboven turned against easier game, the 1,200 innocent Norwegians of Jewish origin—the only celebrities among them being Hambro, who was safely in England, and the great cartoonist, 'Pedro', who escaped.

We here reach the emotional problem of race—the most contro-versial aspect of Quisling's ideology.

It is undoubtedly true that in some ways Quisling promoted anti-semitism, but in fairness to him he must be exonerated from its worst aspects. Although not seeking to excuse his naïve racial views, one should remember that his thinking had the misfortune to be confused, admittedly largely through his own fault, by the barbarous Aryan heresy. This confusion, twisted and exploited by his adversaries, ruined his image and probably contributed more than any other factor to his condemnation and execution. His deadly fear of the 'inter-national Marxist conspiracy', in which a number of Jews played a leading role, may also help to explain how such a clear-headed and basically kind man could have allowed his mythology to become warped.

It must also be stated that Quisling's anti-semitism never ran to genocide. On the contrary, he had saved thousands of Jewish lives during the Russian famine. Before the war he had advocated a 'national home' for the Jews, and he stuck by this. 'Extermination' never entered his vocabulary. In fact it is clear that he was ignorant of what the Nazis were doing, or were about to do, as part of their ghastly 'final solution'.

The first step taken against the Jews in Norway was in May, 1940, when the Gestapo confiscated their wireless sets. This was of course during the period of the Administrative Council when Quisling was in opposition.

On October 26, 1942, during Quisling's National Government, he introduced a law confiscating Jewish property. This was implemented in 125 cases on November 10.

On November 17, 1942, he decreed that all full-Jews, half-Jews and quarter-Jews were to report to the nearest authorities for registration, the definition of 'Jewish' being left to the officials concerned, the State Police and municipal governments. The Jews were given two weeks to register. This gave them sufficient notice to enable 500 to escape to Sweden—some with the help of NS men.

Those who refused to believe that their omission to register would lead to arrest, and those who were unable to escape, hung on. Then the Gestapo pounced. The remaining 782 Norwegian Jews were thrown into Grini concentration camp outside Oslo, together with other Norwegians. This was not a liquidation camp. Indeed it was thoroughly penetrated by members of the underground, who smuggled in comforts and news. Conditions were primitive but tolerable. When Harald Franklin Knudsen paid a visit incognito, at Quisling's request, the Jews did not complain. They and the 'quislings' believed that internment meant what it implied.

Genocide did not enter their thoughts, as is evident from a declaration that Quisling made in the first week in December:

'There are many who say that a Jew cannot be expelled simply because he is a Jew. In my opinion, no such reasoning could be more superficial. . . . A Jew is not Norwegian, not European, he is an Oriental. Jews have no place in Europe. They are an internationally destructive element. The Jews create the Jewish problem and cause active anti-semitism, and it is not difficult to understand why.

'We have many tragedies in Europe today. Jews have married Norwegians; their children are half-Jews and *their* children are quarter-Jews. . . . When the eastern ghettos were opened, Germany was overrun by Russian and Polish Jews in an incredibly short time, and they clamped down like grasshoppers. . . . It was the same in France, Hungary and Bulgaria. So one sees the depth of this problem, which stems from a world problem. The only possible solution is for the Jews to leave Europe and to have some area or another as far away as possible, preferably an island. For us in NS there can be no compromise in this struggle. Those who are not for us are against us.'

Banishment, not liquidation, was his solution. Quisling always maintained that he was not forewarned about the deportation of the Jews and that he took no part in it, but his use of the word 'expelled' in his December 10 declaration indicates that he at least anticipated this development at some time or another. He also maintained that he knew nothing of the 'final solution', and that nothing he had heard in Germany had suggested that the Jews were to be subjected to anything worse than internment or forced labour. Since these events took place some time before the Nazi atrocities were executed with full vigour, it seems reasonable to believe him.

Quisling cannot be acquitted of complicity in some crimes against humanity. Probably he simply turned a blind eye to the realities of Jewish persecution. His crime was one of default rather than of participation.

Actually the one and only public protest against the arrest of the Jews was made by the *NS* Bishop of Oslo, L. Frøyland, who spoke up in his cathedral. This unfortunate man was condemned to ten years' imprisonment after the war for being a member of *Nasjonal Samling*!

At Quisling's trial an appeal made in writing on November 11, 1942, by five bishops, 25 Church organisations and five professors, was cited against him. They condemned the arrest of Jews and the confiscation of their property and begged Quisling, as Minister-President, to intervene. His failure to do so was held by the Court to have 'negligently contributed to the death of several or at least some Jews when ... he collaborated with the German authorities in apprehending Jews and sending them to Germany'.

As Quisling pointed out, the appeal was never submitted to the German authorities, who performed the arrests and the deportation. Theoretically Quisling was head of state, but obviously the last word rested in a matter of this sort with the Reichscommissariat, which is why he battled for years to get rid of Terboven. Had he been factually in power as well as in office, his 'negligence' would indeed have been criminal.

As it was, his share of guilt perhaps deserved a penal sentence, but not death. The Jewish tragedy in Norway cannot properly be dismissed in terms of plain black and white.

Nor were the circumstances of the next atrocity straightforward. On August 14, the Allies and the Soviet Union declared that Norway was an enemy, and Quisling's National Government introduced a Provincial Law for the Maintenance of Law and Order in Wartime. This brought the State Police under direct Military Law, whereas previously they had held civilian status, although they were in effect under Terboven's orders through the medium of his collaborator, Police Minister Jonas Lie.

The Allied declaration was bound to be interpreted as a prelude to armed intervention in Norway, but it was already obvious that a new situation existed. The Germans were being edged back on the Eastern Front and North Norway began to look very vulnerable to an Allied pincer movement. The Swedes were showing signs of partisan support for the Allied cause; eight Companies of Norwegian 'Military Police' were being trained in Sweden as light infantry, and the recruitment of another 12,000 'police troops' was authorised. There was therefore a real threat of invasion, and the Germans were fully justified in taking the strictest measures for their own security in Norway. Any Norwegian who ignored the new situation did so at his peril.

Police Inspector Gunnar Eilifsen must have known this better than most people. The one thing the Germans could not possibly have tolerated was penetration of the State Police, who had been loyal since April 9, 1940, and were the strong arm of the Reichscommissariat. Eilifsen had had a chequered career. He had been a member of *Nasjonal Samling*, whether as a pro-German infiltrator, as a 'Home Front' spy or as a double agent has never been clarified. When he now refused to carry out the orders of Police President Askvig to take into custody two girls who had failed to report for National Labour Service, this could only have been regarded as open defiance.

Eilifsen was arrested on August 9, and on the 15th was condemned to death summarily by a 'People's Court', that is to say a military tribunal, for mutiny under the terms of the Military Laws of May 22, 1902. Quisling's prosecutors charged that he introduced the Provisional Law of August 14, bringing the police under military regulations, deliberately to victimise Eilifsen as an NS renegade. No corroborative evidence has been adduced to substantiate this charge, and indeed Quisling's conduct during this crisis suggests the contrary.

Quisling was never vindictive and never abused his power to take revenge on his enemies. He told Terboven repeatedly on the 15th that he regarded the verdict as unjust, and pleaded for mercy. Terboven, however, threatened to shoot 'a lot more' Norwegians unless Quisling as Minister-President signed the death warrant. After the 'Trondheim massacre' this could not be taken as an idle threat, although Quisling's enemies have always maintained that Terboven was bluffing. Terboven insisted that Eilifsen would be shot anyway, even if Quisling pardoned him. The Reichscommissar also threatened to arrest and deport to Germany 'several hundred policemen' and 'a thousand Norwegian officers'.

As usual, Quisling went home alone to wrestle with his conscience. Maria Quisling, the solitary witness of the ordeal, wrote the following letter to the Court that later tried him:

'On August 15 I was about to say goodbye to my husband and go to Gausdal, when I noticed that he was agitated and looked ill. He did not seem to remember that I was leaving. When I asked what was the matter, he replied that he had not slept the whole night . . . I tried to pump him about what was the matter, but I got no answer. He did not seem at all himself, as if he had had a shock . . . I became frightened and worried and could not bring myself to go away. . . . In the end he said that a death penalty was the trouble, and that it was frightful to have to sign it. I asked why he could not grant a reprieve. My husband answered that he had done all he could, tried everything, but it did not help. . . . The Reichscommissar would not be shaken in his demands. . . . If we do not comply, the Germans will act, and moreover many more (Norwegians) will be taken.'

So Quisling signed the death warrant on the 16th and Eilifsen was shot the same day. Whether Quisling's deadly compromise saved hundreds or possibly thousands of Norwegian lives, can never be known.

The verdict at Quisling's trial was that he 'created a formal opportunity to pass the death sentence on Eilifsen . . . and knew, when the "Act" (of August 14) was issued, what it was going to be used for . . . the defendant is guilty of Eilifsen's death because he also failed to prevent the carrying out of the sentence, something he was able to do by virtue of the right of reprieve which he had vested in himself.'

Quisling's appeal, that he acted 'under duress', was dismissed. The Germans were *de facto* sovereigns of Norway, and therefore Quisling's claim to be leading a National Government, with powers of life and death, was merely symbolic—a transitory stage towards his objectives, peace, the abolition of the Reichscommissariat, and his assumption of real power. The debate will continue, but in any case the extenuating circumstances were formidable.

Whatever the rights and wrongs of the Eilifsen verdict, August 16, 1943, was the moment when Quisling's cause was lost and he should have resigned. If he could not save Eilifsen, his real power was negligible. German factual sovereignty had been demonstrated in the most brutal way. Until then he had legitimate hopes of peace and power. Now they were dashed and his continuation as Minister-President became a meaningless pretence.

Again, one asks, apart from his stubborness, why did he carry on? The answer can only be that he still placed his hopes in Hitler. He continued to bombard the German leader and his other influential German contacts with arguments in favour of peace, an end of the Reichscommissariat and recognition of Norway's claim to a favourable place in the New Order, and in September he received in writing an assurance from Hitler that after the war 'Germany would re-establish Norway's liberty and independence'.

Quisling always attached great importance to this document. It kept alive his ambition to oust Terboven. It ruled out the danger of a Protectorate or German military dictatorship. It also guaranteed Norway's future, whether Germany or the Western Powers won the war. Meanwhile it kept Norway aligned in the crusade against Bolshevism. That was his reasoning, but it is not improbable that Quisling himself was unconvinced by his own arguments.

It is known that he did begin to think of retiring after the Eilifsen affair, prodded to some extent by his wife. He certainly had no immediate financial problems. On his fifty-fifth birthday on July 18, 1942, his oldest political friend and colleague, Frederick Prytz, Minister of Finance, presented him with a cheque for 300,000 *kroner* ($42,000). In 1945 the accusation was made that Prytz had dipped into the Treasury on Quisling's behalf, but this was never proved, and Prytz was dead by that time and unable to answer the charge. He was in any case a wealthy man, and Quisling had many other rich admirers, so there is no reason to believe that the gift was tainted. Quisling was never money-minded, and his salary and expenses, corresponding to pre-war rates, were ample.*

The money from Prytz was earmarked for improvements to Quisling's cottage, Ørneredet (Eagle's Nest), at Asker, 20 miles from Oslo, which was given to him during the war, and for the acquisition of property in Fyresdal, Telemark, his birthplace and his family's home for 400 years.

* 25,000 *kroner* ($3,500) a month, later raised to 30,000 *kroner* ($4,200), covering his salary and representation.

331

At Fyresdal, the farm and parsonage, which once went together, had been shared among relatives—Quisling's immediate family retaining three portions. Then an aunt died, leaving the major part of the estate to Quisling and his two brothers. By the time the legal situation was clarified, Pastor Flatland had left and the parsonage was vacant. Through his Church Ministry Quisling then set about trying to acquire the parsonage, where he was born, and to move Pastor Flatland's successor into a neighbouring house—a reasonable enough course of action since eight of the last twelve holders of the living had been members of the Quisling family.

Quisling was able to take advantage of a peculiar Norwegian law (*Odelrett*), giving citizens the right to acquire an old family property at a nominal price instead of the market value. The Quislings, with eight of the twelve lots, had strong *odel* rights and Vidkun duly obtained the parsonage for 80,000 *kroner* ($11,200).

After the war he maintained that he intended to turn the place into a children's home and an art gallery. Be that as it may, his prosecutor's allegation that he was engaged in some shady property deal is too improbable to be taken seriously.

However, early in 1945—when another atrocity rocked him and liberation was nigh—he proposed to resign office, and tried to persuade his Church Ministry to appoint him to be lay pastor of Fyresdal, where the living was still unfilled. Although he had not been ordained, he felt that he was qualified as a theologian. This would have meant abandoning the children's home, which was supposed to be ready in June, but his application was not granted, and he remained in his post.

His real motives will never be elucidated, but he reminded the court of his 25th anniversary as a student, when he wrote: 'The evolution of popular society rests with the reformation of Christendom as a dynamic organ in life and thought.' He added: 'The present world crisis, like all world crises, has a religious nucleus.'

There is little doubt that the Eilifsen dilemma and failure to achieve independence for Norway in the autumn of 1943 shook Quisling to such an extent that he genuinely wanted to retire and finish his huge life-work on 'Universalism'.*

* This opus lies in Mrs. Quisling's bank, unpublished. For her part, she wishes only to be left alone and, even if she had the funds, she would not very easily

On January 28, 1945, Quisling had a long last talk with Hitler. Eleven days later, Major-General Karl Marthinsen, 49-year-old chief of the Secret Police since July, 1943, and of the *Hird* since June, 1944, was murdered at Slemdal, in the residential foothills of Oslo, on the way to his office. A hail of machine-pistol fire killed him, and his chauffeur was badly wounded. The assassins, doubtless members of the 'Home Front', have never been identified, but their act was bound to be followed by terrible reprisals.

One wonders about the wisdom of this action, for it has since been claimed that Marthinsen's organisation had been penetrated by the 'Home Front' through the enterprise of Sissel Knudsen (now Mrs. Lødner), who pretended to be a friend of Police Minister Jonas Lie and intercepted their correspondence. It is also known that Quisling had got wind of some such escapade several days earlier and had warned notables in touch with the 'Home Front', including Fritjof Heyerdahl, of the inevitable consequences.

The day following Marthinsen's death, 14 Norwegians, none older than 32, who had been under arrest for sabotage for one or two years and earmarked by the Germans for execution in just such an emergency, were shot as a reprisal. According to the Police report, Quisling declined to pardon three of the victims, whereas his consent does not appear to have been sought in the other eleven cases. The official announcements did not state that the executions were connected with the Marthinsen murder, although this was the natural supposition.

Since Quisling had warned the 'Home Front' that matters had gone so far that he could not be responsible for the consequences of an act such as the murder of Marthinsen, and the 'Home Front' having taken no heed, he can hardly be blamed for non-intervention. Moreover,

---

be persuaded to publish the book. 'I am tired and upset,' she informed me. Another difficulty is that some of the chapters have got no further than the headings. The gist of this work, as I gather from the few people who have seen the manuscript, is that heaven (like ideal communism) lies here on earth and not in the next world, if only we would organise our lives rationally; that the root conflict is between science and religion, which Quisling sought to integrate; that the Christian ethic is essential, hence his quarrel with Jewry, which he regarded as competitive ideology, although not as a racial menace. (*Author*)

Terboven again threatened to shoot ten more Norwegians if Quisling did not sign the death warrants.

Nevertheless the subsequent indictment of Quisling contained these words: 'The sentences were submitted to the defendant as "Minister-President" for him to decide whether reprieves should be granted. He, accordingly, had the authority and the duty to decide whether the sentences should be carried out or not. By refusing the reprieves under these circumstances and thus allowing the sentences to be carried out, he contributed to these murders. The defendant claims that he must be exonerated because he was under duress, as the Reichscommissar insisted on these sentences; but this reason cannot be accepted.'

Thus the Marthinsen case repeated his Eilifsen dilemma, which he would have escaped on this occasion if he had followed his earlier inclination to retire. Quisling may well be acquitted by the verdict of history of the five murder charges brought against him—the 'Trondheim Massacre', the loss of the Jews, and the reprisals in the Hansteen, Eilifsen and Marthinsen cases—but he had certainly placed himself in a compromising and vulnerable position.

21

Ancient Rome

'IN dark times,' declared *Fritt Folk* on December 16, 1944, 'the men of the *Hird* must be the torch-bearers of the nation.'

The Red Army were hammering at East Prussia, and the Allies at the Ruhr. Hopes of a separate peace for Germany vanished with the summary hanging of Gestapo criminals in Kharkov. It was too late for secret weapons to turn the tide. Now there was talk in Germany of a 'last bastion', in Bavaria, Bohemia or perhaps in Norway. The Reich was preparing for guerilla warfare with the help of sketchily-trained civilians—the *Volksturm*. Hostages, including General Ruge and Crown Prince Olav's brother-in-law, King Leopold of the Belgians, were assembled for bargaining purposes in South Germany.

As the bleak New Year approached, Quisling told Harald Franklin Knudsen: 'The defeat of Germany will be a defeat for Western Europe and it will come quickly.' As to Norway's future, he said that it depended on many factors: 'I am, however, casting about in my mind for some possibility to lay before Hitler before it is too late. I forbid you to mention this as it is only in the preparatory stage. . . .'

The communiqué issued after Quisling and Hitler had met for the last time, on January 28, 1945, twelve days after the Führer's return to Berlin, where he remained till the end, simply reaffirmed Hitler's promise of September 1943: 'Germany will restore the complete liberty and independence of Norway after victory.' This was meaningless now that East Prussia was encircled and the Red Army was only 110 miles from Berlin.

Notwithstanding, Quisling—stubborn as ever—had a plan. Asked in Court what it was, he answered: 'Those are secrets I shall take with me to the grave.' Fortunately Knudsen has revealed the secret. He says: 'Quisling proposed to Hitler that the German forces in Norway should be joined by their families and sweethearts. Barracks should be built for them until permanent quarters could be provided after the war. Being mostly peasants and artisans, the troops would be attracted by the safe conditions and, having burned their boats, would not want to capitulate or be sent home to their ruined country.

'Having smashed Germany, the Western Powers would face two alternatives—to sacrifice much blood and money in overpowering strongly entrenched positions, at the same time destroying Norway, or to negotiate a Norwegian peace that allowed the Germans to remain and to form the backbone of Nordic defence in any future East-West war. Scandinavia would then be able to muster two million men and the Northern flank against Russia would be definitely secured. Sufficient labour would also be obtained for the reconstruction of North Norway, following its "scorching" by the retreating Germans.'

Quisling believed that an educational programme would induce the Norwegians to accept the Germans, since the unnatural alliance between the West and Bolshevism would soon dissolve and even hardened *jøssinger* would be glad to have the Germans to protect the frontiers in the North. 'The Germans have been living here five years,' he said, 'and have hit it off so well with the Norwegian people that we have a lot of trouble about finding accommodation for German-Norwegian children. Things would be much quieter once the soldiers have their wives sent up here.'

Like the Allies at Yalta, Quisling vastly overestimated the Russians' military strength and underestimated their political offensive. Who in any case would have imagined Eisenhower pulling General George Patton back from Pilsen in Czechoslovakia or Montgomery from beyond the Elbe? Thanks to the Western Powers' behaviour at Yalta and their timidity at the finish, the Soviet Union was saturated with spoils, and the Red Army graciously withdrew from their North Norwegian outpost and contented themselves with sitting on the border while Stalin brought Finland to heel. So the Bolshevik menace that Quisling visualised in North Norway never in fact materialised.

Maybe Quisling's plan for a 'Norwegian bastion' was not so far-fetched as it appears in retrospect. The vast German forces there (420,000 strong) were dug in, with enormous supplies—including 3½ million bottles of wine and spirits at Lillehammer and 1½ million at Bodø—and their morale was unbroken to the end. It is interesting to speculate what would have happened had Hitler accepted Quisling's implicit invitation to fight a last round against Bolshevism in the fells of Norway.

In evidence Quisling said: 'When I talked with Hitler for the last time at the end of January, I asked him precisely what the situation was and he replied that Germany would get by. I believe the Germans based their expectations on "over-valuation" of the German offensive on the West Front (in the Ardennes) at Christmas, and partly on secret weapons that were not ready. Hitler had also said something about his hoping that God would grant him the last eight days of the war.* I had also heard that the Germans actually had a secret weapon of epoch-making character, although few people in Germany had heard of it.'

Quisling himself was a self-taught nuclear physicist and was well aware of the possibilities of a nuclear bomb. Two of his close acquaintances were Sam Eyde and Klaus Hansen,† pioneers of the great Norsk Hydro hydro-electric works in his native Telemark. This was the only plant in Europe capable of large-scale production of 'heavy water' (deuterium oxide), which could theoretically be used in nuclear fission. Quisling would surely have heard that the Germans had ordered production to be raised in March 1942 from 3,000 pounds a year to 10,000—a vast increase, involving the conversion of 100,000 gallons of ordinary water by electrolysis for every single gallon of 'heavy water'.

Such an operation could only have a military bearing and Quisling must also have known that Germany had two experts who were capable of evolving a nuclear device—Professor Werner Heisenberg of the Kaiser Wilhelm Institute, Berlin, and Dr. Otto Hahn, co-discoverer of atomic fission.

* His horoscope told him so.

† He was ear-marked by Terboven to head an alternative 'quisling' government.

The wartime history of Rjukan, the mountain-top Norsk Hydro plant that produced 'heavy water', also pointed to Allied interest in a super-bomb. In November 1942, an Anglo-Norwegian glider attack on Rjukan failed. In February, 1943, the key apparatus, the 'heavy water' concentrator, was eventually sabotaged, and half a year's supply was lost, whereupon the entire garrison was court-martialled. 'The best coup I have ever seen,' said Falkenhorst. This persuaded the Germans to ship the whole plant to Germany for safety, but when it was packed on a long train of flat cars, another marvellous Anglo-Norwegian operation sent it to the bottom of Lake Tinnisjø as it was crossing a ferry on February 20, 1944, so the legend goes.

Quisling was in a particularly good position to know that Germany would not have the bomb in time. He must have realised that it was too late for secret weapons to save Hitler. Evidently, however, Hitler had decided that the twilight of the gods should occur in Germany, not in Norway, so Quisling had to think again.

Quisling now tried to backpedal, but Terboven and the new commander in Norway, General Frans Boehme★ resolved to fight 'to the last man.' Throughout February Quisling was under pressure from Terboven to co-ordinate the *Hird* with the German forces in Norway with a view to a united effort. Following the death of Marthinsen, the argument for amalgamation became stronger, for Marthinsen was not only a former head of the State Police and the head of the Secret Service, but also chief of the *Hird*, on which Quisling was trying to strengthen his hold.

Quisling was therefore obliged to consent to the appointment of a weak new secret police chief, none other than Henrik Rogstad, who had compromised *NS* during the 'Trondheim Massacre'. Under Rogstad, parts of the Norwegian S.S. were placed at the disposal of Jonas Lie's Police Department, Police President Askvig and the Oslo Police.

They were now armed for the first time—their military training having been theoretical up to this point—and were assigned to guard duties at key posts as well as to ordinary police duties. Quisling's long-standing stipulation—that the *Hird* was Norwegian, under his own supreme command, and separate from the German forces—was, however, recognised in principle. It was clearly stated in conference and in public that the *Hird* were not available for regular warfare, but

★ At the New Year, General Rendulic had briefly succeeded Falkenhorst.

in practice, the *Hird*'s new duties relieved the Germans of many military or semi-military chores.

The 'Front Fighters' were another awkward problem. Some 7,000 had by now returned from Finland and the Eastern Front, and about 25 had already joined the pro-German State Police. Quisling could not openly order them to resign from the German ranks, now that they were back home and no longer fighting against Bolshevism, but he pestered the Germans to release them, and told his NS colleagues to try to detach them privately.

As Quisling emphasised in Court: 'I could have got the Germans to fight . . . but my first consideration was to avoid a bloodbath . . . we arranged for the *Hird* to be disarmed during the last days.'

The evidence of those last days bears him out, He did not oppose the 'Home Front', although its supporters pretend that he backed the Germans to the end and that it won some sort of military victory over NS.

Events did not move inexorably to an appointed end in Norway, which muddled through to liberation as she had muddled into war. Norwegian exiles in Sweden reported that the Germans would smash dams and flood valleys, if necessary, so as to force the Allies to negotiate. Then came the mysterious 'Atlantic Radio' report on Sunday, April 28—supposedly from Nazi territory, actually from England—saying that Count Folke Bernadotte was negotiating peace with Hitler's official heir, Himmler.

That Sunday night Quisling called an extraordinary Cabinet meeting at which all his Ministers put themselves at his disposal should he want to bring in substitutes 'from other quarters'—presumably non-NS representatives. A 'transitional government' was to be proclaimed on the radio in the evening, 'to maintain law and order'. The *Hird* were to be told over the air that their duties were confined to police work and must under no circumstances engage in regular warfare.

'Unfortunately,' said Quisling in Court, 'this never came out because one of the Ministers informed the illegal organisations privately without my knowledge.' He was presumably referring to Jonas Lie.

At any rate Terboven scotched the whole scheme when Quisling contacted him after the Cabinet meeting to obtain his assurance that he would not make 'complications'. Terboven pretended that he, too, was thinking of making a proclamation along rather the same lines. Quisling naïvely invited him to Gimle to work out a joint plan, wasting time and allowing Terboven to prevaricate until it was too late to broadcast that night.

He maintained that for Quisling to retire in favour of a 'transitional government' would be to stab Germany in the back, and that if Quisling accepted the resignation of his Ministers, it would look as if he had been deserted.

Thus a vital night went by, and Quisling lost the initiative. He could not now broadcast before the 29th, even had he been certain what he ought to say.

On April 30 Hitler committed suicide. The real test of Quisling's intentions then came.

At 10.20 p.m. on May 1, Grand-Admiral Karl Doenitz broadcast that he was Hitler's heir. 'It is my first task to save Germany from the advancing Bolshevik enemy,' he said. 'As long as the achievement of this aim is impeded by the British and Americans, we shall be forced to carry on our defensive fight with them as well.'

His approach was purely military. If he were to negotiate a separate peace with the West, he obviously had to retain the support of the Armed Forces for bargaining purposes. This meant that the Germans in Norway would have to hold fast to the end, and it ruined Quisling's chance of forming a new government.

'We must take into account the political circumstances in Europe,' Quisling told Terboven by telephone. 'Resistance would mean the complete destruction of our country.' As he added in the dock, he was thinking not only of the German forces, which he regarded in some ways as a 'neutrality guard', but of intervention from Sweden. 'The situation is unchanged', Terboven replied. 'The new German government is not confirmed.'

On May 2, Quisling turned to General Boehme at his headquarters at Lillehammer, reminding him that he had prophesied this situation months before, and complaining that Terboven still 'stood blindly by Hitler'. Boehme, too, rejected Quisling's plea for a peaceful solution, only conceding that Norwegians in German military service should be disbanded, thus reducing the risk of civil war.

Meanwhile Doenitz was moving from Ploen to Flensburg on the Danish-German frontier, where Terboven and Boehme sought him out on May 3. They returned 36 hours later and informed Quisling that the situation was still unchanged. They were as full of fight as ever, determined to defend the highlands south of Trondheim to Telemark and the Swedish border. Their resolution was not even shaken by the surrender of north-east Germany, Holland and Denmark to Montgomery on May 4, not even by Doenitz sending Admiral Hans von Friedburg to surrender to Eisenhower at Rheims on the 5th.

On the 4th, Bernadotte in Sweden learned through his Copenhagen Legation that Himmler's former adviser, Walter Schellenberg, was empowered by Doenitz to negotiate capitulation in Norway. Next morning at 10 o'clock, Schellenberg accompanied Hans Thomsen (German Minister in Stockholm) and a Military Attaché to the Swedish-Norwegian border, but Boehme refused to see them. He would only surrender on direct instructions from the Doenitz Government.

The same day, May 5, Quisling telephoned Terboven concerning the reported capitulation in Denmark and about the reported appointment of Count Lutz Schwerin von Krosigk as Germany's new Foreign Minister. The Reichscommissar would not accept these developments as official until he had confirmation from Flensburg.

Norway was now Germany's last bargaining counter. A precipitate Allied landing or Swedish intervention would still have loosed off an explosion in Norway. With 420,000 troops on the spot—twice as many as the British War Cabinet estimated—the Gestapo, 9,000 pro-German State Police and the *Hird*, the Germans could in theory have put up a terrific resistance. This was the great fear among Norwegians, British officials in Stockholm and the Swedish authorities, although London seems to have been very ill-informed.

Quisling then made his final pilgrimage to Skaugum to try to save the country from another campaign, civil war and total destruction.

Terboven and Boehme were still without instructions and refused to budge, although clearly they realised, orders or no orders, that the game was up.

'I had every chance of escaping, that's a fact,' said Quisling in the dock. 'The last time I saw Reichscommissar Terboven, at Skaugum, he said that a plane and a U-boat* were at my disposal, and I certainly

* It was a long-distance Schnorkel U-boat that could have reached South America.

knew where I could find good friends to care for me and console me during bad times. I thanked him for his invitation and said I could not think of accepting. I had always held the view that one should not desert one's people. I myself had criticised those who had fled from their responsibilities [the King and the Nygaardsvold Government] and I could never bring myself to do anything comparable.

'He said he respected my standpoint and there the matter dropped. He said, in the same connection, that in principle he would not deprive himself of his freedom of action.

'Degrelle* was also there, but not during the conference. Those are the true facts and I think I am entitled to be believed indubitably.'

So Quisling decided to face the music.

II

Boehme's repudiation of Schellenberg and Thomsen increased the alarm in Stockholm. The first effect was to bring Harry Söderman to Oslo. Known as 'Revolver Harry', this great personality was once one of the world's leading criminologists, and the founder of Interpol. He was also the Swedish commander of the Norwegian 'police troops' (light infantry) who had been trained and armed by the Swedish Army but paid for by the London Government.

He made an early visit to Møllergate 19—'Number 19', as Norwegians called this large gaol. Inside, the political prisoners, having got wind of peace, had smashed their tiny windows, thrusting handkerchiefs through the iron bars and waving frantically to the crowd outside. Söderman addressed a line of State Police, saying 'I represent the Norwegian Government and I have come to release your prisoners.' The senior policeman stepped forward and gave the Nazi salute, replying: 'That has been our salute until today, but now I am happy to return to our former customs.'

Then a strange thing happened. Heinrich Fehlis, the head of the German Police in Norway, was greeted as an old friend by Söderman.

* Leon Degrelle had crash-landed in mysterious circumstances at Fornebu and broken a foot. He was the young 'Rexist' leader from Belgium whom Quisling had met in Switzerland in the mid-1930s. Shortly thereafter Degrelle took the bomber that Terboven had put at Quisling's disposal, and reached San Sebastian in Spain. Before he embarked, he telephoned Quisling from the airport to try to persuade him to flee, too, but again Quisling refused, although the liberation of Oslo had begun.

Fehlis helped with the release of the prisoners, and later the same evening, when there was a rumour that desperate 'Nazis', allegedly 'Front Fighters' and *Hird*, but more probably the hard core of Terboven's entourage, were about to try to regain control of the prison, he again came to the rescue. Söderman persuaded him to fetch arms from Gestapo headquarters in Viktoria Terrasen and the danger, real or unreal, passed.

Little wonder that surviving members of *Nasjonal Samling* believe that Söderman was a double agent. Harald Knudsen says that Söderman 'gave Quisling a detailed monthly report on criminal activities of Norwegians in Sweden'. The British Legation in Stockholm treated him almost as one of themselves. Probably he was simply a loyal Swedish policeman trying to do his best for Norway in difficult circumstances.

At any rate Quisling must have known that he had the measure of the 'Home Front' in so far as it might get support from the 'police troops' in Sweden.

The 'Home Front' had only been properly co-ordinated, under Paal Berg, since the autumn, when the Germans had obviously lost the war, subject to a miracle. It is claimed that there were 140,000 members, but the figure was probably nearer 100,000, of whom about 35,000 were lightly armed with weapons dropped from Britain. Norwegians are sportsmen and good shots and these boys, for most of them were in their teens, had a fine time playing soldiers in the wilds. The Germans made little effort to round up smuggled weapons, and did not even bother to chase members of the 'Home Front' into the woods north of Oslo, which area (Nordmarka) was marked on their maps as 'enemy territory'.

The 'Home Front' achieved very little in practice. Some 20,000 tons of German shipping were sunk and another 20,000 tons damaged, there were a few ineffectual attacks on arms dumps and factories; some oil tanks were exploded; and there was sniping at a few soldiers. Much of the 'Home Front' activity was devoted to murdering 'quislings' or to acts of sabotage which were not strictly relevant to the war effort but which justified German reprisals.

NS and the 'Front Fighters' were not worried by the 'Home Front'. Indeed, Quisling refused to have a guard at Gimle until the last six months, when his friends insisted that he might be kidnapped like

Codreano of the Rumanian Iron Guard or Mussolini. It was not until May that he yielded to the entreaties of Rolf Holm, Governor of Oslo, that he should have a personal bodyguard.

Some members of the 'Home Front' were in fact in German pay, and the movement was penetrated by NS. Just before he was murdered, Marthinsen said: 'I could lay my finger on a thousand jøssinger but where is the prison space for them?' The Germans could easily have liquidated the opposition during the last days of the occupation, and one of Quisling's great services to the 'Home Front' was to persuade General Boehme at Lillehammer on May 2 to disband the armed Norwegians under his orders.

Out-manned, out-gunned and out-manœuvred, the 'Home Front' knew that they had no chance of success by their own efforts, and on May 5 their leadership informed the 'quislings' that they would be treated 'fairly'. They also followed Quisling's initiative of April 28-29, when his proposal for a new interim government was leaked, and offered to combine forces in order to avoid civil war. Quisling then sent Orvar Saether, the *Hird* Chief of Staff, to make appropriate arrangements.

Events, however, took place with bewildering rapidity, and there followed one of the most complicated, controversial, and little-known episodes in the Quisling story, involving attempts to negotiate a settlement. The facts are to some extent in dispute, but there can be no doubt to anyone who has investigated the confusing situation that feelers were put out by both sides. A version of the facts that is clearly inspired in some ways is given in a book entitled *Konsentrasjonsleiren Ilebu*,* written under the pseudonym of E. Werner Svendsen.

According to this source, Selmar Alm, a prominent member of the banned Labour Party and Chairman of Eidskog Municipal Council (near Kongsvinger and the Swedish border) conferred during April in Oslo with Christian Astrup, former NS Governor of Bergen who was married to Frederik Prytz's daughter.

Astrup told him that the Oslo 'Home Front' had informed him that a British-backed capitalist coup was imminent in Norway, aimed at sweeping away both the London Government when it returned, and *Nasjonal Samling*. Such an action might well cause civil war.

Astrup argued that an approach should be made to the only man,

* The post-war name for Grini concentration camp.

in his view, with sufficient authority to ensure a socialist solution—
Martin Tranmael, one of the best brains in the Labour movement and
a pre-war opponent of Quisling.

Alm also conferred with Ørnulf Lundesgaard, NS Governor of
Hedemark Province on the Swedish frontier, who had served Quisling
from April 9, 1940, and now informed him of the proposed approach
to Tranmael.

Thirdly, Alm informed Alfred Ljøner, the last Chairman of the
Labour Party before its dissolution, who asked him to continue the
overtures. For some reason, however, Alm lost heart and returned at the
end of April to his country place, Skotterud, ten miles from Sweden.

On May 1, when Hitler's death was announced, the rural mayor in
Alm's neighbourhood informed him that Reidar Hedemann, a Labour
journalist whom he had helped to escape to Sweden, wanted to see him
on the frontier as soon as possible about the political balance of power
in Norway.

Alm assumed that Tranmael was behind Hedemann's approach*
and fixed a meeting for May 6.

Meanwhile Alm returned to Oslo and conferred again with Astrup,
Lundesgaard and Ljøner. This culminated in his having a long discussion with Quisling on May 5.

Quisling, who had expressed interest when he heard of the Tranmael
approach, now said that Tranmael was too close to Moscow in his
political views, but Alm denied this, and Quisling arranged for a car
to fetch Tranmael to Oslo, under safe conduct, for negotiations.

A typewritten record of the Quisling-Alm conversation was made,
and it included this passage: 'The NS Fører and Minister-President
Vidkun Quisling to resign from the post of Minister-President. . . .
A socialist government to be formed. . . . NS and all similar organisa-
tions† to be dissolved and a new socialist party—the Norwegian
Socialist Labour Party—to be established, based on the Labour trade
union organisation and the socialist wing of *Nasjonal Samling*.' It was
also recorded that a 'Norwegian People's Defence', including members

---

* It is only right to point out that Hedemann denied his part in these events
(*Arbeiderbladet* and *Dagbladet*, January 31, 1946). I have included a summary of
them, however, because I believe that, even if 'Svendsen' is wrong about
Hedemann, his story is accurate in important respects.

† i.e. the 'Home Front'.

of the *Hird* and *Mil-org*,* should be established, and temporarily identified with armbands.

On May 6, Alm met Hedemann and Axel Kielland, a Norwegian author, on the frontier and stressed the continued danger of a reactionary coup. Hedemann said that the danger had passed, but added that he was not representing Tranmael, but instead was speaking for 'the whole Norwegian front in Sweden, apart from the Communists'.

Hedemann, according to the Svendsen book, then asked Alm to negotiate a reasonable solution with the Quisling Government with regard to a German capitulation. Alm agreed to try, whereupon Hedemann jumped up from the tree-stump on which he had been squatting and addressed Kielland: 'Now you and I must go immediately to Charlottenberg [inside Sweden]† and telephone to our Legation so that they can name negotiators. They could reach the frontier by air this afternoon.... We must now count in hours, not days.... You must remember my tree-stump so that we can find it again. It will be historical.'

Then they put on record that three negotiators from each party should meet at the frontier at 2 p.m. on the following day, May 7; a representative of the 'Home Front' in Norway should also attend, and that it was desirable that the Germans should be informed of the nature of the meeting.

Astrup drove from Oslo to fetch Alm by car in the afternoon. That evening they collected Lundesgaard and drove to Gimle to tell Quisling to expect a telephone call from Stockholm. The only news he got, however, late at night, was that nobody in Stockholm wanted to serve as a negotiator. That evening they collected Lundesgaard, who drove to Gimle to talk with Quisling. Lundesgaard said that Alm and Astrup would wait for a telephone call from Gimle to come there later. But they waited in vain until late into the night. The only news they received was that no *NS* minister would be appointed as a delegate by Quisling.

Next morning (May 7) they tried once more to get delegates appointed so that they could attend the meeting arranged on the frontier.

Apparently Quisling procrastinated because he was not clear what Hedemann, Kielland and Alm had arranged. Asked if Quisling was

---

* The armed section of the 'Home Front'.

† There Kielland told the author on May 7: 'I am here in a sort of official capacity.'

really ready to negotiate, Alm answered, 'Without doubt', and certainly Quisling seemed to prefer the socialists to a régime imposed from abroad. Fearing, however, that 'without doubt' might be interpreted as 'unconditional surrender', Quisling insisted that capitulation was not imminent and that Alm had gone too far. He was also determined that overtures should not be too eager from his side in case he gave an impression of weakness. Negotiations, he felt, should in any case take place at his quarters in the Oslo Royal Palace.

He therefore refused to send an official emissary to the frontier, but told Alm to keep in touch and to take with him the permanent head of the Culture Ministry, Vig. They did not reach the frontier until 5 p.m. Hedemann and Kielland had gone, the latter having left the message: 'Now it is too late.'

The Swedish afternoon newspapers confirmed that the German capitulation on the Continent was a fact. Unconditional surrender had been signed at Rheims at 2.41 p.m. Bernadotte telephoned Doenitz and von Krosigk and obtained their formal orders for General Boehme to capitulate, too.

Alm drove to the rural mayor at Didskog, where he was surprised to meet three of Quisling's Ministers, and Astrup. Quisling had after all decided to negotiate—presumably after hearing the news from Rheims—but he had missed his opportunity by procrastinating and failing to seize the initiative.

Meanwhile the Germans in Norway clung to power even as it was slipping from their grasp. Very early on the morning of May 7, for example, when the lights were just coming on for the first time for five years, the German authorities were telephoning to forbid the printing of the morning's *Aftenposten* unless it were first censored by them, and were threatening to send SS men to see that their instructions were carried out at the very time when the chief German Press officer was waiting to collect the last issue of the *Deutsche Zeitung in Norwegen*, which was printed under compulsion on *Aftenposten*'s machines.*

General Boehme declared in the *Deutsche Zeitung*: 'After six years of heroic fighting we have been defeated by superior forces. It is for us to see that the shield of honour of the German soldier remains unstained to the last. We stand in Norway unbeaten and in full possession of our powers. No enemy has dared attack us . . .

* The author was an eye-witness of these proceedings.

'We must in the interest of the German people as a whole accept the dictation of our enemy . . . We hope that we now have to do with men of the other side who appreciate a soldier's honour. We expect the Norwegian people to maintain the same discipline with regard to the German soldier, as the German soldier has always shown in Norway. Comrades, grit your teeth, maintain order and obey your superiors.'

In fact the German troops, who on the whole had behaved comparatively well during the occupation, carried out his instructions. The same discipline was not exercised by the Norwegians, certainly not by some of the 8,000 'police troops' who began to filter home on May 8. One of Quisling's last services was to intervene with the Germans who were tempted to take reprisals against the insults of the raw Norwegian volunteers, who had hardly fired a shot in anger during the whole war.

Boehme's provisional capitulation at midnight on May 6-7 was not precipitated by any Norwegian authorities, but by the Swedish Count Folke Bernadotte's telephone call to Doenitz and von Krosigk in Flensburg.

The official act of surrender was made at midnight on May 8-9. Since in Boehme's view Norway and Germany had not been at war since June 10, 1940, he did not surrender to any Norwegian, but waited for General Sir Andrew Thorne of the British First Airborne Division, who arrived on May 8, when the Armistice became effective, representing the Supreme Allied Commander, General Dwight D. Eisenhower. Seventeen officers, led by Brigadier R. Hilton and including two Norwegians, were designated by Thorne for the take-over.

Three days later (May 11), when the 'Home Front' discovered to its dismay that Norway and Germany had been officially in a state of armistice for the last five years, a symbolic surrender was arranged for publicity purposes at Akershus Fortress. A formidable German general was photographed saluting a bareheaded Norwegian boy in plus-fours and sports stockings. Nine Norwegians out of ten believe that this picture, hanging in homes throughout the country, represents the *Wehrmacht* surrendering to the 'Home Front', and that this was the official capitulation.

Rather more than 24 hours thus elapsed between the breakdown of frontier talks late on May 7, when Alm returned empty-handed, and early on May 9, when Quisling was tricked into custody.

348

He was not idle during that time. He continued to work for an orderly transition and the avoidance of reprisals by either side, in the spirit of his last radio speech stressing that his National Government was 'Norway's only lawful and factual government . . . that there would be none other until it has been replaced by lawful means by another lawful government inside the country.' He added: 'We are willing to sacrifice anything to save our people's future, but we are not willing to make sacrifices and concessions that might endanger the evolution of the future. We are not going to weaken our case and to abandon our country, our people and our comrades to lawlessness and Bolshevism.'

This principle, which was semi-officially accepted by the 'Home Front' on May 5 and tacitly conceded by the attempted frontier negotiations on May 6-7, had been endorsed by an extraordinary Cabinet meeting on April 29 and again on May 5, the day the Danish capitulation became effective.

Ministers prepared to hand over their portfolios in good working condition. No attempt was made to burn controversial papers. No plans were laid for flight or hiding. Quisling and all his men trusted in the assurance of the 'Home Front' that they would be given safe conduct to a villa in Holmenkollen that had been rented by the Gestapo second-in-command, Siegfried Fehmer, who had disappeared. This arrangement was guaranteed by the Red Cross and the further assurance was given that the 'quislings' would be treated 'according to Norwegian law'.

Supporters of the 'Home Front' did not dare show their faces in numbers until May 8, when Boehme signed his provisional capitulation. They were still hopelessly outnumbered by the German forces, although they had been reinforced by advance 'police troops' from Sweden. Nevertheless, the Gimle guard was brought up to about 150 armed *Hird* in case the 'Home Front' went back on their promise.

At 7 a.m. on the 8th, Bjørn Foss, a 40-year-old doctor in Air Raid Precautions, was telephoned at home by Lorentz Brinch, a barrister who was head of D 13, the 'action group' of the *Mil-org* underground organisation, ordering him to 'Number 19' to be briefed about contacting Quisling. A State Police captain telephoned Gimle, and a meeting between Foss and Quisling was arranged. It was postponed twice, first by Quisling and then by Foss, suggesting some possible confusion. Quisling clearly wanted all his Ministers by him, and in fact by 11 a.m. all except Riisnaes (Justice), Lie (Police) and Whist (Supply) had reported at Gimle, some of them with suitcases containing clothing, toilet requisites, sandwiches and drinks.

When Foss arrived, Quisling, supported by two of his Ministers, received him in the 'golden salon'. They all bowed. After a long silence, when Quisling passed the cigarettes, Foss said: 'No thank you. You know why I am here. I have authority to invite you and your wife to a villa on Holmenkollen, under the protection of the "Home Front", until your case comes up. You and your wife may take all your things with you.'

Quisling then talked for half an hour on how the Germans had deceived him and how he had striven for Norway. He said that the simplest thing might have been to take his own life, and that he had thought of it. 'I am disappointed with the Norwegian people. In ten years they will see that I was right,' he continued. 'They will recognise the danger from the East.'

At that moment the Red Army was bearing down through North Norway, collecting tens of thousands of Communist prisoners of war on the way,* and conspiring with the powerful Communist element in *Mil-org*. As events shaped, it seems that Quisling exaggerated the danger of a Communist coup in Norway, but still the threat existed, as half-hearted Communist collaboration within the 'Home Front' indicated and the forthcoming election of 12 Communists to the *Storting* proved.

'I know,' Quisling continued, 'that I am condemned to death by the Norwegian people and that the simplest thing would be to end my life, but after mature consideration I have decided to see history's judgment on it—and, believe me, in ten years I shall be another Saint Olav!'

Then he reached the crux of his argument. 'I have 30,000 men in the Oslo area. *Mil-org* has only 4,000. I therefore know that I can win the battle today. But it is also clear that I should lose the second round. For *you* will have the help of the Allies. I do not want Norway to be a battlefield once more.'

Foss thanked him, saying: 'That's good. What you say is right.

* 12,000 Red Army prisoners and forced labourers were buried in Norway during the German Occupation.

Fighting would mean unnecessary bloodshed. I am glad the outcome is decided and that the transition will be peaceful.'

Quisling then agreed to go to Holmenkollen, provided that this arrangement covered his Ministers. 'I will not desert my friends who have stood by me during the most difficult years of my life.'

Foss raised no objection. As he left the room, Quisling put a hand on Foss's shoulder and said: 'I give you my word there will be no fighting.'

'Thank you for that', Foss replied. 'If you want to talk to me again, telephone me at Number 19.'

Later that afternoon Quisling in fact rang Number 19, but 'because of a misunderstanding'—so the history of *Mil-org* says—it was stated that Dr. Foss was out. Already in fact the 'Home Front' was beginning to go back on its word.

Quisling wanted to use the shrewd Alf Whist to continue negotiations, but Whist stayed at home, so the Minister of Social Affairs, J. L. Lippestad, was sent to Number 19 instead. He was given a free hand. He found the acting police chief Heinrich Meyer, a very reasonable man, ostensibly in control, for the real 'Home Front' leaders had still not ventured into public.

Discussion of a 'fair solution' had not gone far before Sven Arntzen burst in from an adjacent room where he had been listening. 'No,' he shouted angrily, 'the case must be tried by Norwegian law.'

This was the turning point of subsequent Norwegian history, when the 'Home Front' first showed its hand. Arntzen was one of the lawyers who had joined Paal Berg, ex-Judge Schelderup, Emil Stang (a future Chief Justice and former Communist opponent of Quisling) and Annaeus Schjoedt (Quisling's former Moscow companion and future prosecutor) to oppose Quisling and his followers.

The Lippestad-Meyer negotiations ended abruptly and the Minister returned to Gimle empty-handed. It was now evening and the *Hird* had been joined by groups of 'Front Fighters' and Germans. They were amply armed, and the Quisling hierarchy could have gone down fighting, but Quisling still refused to let 'Norwegian fight against Norwegian'. He accepted Arntzen's word that his case would be 'tried by Norwegian law', little knowing that the law had been changed in London!

Quisling did not know that Orvar Saether, whom he had sent to

351

negotiate a peaceful transition with the 'Home Front', had already been arrested surreptitiously. Nor was he aware of the true status of *Mil-org*. Until November 20, 1940, its founder, General Olaf Helset, and his few collaborators, had operated under orders from General Ruge given before the secret Armistice of June 10, 1940. Then the London Government secretly brought *Mil-org* directly under the so-called Norwegian 'Army' in England, and termed it the 'fourth line of Defence'.

The official history of *Mil-org* says that Quisling was given an 'ultimatum on the night of May 8 to report at Number 19 the following morning'. He was at the time ignorant on three counts. He did not know that Norwegian law had been fabricated in London by the introduction of secret, provisional decrees; he did not know that 'quislings' were already being arrested; and he did not know that the *Mil-org* section of the 'Home Front' had been given bogus military status. In fact he had behind him the assurances that the 'Home Front' had asked him to go, under safe conduct, to his cottage at Asker, and that Dr. Foss had later asked him to go instead to the Holmenkollen villa, with his wife and Ministers, under the auspices of the Red Cross.

He therefore had no reason to suspect that the 'Home Front' offer of 'fair treatment' had been withdrawn. He had acted in good faith, disarming the *Hird*, disengaging the 'Front Fighters' from German orders, discouraging the Germans from a last stand, refusing to flee, and negotiating a peaceful transition. Naturally he expected good faith in return.

In this expectation he was cruelly deceived. He was lured into a trap and seized under false pretences.

The *Norsk Biografisk Lexicon* says that Quisling 'surrendered' at 7 a.m. on May 9, a few hours after the capitulation had come into effect. Actually, he drove to Oslo with overnight baggage for the villa promised him at Holmenkollen, intending to hand over authority to the 'Home Front' in an orderly manner, as arranged.

He found, however, that his opponents had very different ideas. '. . . it seems poor treatment,' he later said at his trial, 'that one has received after five years at the head of this country's management—that one should report to the police station and be treated like a common criminal'. His baggage was seized. He was cross-questioned and bodily searched like an ordinary prisoner, and not even allowed to specify his profession as 'former Minister-President'. Then he was charged with treason in April 1940 against the mobilisation order, seeking to bring Norway under a foreign power, bearing arms and encouraging others to do so against Norway, attempting to change the Constitution unlawfully, and murdering Eilifsen. Next he was submitted to a gruelling physical examination by Dr. Jon Leikvam and Dr. Johan Loftus, who found he was sane, whereupon he was placed in a cell and half-starved.

The Criminal Police Chief, Lars L'Abee-Lund gave a curious version of the story in an interview in *Dagbladet* on February 14, 1964: 'The police rejected all (Quisling's) proposals. He was told that there was no basis for negotiations. The moment the Germans handed over power he would be arrested and taken in charge in the ordinary way. We made it plain that if necessary he would be fetched by force. Then we heard from Quisling that he would come voluntarily. For safety's sake we surrounded Gimle and all the roads into town . . . We could do nothing until the Germans had signed the capitulation. That was done by General Boehme, and in that moment he transferred power to the Allies.★ Then the secret police organisations could carry out orders from the State Police Chief Aulie in London. It was then that we first received formal authority to come to grips.' Thus we see that the very first act of the hitherto powerless London Government was vengeance, unadulterated by self-criticism or humility, magnanimity or mercy.

Quisling had made arrangements to hand over his complete archives for the historical record. Early on May 9, he told the leader of the Gimle guard, Bjørn Østring, that he did not want his private papers hidden or destroyed. He ordered his secretary, Per Jahr, to tell Sverre Aastorp, 27-years-old head of the *Hird* membership department, who was also a member of the guard, to move the papers to safety before they could be destroyed or pilfered by the 'Home Front'.

The plan was to take the archives, packed in three briefcases, to the home of Ole Stang, father of Quisling's young Sports Minister, Axel Stang, in Prinsesse-Alle, Oslo. Since the father was not a member of *Nasjonal Samling* and the mother had been a Lady-in-Waiting to Queen Maud, it was thought that their custody would be respected.

★ NB. Norway was *not* one of the Allies. At the capitulation, sovereignty passed to the British liberation forces and this was marked by the presence of a British Security officer (MacRoberts), who supervised the Norwegian police.

Aastorp and his two companions, who were carrying the papers, had the misfortune to run into a patrol outside Bygdø police station, the police having just been told by State Police headquarters in Oslo to watch all roads from Gimle. The trio bluffed their way through, but the surprise stoppage decided them to abandon the trip near Skøyen and to make haste, while there was still time, to hand over the documents safely to the senior official at police headquarters in Oslo.

On arrival at Number 19, the three men were received by Heinrich Meyer, who took note of their request that the three portfolios should be handed to Quisling's lawyer. No receipt was given by Meyer, but his acceptance of the cases was recorded in his notebook. Meyer then said, 'Do you mind if I arrest you?', and apologised when he was told 'No'.

According to Aastorp,* he was cross-examined by the well-known sportsman, Erik Stai, who was officiating as Criminal Police Inspector at Aakerbergsveien Prison in Oslo. Stai insisted that Aastorp had hidden or destroyed part of Quisling's archives, but Aastorp denied this categorically.

The extraordinary thing is that, in evidence during Quisling's trial, only one briefcase was produced. The following record is instructive:
Defence: 'Have you destroyed any of your archives?'
Quisling: 'Not one paper . . . I could have destroyed them very easily because I had the special papers, which have been used against me, alone in one portfolio. I could have thrown it into the central-heating. I did not do that—as I told the police.'
Prosecution: 'Does the accused mean to maintain that he had no other papers than the little portfolio we have here?'
Quisling: 'They took all I had out there [at Gimle].'
Prosecution: 'All you had there at that time? But your archive was not so small earlier.'
Quisling: 'I have not destroyed anything, not one paper, since I had this situation in mind [his trial].'
Defence: '. . . in your office at the palace, some things *were* burned. Did that happen on your instructions?'
Quisling: 'No. I had my own archives at the palace but they were old

* Aastorp's information was given to the author in an affidavit on May 5, 1964.

354

papers . . . public documents that were not my private affair . . . I deliberately did not destroy one of my private papers.'

The suspicion is more than strong that, although time and again the Norwegian Press stated that all Quisling's private papers had been 'saved', about two-thirds of them were suppressed by his enemies. The small yellow pigskin briefcase was produced, containing papers damaging to Quisling, but not the two larger cases described by Aastorp, and the trial was peppered with references to vital missing documents.

The Attorney-General, Sven Arntzen, said in a Press interview: 'We had no reason on May 8 to condemn Quisling to death, but then we got his papers.' Among the many missing papers, however, were Quisling's letter to General Laake saying that he would not serve under the subversive Labour Government, and the General's sympathetic reply; Quisling's 'Europa Pact' defining Norway's free and independent role in a future Continental settlement; annotations to his written request to be named Pastor of Fyresdal; the Soviet letter thanking him for his services to Russia during the famine; the list of distinguished Norwegians who were standing by to serve Terboven as an alternative to Quisling's National Government; Quisling's 1945 orders to the *Hird* removing them from German control; Orvar Saether's protest to Terboven against German encroachments on the *Hird*, and his order calling the *Hird* throughout Norway to rally to Quisling; and Quisling's long, lifework on 'Universalism' or 'Social-Individualism'.

There was such bitterness* against Quisling that suppression of these and a great many other documents that may have helped him, or embarrassed his opponents, cannot be ruled out. At what level the

---

* As an example of bitterness, at the end of my audience with King Haakon in London a year earlier I had ventured to ask: 'And what are you going to do, Sir, with Quisling?' His Majesty replied without hesitation: 'We shall hang him, yes, we shall hang him *three times*!'

I suppose I looked astonished, because the King explained: 'You see, the first time the trap door will fail to open. Then we shall say "We are very sorry, Major Quisling, we shall have to try again later." Then he will be taken back to his cell. The next time, you see, the rope will break! Once more we shall apologise and say "We are very sorry, Major Quisling, this has happened again. We shall see if we can do better next time." Then he will be taken back to his cell. The third time will be lucky! You see?'

suppression took place, and whether the rumours are true that documents are hidden in the Law Courts, must remain matters of speculation. Without impugning the integrity of any individual—the judges and prosecution lawyers could only deal with papers in their possession —there can be no doubt that many documents favourable to Quisling (which he would have no reason to destroy) were never produced.

Quisling was a victim of the mob. Outside 'Number 19', on the morning of May 9, after he arrived, thousands of Norwegians were screaming mad, brandishing knives and spitting at 'quislings'. The new authorities yielded to this savage mood.

Despairing of any mercy, three leading 'quislings' barricaded themselves in Skallum Court, the Norwegian police centre for senior officers in Baerum suburb. There Henrik Rogstad of the 'Trondheim Massacre', who had succeeded Marthinsen as Security police chief, blew his brains out, four days after his marriage. Jonas Lie drank enough *akevitt* to bring on a fatal heart attack, knowing that this would happen in his malarial condition. Sverre Riisnaes, Minister of Justice, also drank himself into a stupor and went off his head at the time—later to survive 12 years' imprisonment.

Out at Skaugum Palace, Terboven—faithful to his Führer unto death—and Rediess, the German Police chief, blew themselves up with hand-grenades. Weiner, the dreaded Gestapo chief with supposedly hypnotic eyes, was captured and put in the 'condemned cell' in the ancient Powder Tower in Akershus Castle. There he later seized a gun from his Norwegian guard, whom he bundled into the cell, and then turned it on himself.

Weiner's second-in-command, Wolfgang Fehmer, escaped to South Norway, but was eventually captured when he contacted his Norwegian mistress, to ask after his pet fox-terrier. He, too, was then confined in the Powder Tower, where he wrote a long and still extant account of his stewardship in Norway. Then he was summarily tried, condemned to death and supposedly shot, but it is widely believed that he was spirited away and is now working for the Americans' Central Intelligence Agency.

A colossal witch-hunt also began on May 9 through the length and breadth of Norway. Nothing similar has ever occurred in Northern Europe—not even in Finland after the terrible Civil War or, as the Finns prefer to call it, the War of Independence. It would require a book in itself to detail the shameful horrors that ensued. Contrary to the principles of Western jurisprudence and to practice in other liberated countries, 'guilt by association' became 'law', and so thousands of members of *Nasjonal Samling* automatically became 'criminals' and were gaoled for up to fifteen years. 'Informing' became a national preoccupation. One Norwegian collected 80,000 advertisements by his fellow-countrymen in German and *NS* newspapers and presented them to the Attorney-General's office. Paying off old scores—political, business and personal—became a mania. Victimisation continues even today in the government, Courts, municipalities, universities, schools and private relationships. A leading industrialist and humanitarian, for example, has not spoken for twenty-five years to his sister, the wife of a high Army officer, because she was a member of *Nasjonal Samling*! There are still thousands of these feuds embittering private life in Norway today.

Elderly professors, men with international reputations such as Adolf Hoel and Gustav Smestad, who had served Norway's territorial interests in the Arctic for decades, were man-handled, insulted, starved and put to forced labour.

Knut Hamsun, the greatest of all Norwegian authors, aged 81, was seized from his family and home, robbed of his literary earnings, and placed under arrest in a poorhouse and later in a psychiatric clinic. Trygve Lie and Terje Wold (London Minister of Justice and now Chief Justice) actually boasted about Hamsun's treatment. When in Moscow Molotov suggested that they were treating a great writer harshly, Wold had the audacity to say to Molotov of all people: 'Don't be soft.'

Ragnar Skancke, the former Director of Trondheim Technical High School and pioneer of radar who became Quisling's Minister of Church and Education, was actually executed, after three years in gaol, despite a petition by 800 clergymen and professors! One firing squad refused to do the job. Another was so horrified that it failed to kill him outright. He lay writhing on the ground and had to be despatched with a bullet in the neck.

50,000 alleged 'collaborators' or 'Nazis', as they were collectively termed, were arrested and thrown in gaol, often for years without charge or trial. The warders' methods aped the Germans'—interrogations up to eight hours at a stretch without rest, exhausting punishment-exercises under threats of violence, 'eeling' (dragging prisoners

357

back and forth across broken stones), and starvation diet (800 calories a day). Many prisoners died of malnutrition or starvation, and limbs swollen from privation were a commonplace. Hundreds, if not thousands, died of dysentery and tuberculosis epidemics. Hundreds more bear the scars of the kicking, beating and brutality of their guards.

Norway simply exchanged the terror of the Gestapo for the terror of the 'Home Front', which unfortunately lasted twice as long as the German Occupation. The last political prisoners have only come out of gaol during the last year or so, having served sentences twice as long as the average murderer.

It is estimated that there were a million denunciations in a country of three million inhabitants, where 'everybody knows everybody' and therefore the repercussions were especially unpleasant. Attorney-General Arntzen spent eight years sorting out the guilt. *Kartoteket over Landssvikere* (The Catalogue of Traitors) says they numbered about 130,000 persons, but the most reliable official breakdown is as follows:

> 17,000 imprisoned after trial
> 3,450 fined after trial
> 3,120 punished directly by the police
> 25,118 fined directly by the police
> 5,500 charged but not tried
> 37,150 investigated
> 1,375 not guilty

Thirty Norwegians were condemned to death for high treason and fifteen for war crimes. Twenty-five of the former were executed, one died under sentence and four were pardoned. The convicted war criminals were all executed. In addition, it is estimated that there were more than 200 unofficial liquidations.

As the Norwegian Association for Social Redress wrote to the International Commission of Jurists on June 15, 1964: 'The hatred of *NS* members was so intense that there was almost no risk in murdering them. Even robbers and murderers of a Jew and his wife were acquitted in Court after 1945, because they were members of the resistance movement. . . . No member of *NS* has harmed any Jews.'

The economic reprisals were equally staggering. The treason catalogue states that *NS* members were directly fined 280 million *kroner*

($39.2m.)*. For instance, a university professor, such as Gustav Smedal, was fined 150,000 *kroner* ($21,000). A High Court judge, such as Sverre Helliksen, was fined 442,500 *kroner* ($62,000). Millionaires, such as Hildisch (the margarine king), Fermann (the hard-bread magnate) and Petter Østby (the winter-sports gear inventor), were bankrupted. Their international businesses were taken away from them and run by less competent officials in a Compensation Directorate. Innumerable cases of this sort are estimated by Marta Steinsvik in *Frimodige Ytringer* (Open Talk) to have cost the state between three and four milliard *kroner* ($420m.-$560m.). But for various forms of American aid and loans, which financed the expansion of shipping, industry and electric power, anti-*NS* economic reprisals would have bankrupted Norway.

The ramifications of economic reprisals are endless. For instance, a man who lived in a tiny cottage in East Norway on 200 *kroner* ($14) a month during the occupation, running a shuttle service to Sweden for hunted members of the Resistance, had to wait until 1964 to inherit the great house and estate left by his father, one of the richest men in Norway—the reason being that the father was fanatically anti-Communist and therefore supported Quisling. Father and son did not speak to each other for years on end because of their political quarrel. Yet the son was put to vast legal expense, twenty years of worry and family misery, during which time the house fell into such disrepair that it will cost 500,000 *kroner* ($210,000) to set it in order!

One could continue in this vein almost endlessly. Everything must have seemed wonderful, however, on the surface during the merry month of May in 1945. Millions of bottles of German drink propelled the nation on an eighteen-month binge, and practically all edible food disappeared from restaurants during the endless festivities. General Thorne, commander of the First Airborne liberation troops, moved into Gimle, and within a week the British had coined the phrase 'going Norwegian' to apply to anything that went wrong. Norwegian officers and men gave up any serious attempt to combine forces and simply handed over the demobilisation to the German commander, General Boehme, who performed the whole huge operation without a hitch, even to the extent of sending the German Military Police to help the 'Home Front' with a truculent German submarine crew in

* Ex-Finance Minister Gunnar Jahn has said 270m. *kroner*.

Oslo Fjord. There was a race for the enormous German stores and equipment—including the hulk of the biggest battleship in the world —the *Tirpitz* in a fjord near Tromsö.

Crown Prince Olav stepped jauntily ashore on May 13 as Commander-in-Chief, in British uniform, a post that had been delegated to him by his father. He received a tumultuous welcome, partly because he is genuinely 'one of the people' and it was widely known that he had always wanted to share their fate during the occupation. He was allotted a small token force of Norwegian volunteers in British service, fostering the illusion of the liberation of Norway by Norwegians.

Once Crown Prince Olav had returned, the way was safe for the Nygaardsvold Government to return also. At first it was intended that they should accompany the Crown Prince, but a bitter controversy had already broken out—and still persists—between Hambro, the architect of the government in exile, and Berg, the official leader of the 'Home Front', which was now in ostensible control of the country and basking in spurious glory. Hambro wanted to return to the old pre-war political system of parties, minus Quisling; Berg sought to perpetuate the 'Home Front' as an entity, either as a government or at least as a participant in a new government.

This is not the place to cover post-war political developments in detail, particularly since the facts are only now coming to light. It suffices to say that King Haakon, the London Government and the 'Home Front' soon made common cause. Thus nearly everyone for different reasons pursued a policy of putting all the blame on Quisling for the German Occupation.

Hambro, Nygaardsvold and the other exiles eventually returned on May 31. The King returned on June 7, the anniversary of the day he fled, aboard the *Devonshire*, which had taken him to Scotland.

One Viking rite still had to be performed—the humiliation of the enemy and the final human sacrifice.

The well-tried authoritarian technique of attacking a man through his wife was not neglected. Maria Quisling was seized from her flat, taken into custody with the wife of Carl Bernard Askvig, and kept incommunicado. No charge could be preferred against her, and the only object of her imprisonment was clearly to worry Quisling.

Eventually a few conscience-stricken members of the 'Home Front', including Odd Nansen, who had been in a German concentration camp and resented Quisling's use of Fridtjof Nansen's name, came to her rescue. She was released and able to visit her husband in his tiny cell in Møllergaten 19. She was, however, reduced to poverty. Her possessions, including Old Masters, were stolen. All she was allowed to keep was 250 *kroner* ($123), one bed, one table and one chair. Mercifully she found lodging with a widow of Frederik Prytz, who had influential relatives and saved a few pennies from the wreck.

Not until years later did Odd Nansen and other pre-war friends manage to retrieve her flat, most of her pictures and her pension as the widow of an Army Captain. Now she lets rooms. She is a nervous wreck, aged over 60, forbidden by her doctors and lawyers to see anybody. She spent the summer of 1964 in a rest home. One of the conditions that the 'Home Front' extracted before her release was an undertaking not to publish her husband's lifework on 'Universalism' or any of his other surviving papers, and not to take part in politics. In law she is a 'good Norwegian'—just as good as any member of the 'Home Front'—but she is socially ostracised.

Quisling in gaol bore up against the persecution of his wife with stoicism. He insisted on sparing her the ordeal of giving oral evidence in Court on his behalf before the eyes of the world. He also dissuaded her from taking her life so that she could 'go with him'.

His opponents also tried to break him physically. His prison diet was kept at 700 and 800 calories a day, instead of a proper 3,000. By the time he was brought to Court, nearly four months after he was seized, he had lost 49 pounds. On August 20, when the case opened, *Aftenposten* wrote: 'He has grown thinner. His dark suit hangs loosely on him.'

Harald Franklin Knudsen was moved into the condemned cell a few hours after Quisling's execution, before his bed had been remade, and has described the conditions as follows: 'A small window with iron bars, dirty grey stone walls, a plank bed with a palliasse, a wash bowl, a toilet bucket, a small table and a hard chair.' Such were the cramped circumstances under which Quisling had to prepare his defence, covering fifteen years of complicated history and the details of his varied life from infancy. Thanks to his prodigious memory and physical strength, he was able to overcome all handicaps.

In the world at large a campaign was run to disparage his personal life and to prepare the public for his condemnation, although the case was *sub judice*. Two bottles of brandy and a box of cigars were found in the baggage that he had packed to take to the promised asylum at Holmenkollen. This discovery was adduced as evidence that he was a drunkard and spendthrift, although his asceticism was well known. It was said that he lived in luxury off black-market food during the war, although it was known that he had issued standing orders to the contrary; his simple habit of pushing his plate towards a friend at meals, saying 'Have a bite', was a public joke. He was even said to be a fornicator, although his shyness with women and his devotion to Maria were proverbial.

Aftenposten reported on the second day of the trial: 'If one studies the picture totted up by the indictment—treason, swindling, cheating and the immense private expenditure—the decadent Roman emperors suggest themselves as the natural historical parallel. Physiologically something reminds one of the bust of the late Roman emperors.'

Thus the Quisling drama ended in the atmosphere of Ancient Rome —as it had begun, on the eve of April 9, 1940, with the King and his officers banqueting like Lucullus.

What the world was about to witness was not a trial, based on the canons of Roman Law, but a gladiatorial show for the masses in the spirit of that Colosseum, throwing a Christian to the lions.

III

Few realists would complain if the 'Home Front' had shot down Quisling in anger at the time of the liberation, as happened to Mussolini. However, they were determined to kill him, and to do so with the full authority of the law, even if it was a law enacted specially to condemn him and his followers. Every authority in Norway from the King and Nygaardsvold downwards, including Quisling, had flouted the Constitution—simply because the laws of 1814 never allowed for the exceptional circumstances of 1940-45. The Law for Traitors of December 15, 1944, under which Quisling was convicted, had no validity, except the sanction of brute force.

The Prosecution freely admitted that it had no hope of securing the death sentence on the basis of the charges levelled against him in May, particularly after a telephone call to the British Home Office in London, asking what it was proposed to do about collaboration in the liberated Channel Isles, had solicited the unhelpful reply that, since inevitably many Channel Islanders had collaborated with the Germans, the British preferred 'official glorification.'

The Prosecution then broadened their attack. On June 21, the charges against Quisling were extended to cover the murders of Viggo Hansteen in 1941, the Norwegian Jews and the 14 Norwegians shot as reprisals for Marthinsen. There were also charges of theft and receiving stolen goods.

Quisling carefully prepared his defence, and his optimism about acquittal, or at any rate escaping the death sentence, was not entirely unjustified until five days before the opening of his case when affidavits from Rosenberg, Ribbentrop, Göring, Keitel and Jodl were suddenly sprung on him. He had completely to revise his defence in a short time, and without any opportunity of calling rebutting German evidence. Only a few paragraphs from his original opening speech could now be used in the new context.

We have seen how all the big Nazis were working for their own ends, and obviously under interrogation in 1945, they were under duress and anxious to pass their blame onto other shoulders. Little or no reliance can be placed on their statements, as later historical revelations have proved. Astonishingly, the affidavits were taken by the Court as gospel truth, without Quisling been given any opportunity to cross-examine. Equally astonishingly, the Germans who might have helped him were never called as witnesses, although such men as Scheidt, Schreiber, Falkenhorst, Raeder and Admiral Boehm were readily available.

Furthermore, no evidence was called from the British side to show that an Allied invasion was under way on April 9, 1940, which would have underlined the dubious position of the Nygaardsvold Government and explained Quisling's initiative on that fatal day when he rushed into the breach. Quisling had to rely on extracts in the Norwegian Press from Paul Reynaud's forthcoming war memoirs, the full text of which was not yet available.

The trial, with its complicated issues, was rushed through in eight effective days' hearing, less than it takes for simpler cases in Norway and elsewhere. In the middle, on August 27, Quisling was subjected to the most painful brain investigations, which would normally have demanded an interruption of legal proceedings for several weeks.

A grave responsibility rests with the Norwegian legal profession for

363

the conduct of the Quisling case. No attempt was made in advance to investigate the legality of the 'London laws', which were simply accepted at their face value. The President of the Federation of Judges suggested that they should hold a joint session and accept the Prosecutor-General's view that the 'treason settlement' was in order. The President of the Federation of Attorneys remained silent.

The Law was one of the most compromised of all the professions in Norway. The Supreme Court had first invalidated itself by entering politics and had later deserted its responsibilities in the act of resignation. The other judges had remained in office under the occupation, and the lawyers had enforced NS laws, without questioning their validity. Only a handful had risked German displeasure and been interned.

The only way to have ensured that justice was seen to be done would have been to have invited unprejudiced foreign lawyers to form a tribunal. As it was, the principal legal figures in the case were not merely Quisling's ideological opponents but in some cases his active enemies. However well Chief Justice Paal Berg may have been able to prevent his personal views from influencing his judicial judgement, he can hardly be described as a disinterested man. Yet he was one of the men who rejected Quisling's final appeal. Another was Emil Stang, who had been a leading Communist and one of Quisling's bitterest opponents.

The Chief Judge in the Quisling case was Erik Solem. The authoritative Norwegian-American magazine, *The Norseman*, said in its November-December issue in 1945: 'It was a fair trial, though it certainly was not impartially conducted. The presiding judge, Erik Solem, illustrates this point. . . . If he had chosen the stage as a career, he would inevitably have found himself presiding, night after night, over courts of law. He had a keen, thin face, penetrating eyes under bushy brows, a generous forehead and thin greying hair. His voice is usually low and clear, but it can be cutting in sarcasm, incisive and commanding. Now and then he raised it to flash back at Quisling when his oratory, usually indulgently received, went too far.

'When Quisling complained of his treatment since he gave himself up and said he had lost some two and a half stone, the judge replied: "That is nothing to what some of our people lost when you put them in your concentration camps: men who weighed ten stone came out weighing five." And everybody in Court knew Solem had been an

364

underground leader who knew the inside of a concentration camp. He was not impartial, but he was fair.'

Being fair without being impartial cannot have been an easy task, and the trial did not help Solem's reputation. He had been legal adviser to the Germans, and there were members of *Nasjonal Samling* who identified him with Gestapo agent number 13. He appears later to have relented, and said that the 'Front Fighters' had been punished enough by their experiences on the Eastern Front, but when he visited them in prison, they spat at him.

Eventually the Quisling case weighed so heavily on him that he went off his head. In delirium he screamed: 'Take your blazing eyes off me.' He was haunted to the end of his life by Quisling's ghost.

Henrik Bergh, the defence counsel whom Quisling was allotted in default of any other lawyer who was prepared to take the case— Quisling's own supporters were all in prison—told Quisling that he was 'always a *jøssing*', according to a United Press interview in the Swedish evening newspaper *Expressen* on August 6, 1945.

Looking back on the trial—apart from Pétain's, the first of the great war trials—it is easy to see that everyone was still indoctrinated by five years of propaganda. Winning the war had been the supreme objective, and there was no reason why the Norwegians, sitting in judgement and hollering for revenge outside the courtroom, should not have believed the worst. At the time everyone took the Rosenberg diary and other German evidence at its face value, never realising that it was slanted. Quisling's own protestations that he was 'the saviour of Norway' or that he did not 'feel guilty of a single charge' seemed incredible. When his cheeks flushed with anger, when he banged the table or turned indignantly to address the public, he seemed to be up to the tricks of a past dictator. Hardly anyone credited him with sincerity.*

Somehow, however, he maintained his dignity, and there was some feeling of sympathy for the underdog faced with the interruptions and sarcasms of the presiding judge. He was not the ranting maniac that he had been represented as being, but a cultivated man, mistaken

* I was as completely prejudiced against him as anyone else. Covering the trial, on the second day I wrote: 'The mountain of documentary evidence produced today seems enough to condemn him, and to prolong the hearing another week seems superfluous.'

maybe, but still no Hitler. Often he had to make a dash from the dock to the toilet because of a recurrence of his old kidney complaint, which recalled his sufferings in Russia. The details of how wires were pushed into his cranium in the middle of his case in order to test his sanity sent a shiver down the spine and built up further sympathy.

Considering the overwhelming weight of evidence against him, he argued with extraordinary conviction, but on September 10, he was condemned to death.

There is no need in this context to review the trial in detail. The result was almost a foregone conclusion. It is only now looking back on events that one begins to doubt what seemed so apparent at the time. 'Norway would stand far higher,' says Odd Nansen, 'if nobody had been executed. As for the "Front Fighters", they were disgracefully treated and should have been exonerated. They were brave men who obeyed their consciences. Quisling's five years as Minister-President were hell for him.'

J. Bernard Hjort, now the leading defence counsel in Norway, says that: 'Quisling was a tragedy. He was inspired by the patriotic feelings of 1905. At the worst he should have been court-martialled and shot for desertion.'

The distinguished Swedish lawyer, Hemming Sjöberg, who attended the trial professionally, has condemned its legality and the sentence out of hand.

The Norseman concluded its account of the trial thus: 'We may still be too close to events to distinguish between different kinds of treachery. But we must eventually learn what makes dictators tick, as this is an essential step towards preventing them from troubling the world again . . . Quisling ticked because he saw an explosion ahead and was convinced that the "lazy democracies" would do nothing about it. He was nearly right, and if we are to have no more of his kind, democracy must offer something more than ease and comfort until its blind eye is suddenly opened by economic disaster and its younger brother, war.'

Two interesting comments about Quisling's attitude to his trial are offered by the Swedish magazine *Vi* and by *The Norseman*. Elly James, writing in *Vi*, said: 'Quisling's defence was many-sided . . . but it had its effect on us foreigners . . . the Norwegians took the whole story more coldly . . . he was a phenomenon . . . when he was allowed

366

to talk freely in his own way he was impressive; but when he was interrupted and confronted with details, he was put out of his stride.' *The Norseman* commented: 'The minor charges were what stung him to fury. What the prosecution was trying to do was to remove any trace of dignity from the puppet. Hence accusations of theft, drunkenness and debauchery.'

Quisling's final speech, however, before the death sentence, was a *tour de force*. He spoke for eight hours without a note, without hesitation and without a mistake, reviewing with clarity and cohesion his lifework and all the complicated political details of his career. He raised the proceedings of the Court to a higher level and preserved his dignity to the last. He made his tormentors look very small indeed.

His last words produced the desired effect: 'If my work has been treason, then I pray God, for Norway's sake, that very many sons of Norway will be traitors like me, as long as they are not thrown into prison.'

Elly James described how he heard himself condemned to death: 'He took it like a soldier, tight-lipped, one hand gripping the rail of the dock and one wiping cold sweat from his forehead. Twice he drank water and changed his posture and sank his head in his hand until the flesh folded over his ears.' His worst enemy could not deny his courage.

A month later, on October 13, Chief Justice Paal Berg and three of his fellow judges rejected Quisling's appeal, and he surrendered himself to the judgement of history in these terms:

'I am the same man I have always been. I have not changed in any way at all. Can you point to a single instance of my taking revenge during these last six years? There are many walking freely in Oslo and elsewhere today who have done me dirty tricks politically, but I have not touched one of them in any way, never. Revenge is not a proper political motive and I, for my part, leave it to others.

'This case is not of a merely judicial nature. It is first and foremost a political case. It is, indeed, more than that. It is an historical event, and as such it also has a religious core.

'In all my actions and all my thoughts, I have been guided by two motives—my love of Norway and the Norwegian people. And that has to do with what I call the Will of God.

'I thought I was able to see the world problems in perspective; I had learned to do that, not least from the Bolsheviks, who, in my judgement, understood the world situation best and analysed it best. I thought I could make a contribution to my own country in this respect by what I did. In the midst of all the difficulties I ran up against, I thought that politics were a means towards serving something higher. They are a means in the process of historical development, in the work of the divine. Just as we military men say that strategy must be a vehicle for politics, I believe this is so in the present case. This is the point of view with which I have regarded the case.

'Many years ago—twenty years back—I became clear about these matters. I can now say—having received a certificate that I am not insane—that I am clear that there exists in the Universe a divine power connected with the inhabited planets; that what is now happening in these great times on earth is a great change, when the Kingdom of God is beginning to take form here on this earth, in the real sense of the term.

'Formerly, it was supposed that the Beyond was the real Kingdom of God. I am of the opinion that we are more and more coming to realise that the Kingdom of God is here on earth. The Marxists are saying that the Millenium is to be created here on earth, but they want to make it material, on the lines of Dialectic Marxism. But what in fact will save the world is the spiritual basis for this practical Kingdom of God. This is practical altruism.

'The platform of *Nasjonal Samling*—which is no German replica— was put into form by me as early as 1918 in Russia. It was an attempt to create practical altruism—with results obvious to one and all. The platform itself is, however, a move in the same direction—the object of all my efforts. That is what I have tried to open up the way for. I know that understanding of it will go on growing and growing out of what is now happening in the world.

'I thought I should be able to do something about it at the time in Russia and I spoke to the Communist leaders in the Ukraine on the subject—about the material basis of Bolshevism, the economic principles of which are not in themselves entirely vicious in relationship to industrial arts, etc. I sought to place it (Communism) on a spiritual basis. I have discussed this subject with the Germans. I told Hitler that National Socialism in Germany was materialistic, that he would not be able to carry it through; that it would bring him to the

368

ground—"Blood and Soil" is merely masked materialism; that materialism merely leads to total egotism and all its extreme consequences.

'I mean that I have recognised and worked for this new Kingdom of God. It is only this which has motivated me, together with my patriotism and my sense of duty. I mean that here one was confronted by something more than faced Harald Fairhair and St. Olav. Sentence can be passed on me, if so willed, but in so doing a blood-guilt will be brought upon the whole Norwegian people. I have done nothing that deserves either death or imprisonment. Not that I fear death for myself. I regret it for my near relations. I fear it for the whole Norwegian people.

'One must understand that. It is certainly plain to see, and I may well say that I am now speaking after the event—standing face to face with death. One must understand that one is facing a problem in my person itself—a problem which cannot be got round as easily as this.

'I have fought like an honest Norwegian. I have not sought power. I have not been an opportunist. I have tried to find out what is going to happen in this world, what has to be done, what I was to do, and what contribution I could make to this world.

'I have made my contribution. It has perhaps failed in certain respects, but one knows that the path is being cleared. A way is being paved anew, and I see what is now coming. I see where the right way lies here at home.

'The Hohenzollerns have fallen in Germany. The Hapsburgs have fallen in Austria. The Germans had to lose this war, too, as things turned out. But I had to reckon on their victory up to the last moment because of their possession of certain secret weapons, which might supposedly have turned the scale. And they could have won earlier on if they had, in my opinion, avoided gross military and political mistakes, of which Norway was one—and not the least, politically.

'Hitler told me in January this year that Germany would regain supremacy in the air and, he was convinced, be victorious. This one may take for what it is worth. I had, however, to take that consideration into account and keep going in order to preserve Norway from German potentialities.

'In practical politics I have worked for my country on the basis of the religious conviction and faith which I hold. It goes wide of Law, wide of sectional interests. Anyhow, it is the master-spring that has motivated me. Those who hold power in our own time cannot, I believe, blot out one's memory from the ages to come.

'I know I am being judged objectively under law. But I also want to ask that consideration be given to the facts I have mentioned elsewhere. I believe that the facts have not been sufficiently elucidated in the present case. My work and contribution have not in any way been made properly clear. Nor in any way has the background of our work. The failings of the men formerly in power are really what is to blame —not me.

'I have indicated my inner motives. I considered it my bounden duty to do so before the Supreme Court of Norway—and thereby to the Norwegian people.'

The speech told severely on him, but he controlled himself, and walked back to his seat with firm steps, the sweat pouring down his cheeks.

Before the Court rose, he asked to shake hands with the stenographers. During his trial he had been moved to the ancient Powder Tower of Akershus Fortress, up a single-file winding stone stairway and into a tiny room, now used for storing camera equipment, under the eaves, where there was just room to turn round.

On October 13, when his appeal was dismissed, he was moved into the condemned cell, number 34, at Møllergaten 19. He was still allowed to wear civilian clothes, which hung around his emaciated body like sacking, but his Hitler lock of hair was shaved away. His diet remained on the starvation level and the solitary pickled herring that he got for lunch was photographed by the Press with some glee. His wife brought him food parcels daily, but there is no evidence that they ever reached him. Their few meetings were terrible. She repeatedly threatened suicide, but his calm and self-possession stopped her. By all accounts he was a model prisoner.

His last public appearance was on October 18, when he gave evidence for Hagelin, who by this time looked a beaten man. Under cross-examination Hagelin pleaded loss of memory. Loyally, Quisling related how Hagelin had collected a file of Terboven's misdeeds to show to Hitler and other Nazi leaders so as to help to secure the Reichscommissar's dismissal. This did not help, and Hagelin, the real instigator of the April 9 coup, was duly condemned to death.

Quisling did not petition King Haakon for a reprieve, well knowing his Sovereign's temper, and contented himself with writing a letter protesting that he had been condemned unlawfully. No reply was called for and none was received. So their acquaintance, which had begun with mutual admiration and lapsed into misunderstanding, ended in the prevalent hate.

On October 23 Quisling was informed that he would not be pardoned.

Not even this news shook his monumental composure. Throughout those last 44 days before he was executed, up to the last moment, he appeared perfectly normal, convinced of his innocence, his martyrdom and his future pedestal in Norwegian history.

He wrote a 20-page summary of 'Universalism' for posterity, and, sitting alone in his cell, in a blue dressing-gown, he seemed to lose himself in the Bible and the book written by his father on 'The suffering and death of Jesus'.

With visiting clergy, including the present Bishop of Tønsberg, Dagfinn Hauge, he liked to discuss higher mathematics, relativity, theology, history and philosophy. 'I have the satisfaction of having governed Norway equally as long as Olav Trygvason, and no worse, everything considered,' was a phrase he often used. 'I handed over Norway to the King in good order. What would Norway have done without me?' was another of his themes.

The last message that he sent out to his followers bade them: 'Do not handicap yourselves with the idea of revenge, because the trend of events will avenge the wrongs that you suffer, not only in the case of the individuals who initiated the prosecutions, but also of the society that has permitted this lawlessness.'

Dr. Jon Leikvam, who attended Quisling in prison, said: 'Quisling is quite clear that he must die, but I am convinced that he dies a martyr.'

Even in the police car from Møllergaten to Akershus for the execution, he told the driver calmly: 'I am guiltless and condemned unlawfully. My case was never thoroughly heard and was illegal. I go to a martyr's death.'

When he was fetched from his cell at 2 a.m. on October 24, 1945, the last words he spoke to his warder were: 'I hope your new electric razor works all right.'

He left his Bible open with this text underlined: 'He shall redeem their soul from defeat and violence and precious shall their blood be in His sight.'

In throwing back his rough blanket when he was suddenly aroused, he disturbed a little posy of roses from his wife, and the petals lay scattered on the ground when his faithful friend and adjutant was moved into the condemned cell—uncharged and untried—a few hours later.

Under the brown stone walls of Akershus, a stake had been driven into the ground and surrounded by a man-sized box—in sight of the grave where the 14 Norwegians, shot by the Germans for Marthinsen's murder, now rested.

There Quisling was kept waiting more than an hour in the cold autumnal air while scores of sightseers, including Judge Erik Solem, assembled on the ramparts overlooking the fjord. As he cast an eye over the crowd, Quisling remarked: 'It is just like Ancient Rome, where it was entertainment to watch people die.'

He then asked to be allowed to shake hands with the ten-man firing-squad. This was agreed. 'Don't allow your conscience to trouble you in later years,' he said to the boys. 'Not on my account. You are acting under orders and are only doing your duty as soldiers, like myself.'

His request to face the firing-squad un-blindfolded was refused.

As they bound him to the stake, he played his last trick. While being fixed to his cardboard outline on the stake, he brought his mathematical mind to bear and balanced his body like a statue so that it would remain standing when he was dead.

So it worked out, after six or seven bullets had struck his heart. He seemed to be still alive when the thongs were undone and the bandage was removed from his staring eyes. The onlookers were aghast.

Then his corpse was taken down to the Møllergaten 19 garage and put on view for all and sundry. Many 'good Norwegians' came to see that the prototype 'quisling' was really dead. For their benefit the covering was thrown back. People prodded the body and made ribald remarks.

Even in the grave the decencies were not observed. When his ashes were returned to his widow many years later, and interred beside his beloved mother at Gjerpen in his native Telemark, his last resting-place was defiled.

Oslo, December, 1963–December, 1964

Appendix

Programme of *Nasjonal Samling*

I. *The State and the Community*

1. The National Government to act independently of party politics.

2. The cultural life of the nation and its livelihood to be organised in self-governing bodies and associations. These to be the links between the individual and the State, and controlled by the latter.

3. The management of the State to be rationalised by strongly increased influence of experts and the inculcation of personal responsibility and authority among officials and employees. General management and business management to be separated.

4. The self-government of communities to be transformed and their authority to be underwritten by the State. The power of Mayors to be strengthened in the counties. The duties and responsibilities of the State and Communities to be more effectively separated so as to clarify financial obligations.

5. Law and Justice to be rigorously enforced. The State to assume control of the Police. Corruption and dishonesty to be counteracted by all possible means and respect for Justice raised. The use of inexpert jurymen to be reduced accordingly.

6. State Finances to be staggered in accordance with an economic plan of several years' duration. Strict economy and minimum taxation of trade, industry and other enterprises. A uniform scale of taxation throughout the country, with taxes being reduced to a reasonable level. The same scale to apply to town and country. Expenses to be reduced to a minimum.

7. Voluntary labour service to be introduced for all healthy youths in order to strengthen the feeling of solidarity in the nation and to create a bond in building up the country.

II. *Working Life*

8. Everybody to have the right and duty to work. Brain-work and manual-labour to be equally respected.

9. Private enterprise and property rights to be protected within the framework of economically planned organisations for trade and production. All national resources to be utilised. The State and Communities not to engage in trade or industry on their own account, unless social considerations demand it. Co-operative trade to be non-political.

10. The extension and modernisation of communications by land, sea and air, and the transformation of waterfalls into hydro-electric power, to be promoted by private enterprise.

11. Lockouts and strikes to be banned. The rights and duties of employers and employees to be fixed by law, defining their terms of co-operation and conditions for settling disputes about working conditions. The responsibility of banks and financial institutions to be changed and the responsibility of their management increased so as to protect commercial and industrial undertakings as well as the benefits of employees.

12. Unemployment to be abolished in accordance with a national economic plan. Working hours and pensions to be regulated in accordance with technical development so that all young people obtain employment. Available jobs to be dispersed in a just and reasonable manner. Double employment and promotion through private influence to be strictly avoided. Relief organisation to be superseded by general and systematic social reform. All able-bodied persons to be found work instead of relief.

13. A rational monetary system to be established on a fixed level of value so that work is properly rewarded.

14. Banking services to be changed in accordance with the demands of the time. Nationwide credit to be made available to enterprises large and small. Capital to serve the productive life of the country, and interest rates to be reduced. Unsound speculation and too much reward for too little work to be stopped. Savings, old-age pensions and life insurances to be promoted and protected.

15. A national agricultural policy to promote a class of large and small freehold farmers, to secure the national food supply, to facilitate new cultivation and to encourage the building of new farms. Debts to be settled, prices and distribution to be arranged, taxes and dues to be regulated so as to make agriculture pay.

16. Forestry production to be increased through rational cultivation and management and the construction of new roads, thus providing all-the-year round work for forest workers and improving their conditions—also increasing their opportunities for becoming independent owners.

17. Fishermen to be supported by the assistance of organised co-operatives, through the improvement of fish products, improved export, an increased home market, the settlement of debts and easier opportunities to combine fishing with farming. Control of foreign trawlers to be more efficient.

18. Cottage industries, small enterprises and small craft to be energetically supported.

III. The Individual: the race and health of the nation

19. Responsibility for the maintenance of living standards to be strengthened. Everybody to be placed so as to use his or her gifts and abilities to the advantage of all.

20. The family and home to be protected. Respect for women's homework and motherhood to be raised. Equal political and employment rights for men and women. Economic support for children and the disabled to be achieved. Old-age pensions for all.

21. National health to be improved by better sanitation and accommodation as well as opposition to the misuse of alcohol and the promotion of sport and exercise.

The race to be protected. Habitual criminals, the insane and hereditary imbeciles to be sterilised after examination by experts and certification that they cannot beget sound children.

IV. Schools and Intellectual Life

22. The fundamental value of the Christian religion to be protected.

23. Better and quicker school education, with special attention to the formation of character, social consciousness, physical development and practical life. A general school plan offering full facilities for pupils to specialise according to their gifts and their plans for the future—in accordance with the needs of society. The State to pay for pupils with special gifts. Research institutes and specialised schools to be founded and developed.

24. Self-governing intellectual organisations to receive financial support under the supervision of the State.

25. The press, theatres, cinemas, broadcasting and other cultural institutions to support the interests of the nation. Anti-social propaganda and the spreading of class-hatred to be strictly forbidden.

26. The natural amalgamation of the two Norwegian dialects into one written language to be promoted but not enforced.

V. Defence and Foreign Policy

27. Defence to be strengthened, especially the Navy and Air Force. The three Services to be combined.

28. The Foreign Service to be practical and efficient and to be conducted along lines designed to further a determined trade and foreign policy.

29. Trade policy to strive for the consolidation of the national homestead, increased exports and increased shipping. Goods which can be produced at home in sufficient quantity and quality to be excluded from imports. Self-sufficiency apart, foreign trade to be based upon reciprocity.

Norwegian Mercantile Marine activities abroad to have determined political support.

Norwegian Arctic and Antarctic interests to be strongly and alertly asserted.

30. Large contributions to be made towards the world community of nations. Norwegian foreign policy to seek worldwide connections with related peoples in culture, race and interests. Everywhere, however, the interests of the nation to precede the interests of individuals, parties and countries.

SELF-INTEREST THROUGH COMMON-INTEREST!

NORWAY WAS A COUNTRY. IT IS TO BE A NATION!

Index

INDEX